D0425503

The Curve of Life

THE CURVE OF LIFE

Correspondence of Heinz Kohut

1923–1981

Edited by Geoffrey Cocks

THE UNIVERSITY OF CHICAGO PRESS

Chicago and London

HEINZ KOHUT was the author of several books, including
How Does Analysis Cure? also published by the
University of Chicago Press.

GEOFFREY COCKS is professor of history at Albion College.

With appreciation for permission to use Anna Freud's
letters to Heinz Kohut: The letters of Anna Freud © 1992
The Estate of Anna Freud, by arrangement with
Mark Paterson & Associates, Colchester, UK.

The University of Chicago Press, Chicago 60637
The University of Chicago Press, Ltd., London
© 1994 by The University of Chicago

All rights reserved. Published 1994
Printed in the United States of America

03 02 01 00 99 98 97 96 95 94   1 2 3 4 5

ISBN: 0-226-11170-9 (cloth)

Library of Congress Cataloging-in-Publication Data

Kohut, Heinz.
    The curve of life : the correspondence of Heinz Kohut, 1923–1981 /
edited by Geoffrey Cocks.
        p.   cm.
    Includes bibliographical references and index.
    1. Kohut, Heinz—Correspondence.   2. Psychoanalysts—
Correspondence.   I. Cocks, Geoffrey, 1948–   . II. Title.
RC438.6.K64A4   1994
150.19′5′092—dc20   93-40922
[B]   CIP

♾ The paper used in this publication meets the minimum requirements of the American National
Standard for Information Sciences—Permanence of Paper for Printed Library Materials,
ANSI Z39.48-1984

In Memory of
Elizabeth M. Kohut 1912–1992
and
J. Fraser Cocks, Jr., 1906–1991

Contents

Illustrations

Chronology

1913	Born May 3, Vienna
1914	*August:* First World War begins
1916	*November:* Austrian Emperor Franz Joseph dies
1918	*November:* First World War ends; Austro-Hungarian Empire dissolves
1931	*May:* Vienna Creditanstalt fails; Depression
1932	*June:* graduates from Döblinger Gymnasium
1934	*February:* Socialist uprising in Vienna suppressed
1937	*November:* father dies
1938	*March:* Nazi Germany annexes Austria
	June: witnesses Freud's departure
	November: in hiding during "Night of Broken Glass"; receives medical degree from University of Vienna
1939	*March:* leaves Vienna for England
	September: Second World War begins; death of Freud
1940	*February:* leaves England for America
	March: arrives in Chicago; mother arrives
1941	Resident in neurology at the University of Chicago Hospitals
1942	Assistant in neurology
1943	Instructor in neurology
1944	Instructor in neurology and psychiatry
1945	*July:* becomes United States citizen
	August: Second World War ends
1947	Assistant professor of psychiatry
1948	*October:* marries social worker Betty Meyer
1950	*March:* son, Thomas August, born
	October: graduates from Institute for Psychoanalysis, Chicago
1951	First annual vacation in Carmel, California
1953	Faculty, Institute for Psychoanalysis
1957	*August:* first return to Vienna
	November: "Introspection, Empathy, and Psychoanalysis" presented at the twenty-fifth anniversary celebration of the Institute for Psychoanalysis, Chicago
1963	*November:* assassination of President Kennedy
1963–64	President, Chicago Psychoanalytic Society

xi

1965–73 Vice-President, International Psycho-Analytical Association

1966 "Forms and Transformations of Narcissism"

1968 *December:* Sigmund Freud Lecture of the Psychoanalytic Association of New York: "The Psychoanalytic Treatment of Narcissistic Personality Disorders"

1969 *October:* German Peace Prize Laudation for Alexander Mitscherlich, Frankfurt/Main

1970 "Scientific Activities of the American Psychoanalytic Association: An Inquiry"
October: Address at the fiftieth anniversary celebration of the Berlin Psychoanalytic Institute

1971 *The Analysis of the Self*
October: diagnosed with lymphatic cancer
November: A. A. Brill Lecture of the New York Psychoanalytic Society: "Thoughts on Narcissism and Narcissistic Rage"

1972 *October:* mother dies

1973 *June:* Chicago Conference on "Psychoanalysis and History" in honor of sixtieth birthday
November: Honorary Doctor of Science, University of Cincinnati

1977 *The Restoration of the Self*
Austrian Cross of Honor for Science and Art

1978 *June:* voted off governing council of Chicago Institute for Psychoanalysis
October: First Annual Conference on the Psychology of the Self, Chicago

1979 *January:* heart surgery, postoperative complications
October: Second Annual Conference on the Psychology of the Self, University of California, Los Angeles

1980 *June:* Conference on Psychohistorical Meanings of Leadership, Chicago
November: Third Annual Conference on the Psychology of the Self, Boston

1981 *October:* Fourth Annual Conference on the Psychology of the Self, University of California, Berkeley
Dies October 8, Billings Hospital, Chicago
November: son Thomas edits and presents "Introspection, Empathy, and the Semicircle of Mental Health" at the fiftieth anniversary celebration of the Institute for Psychoanalysis, Chicago

Acknowledgments

This project originated from and was nourished by the trust, dedication, knowledge, and generosity of Betty and Tom Kohut. The publication was supported in part by NIH grant LM 05166 from the National Library of Medicine; additional funding was provided by the Heinz Kohut Memorial Fund of the Chicago Institute for Psychoanalysis and by the Faculty Development Committee of Albion College.

I am grateful also to the following individuals and organizations for their assistance: Thomas Aichhorn, the American Psychoanalytic Association, Jacob Arlow, the Association Internationale d'Histoire de la Psychanalyse, the Austrian Consulate General of Chicago, Michael Basch, the Berlin Document Center, Joan Bossert of Oxford University Press, Shirley Braverman, Charles Brenner, Chicago editors T. David Brent and Lila Weinberg, Michael Burlingham, H. Wayne Carver, the *Chicago Sun-Times*, Theodore Cohen, David Deckelbaum, John Demos, Douglas Detrick, Miriam Elson, Lloyd Etheredge, Helen Fischer, Patricia French of the Hoover Institution at Stanford University, J. William Fulbright, Peter Gay, John Gedo, Arnold Goldberg, John Hayward, Ludger Hermanns, the John Fitzgerald Kennedy Library, Michael Kater, Jerome Kavka, Charles Kligerman, Robert Knight, Susan Kohut, Franz Kraemer, Walter Lampl, Siegmund and Norma Levarie, Leykam-Mürztaler AG, Janet Malcolm, Ana Marquinez-Castellanos, the *Medical Tribune*, Rolf Meyersohn, the Michigan Psychoanalytic Institute, Alice Wiley Moore, the New York Psychoanalytic Institute, the *New York Times*, Max Noordhoorn, the *Österreichische Hochschulzeitung*, the Österreichisches Staatsarchiv, Paul Ornstein, Jacques Palaci, Mark Paterson, *Die Presse*, Susan Quinn, Peter Richter, Paul Roazen, Thomas Roberts, Andrew Rolle, Heidi Rosenberg, the Sigmund Freud Archives, the Sigmund Freud-Gesellschaft, Elise Snyder, Morris Stein, Edward Teller, David M. Terman, Nellie Thompson, Marian Tolpin, Paul Tolpin, Michael Van Houten, Eugen Weber, W. Marc Wheaton, the Wiener Psychoanalytische Vereinigung, Euzetta Williams, Ilse von Witzleben, Ernest Wolf, Emmanuel Yewah, and Elisabeth Young-Bruehl.

G.C.

Albion, Michigan
December 1993

Abbreviations

APA	American Psychoanalytic Association
IJP	*International Journal of Psycho-Analysis*
IPA	International Psycho-Analytical Association
JAPA	*Journal of the American Psychoanalytic Association*
Search	Heinz Kohut, *Search for the Self*, 4 vols.

Introduction

The curve of psychoanalyst Heinz Kohut's life began in Vienna on May 3, 1913, and ended in Chicago on October 8, 1981. The conception of the course of human life as a curve was his own (see below, March 3, 1969). It is a conception which reflects not only the essence of the "psychology of the self" Kohut developed during the last decade of his life but also Kohut's life experience as a whole. In 1978 he wrote that the "concept of a nuclear self . . . has, from the beginning, a destiny, a potential life curve," by which Kohut meant that the course of life is not a hostage to childhood conflicts, as Freud had argued, but the developing experience of a self.

Kohut's last paper was edited and delivered posthumously by his son on the occasion of the fiftieth anniversary celebration of the founding of the Chicago Institute for Psychoanalysis on November 7, 1981. The paper was entitled "Introspection, Empathy, and the Semicircle of Mental Health." The first half of this title referred to the paper Kohut had presented for the twenty-fifth anniversary of the institute, while the second half of the title was inspired by the post-Homeric story of Odysseus and his infant son Telemachus. Odysseus is reluctant to leave his young wife and son for the war against Troy and so feigns mental illness by sowing his field with salt. But one of the delegates of the Greek state, suspecting a trick, throws Telemachus in front of the plow. Odysseus immediately makes a semicircle around the baby and thus demonstrates his mental health by saving his son's life.[1] Kohut sets this story against Sophocles' Oedipus, the doomed figure who inspired Freud's view of human development. For Kohut the story of Odysseus is symbolic of "that joyful awareness of the human self as being temporal, of having an unrolling destiny: a preparatory beginning, a flourishing middle, and a retrospective end; a fitting symbol of the fact that healthy man experiences, and with the deepest joy, the next generation as an extension of his own self."[2]

Thus the image and shape of a curve embrace Kohut's critique not only of Freud's notion of "the child as father to the man" but also of the Western tradition of what in a letter to a colleague in 1978 he called

---

1. *Search*, 4:562; Kohut wrongly ascribes this story to Homer. See also Kohut to the Chicago Institute for Psychoanalysis librarian Glenn Miller, April 9, 1980.
    2. *Search*, 4:563.

"fearless self-sufficiency."[3] While sharing the psychoanalytic view of the importance of the psychodynamics of early life, Kohut came to see childhood as something other than a rock of Prometheus—or, perhaps better, Procrustean bed—to which the adult is bound. Rather, childhood is a time when a properly empathic parental environment can mobilize the child's potential psychological strengths. Kohut, therefore, rejected the biological aspect of psychoanalysis which sees human life as a struggle between sexual and aggressive drives and the social environment. For Kohut psychoanalysis was a pure psychology dealing with the experiential rather than with the biological. Moreover, Kohut argued that psychoanalysis had imbibed a peculiarly modern Western ideal of independence while self psychology had shown the ongoing importance of human relationships in the development of character. Kohut's curve, therefore, expresses nurture and enclosure within as well as across generations—this in contrast to a lonely trajectory of attempted escape from the gravity of origins.

While much has been published on Kohut's theories, and while Kohut himself has offered glimpses of his life in his own writings, he always remained a very private person. The correspndence contained in this volume thus offers a more detailed and nuanced look at his life and career than has ever been possible before. That Kohut embraced Freud in his own way is a reflection of the life that emerges in these letters. Even though he was born in Freud's Vienna, Kohut was a child of the twentieth century just as surely as Freud, born in 1856, was a child of the nineteenth. Kohut admired such contemporaneous musicians as Arnold Schoenberg, Anton von Webern, and Alban Berg; writers like Thomas Mann, Robert Musil, Eugene O'Neill, Franz Kafka, Ezra Pound, and James Joyce; and artists such as Pablo Picasso, all of whom "were active in depicting the broken-up self and its artistic re-creation."[4] And Kohut's view of empathy as a means to knowledge also reflected a modern appreciation of the interdependence of observer and observed, while Freud maintained a nineteenth-century faith in the classical "distinction between observer and observed."[5] It is as instructive as it is ironic that the year Kohut was born, 1913, was the year in which Freud wrote "On Narcissism."[6] Fifty years later and

3. Search, 4:572.

4. Search, 3:331. See also below, April 7, 1977; and March 24, 1981; on Musil, see Kohut to Siegmund Levarie, September 19, 1938.

5. Paul H. Ornstein, "The Unfolding and Completion of Heinz Kohut's Paradigm of Psychoanalysis," in Search, 3:10.

6. Peter Gay, Freud: A Life for Our Time (New York, 1988), p. 338; "On Narcissism" was published in 1914.

a hemisphere away, Kohut was to make his most decisive contributions to traditional psychoanalysis on the subject of narcissism and then use that subject as a point of departure for his own psychology of the self.

But it was Kohut's early years in Vienna which provided the basic emotional and intellectual stimulation for his creative and scientific work in psychoanalysis, on narcissism, and toward self psychology. These years also embodied a point of departure in the literal as well as the metaphorical sense. For both Freud and Kohut were forced to leave Vienna as a consequence of Nazi Germany's annexation of Austria in 1938, and their departure within six months of each other would also come to symbolize both Kohut's moving toward and moving away from (or, as Kohut himself might put it, beyond) Freud. While Freud left Vienna in June 1938 for exile and death in England, Kohut escaped to England in March 1939 on his way to the United States. Like Freud, he started with neurology but, also like Freud, changed to psychiatry on his way to becoming a psychoanalyst. For Kohut, the transplantation of psychoanalysis into the United States which had begun in the 1920s and had accelerated in the 1930s was to provide a solid basis not only for a career as a psychoanalyst but for the construction of his own brand of the discipline. Psychoanalysis was also a means for Kohut to maintain a connection with his life in Vienna; his own analysis with Aichhorn had been interrupted by the *Anschluss* (see below, April 29, 1939). American psychoanalysis comprised a strong trend toward ego psychology first pioneered by Freud himself (and his daughter Anna) as well as an insistence on the medical control of psychoanalysis against which Kohut, following Freud, would rebel.

Vienna in 1913 was a city of established culture and incipient crisis. It was a city associated with the work of composers such as Schoenberg and Gustav Mahler, writers like Hugo von Hofmannstahl and Arthur Schnitzler, artists such as Gustav Klimt and Oskar Kokoschka—and, of course, thinkers like Sigmund Freud, who in 1900 published *The Interpretation of Dreams*, the first great work of a new science of the mind called psychoanalysis. But, particularly after 1900, representative government in the Austro-Hungarian Empire had degenerated into imperial bureaucratic authoritarianism, while a newly virulent brand of mass politics was beginning to crystallize around charismatic figures like the anti-Semitic mayor of Vienna, Karl Lueger.[7] The Empire as a whole, moreover, was beginning to come apart as a result of ethnic and nationalist agitation. Within a year a crisis with Serbia over the

---

7. Carl E. Schorske, *Fin-de-Siècle Vienna: Politics and Culture* (New York, 1980), pp. 116–80; and see Kohut to Siegmund Levarie, February 21, 1980.

recently annexed Austrian province of Bosnia-Herzogovina would explode into war.

It was into such an environment that Heinz Kohut was born in May 1913. That same month a "rough beast"[8] named Adolf Hitler left Vienna and slouched toward Munich on a path that would lead back to the Austrian capital twenty-five years later and end Kohut's years in his homeland. Heinz's father, Felix, was in the paper business (Fa. Bellak & Kohut) and was also an accomplished amateur pianist. His mother, Else (née Lampl), was also musical, blessed with a fine singing voice. Music thus became an important part of Heinz Kohut's life. Heinz took piano lessons as a boy and cultivated an educated taste in music ranging from German and other classical composers to jazzman Louis Armstrong. His first published psychoanalytic paper, which appeared in 1950 and was coauthored by musicologist and old friend Siegmund Levarie, was "On the Enjoyment of Listening to Music."[9] The Kohut family was solidly upper-middle class, and Felix and Else vacationed in Italy and Switzerland. During Kohut's childhood, the family first lived in an apartment in the Alsergrund district and then moved to a big house at Paradiesgasse 47 in Grinzing, a village within the Döbling district north of the city center.

The First World War took Felix Kohut away from home and brought the paper business under increasing government and military control.[10] For the next five years Heinz and his mother also had to endure at least some of the hardships that ensued from a long war of attrition and the Allied blockade of Germany and Austria. It seems that it was during this period that Kohut's character was formed most decisively and in such a way as to give both form and content to his subsequent contributions to psychoanalytic thought.

The most revealing account of Kohut's early years is most probably contained in his famous case study, "The Two Analyses of Mr. Z." It is likely that this essay describes Kohut's training analysis with Ruth Eissler in the 1940s (see below, September 2, 1946) and a subsequent self-analysis in the 1960s. Kohut never told anyone that he was Mr. Z., but both his wife and son became convinced that this was the case, and since publication of the case several of Kohut's colleagues and friends have intuited this relationship. The dominant parental figure

8. William Butler Yeats, "The Second Coming" (1919), in *The Collected Poems of W. B. Yeats* (New York, 1956), p. 185.

9. *Search*, 1:135–58. This was Siegmund Löwenherz who upon arrival in the United States in 1938 Hebraized his name to Levarie (both names meaning "lion heart").

10. David Mitrany, *The Effect of the War in Southeastern Europe* (New Haven, 1936), pp. 83–84, 86, 101, 122.

in "The Two Analyses of Mr. Z." is the mother, whose controlling behavior and paranoia breed insecurity and self-doubt in her son. Kohut, in published recollections of his childhood, dwells on the absence of his father rather than on the presence of his mother. But the absence of the father would more than likely only have aggravated the intrusive presence of the mother and thus intensified the wish to have the father at home. And, following psychoanalytic reasoning, what is unmentioned is just as—if not more—significant as what is mentioned: Kohut was able to treat the absence of his father publicly; the early influence of his mother he was not. That Kohut waited until 1979 to publish "The Two Analyses of Mr. Z." would seem to demonstrate the insecure personal status of what he regarded as the seminal case for self psychology.[11]

An examination of the case study in fact reveals only lightly camouflaged events in Kohut's life. In the second analysis, in fact a self-analysis probably facilitated by a mental crisis late in Else Kohut's life, the image of Kohut's mother is of a possessive, domineering, and seductive woman who "emotionally enslaved those around her and stifled their independent existence."[12] Else also displayed paranoid tendencies which further oppressed Heinz and the gentle, easygoing Felix. Mr. Z., who has "the face of a dreamer and a thinker,"[13] is, like Kohut, an only child. His father is a successful business executive who is away from the family early in the son's life. He returns, as Felix did from the First World War, when the boy is five years old. But the father remains distant, driven to other women in "flight from the mother."[14] Unlike Odysseus with Telemachus, "the father had tried to save himself, and in doing so had sacrificed his son."[15]

11. *IJP* 60 (1979): 3–27; *Search*, 4:395–446. There is no mention of the case in Kohut's correspondence before 1979 and from then on only scant reference: see below, February 2, 1979; September 25, 1979; and August 7, 1980. The case also appears in a revised German translation of Kohut's *The Restoration of the Self* (New York, 1977), *Die Heilung des Selbst*, trans. Elke vom Scheidt (Frankfurt am Main, 1979), in place of "From the Analysis of Mr. X"; see Kohut to Anita Eckstaedt, October 11, 1975; February 10, 1976; and March 26, 1977; see also discussions of the case beginning in 1978 in *Advances in Self Psychology*, ed. Arnold Goldberg (New York, 1980), pp. 449, 450, 552–53, 511, 513.

12. *Search*, 4:417; see also Kohut, *How Does Analysis Cure?* (Chicago, 1984), pp. 16–17, 148–49; and the similar cases described in *Search*, 3:295, 297–98; and Kohut, *The Analysis of the Self* (New York, 1971), pp. 81–82, 146–47. The radical Emma Goldman (1869–1940) also viewed the "woman as mother . . . [as] 'the greatest deterrent influence' in the life of her children, treating them as her own possession and robbing her offspring of any independence." Alice Wexler, *Emma Goldman in America* (Boston, 1986), p. 195.

13. *Search*, 4:396.

14. *Search*, 4:417.

15. *Search*, 4:417.

Although the boy's first two years were happy ones, the nurture his mother provided her infant son became increasingly disruptive of his autonomous development. She regularly examined his feces. Later, she systematically inspected his skin for blemishes and popped any offending blackheads. She subjected him to constant criticism, something to which Kohut would remain sensitive all his life.[16] When Mr. Z. got his own room she would not allow him to close the door. His masturbatory fantasies, commencing around the time his father returned from the war, were masochistic ones of being controlled by women. Most often they adopted a slave motif drawn from *Uncle Tom's Cabin*, which his mother read aloud to him when he was a child.

Both the mother and the father contributed to a sense in Mr. Z. of his being denied value as a person: she by treating him as an object and as a part of herself; he by deserting him. Nor did his father's return satisfy Mr. Z.'s psychological needs: "I was deprived of a young, vigorous father," Kohut told an interviewer in 1978. "He was replaced by an old man, a grandfather, and that was not the same."[17] This observation reflects the denigration of the father by the mother described in "Mr. Z."

Though until 1921 Heinz was indulged as the only child in the Lampl clan, after the war his parents' busy business and social life isolated him (see below, December 4, 1973). He was also sent away on summer vacations in Austria, France, Switzerland, and Germany, although his mother often accompanied him (see below, July 15, 1923; and July 4, 1963). He later recalled to a friend that he once became ill while staying with friends and neither his father nor his mother visited him. Another story, repeated in "The Two Analyses of Mr. Z."[18] was a skiing trip he took with his father. Heinz was disappointed to sense what was an occasion for closeness between father and son was also an opportunity for the father to meet his mistress.

Kohut, largely left to own devices, was diverted early on not only by hiking, scouting, boxing, and soccer (see below, July 4, 1963; and September 12, 1971) but also by stories of space travel and membership in an adolescent secret society.[19] He also had an intense and intellectually stimulating relationship with a young tutor, Ernst Morawetz, who, it seems, is represented by the young counselor with whom Mr. Z.

16. See, for example, Lutz Rosenkötter to Kohut, October 13, 1980; and below, July 19, 1977.
17. *People*, February 20, 1979, p. 61.
18. *Search*, 4:433–36.
19. *Search*, 2:661; Kohut, *Self Psychology and the Humanities* (New York, 1985), p. 241.

had one or two homosexual encounters. Together with Morawetz, Kohut immersed himself in the world of museums, music, and the works of Kant, Nietzsche, and Schopenhauer. He was the beneficiary of a classical education ("eight years of Latin and six years of Greek")[20] in Vienna, but he also spent a couple of summers at boarding schools in Switzerland and France. This aggravated the isolation he felt from his parents: "Royalty was around, but that did not make up for an essential deep loneliness. I would get postcards from my father from one end of Europe and from my mother at the other end."[21] Even when the family was together, the distance between parents and son remained great. Two days after his sixty-seventh birthday and in the midst of difficulties stemming from the Chicago institute's hostility toward his challenge to psychoanalytic orthodoxy, he wrote to colleague Arnold Goldberg and underlined the *"emptiness"* (see below, May 5, 1980) of the birthday parties he had as a child.

As a result, Kohut idealized his tutor and many of his teachers in school—in particular a high school history and geography teacher, Ignaz Purkarthofer[22]—and later spent a great deal of time with his young uncle, Hans Lampl, sharing his active cultural and social life. When Kohut returned to Vienna for the first time in 1957, he made a point of visiting Lampl, who was ill and would die soon afterward.[23] As early as grade school, Kohut recalled many years later (see below, October 13, 1978), he had developed an interest in medicine, an interest Kohut says his artistically inclined father could not appreciate. It was not until Heinz was in medical school that his father came to value his son's work. This acknowledgment was, as Kohut recognized later, also an affirmation of the identity he had managed to forge from positive and nurturing aspects of both his mother's and his father's personalities. According to his cousin Walter Lampl, Heinz was devastated by his father's death from leukemia in 1937.

Kohut in the meantime had become the quintessential young Viennese intellectual, frequenting the coffeehouses that were centers for discussion and debate (see below, June 20, 1980). Many of these discussions were with his friend Siegmund, whom he had met in 1924

20. Kohut to Marquis Biographical Library Society, July 1, 1972.
21. Mark Perlberg, "A New Mirror for Narcissus," *Human Behavior* 6 (February 1977): 21. More than one summer was spent at St. Quai-Portrieux near St. Malo in Brittany: see Kohut to Jacques Palaci, October 4, 1976. See also below, December 4, 1973.
22. *Search*, 2:771–72. Kohut dedicated his last book, *How Does Analysis Cure?* to Morawetz and Purkarthofer, but he misspells the latter's name.
23. *Search*, 2:663–64; Kohut to Stephan Stewart, October 16, 1957.

and with whom he would tour Paris and Brittany in the summer of 1929. Döbling itself was famous for its cultural salons, and the Döblinger Gymnasium, where Kohut received his classical education, was one of the secondary schools which trained students for entry into the university.[24]

Kohut passed his graduation examinations (*Matura*) at the Döblinger Gymnasium in 1932. He went on to study medicine at the University of Vienna; he also interned for a year at hospitals in Paris (see below, March 24 and 25, 1936). Kohut, like many Viennese intellectuals, had for some time been interested in psychoanalysis and began his own analysis in the 1930s, first briefly with Walter Marseilles and then with August Aichhorn. He received his medical degree in November 1938, but in March of that year Nazi Germany annexed Austria. As for so many others, this represented a personal disaster for Kohut. Although the Kohuts were not religious, they were legally members of the Jewish Community (*Israelitische Kultusgemeinde Wien*) and thus their "racial" background was Jewish.[25] Kohut could not remain in Austria.

In a sense, he left Vienna twice. On the afternoon of June 4, 1938, acting on a tip from Aichhorn, he went to the train station in Vienna to witness the departure of Freud into exile (see below, October 12, 1952). With this event, he recalled many years later, "I had the feeling of a crumbling universe."[26] Kohut could certainly identify with Freud and surely could see himself leaving Vienna under similar circumstances in the near future. Moreover, his friend Siegmund emigrated in July.

But first there was the matter of his medical exams. The Nazis initially threatened the immediate expulsion of all Jewish university students. But in June it was decreed that those in their last year could

---

24. Steven Beller, *Vienna and the Jews: A Cultural History, 1867–1938* (Cambridge, 1989), pp. 40–53.

25. Kohut himself never made much at all of his Jewish background, although he did once take the opportunity to attend a United Nations Security Council debate on Palestine. See Kohut to August Aichhorn, May 29, 1948. According to Walter Lampl, the Kohut family did not observe the Sabbath, but they did reserve seats at the temple in the Ninth District near the Liechtenstein park. On Yom Kippur, however, "Felix, observing Jewish religious law and customs, would walk from Paradiesgasse some three miles to attend services; Else would drive her car to the temple's vicinity and walk from there." Walter Lampl, personal communication, March 10, 1993.

26. Susan Quinn, "Oedipus vs. Narcissus," *New York Times Magazine*, November 9, 1980, p. 120. See also Mitchell G. Ash, "Central European Emigré Psychologists and Psychoanalysts in the United Kingdom," in *Second Chance: Two Centuries of German-speaking Jews in the United Kingdom*, ed. Julius Carlebach et al. (Tübingen, 1991), pp. 101–20; and VA K 139: Österreichisches Staatsarchiv, Vienna.

take their oral exams.[27] In early October Kohut was notified that he would have to take eight examinations within a period of four weeks starting immediately; he finished on October 26.[28] Then in early November Kohut and his mother had to hide during the anti-Semitic riots which began on November 9 during "the night of broken glass." What before had been demoralizing and threatening had now become dangerous: when the night before Kohut had written Siegmund, in a letter that was resumed only on November 16, about the "crazy act in Paris," he parenthesized ominously that in Vienna that evening there had been both an earthquake and an eclipse of the moon (see below, November 8, 1938). Moving from their exposed single dwelling in Grinzing the Kohuts spent "crystal night" with Siegmund's parents at their apartment and then a few nights elsewhere with non-Jewish friends until the terror abated. Josef Löwenherz was the leader of the Jewish Community and his wife, Sophie, felt that the apartment would not long be safe.

It was Löwenherz who, together with Kohut's uncle Hans operating in England and in Switzerland, procured a transit visa for England for Kohut in February of 1939.[29] Until then Kohut was able to get a tedious clerical job in the Rothschildspital, the hospital of the Jewish Community in Währing, under the official protection of Quaker Pastor Frank van Gheel Gildemeester and Rabbi Benjamin Murmelstein.[30] So the near future Kohut had been anxiously anticipating ever since Freud's departure eight months before arrived in March 1939 when he led a group of Jews by train through Germany and thence to freedom in England (see below, March 18, 1938; and June 2, 1946). He was placed in the Kitchener Camp at Richborough near Sandwich, Kent, where he worked in the first aid station.[31] He caught pneumonia, however, and was allowed to stay with his uncle Hans in London; Hans Lampl,

27. Norman Bentwich, "The Destruction of the Jewish Community in Austria 1938–1942," in The Jews of Austria: Essays on Their Life, History and Destruction, ed. Josef Fraenkel (London, 1967), p. 470.

28. Kohut to Siegmund Levarie, October 5 and 26, 1938; and below, August 23 and 25, 1938. Kohut's Jewish professors were replaced for the exams by Nazi professors.

29. Kohut to Siegmund Levarie, February 14 and June 28, 1939. The elder Löwenherz stayed in Vienna until the end of the war as head of the Jewish Community; see Raul Hilberg, The Destruction of the European Jews (Chicago, 1961), p. 292; and below, September 2, 1946.

30. Kohut to Siegmund Levarie, December 12, 1938; Bentwich, p. 469; and Herbert Rosenkranz, "The Anschluss and the Tragedy of Austrian Jewry 1938–1945," in The Jews of Austria, pp. 479–526.

31. See below, May 22, 1939; on the Kitchener Camp, see Ronald Stent, "Jewish Refugee Organizations," in Second Chance, pp. 591–93.

an executive of the Austrian paper firm Leykam-Josefsthal A.G., had
emigrated to England in 1938.[32] Kohut's stay in England was contin-
gent on his receiving a visa to enter the United States; this he secured
through an affidavit signed by the Chicago business partner of his
friend Siegmund's uncle (see below, August 31, 1938). At the end of
February 1940 Kohut sailed for the United States in a convoy across an
Atlantic Ocean prowled by German submarines. He settled in Chicago
where Siegmund was teaching and conducting at the University of
Chicago.

The legacy for Kohut of his years in Vienna was twofold. Although
he did not speak German at home out of a desire to become an American, he preserved a strong love for his homeland (see below, September 10, 1951; and May 6, 1973). He once recalled with genuine pleasure
an occasion during a visit to Amsterdam when "my old Viennese began to come bubbling out" (see below, September 25, 1965). To be sure,
Kohut was still ambivalent about this. Almost all of his relatives had
died in Nazi concentration camps (see below, June 2, 1946). He spoke
of "playing with psychological fire" (see below, September 15, 1975)
in returning to Vienna for the first time in 1957; and as late as 1970 he
was telling colleague Margaret Mahler that she was "brave to have
accepted a scientific assignment in Vienna," adding that he had "so far
declined all such invitations."[33] But when friend Henry von Witzleben
commented that Kohut resisted using German,[34] he responded that it
was only when he could "speak and think German" that he felt really
content, and how wonderful it was to be in Austria and to hear people
speaking "normally." Kohut conceded that his friend must have detected something in his letter that he had in the meantime forgotten.
But late in his life he responded to contacts from gymnasium friends
who had learned of his fame (see below, September 14, 1973) and was
looking forward to a reunion with them in May 1982 on the fiftieth
anniversary of their graduation.[35] Kohut was also very pleased in 1977
to be honored with membership in the Austrian Academy of Sciences
(see below, October 6, 1977) and even more pleased at receiving the
Austrian Cross of Honor for Science and Art that same year.[36] And

32. Lampl resumed his post as director during 1947–50; see also Kohut to August
Aichhorn, February 2, 1947. On Kohut in London, see Kohut to Siegmund Levarie,
October 27, 1939.

33. Kohut to Mahler, May 23, 1970.

34. von Witzleben to Kohut, February 23, 1963; Kohut's reply is undated and his
original letter to von Witzleben is missing.

35. Walter Neudörfer to Kohut, June 15, 1981.

36. As he wrote to Hertha Firnberg, Austrian Bundesminister für Wissenschaft und
Forschung on November 7, 1977: "[T]he values of the Austria that I had known seemed

only two years before his death he privately expressed a particular nostalgia for Germany, a view in keeping with his paternal grandfather's greater German (*grossdeutsch*) predilections (see below, February 24, 1979).

The second aspect of the legacy of Kohut's Vienna years consisted of his lifelong concern with the human capacity and need for empathy. This concern was part of an intellectual commitment common in Europe to psychoanalysis as a broad humanistic discipline rather than simply a medical one. Such a view would conflict with the American emphasis on medical training for psychoanalysts but also exploit powerful postwar trends in America and elsewhere toward supplementing (or even replacing) the biology of drives with a psychology of intentions and social interactions (see below, August 4, 1964). Empathy for Kohut was a matter of nurture ("was one fully accepted by one's parents or not?"),[37] but it was also an intellectual tool, a means to knowledge, an idea Kohut acquired as an adolescent from Immanuel Kant's idea that one cannot separate what one knows from how one comes to know it. The essence of reality is unknowable, Kant argues, therefore, Kohut argued ("because I was from earliest childhood on emotionally prepared for this insight"),[38] only introspection and empathy can reveal the inner life of human beings. Self psychology would, therefore, be an experiential psychology.

Kohut's own childhood and adolescent experiences with parents who were distant and unempathic, coupled with his innate brilliance and the intellectual atmosphere of Vienna, were to sensitize him to patients suffering from narcissistic disorders who were the psychological casualties of modern families in which there is insufficient nurturing of the infant's and child's sense of self-worth and self-confidence: "Parents are away a lot. Daddies are not around, or they don't feel any pride in themselves. Children feel abandoned and depressed."[39] Such children can become "narcissistic personalities" who crave attention and affirmation. Kohut himself was susceptible to feelings of narcissistic injury, and his "disinclination to talk about particular chapters of my early life" (see below, October 27, 1973) was an indication of the pain he felt over his experiences, a pain certainly deepened by the

---

again to come alive and a wound that I thought could never heal seemed finally to close." Kohut was also named to honorary membership in the Österreichische Studiengesellschaft für Kinderpsychiatrie: see Kohut to Lore Watzka, July 2, 1976; and Wolfgang Huber, *Psychoanalyse in Österreich seit 1933* (Vienna, 1977), pp. 122, 203.

37. Perlberg, "A New Mirror for Narcissus," p. 18.

38. *Search*, 4:447–48; see also *Search*, 4:551–52.

39. *People*, p. 61.

Nazi annexation of Austria, an event which seemed to Kohut to justify
the paranoia of his mother that was the psychological complement to
her desire to control those around her. All his life Heinz had struggled
with the question of who was crazy, he or his mother: now the arrival
of the Nazis appeared to have confirmed her suspicions of the outside
world. Kohut's old friend Charles Kligerman recalled at the memorial
service for Kohut in Chicago in 1981: "The rise of Hitler and the destruction of the idealized Viennese world in which he had become
persona non grata were tremendous blows to his self-esteem."[40] These
feelings were aggravated by the fact that Kohut, raised in a nonreli-
gious and assimilated family environment, regarded himself as Austrian rather than as Jewish. He would tell his son that, unlike the Jews,
he was not able to comprehend why he had to leave Austria, since in
spite of his Jewish ancestry he did not have a Jewish identity. As he
put it in 1980, "[A]ll of a sudden, these bullies came along who claimed
they were the real Germans and I was all of a sudden a foreigner and
didn't belong."[41]

Kohut was at first able to obtain only a low-paying internship at the
small Roseland Hospital in Chicago. He later claimed to have learned
English primarily through reading the works of Lewis Carroll (see
below, October 10, 1956; and January 31, 1967), but he had received
some tutoring in the language in Vienna in 1938 (see below, November
8 and 16, 1938) as well as some instruction in it in the transit camp
during 1939.[42] He received his Illinois medical license in August 1941
and became a resident in neurology at the University of Chicago Hospitals the same year (see below, September 2, 1946). By 1944, however,
he had begun to make the turn from the temporary professional haven
of neurology (see below, October 12, 1946), the study of the nervous
system and its diseases, to psychiatry, the study and treatment of

40. Charles Kligerman, "Memorial for Heinz Kohut, M.D., October 31, 1981," *Annual
of Psychoanalysis* 12–13 (1985): 12.

41. Quinn, "Oedipus vs. Narcissus," p. 124. As Betty Kohut has recalled, this experience sharpened Kohut's concern over the rabid anticommunism of the postwar years
in the United States. Among his letters is an address by University of Chicago Chancellor
Robert Maynard Hutchins concerning investigations of Communist influence at the
school: The University of Chicago Senate, "Annual Report of the Chancellor (Investigation by State Legislature)," May 6, 1949, pp. 1–3.

42. Kohut to Siegmund Levarie, June 25, 1939; Kohut sent two letters to Levarie in
excellent English on September 3 and October 13, 1939. Kohut wanted to serve in the
military but only as a doctor. (See below, June 2, 1946, where he wrongly claims that
not being an American citizen also kept him from military service.) Levarie, also not a
citizen, served in the Pacific theater from 1942 to 1945; see Kohut to Levarie, March 12,
1945.

mental disorders, by becoming an instructor in that discipline as well.[43] He received his board certification in neurology in 1946 and in psychiatry in 1949. From 1947 to 1950 he was an assistant professor of psychiatry at the University of Chicago School of Medicine. In the fall of 1946 Kohut had begun training at the Chicago Institute for Psychoanalysis, from which he graduated in 1950. He became a member of the institute in 1953. Near the end of the war in 1945 he had gained United States citizenship and had married an institute social worker, Betty Meyer, in Milwaukee in 1948.[44]

Kohut's mother had remained in Austria until February 1940 before moving to the United States via Italy. After arriving in Chicago in March, she, in characteristically fearless fashion, opened a small notions store named "De Else" on 47th Street. After her son left Vienna, she not surprisingly kept to herself; Aichhorn reported to Kohut in 1939 that he had not responded to his many invitations to visit.[45] In response to a Nazi decree of February 21, 1939, which required Jews to hand over all gold, platinum, silver, precious stones, and pearls,[46] Else had taken some of the family's valuables to the Dorotheum, the state-owned auction house and pawnbrokerage. Twenty-one years later she would apply for and receive restitution payments from the Austrian government.[47] In February 1939 Else had had to sell the family's home at a significant loss (see below, March 7, 1947), moving into an apartment on the Währingerstrasse near the stationery store she had also had to sell (see below, August 23 and 25, 1938; and September 2, 1946). Soon after the war Aichhorn—to whom Kohut was sending food, books, and even coal—wrote that he had run into the man who

43. In 1969 Kohut would resign from the Chicago Neurological Society; Kohut to Joel Brunlik, November 14, 1969. But he remained a lecturer in the University of Chicago Department of Psychiatry from 1958 to 1981 (see below, December 17, 1962); and in 1979 he was named an honorary member of the Michael Reese Hospital and Medical Center Department of Psychiatry.

44. See Kohut to August Aichhorn, December 28, 1948; in this letter Kohut reports their great good fortune in finding an apartment in the midst of a severe housing shortage. Before the war Betty Kohut had gone to Vienna to be analyzed and had taken a seminar for pedagogues from Aichhorn; see Kohut to Aichhorn, May 18, 1949. She continued her work as a psychotherapist after her marriage.

45. Aichhorn to Kohut, July 23, 1939; this letter was written from Budapest.

46. "Dritte Anordnung auf Grund der Verordnung über die Anmeldung des Vermögens von Juden. Vom 21. Februar 1939," Reichsgesetzblatt (1939), I:282.

47. Edward K. Fliegel to Kohut, December 19, 1960; and VA 17.666, VA 37.820, HF-Abg.F. 679, HF-NHF I: Österreichisches Staatsarchiv, Vienna. The Dorotheum auction house was the place where most of the officially "aryanized" goods from Vienna were brought. See Robert B. Knight, "Restitution and Legitimacy in Post-War Austria," Leo Baeck Institute Yearbook 36 (1991): 413–41.

was now living in the Kohuts' house, and he had given Aichhorn the distinct impression of feeling somewhat guilty about how he had come to own the property.[48]

During the 1950s Kohut rapidly established himself as a major force at the Institute for Psychoanalysis. He quickly became a training analyst, one of those who analyze students and supervise their analyses of patients (see below, November 13, 1963; and October 16, 1964). He participated in the recasting of the curriculum and taught the core theory sequence "in a manner," according to Kligerman, "that set the standard for every subsequent teacher."[49] Kohut's brilliance allowed him to teach extemporaneously; in the theory course there was no syllabus—in his own words, he "taught off-the-cuff and different each time."[50] He received high marks from the students; on one occasion the only criticism, not surprising given the depth and breadth of his knowledge and his need to be the center of attention, was that he was much more effective as a lecturer than as a discussion leader.[51] This brilliance and self-confidence could also on occasion manifest itself as a self-righteous dismissal of opposing points of view and what he regarded as inadequate or irrelevant formulations. Kohut always took great pride in his erudition (see below, May 16, 1967). Finally, Kohut had a thriving clinical practice which provided much of what he liked to call the "experience-near" material with which he would construct his later "experience-distant" theories on narcissism and the self.

Kohut also rapidly gained professional stature on the national level. These were the boom years for psychoanalysis, particularly in the United States, where the numerous refugees from Europe and the American wartime mobilization of psychological services had promoted unprecedented growth in the field. He became a member of the editorial board of the *Journal of the American Psychoanalytic Association* in 1955 and spoke out on the issue of factional infighting within and among psychoanalytic institutes (see below, June 15, 1956). Kohut also

48. Aichhorn to Kohut, November 19, 1946; see also Aichhorn to Kohut, February 19, 1947. After the war the house and Else's store were placed under the trusteeship of an aunt who had survived the war: see below, September 2, 1946. Else's Citroen C6 automobile was also confiscated; see Verzeichnis über das Vermögen von Juden, July 12, 1938, p. 3; VA K 71/34: Österreichisches Staatsarchiv, Vienna.

49. Kligerman, "Memorial for Heinz Kohut," p. 11.

50. Kohut to Eli Zaretsky, February 14, 1980.

51. Institute for Psychoanalysis Teaching Evaluation, n.d.; see also Janice Norton to Kohut, May 31, 1961; and Ana Marquinez-Castellanos to Kohut, April 9, 1979. While Kohut's written style is often (but not always) dense and complex, his spoken style (reflected in published extemporaneous remarks) was "simple and lyric": Paul Tolpin to Anders Richter, November 28, 1979.

established close relationships with, among others, prominent fellow Viennese colleagues Kurt Eissler, Heinz Hartmann, and Marianne Kris. His reputation was further enhanced by ventures in "applied psychoanalysis," most significantly a paper on Thomas Mann's novella *Death in Venice* (see below, November 26, 1956; and January 1, 1957).

Most important during these years, however, was the fact that Kohut had begun to think critically about psychoanalytic theory and practice. He was typical of the time in that he adhered to a psychoanalytic ego psychology that stressed the ego's autonomy from, as well as its mediation between, internal drives and external environment (see below, May 16, 1966). But he was concerned about the Freudian mixing of biology and psychology.[52] This early concern would eventually find expression in his psychology of the self as an insistence on psychoanalysis as a pure psychology devoted to the study of human experience *by means of* human experience. A drive, an ego, or an id cannot be experienced, but a self can, Kohut would argue.

His first major statement on the experiential basis of psychoanalytic knowledge came in a paper read at the twenty-fifth anniversary meeting of the Chicago Institute in November 1957. Kohut claimed that the inner life of human beings can be observed only "through introspection in ourselves, and through empathy (i.e., vicarious introspection) in others."[53] Kohut acknowledged limits to such introspection and retained in this paper a belief in the primal nature of the sexual and aggressive drives. This paper was published in 1959 and had a mixed reception: praise for its careful clarification of the investigative method special to psychoanalysis, criticism for being "lop-sided" and arguing for the obvious.[54] Its significance for Kohut's work as a whole, however, is that it argued for what was unique about psychoanalysis and against attempts either to reduce psychoanalysis to biology by emphasizing the drives or by diluting it into sociology by stressing what ego psychologist Heinz Hartmann called "adaptation" to external conditions.[55] Within the curve set by his own life experience this essay would form the basis for a thoroughgoing critique of psychoanalytic theory and practice.

The first five years of the new decade, however, were chiefly ones of involvement in the national politics of psychoanalysis, while the

52. Paul H. Ornstein, "The Evolution of Heinz Kohut's Psychoanalytic Psychology of the Self," in *Search*, 1:25.

53. *Search*, 1:206.

54. "Journal of the A. Psa. A. re Introspection and Empathy," n.d.; see also below, November 22, 1959.

55. *Search*, 3:97n.3; see also below, May 16, 1966.

latter half of the decade was to see Kohut's growing participation in the international affairs of the discipline followed by a decisive break. This break, and the experiences that immediately preceded it, would help bring Kohut's earlier work to fruition in the 1970s. During 1963 and 1964 he was president of the Chicago Psychoanalytic Society, and then was president of the American Psychoanalytic Association from May 1964 to May 1965 (see below, March 7, 1965). The APA had around 1100 members, the great majority of whom were physicians, who were seeing roughly 11,000 patients a year. It was at this time that Kohut became known to many as "Mr. Psychoanalysis," loyally and publicly asserting that his discipline's "scientific aspects are outstanding and that it is primarily a biological science."[56] In his inaugural address in Los Angeles Kohut emphasized the importance of scientific advances for greater understanding of human psychology in the long term as opposed to the limited therapeutic gains psychoanalysts could hope to make given the small numbers of analysts and analysands. He also stressed the need to combat "our worst disease, an excessive tendency toward dissension."[57] But Kohut was in fact not a defender of the status quo in American psychoanalysis. In his valedictory as president in New York the following year, Kohut highlighted controversies over the place of child psychology in the APA and the issue of the training of nonmedical analysts.[58] In both of these areas Kohut backed unsuccessful efforts to expand the boundaries of the discipline (see below, August 4, 1964).

The insights Kohut was gaining through his ongoing clinical work were reinforced by his organizational experiences during these years. At the time (see below, May 17, 1966) and later he maintained that by observing himself and others in the administration of psychoanalysis he learned a great deal about inflated pride and narcissistic wounds.[59] He also commented that he must have fled into administration in the first place to escape tension over his growing sense of challenging psychoanalytic orthodoxy in his clinical practice and writing.[60] During this time Kohut's seminal contributions on the subject of narcissism were contained in three papers: "Forms and Transformations of Nar-

---

56. Emma Harrison, "Analysis Appeals to the Educated," *New York Times*, May 2, 1964; see also Kohut, "On the Occasion of Heinz Hartmann's Seventieth Birthday," November 4, 1964, p. 2; and see below, February 10, 1965; and August 9, 1968.

57. *Search*, 1:392.

58. *Search*, 1:395–404. On nonmedical training, see *JAPA* 17 (1969): 645.

59. *Search*, 2:772; Kohut, *The Kohut Seminars on Self Psychology and Psychotherapy with Adolescents and Young Adults*, ed. Miriam Elson (New York, 1987), pp. 31–32.

60. Kohut, *How Does Analysis Cure?* pp. 87–88.

cissism" (1966), "The Psychoanalytic Treatment of Narcissistic Personality Disorders" (1968), and "Thoughts on Narcissism and Narcissistic Rage" (1972). These contributions to psychoanalytic theory and practice would gradually evolve into the psychology of the self that Kohut would work out most significantly in three books during the ensuing decade: *The Analysis of the Self* (1971), *The Restoration of the Self* (1977), and *How Does Analysis Cure?* (1984).

Kohut argued that his clinical experience and that of many others had shown that the traditional psychoanalytic emphasis on sexual and aggressive drives and conflicts was no longer adequate to explain and treat many psychoanalytic patients. He had discovered three types of narcissistic transferences: mirroring, twinship, and idealizing. Transference is the process by which the patient transfers or projects his or her unconscious needs and wishes onto the figure of the analyst. These needs and wishes are then available for recognition and analysis, for "working through" by the patient. Kohut argued that common patient objections to psychoanalytic interpretations he encountered in his practice were not just resistances to dealing with repressed unconscious oedipal wishes, as traditional theory held, but were often symptoms of narcissistic needs stemming from early emotional deficits. Kohut maintained that contemporary family structure, or the lack thereof, had created a psychological environment of loneliness in place of the close Victorian family atmosphere of supercharged sexual tension (see below, February 7, 1977). In 1981, for example, Kohut spoke of

> the poor rich people's children who[m] I now treat, who grew up on the wealthy North Shore, whose parents were always unapproachable. They were playing bridge, going out. There was nobody but hired help, but you could never get at them.[61]

For Freud and most psychoanalysts the child is a bundle of drives coming into conflict with civilized restraints. This culminates in the Oedipus conflict whereby the child is to renounce desire for the parent of the opposite sex and reorient himself or herself eventually to normal genital sexuality with adult partners outside of the family. The universal phenomenon of neurosis, psychoanalysts believe, is the result of the imperfect resolution of this fundamental conflict. Kohut, in part drawing upon a post-Freudian tradition of psychoanalytic thought and practice which emphasizes the pre-oedipal relationships of young chil-

---

61. Dr. Robert L. Randall, "First Meeting with Heinz Kohut, M.D., March 22, 1981," p. 5 (typescript). The reference to parents hiding behind bridge hands may have been taken from Kohut's own childhood. Such characters also inhabit the Chicago novels of Sara Paretsky.

dren and their parents, primarily the mother, ultimately developed the idea of the "self" as a substitute for the mechanistic Freudian structure of id, ego, and superego. Kohut also rejected the "Kleinian" view of the psyche as determined by inborn sexual and aggressive drives channeled by the infant's relations with objects in the first months and years of life (see below, October 11, 25, and 28, 1966; and March 3, 1975). Melanie Klein, Donald W. Winnicott, and Margaret Mahler, following Freud, were typical of the prevailing psychoanalytic view that narcissism was often an impediment to proper emotional relationships with others.[62] Kohut elaborated on the notion that narcissism per se is not pathological and has a line of development from archaic to mature as an end in itself. The self thus develops in interaction with the environment throughout life by means of the creation of "selfobjects," other people who are experienced as part of the self. Ultimately, Kohut conceived of the self as "bipolar." One pole comprises the self's need to be affirmed ("mirrored") by the parents.[63] The other pole consists of values internalized as a result of identification with idealized early caregivers. The mature self, the product of empathic parenting, has an affirmative yet realistic sense of its own capabilities and limitations. The immature self is brittle and hollow, anxiously seeking validation from external sources.

One signal indication of Kohut's own validation in the science and profession of psychoanalysis during these years was his growing relationship with Anna Freud. Freud's youngest daughter had established herself at the Hampstead Clinic in London as an expert in working with children and was the author of the influential *The Ego and the Mechanisms of Defense* (1936). Kohut's correspondence with her began in 1963; she was a guest in the Kohut home during a visit to Chicago in December 1966 to receive an honorary degree from the University of Chicago;[64] and during 1968 and 1969 she was one of those who urged Kohut to allow his name to be placed in nomination for president of the International Psycho-Analytical Association. Anna Freud shared Kohut's critical Old World view of the domination of psychoanalysis by the medical profession in America as well as of the various

---

62. Paul H. Ornstein, "From Narcissism to Ego Psychology to Self Psychology," in *Freud's "On Narcissism: An Introduction,"* ed. Joseph Sandler et al. (New Haven, 1991), p. 179.

63. Douglas Detrick, "Self Psychology and the Empathic Environment," *The Humanist* 41 (May/June 1981): 28. Polarity was one of the two principles of nature, according to Kohut's beloved Goethe, the other being increase.

64. See Heinz Kohut, "Notes Concerning Anna Freud in Chicago; December 1966," December 1966 (typescript).

groups "pulling away from analysis" (see below, November 24, 1968); and she viewed Kohut as one of the few genuinely creative minds among the world's psychoanalysts. For his part, Kohut displayed great deference toward "Miss Freud" (it was not until 1975 that he would begin a letter to her as "Dear Anna Freud"), and in his correspondence with her he took the opportunity to be exceptionally harsh in his criticism of Anna Freud's bitter rival Melanie Klein (see below, especially October 28, 1966). However, by 1978 at the latest, Anna Freud had concluded that Kohut "had become antipsychoanalytic."[65] While there are no traces of conflict or even of significant disagreement anywhere in their correspondence, their contact diminished steadily after 1969 and became almost completely confined to personal, social, and organizational matters. This would seem to indicate a widening scientific divergence, although in 1972 she did write an appreciative note to him about how helpful his essay of that year on narcissistic rage had been in her thinking about one of her patients.[66]

Kohut's bid for the presidency of the IPA was preempted by the failure of certain key individuals and groups to lend him their support (see below, February 10, 1969). He expressed great disappointment to Anna Freud over this (see below, February 16, 1969) and also wrote that day in the same vein to Ruth Eissler:

> But much as I dreaded the humdrum of an administrative job, the emotional hardships of being the leader of a heterogeneous group, and especially the imprisonment by work which I do not enjoy, once I had made up my mind to undertake the job if it were offered, the emotional situation changed. Plans were beginning to form in me: about programs, about organizational moves, about addresses to be given—and to turn away from them now is not easy. But, as I wrote to Miss Freud, after one disturbed night I am again sleeping soundly and the waves of resentment and hurt pride which overtook me for a day or two have receded.

Along with feelings of disappointment and rejection—as well as any narcissistic injury which may have helped further spur Kohut's creative turn from psychoanalytic orthodoxy during the ensuing decade—there was a significant amount of genuine relief. Kohut had always been ambivalent about holding office because it interfered with his teaching, practicing, and—most important to him—his writing (see

---

65. Elisabeth Young-Bruehl, *Anna Freud: A Biography* (New York, 1988), p. 440.

66. Anna Freud to Kohut, June 21, 1972; "one of my favorite papers": Kohut to Jacques Palaci, April 23, 1974. But cf. below, August 23, 1971, on defections.

below, September 26, 1977). In 1969 he was finishing the manuscript of his first book, *The Analysis of the Self*, which would appear in 1971.

Most crucially, however, it was also during this time that Kohut went through his period of self-analysis reworking the training analysis he had undergone with Ruth Eissler. The self-analysis coincided with a crisis in the life of his mother Else, who began to suffer from "a set of circumscribed paranoid delusions."[67] She would subsequently suffer a stroke and die in 1972 at the age of eighty-one. Shortly before her death she would embrace the Catholicism in which she had been confirmed as a little girl and would be buried in a Catholic cemetery.[68] His mother's mental difficulties reactivated old conflicts in Kohut which he claimed led directly not only to greater self-understanding and happiness but to what he considered the psychoanalytic breakthrough represented by self psychology. The famously difficult prose of *The Analysis of the Self* may well reflect the personal and professional conflicts Kohut himself had to work through during these years.

The self-analysis as reported in "Mr. Z." focuses on the struggle of the patient's self "to disentangle itself from the noxious self object, to delimit itself, to grow, to become independent."[69] This represents a change from the first analysis which in classic psychoanalytic fashion focuses on the oedipal dynamics of a strong tie to the mother and resultant ambivalent attitudes toward the rival father. The conclusion of the first analysis in "Mr. Z." is that the patient's narcissism is a defense against oedipal wishes. The second analysis, however, validates the patient's perception of the mother's psychopathological intrusiveness and paranoia and appreciates his need to establish psychological autonomy. It must be said that there would seem to be a middle position in which oedipal dynamics and maternal disorder are not mutually exclusive. Be that as it may, for Kohut his mother's crisis revealed once and for all the pathological features of her personality and established the correctness of the latter analysis and relieved him of much of his doubt about himself. In a very deep sense, Kohut had spent his life worrying about who was crazy—himself or his mother. Now he believed he knew.

By the time *The Analysis of the Self* was published Kohut would have another reason to husband his time and energy in order to continue

---

67. *Search*, 4:412. Since Else's emigration to America, there had always been tension between her and her son and his wife (see below, August 16, 1948).

68. Kohut gave a memorial speech at his mother's funeral, but unlike the similar addresses he gave for August Aichhorn, Max Gitelson, and his mother-in-law, Doris Meyer, no copy of the memorial to his mother exists in the correspondence.

69. *Search*, 4:416.

his writing. In the fall of 1971 he was diagnosed with lymphatic cancer. Intruding as it did upon the great personal and professional satisfaction Kohut had derived from his work over the past five years in particular, this was an especially bitter blow and one which would force him from then on to decline invitations to give lectures, hold seminars, and receive awards.[70] Although his cancer entered a long period of remission, Kohut had to suffer a great deal during the last decade of his life. In January 1979 he underwent a coronary bypass and endured a long convalescence as a result of a series of complications.[71] These sequelae included labyrinthitis which Kohut with characteristic wit described as "an inner ear problem that makes me feel seasick without the compensation of ocean breezes."[72] And in late 1980 he fell ill with a life-threatening pneumonia following upon the rigors of a self psychology conference in Boston (see below, December 6, 1980).

The absolute priority Kohut gave to his profession and to his creative work meant that the exhaustion which came with illness and age caused him to have to give up even more of the social life he cherished (see below, February 6, 1968).[73] This was not easy for him to do; as he told *People Magazine* in 1979, "I'm no ascetic."[74] His narcissism demanded attention and affirmation by others, as witnessed by an almost childlike joy in the telling of stories, the presentation of ideas, the exhibition of skills, and the bestowal of honors. Although his was hardly a life of unbroken happiness, Kohut was full of humor, charm,

70. Kohut to Frederick Hacker, December 7, 1971; and to Anna Freud, December 25, 1971. See also Kohut to George Pollock, November 14, 1971; and below, May 9, 1972. In the 1950s Kohut had stopped smoking (see below, July 5, 1960) and started running a mile or more a day; he also played tennis regularly and as a result lost a great deal of weight. See Kligerman, "Memorial for Heinz Kohut," p. 14; and Kohut to Ignazio Matte-Blanco, August 21, 1969.

71. See Kohut to Douglas Levin, June 23, 1979; and to Nathaniel London, July 17, 1979. Ironically, when Kohut was searching unsuccessfully for a letter by German heart specialist Karl Friedrich von Wenkebach as a present for his cardiologist, he inquired at the same Dorotheum auction house to which his mother had been forced to take the family's valuables in 1939. See Kohut to Dorotheum, December 22, 1980; and for a sunny appraisal, John Dornberg, "Vienna's Dorotheum," *Smithsonian* 21, no. 9 (December 1990): 110–20.

72. Kohut to Ursula Mahlendorf, October 28, 1979.

73. Kligerman, "Memorial for Heinz Kohut," p. 14. In a letter to his son on November 11, 1978 (before his heart operation), Kohut reported that he was regularly rising at 6 A.M. to work.

74. *People*, p. 61. Kohut expressed his reaction to the very brief article which emerged from the time-consuming photographing and interviewing in a letter of February 23, 1979, to his son and daughter-in-law: "What an anticlimax!"

and playfulness (see below, November 1960; July 5, 1967; Kohut to Solms-Rödelheim, March 3, 1973; and December 26, 1976). He could laugh at himself and display a vital joie de vivre, as evidenced by his closing a letter to a young German colleague with this observation in anticipation of his annual vacation: "There seems to be a serious water shortage in California, but who cares? The California wines are getting better and better."[75] Although he worked during his vacations in the village of Carmel-by-the-Sea, he also looked forward eagerly every year to the rejuvenation he could find in the slower pace and scenic beauty there (see below, September 10, 1951). Nowhere else was Kohut happier.

The last decade of Kohut's life constituted a creative burst which brought with it fulfillment and frustration. *The Analysis of the Self* generated both praise and criticism, but it attempted to integrate a "narrower" concept of the self into the traditional psychoanalytic model of the mind. *The Restoration of the Self*, published six years later, would establish "a self psychology in the broader sense"[76] wherein the "bipolar self" formed the basis of the entire personality. These works attracted a significant number of serious and devoted adherents in Chicago, throughout the United States, and abroad. But alongside these came three forms of the "misunderstanding" of his work which so upset and frustrated Kohut: criticism, cultism, and popularization. Psychoanalysts have always been given to bitter and even vicious attacks. Given the comprehensive and synthetic nature of *The Analysis of the Self* (not to mention its difficulty), Kohut came under fire for allegedly having merely restated in his own words the work of many other predecessors; in one instance he came close to being charged with plagiarism in the pages of the *IJP* (see below, June 18, 1973).[77] Such misunderstanding arose at least in part out of the fact that Kohut's own intuition and creativity during this time likely caused him not to read much of the contemporaneous literature in the field of psychoanalysis, such as D. W. Winnicott (see below, July 2, 1973) and other members of the British school who were mentioned in the accusation of plagiarism. At the same time, Kohut's ideas and person

75. Kohut to Tilmann Moser, March 23, 1977; see also a parody which, according to Siegmund Levarie, Kohut enjoyed immensely: Donald Barthelme, "Conversations with Goethe," *New Yorker*, October 20, 1980, p. 49.

76. Ornstein, "Heinz Kohut's Paradigm of Psychoanalysis," p. 2.

77. See also Kohut, *The Restoration of the Self*, pp. xix–xx. According to the editor and proprietor of the papers of psychoanalyst Erich Siemenauer of Berlin, Siemenauer was privately bitter over what he felt was Kohut's usurping of his position as a pioneer in the research on narcissism. Ludger Hermanns, personal communication, January 21, 1992.

began to attract the type of attention and support he, displaying the elitism common among psychoanalysts, feared might lead to cultism. This danger was compounded, he believed, by the potential and actual popularization of his ideas in the United States as a result of the cultural movement surrounding "the new narcissism" (see below, February 18, 1978; and June 24, 1981). Although Kohut said that lay people often understood his ideas better than many of his professional colleagues, his ideas on narcissism were also popularly misunderstood; as he wrote concerning an "erroneous impression" of his work in *Newsweek* in 1978, "I do not share in the prevailing pejorative outlook on narcissism."[78] But he also recognized that his own emphasis on empathy and human contact as well as his visibility as a figurehead, effectiveness as a speaker, and desire for attention heightened this danger.[79] He summed up his feelings in this regard in a letter to his son and daughter-in-law on November 30, 1978:

> My professional position is peculiar. I get buffeted around by nasty rejections and warmest praise—I could do with less of both but must admit that I am sometimes quite upset about it all.

Although in 1973 Kohut could write that "my ideas have led me into new regions,"[80] in 1978 he would still maintain that "what we are doing is in the very center of psychoanalysis."[81] But by 1978 very many psychoanalysts, while acknowledging in particular the importance of Kohut's ideas on narcissism, judged Kohut's theories as being outside the pale of the discipline. By this time Kohut had dethroned (but not banished) the Oedipus complex. The oedipal *phase* was ubiquitous, as was the oedipal *conflict*, but this, Kohut thought, did not make such conflict normal. It was determined not by biology but by parental response to the child's growing assertiveness and affection. As Kohut sees it, classical analysis deals essentially with "Guilty Man," while self psychology concerns itself more with "Tragic Man," the product of an unempathic mother and an absent father. The former stresses pathology, conflict, and failure, and the latter with some qualification emphasizes the potential for growth, adjustment, and success. As he wrote to a colleague in 1981:

78. *Search*, 4:569; and *Newsweek*, February 27, 1978, p. 11.
79. Kohut to Jerome Oremland, October 9, 1977; to Victor Monke, October 22, 1979; and to University of California, Berkeley, January 22, 1980. Kohut was not interested in writing for the general public: see below, March 2, 1979; and Kohut to Sydelle Kramer, May 21, 1979. But he was interviewed regularly and once gave a television speech in Italy; Lyda Gairinger to Kohut, October 14, 1969.
80. Kohut to Siegmund Levarie, May 5, 1973.
81. Kohut to Nathaniel London, October 4, 1978.

What you said about the difference between classical analysis and
self psychology, "in classical analysis we end up with what was
and what is, while in self psychology we end up with what might
have been, and what can be," is very nice to read and I think—I
hope—that it is true.[82]

In this, to return to the ancient image of "the semicircle of mental
health," Kohut is counterposing a liberal tradition of "striving, re-
sourceful man" as represented by the "modernist" Greek playwright
Euripides against the idea of the "sacrificial he-goat" as dramatized by
the conservative Sophocles in Oedipus Rex.[83]

Kohut was no radical, much less a utopian. His father had been a
Social Democrat, but Kohut displayed a certain conservatism characteristic of a nineteenth-century liberal. He was, however, socially conscious (see below, August 21, 1964; and Kohut to Everett Dirksen,
June 18, 1968), at one point, for instance, contributing to a fund to
help Hungarian colleagues suffering under government oppression.[84]
Nor was he philosophically or scientifically naive. He retained a strong
Central European tradition of skepticism, intellectual rigor, and historical consciousness. All his life he continued to be influenced by the
works of Kafka, seeing in them an expressive rendering of modern
anxiety and anomie (see below, February 26, 1971). He found the shallow and self-indulgent narcissism of the "me-decade" disturbing, especially in terms of parental neglect of children.[85] He ultimately
thought psychoanalyst Erik Erikson's theories of identity formation
deficient because they describe the adolescent and early adult surface
rather than the childhood depths of the personality and because they
"are really value judgments disguised in scientific terms."[86] Unlike
Freud, he believed religion, together with art and science, to be "one
of the three great cultural selfobjects of man."[87] He associated himself
with Unitarianism and felt it was particularly important for his son to

82. Kohut to Roger Petti, February 17, 1981.
83. Search, 4:561; and see below, August 7, 1980.
84. Kohut to Barbara Lantos, May 25, 1955; see below, Kohut to Etheredge, September 26, 1977.
85. Lois Timnick, "Rift Threatens Freudian Theory," Los Angeles Times, October 27,
1979.
86. Kohut, The Kohut Seminars, p. 224. As was the case with American object relations
specialist Otto Kernberg, Kohut was not in touch with Erikson, although Erikson did
attend a session at a self psychology conference; see Anna Ornstein to Kohut, January
31, 1979. See also below, Kohut to Philip Gradolph, February 13, 1977.
87. Randall, "First Meeting with Heinz Kohut," p. 7. See also below, September 28,
1966; and Peter Steinfels, "Psychiatrists and Pope to Discuss End to Longtime Hostility,"
New York Times, January 3, 1993.

have an appreciation for religion. But he was not interested in the unworldly perfection of heavenly salvation—as he once put it in musical terms he borrowed from Siegmund Levarie:

> Great music is not just a perfect chord. Great music is always a deviation into dissonance and a complex way of coming back again to the consonance. This is what drives music through the tunes and harmonies until it finally rests or alludes again at the rest of balance. And so we are spurred on by the necessary shortcomings of that early grace, if you want to use the religious term, of acceptance and perfect mirroring, perfect calmness as we were uplifted, and the perfectly graspable alter-ego environment of other human beings. Which child grows up in a perfect milieu? Some scars, some trauma, some shortcomings belong to life.[88]

In short, Kohut remained suspended between a European and an American view of life—not pure pessimism versus pure optimism, to be sure, but rather a deep concern for human problems as well as for human potentials. This is the reason the title for *The Restoration of the Self* embodies lines from Eugene O'Neill's play *The Great God Brown* (see below, July 25, 1976): "Man is born broken. He lives by mending. The grace of God is glue."

Together with close Chicago colleagues such as Ernest Wolf, Arnold Goldberg, Michael Basch, and Paul and Marian Tolpin, as well as Paul and Anna Ornstein of Cincinnati, Kohut was involved in attempts to institutionalize the training and practice of psychoanalytic self psychology in Chicago (see below, February 21 and November 23, 1978). As early as 1976 the Curriculum Committee of the institute had "agreed to the desirability of giving the students an overall picture of the analytic scene in the first year, including the psychology of the self."[89] Actual training in self psychology first took the form of Saturday workshops, then the establishment of postgraduate courses, and finally the setting up of a popular curricular track.[90] Although Kohut himself progressively tended to perceive rejection of his work (see below, November 23, 1978), interest in self psychology has manifested itself to

88. Robert L. Randall, "Second Meeting With Heinz Kohut, M.D.," April 12, 1981, p. 8 (typescript). See also below, June 7, 1981.

89. Institute for Psychoanalysis, Curriculum Committee, January 13, 1976, p. 1. At this meeting Kohut emphasized that he was now more interested in writing than in teaching and that younger colleagues would have to take the lead in this realm (pp. 2, 3).

90. Ernest Wolf to Heinz Walter, April 15, 1981; see also Kohut to Wolf, July 7, 1978; and to Joris Duytschaever, June 2, 1979. Self psychology is also a curricular track in Los Angeles.

varying degrees at institutes around the country and around the world.[91] Various of Kohut's works have been translated into German, Italian, French, Spanish, Portuguese, Swedish, and Japanese, while in the United States self psychology was promoted most effectively by annual conferences. The initial conference in Chicago in 1978 drew 450 participants, the second in Los Angeles attracted 600, and the third in Boston saw 950 attend.[92]

Generally, Kohut's work was most popular among younger analysts for whom his emphasis on empathy fit their postwar cultural and educational experiences. And even though the psychoanalytic establishment in the United States managed to limit severely the number of nonmedical candidates, there has been longstanding and continuous pressure from within and without the psychoanalytic community for expansion of the discipline's popular and practical base which culminated in 1989 in a successful class-action lawsuit (see below, August 4, 1964). One example of Kohut's appeal along such lines is the argument for self psychology as supportive of feminism. While it is the case that the psychoanalytic movement has for a long time been more open to contributions by women than the fields of medicine and psychiatry in general, Freud's theories have long been criticized for their cultural bias against women. But the move in psychoanalysis toward an emphasis on the pre-oedipal relationship with the mother—work pioneered, among others, by Melanie Klein and Anna Freud—has undercut much of this traditional fixation on the male as the norm in psychoanalysis. And with the opening of psychoanalytic ranks in 1989 to nonmedical practitioners, many of whom are women, a significant part of the current agenda in psychoanalysis involves work on and by women. It is true that Kohut built his theories largely on experience with male patients (see below, October 28, 1973) and that he retained a psychoanalytic emphasis on sexuality (see below, March 14, 1980). It seems likely that his theories stemmed from a childhood marked by a desperate search for masculine identity as an escape from maternal domination and paternal neglect. In spite of these things, self psychology appears to be compatible with feminist values in three respects: aside from its pre-(or supra-)oedipal orientation, "it separates value acquisition from an oedipal superego that is based on castration anxi-

91. See, for example, Philadelphia Psychoanalytic Institute to Kohut, February 15, 1980; Franco Paparo to Kohut, n.d.; and Tilmann Moser to Kohut, October 25, 1970.

92. Kohut to Fernando Cesarman, March 13, 1981. These conferences have taken place ever since. Kohut's last was the fourth at Berkeley, California, in 1981; the editor's note in *Search*, 4:525, incorrectly identifies this conference as the fifth.

ety; and it places a special value on empathy."[93] Moreover, the whole idea of the self and the realization of its potentials offers a model which, in addition to preferring relatedness to Freudian individuation, emphasizes common human psychological and social options rather than biologically based gender differences.

Kohut's influence also spread because of the interest in his work, not only in fields allied to psychoanalysis such as social work (see below, March 10, 1977), pastoral counseling, and various psychotherapies but in the social sciences and humanities in general (see below, May 19, 1977). While psychoanalysis had traditionally influenced fields outside medicine and psychology, Kohut's work seemed more applicable to a whole range of "nonpathological" human phenomena. While this interdisciplinary trend has ebbed somewat since Kohut's death, it was particularly pronounced in the field of history during the last years of his life. For some time a number of historians had been using psychoanalytic perspectives in their work (see below, January 28 and December 31, 1974). Kohut himself was very interested in history and in the contribution his ideas could make to understanding individuals and groups in the past. He was especially concerned with the leaders and those who were led in the charismatic mass movements of the twentieth century (see below, May 14, 1979), the most fateful of which had affected him and his family directly.[94] His son, after graduating as a research psychoanalyst from the Cincinnati Psychoanalytic Institute, earned a doctorate in history (see below, June 17, 1975), and Kohut took special pleasure and pride in participating with him in a psychohistory conference in 1980 (see below, July 9, 1980).

Matters in Kohut's own field during these years, however, were less than serene. Criticism of Kohut's theories ran broad and deep within the psychoanalytic community. Kohut himself not only complained about being misconstrued and misunderstood which—given the sophistication of his thinking and the more than occasional confusion in the course of his formulation of new ideas—should not have been a surprise, but he was particularly pained by what he felt were personal attacks and snubs from many of his colleagues. While some friendships survived professional disagreement, others did not. Particularly painful cases of the latter involved Kurt Eissler (see below, December 11, 1978) and Martin Stein. Another was junior colleague John

93. Judith Kegan Gardiner, "Self Psychology as Feminist Theory," *Signs* 12 (1987): 767; see also *Search*, 2:783–92; Arnold Goldberg to Edward Jones, October 1, 1980.

94. See Charles B. Strozier, "Introduction," in *Self Psychology and the Humanities*, pp. xxvii–xxx.

Gedo, an early admirer of Kohut's work whom Kohut regarded as "one of the finest minds of the younger generation in psychoanalysis."[95] Gedo played Jung to Kohut's Freud. At the celebrations in 1973 honoring Kohut's sixtieth birthday, Gedo gave an embarrassingly florid laudation in which he compared his mentor to Euripides (see below, October 23, 1973). Within two years, however, the two men would be scientifically and personally estranged.

Perhaps what Kohut regarded as the cruelest blow came in the spring of 1978. At that time a number of his colleagues at the Chicago institute (and elsewhere) were afraid that he and his followers were planning to split off (see below, May 1, 1978). Perhaps more as a result of personal resentments than of concern over the possibility of a secession, Kohut was subsequently not reelected to the institute's governing body, the Psychoanalytic Education Council.[96] As with the earlier rebuff in seeking the IPA presidency, Kohut was happy not to have to bother with such official duties, especially since he more than ever was committed to research as well as being increasingly weakened by illness. He was also entering that stage of career when official capacities are as a matter of course laid aside: in 1981 he became inactive as a supervising analyst and became training analyst emeritus.[97] But this rejection hurt terribly and, although he would be reelected to the council for a three-year term in 1980, the original defeat was emblematic of the problems in general Kohut encountered as a result of going his own way in psychoanalytic theory and practice.[98] Even his presentation scheduled for the fiftieth anniversary of the institute in November 1981 was problematic. Originally, Kohut's lecture for this occasion was to be given the status of an "Academic Lecture," but then this status was rescinded. As a result, Kohut insisted on arrangements he felt would assure a proper forum and reception for his paper (see below, May 29 and June 9, 1980). He died of congestive heart failure almost a month to the day before the celebration, and his son Tom edited and read the paper for him.

As a final demonstration of the fruitful intertwining of Kohut's life

95. Kohut to Selma Kramer, June 13, 1972; see also below, July 12, 1968; and June 22, 1977. Gedo also became an editor of *JAPA* on Kohut's recommendation; see Kohut to Eugene Pumpian-Mindlin, May 10, 1971.

96. George Pollock to Kohut, June 9, 1978. There was outrage expressed over this: see Kay Field to Kohut, June 19, 1978; and Debbie Cardon to Kohut, June 20, 1978.

97. George Pollock to Kohut, July 14, 1981. Faculty emeritus status would follow at age seventy.

98. George Pollock to Kohut, May 29, 1980; see also below, May 5 and 6, 1980. Kohut was also subsequently named to Life Membership in the Chicago Psychoanalytic Society; Robert Leider to Kohut, March 9, 1981.

and work, we must return to the theme of empathy within and across generations. Kohut was passionately concerned with the promise represented by youth for the interdependence of human beings within and across generations. His praise for President Kennedy after the assassination and his note to Mrs. Kennedy (see below, December 29, 1963) both struck the theme of youth, the former by recalling Robert Frost as "the old youthful poet" (see below, November 26, 1963) at Kennedy's inauguration, and the latter by dedicating the eulogy to Kennedy's son. Kohut's enthusiasm for Arkansas Senator J. William Fulbright (see below, March 4 and April 7, 1980) was based largely on Fulbright's juxtaposition of the idealism of youthful protestors against the war in Vietnam with the aged cynicism of the war's political and military sponsors.[99] Although Tom recalls that he and his father clashed violently over American policy in Southeast Asia, the fact that his own son actively opposed and resisted the war (see below, November 17, 1968; February 4 and 5, 1969; April 10, 1969; May 11, 1970; and December 25, 1971) eventually engaged and strengthened Kohut's idealistic orientation.

Even though Kohut was frequently apart from his family due to travel and work, he cultivated an especially warm relationship with his son and wrote him frequent and loving letters over the last twenty years of his life. Kohut dedicated *The Restoration of the Self* to "G and his generation," that is, to Tom (middle name August, or, familiarly, "Gustl").[100] Tom might have represented for his father both Telemachus and Odysseus ("the first would-be draft evader in literature"),[101] not only the son but also a father who, unlike Odysseus and Kohut's own father, did not go off to war and abandon the son to the mother. The leitmotif here is the preservation of empathic relations, although, sadly, Kohut's dedication to the scientific elaboration of such relations had to claim much of the time he could otherwise have devoted to his own family. Finally, for Kohut's son to become a historian and write a book using in part his father's theories to analyze the psychological basis for the mass appeal Emperor Wilhelm II exercised in leading Germany into war in 1914 describes circles upon circles in the Kohut family history (see below, February 24, 1979).[102]

99. See the postscript below, July 31, 1968. On Kohut's own description of his "characteristic . . . adolescent idealism," see *Search*, 2:661.

100. Tom's middle name was given in honor of August Aichhorn; see below, June 2, 1946.

101. *Search*, 4:562.

102. Thomas A. Kohut, *Wilhelm II and the Germans: A Study in Leadership* (New York, 1991); see below, May 14, 1979.

Young colleagues like John Gedo, Tolmann Moser, and Arnold Goldberg, among many others, were typical of Kohut's appeal to the youth of his profession to challenge their elders. In 1973 he placed this appeal in the context of the first opera he had ever seen, Richard Wagner's *Die Meistersinger von Nürnberg* (1867). Kohut's father had taken him to see this opera, the reason why Kohut would in turn take his son to see it (see below, August 3, 1968). Kohut interprets the opera as a lesson in the importance of graceful aging (see below, January 11, 1969) and in the perils for the psychoanalytic community of "tool-and-method pride." What Kohut means by "tool-and-method pride" is the tendency for specialists to exalt means over ends and to ignore or disparage "the creative rebel" in their ranks. Because he felt some conflict over challenging psychoanalytic orthodoxy, conflict reflected in the density of his prose during these years, Kohut does not issue a call to arms. Rather he emphasizes the words of hero Hans Sachs in *Die Meistersinger:* "Do not hold the masters in contempt, but [*sic*] do revere their art!"[103] For while Kohut saw himself as a pioneer with the emotional disposition and cognitive ability "to look at things as if I were seeing them for the first time" (see below, Kohut to Philip Gradolph, February 13, 1977), he disliked polemics and personal confrontations (see below, January 28, 1969; and August 10, 1977).

Orthodox psychoanalysts would tend to see in this dual wish to challenge authority yet avoid confrontation an oedipal symptomatology aggravated by the early omnipresence and domination of the mother and the absence of the father during the first five years of life.[104] From this perspective, Kohut's emphasis upon narcissism and the self—as well as his recollection of the distance of *both* his parents—are defense mechanisms against an unresolved Oedipus complex. Such psychodynamics would also have caused resistance to the findings of his training analysis with Ruth Eissler. On the other hand, as

103. *Search*, 2:691. Siegmund Levarie points out that this line from *Die Meistersinger* in fact reads: "and do revere their art!" (*und ehrt mir Ihre Kunst*). Kohut's substitution of "but" could be interpreted as an expression of unconscious aggression since that conjunction makes sense with "Hold the masters in contempt." Kohut also manifested a lifelong Germanic and Enlightenment respect for reason, order, authority, and documentation. See his (also narcissistic) concern about CME (Continuing Medical Education) credits for the 1979 UCLA Self Psychology Conference: Kohut to Shulamite Ash, December 20, 1979; and February 14, 1980.

104. Historian Peter Loewenberg has analyzed the drastic political consequences in Germany among less stable and more afflicted individuals of the oedipal dynamics of the conjunction of wartime absence of fathers, malnutrition, and military defeat in "The Psychohistorical Origins of the Nazi Youth Cohort," *American Historical Review* 76 (1971): 1457–1502.

Kohut himself put it in his critique of the classical conception of the Oedipus complex:

> Is it not the most significant dynamic-genetic feature of the Oedipus story that Oedipus was a rejected child? . . . The fact is that Oedipus was not wanted by his parents and that he was put out into the cold by them.[105]

Criticisms of Kohut's theories abound, and the influence of his ideas among psychoanalysts remains severely restricted. There are arguments about whether self psychology can replace the orthodox psychoanalytic paradigm or can be integrated into it, whether narcissistic disorders represent a significant percentage of psychoanalytic cases, the extent to which the "self" itself is an abstraction rather than an experience, and the like. It is not clear what the future holds for the development and influence of Kohut's ideas. But the story of Kohut's life and career reveals the close and fruitful link between the personal and the scientific inherent in the subject matter and method of psychoanalysis. In Kohut we see the conjunction of a special set of early life experiences, an innate brilliance and creativity, and, within the cultural milieu of fin-de-siècle Vienna, the unique intellectual and emotional stimulation of pscyhoanalysis. The curve of Heinz Kohut's life would bear all these lineaments toward new worlds across space, time, and thought.

105. *Search,* 4:564; for Kohut's responses to criticisms of "The Two Analyses of Mr. Z," see *Search,* 4:514–20, 570, 573–74, 688–90; and Kohut, *How Does Analysis Cure?* pp. 84–91.

Editor's Note

The correspondence in this volume excludes those letters to, from, and about Kohut's patients, all of which, in accord with Kohut's instructions, were destroyed upon his death. The correspondence as a whole also does not, with a few exceptions, include reports on oral communications. Ninety-three letters from the last twenty years of Kohut's life have already appeared in *The Search for the Self: Selected Writings of Heinz Kohut* (volumes 2 and 4) and two letters appear in *Advances in Self Psychology* (1980), but the subject matter of those letters is largely restricted to professional and theoretical matters, while many of the letters are excerpted and often do not name the correspondent.

Kohut's letters in English were either dictated or typed from drafts written in his own style of shorthand; Kohut himself typed the letters written in German. Some letters, especially from the later years, were handwritten. In this collection references to letters printed in the volume are contained in brackets (or occasionally in footnotes) and include the word "above" or "below" and the date (without the year if in close sequence; the correspondent's names are indicated only if more than one letter appears on that date). References to unpublished letters are contained in the footnotes and include the names of the correspondents. The entire professional correspondence will eventually be made available at the Chicago Institute for Psychoanalysis. All letters by Kohut in this volume after 1939 were, unless otherwise indicated, written in Chicago. British spellings and Germanisms are retained. Some substantive errors in spelling and grammar as well as characteristic habits of punctuation have been preserved insofar as they may reveal the state of mind. The letters appear in chronological order except in a few instances where, for the reader's convenience, the letters in an exchange with a single correspondent are placed in sequence; all such cases involve only the reordering of days and not months or years. There are a few omissions of confidential (or extraneous) material contained in the letters: personal and place names are replaced by underlined spaces, while phrases, clauses, or sentences (or addresses in the body of a letter) are replaced by ellipses. The designation of years as "chapters" is only generally related to historical substance and is largely intended to divide the correspondence into manageable sections. Save for the poem in the letter of May 5, 1980, which was translated by Max Noordhoorn and Emmanuel Yewah, and some assistance elsewhere from Siegmund Levarie and Betty and Tom Kohut, all translations are my own.

1923–1948

"bury myself in Freud's life work"

Oetz/Tyrol, Austria, July 15, 1923 [original in German]
Dear Daddy,

As you know from my postcard, I was at the Bielefelder hut [for climbers and hikers], which I enjoyed very much. It is so hot here that it is 35 degrees [Celsius] in the shade. Today in Oetz there was a big twenty-fourth jubilee celebration for the pastor. First thing I took a dip, because in this heat it is no pleasure to walk for three-quarters of an hour. This morning we[1] were awakened very early by continuous cannon firing. Last night was the big torchlight procession, everywhere there were Chinese lanterns hanging in the windows and the whole village was decorated. There was also supposed to be a big [bon]fire, but it was not held because of the danger of forest fire. We are taking a lot of walks and picking strawberries. How are you, daddy? Are you well? Write to me sometime.

Many kisses,
Heinz

1. According to Charles Kligerman, Heinz's mother often accompanied him on his summer vacations.

Paris, March 24, 1936 [original in German]
Siegmund Löwenherz
Vienna
Dear Siegmund!

Now that was really a thoroughly charming idea of yours to use the roundabout method of Goethe's sign language to remind me to write. I think that was the only possibility of awakening me from my writing lethargy, a lethargy so great that—everything notwithstanding—it is only the difficulty of procuring violets in Paris you have to thank for the fact that I'm getting around to it at all.[1] When I opened your letter—I recognized your handwriting [Klaue] right away!—I must have looked a little confused at first, but the very next moment I was enjoying immensely the wonderful—and here in the middle of this entirely Parisian environment (I was standing in a bistro eating my breakfast) so *strange*—idea which transported me in the most remarkable way to Vienna. But then in the third instance I was scratching my head. For where in Paris could I lay my hands on a "Goethe"—in particular the *Noten und Abhandlungen zu[bessere]m [Verständnis des]*

West-östlichen Divans?[2] But it turned out not to be too difficult after all! After lunch, being in the [Latin] Quarter, I went to the library of the Sorbonne and searched out the relevant volume in a German edition of Goethe's collected works from 1840, sat down—with pleasure!—at a table and with studious expression began to leaf through the book until I had found the place. It was a real adventure!

Otherwise everything's fine and I am doing very well. Up until now I have worked at the Hotel-Dieu, one of the largest Parisian hospitals (right next to Notre-Dame), in an internal ward and it was wonderful since everybody, as I was the only foreigner working there, assisted me in the nicest manner. Tomorrow I transfer to the Hôpital St. Louis, not far from the Gare de L'Est, for a few weeks of a "dermatological stage" [*"dermatologischen Stage"*].

March 25, 1936

Last night I was brusquely interrupted by an acquaintance who was picking me up for dinner and so I am continuing today. You have no idea how beautiful Paris is now. Really almost overnight everything has turned green—and what a marvelous green. Delicate light green through which one can see the houses and the sky. As I write this I think above all of the "Luxembourg" [Gardens] in which every day I spend an hour after eating and usually also a while in the late afternoon and which I love very much. Do you know it?

Today for the first time I was at the Hôpital St. Louis and it seems to me to be very good. But what one sees there is truly dreadful. You have no idea (and I had none as well) how hideous this syphilis is. (The Hôpital St. Louis is reserved almost exclusively for this disease.) I don't think I'll soon forget what I saw today: a Negro who with a sorrowful expression (who knows, maybe it only appeared that way to me!) displayed his sores to me—it's really something what a person can endure.

Well, dear Siegmund, enough for today. I thank you once again for your delightful idea and only ask you to write me again when you feel like it. Life is downright strange [*recht komisch*]—what with the green of trees and syphilitic sores—but sometimes on the whole rather beautiful, is it not?

Heinz

---

1. A word play in "Blumen- und Zeichenwechsel," in *Goethes Werke* (Hamburg, 1962), 2:191

2. Goethe's explanatory essay for a collection (1819) of poems, of which the aforementioned sign language was a significant component.

Vienna, August 23, 1938 [original in German][1]
IV. (see last page!)
Siegmund Levarie[2]
Chicago
Dear Siegmund!
Your letter arrived today. You can imagine how anxiously I was
waiting for it. The best: the wonderful matter-of-factness with which
you undertake the great efforts connected with all of this and which
has allowed me and you to grow together into a common "we." You
know: Gratitude is a state of being!
Naturally I (and probably you too) expected difficulties least of all
where they now apparently lie. That a stipend would be easier to
obtain than admission to a university was really not to be foreseen.
As far as the completion of my studies in Europe goes, I naturally will
do everything to make it possible. As for the chances of success, I can,
as you can imagine, hardly make predictions. I don't even know how
things will go in Vienna—whether we shall be given a date at all and
what this span of time, in which I am to take 8 exams, will look like.
Switzerland is at the present as good as shut off and study in Prague
would take 2½ years, which is out of the question. Anyway I consider
your "angler" tactic completely right and maybe we shall be lucky and
one of the eight universities will bite.
Only one problem: What are the possibilities if by luck I show up
with a European diploma? Until my degree is approved [*Nostrifikation*],
I would hardly be able to get a stipend. Or—since we cannot entirely
exclude the possibility of finding a place at an American university—:
Which would be more advantageous—study without a doctorate or
no study with a doctorate? You understand what I am asking![3]
Up until now I had always assumed that the first option was the
better one—not simply because of the "American" doctorate (which
according to your report is apparently not the case), but also because
of the availability of a stipend which would provide me a certain financial basis for the initial period.

August 25
The evening before last I was so tired I almost fell asleep while
writing, yesterday I was again tired and depressed and simply not in
any condition to continue the letter. Today as a precaution I am writing
after dinner, at a time when I am in halfway good form. Outside it is
so stormy and rainy that I can scarcely remember experiencing the like
of it in Vienna—and it is so cold—if it were not a shame to do so in
August—one could imagine lighting a fire.
There is nothing special to report from here. A buyer has presented

himself to my mother and we hope that everything will go quickly and painlessly. I am working a fair amount and not too badly—some of it is nice and interesting (psychiatry), some boring.

An earnest request: write! and not just the practical, but also about you, what you're doing, how you're doing.

And now farewell—6 months seems a long time to me, but it will pass "in the interests both of science and humanity." [English in original]

Heinz

Please number your letters so that no errors crop up! Hitherto written:

1. letter to Italy
2. newspaper to Lisbon
3. letter to Winnetka
4. this letter

Received:

1. letter (stamp: Naples)
2. card from Algiers
3. letter with enclosures (registered)

1. This letter was registered. Kohut and Levarie also assumed that their letters were being opened by censors.

2. As noted earlier, after leaving Austria Siegmund Hebraized his name from Löwenherz to Levarie, both names meaning "lion heart."

3. Fearing an oversupply of doctors, the American Medical Association had become increasingly concerned over the influx of foreign physicians during the 1930s. As a result, "medical licensing boards adopted more rigorous standards for foreign physicians." Paul Starr, *The Social Transformation of American Medicine* (New York, 1982), p. 272.

Vienna, August 31, 1938 [original in German]

V.

Siegmund Levarie

Chicago

Dear Siegmund!

Your letter of August 16 came today with notification of the affidavit. It made me very happy.

I am so tired that today I don't want to write you more than this— the practical questions demand clearer and more alert reflection than I can muster at the moment.

So in brief only what occurs to me:

I don't know whether a Swiss diploma is valid in the USA—please try and find out since reliable information is not available here.

Further: The idea of transferring the scholarship is excellent. Main difficulty for study in Switzerland is, however, the permission for entry and stay. If I don't have a visa for the United States Switzerland won't let me in, and if I have it it expires in 4 months, and to finish my studies in Switzerland would take about 8 months. (Everything is figured in: one must merely register for 1 semester.) The question therefore is: Is there some sort of verification (for the Swiss officials) that my entry into the USA is assured without thereby initiating the period of time for which the visa is valid?

As for study fees, they are much lower in Switzerland than in America.

About chances here there is still nothing I can find out—I work as if I were certain of a date: hence I don't want to exclude fully the possibility of coming over with a Vienna doctorate. In any case that would be the most advantageous possibility.

Something else: [August] Aichhorn has a friend in Chicago [Kurt Eissler] who would probably offer me the opportunity to continue my work over there. I am writing you this so that you too are informed about me in this matter and so that you can balance given chances against one another.

Now that I've gotten a bit into the flow of the letter—I am less tired and must apologize only for my muddled style.

Perhaps the cigarette I've just lighted will help!

Another question: How should I conduct myself toward my old friend Mr. Nordhaus (a letter of thanks?!?)?[1]

For the present I will wait for your instructions—meanwhile thank him for me in whatever form you find appropriate!

Why do I not hear anything about you? In general, from the way in which you write, also from your handwriting I infer (or at least believe) that you are in good shape. I would like to hear this directly from you. Tomorrow I hope to learn more about you from your mother, since she told me on the telephone that she had received a letter from you.

I really must stop now! As a child I remember that every night before going to sleep I had to say a little bedtime prayer with an improvised ending, which asked that my father (who at the time was away at war) return home safely. Those were simple, clear times! In principle, however, I think it is no different when I say to you now, within the limits of the affection which we allow each other, farewell.

Heinz

1. Nordhaus was the business partner of Siegmund's uncle who signed the affidavit guaranteeing that Kohut would not become "a burden on society." Kohut, of course, had never met this "old friend."

Vienna, November 8, 1938 [original in German]
Siegmund Levarie
Chicago
Dear Siegmund!
—still I wonder why I haven't heard anything from you. I have recently been to your house on several occasions and read all your letters as well as the university newspaper. I don't need to tell you how much I enjoyed that.

In the meantime I have received my degree and already have my diploma together with two copies. Please write and tell me what besides the diploma I should have uniformalized or translated, respectively, and which other documents I might need. Above all write and tell me whether there is anything you can do before I come over and whether I need to send you any documents. In any case I shall send you my diploma when I have gathered together all the approvals and stamps.

I have begun to concern myself about my emigration: attorney—notary—tax advisor, and whoever else. Nevertheless up until now I have not secured anything for myself except a feeling of complete incalculability as to when I will be able to bring all of these things to an end.

The mood here since yesterday's crazy act in Paris[1] is once again very sinister (into the bargain tonight there was an earthquake and a lunar eclipse)[2] and I am anxious about what the next few days will bring.

For all these reasons I beg you very much to write to me. It is a great comfort to receive a nice, encouraging letter from outside—so try hard!

Today my head is empty and gloomy and in spite of the pressing need I felt to write you again I produce only colorless scribbling. You understand—and also that now I stop.
          H.
                                              November 16, 1938
I received your letter of November 4 a couple of days ago and the great joy it gave me helped me endure many things more easily. You have certainly known for some time about the results of the exams and my graduation. Your other question as to when approximately in

this century I will receive my visa I can unfortunately not yet answer. In this regard I am hopeful about the help of your father and am waiting for his return from England. At the moment I unfortunately cannot undertake anything at all to hasten my emigration. The only positive thing that I am presently doing is devoting myself rather intensively to the study of the English language and having Mrs. Kaan tell me jokes.[3] Yet I rather fear the various difficulties of a practical nature that will at first arise over there. Once more I repeat what I have already written to you, that Chicago appears to be exceedingly advantageous to me, since Aichh[orn]. has many friends there who certainly will be able to help me on in their field.

Enough for today. Now once again all my gratitude for your always so naturally manifested willingness to help and farewell!

H.

Again: whatever occurs to you that I could use or get over here!—When you write to Ada [Siegmund's sister]: she could occasionally write me a few words.

1. The assassination of a German diplomat in Paris by a young Jew on November 7 provoked Nazi pogroms against Jews in Germany and Austria which came to be known collectively as *Reichskristallnacht*, or "night of broken glass" of November 9–10.

2. "Quake Damages Vienna Houses," *New York Times*, November 9, 1938; "Clouds Hide Eclipse in London," *New York Times*, November 8, 1938.

3. Within the month Kohut had to abandon the English lessons because the Englishwoman, Mrs. Kaan, was no longer allowed to have contact with Jews; see Kohut to Levarie, November 29–30, 1938.

Vienna, March 1, 1939 [original in German]
Siegmund Levarie
Chicago
Dear Siegmund,

This is the second sample of the new stationery ["Heinz Kohut, M.D."], although I am not quite sure that I am justified in calling myself an M.D.—or does my local diploma suffice for that?

Yesterday Richard's [Siegmund's cousin] long-awaited letter finally arrived. It was unbelievably blunt, and astounding in its lack of personal comprehension of the present situation. "Work hard at your studies and grind it out!" he writes to me, meaning that I should begin preparing here for the exams in the U.S.A. No, that won't do, quite apart from my Gildemeester-occupation.[1] I can't conceive of anyone here who in the middle of all the daily agitations could muster the peace and quiet to sit for hours with a book.

Yesterday the formalities of my emigration moved a step further: the Reich Emigration Tax Office, upon payment of RM [*Reichsmark*] 20,000, has no more objections to my emigration. The only thing I am still stuck with are some small tax arrears of my mother's, but those are a matter of a few days. So I can count on having my emigration papers, including the issuance of the passport, all together in about 10–14 days. As far as immigration goes, the transit camp in England comes first. Such a thing is certainly not an ideal situation, but what can one do—the main thing is that one can get out at all.

Yesterday I finally finished typing the table of contents for the [*Goethes Werke. Vollständige*] *Ausgabe letzter Hand* [60 vols., 1827–42] and now will have it bound. *Tempora mutantus* [Times change]—how different it was when we began it.

Servus [Greetings] Siegmund! I await your report about the big concert with excitement. How I would like to be face to face with you: the chessboard between us, as I picture it, on those first evenings— and the pieces untouched after the inevitable "Oh my" at the queen's gambit because there will be much to talk about.

And once again: farewell! Believe me, life can become quite bitter.

Heinz

Thanks for the Renoir: it's wonderful and gives me great pleasure.

1. Quaker Pastor Frank van Gheel Gildemeester assisted Protestant and nonconfessional Jews after the Anschluss; see George E. Berkley, *Vienna and Its Jews: The Tragedy of Success, 1880s–1980s* (Cambridge, Mass., 1988), pp. 327–28.

Vienna, March 18, 1939 [original in German]
Siegmund Levarie
Chicago
Dear Siegmund!

Here are a couple of lines as a sign of life from out of frightful turmoil. My emigration appears imminent—America, of course, will still take quite a while longer. I have all my documents ready: passport, tax license, etc., and have been designated by Dr. Murmelstein, who is in charge of camp matters for the K.G. [Kultusgemeinde], as leader of the first transport to the so-called transit camp in Richborough, Kent (between Dover and London).[1] Our passports—125 people are travelling with us—are at the English Consulate and should be ready within the next few days.

I am not thinking much about what will happen abroad. Perhaps it will be possible to get away from the refugee camp, where things certainly won't be ideal—*on verra* [we shall see]. I only think, and the last few days have only reinforced this belief in me, that it will in any case be good to get out and that whatever follows will be dealt with somehow.

Et vous, Monsieur? And you, Mister [English in original] Löwenherz? One doesn't hear anything from you [*Ihnen*, formal "you"]! Only indirectly did I hear that your concert was a great success and that [Paul] Hindemith spent quite some time with you. Nevertheless I am keeping my congratulations to myself until I hear something authentic from the maestro himself. And now *Addio*, my dear fellow. Cross your fingers for me once again that everything will go well and that not too long from now you will receive, even if not me in full life-size, a short letter in my handwriting with an English stamp glued on it.

Farewell!

Heinz

1. Rabbi Benjamin Murmelstein had been Kohut's religion teacher at the Döblinger Gymnasium.

Kitchener Camp, April 29, 1939 [original in German]
Siegmund Levarie
Chicago
Dear Siegmund,

I waited a long time for your letter which came yesterday, but now it has come and the waiting is over.

First the essential: You have received no money for me and that is very bad. I had counted on having around 70 pounds sterling. Maybe the money is somewhere else, but it will not be too easy to get. Once again: Thanks for your willingness to help. I shall try to become as great in taking as you are in giving. The boxes, as I believe I already wrote you, left Vienna some time ago. They were sent to your uncle's Chicago business address. If you want to, you can perhaps open the box of books and keep the "Goethe." I would like to know it is in human hands.

Concerning the affidavit for my mother: she was born on November 24, 1890, in Vienna. I don't think you need any other data. At the beginning of July she registered with the U.S. Consulate in Vienna. Many thanks here too for your help. She is very desperate but since I left, I have heard, also brave. With regard to the journey by car from New York to Chicago there seems to be little hope. Rumors have it that this year only those who registered before June 20 will be processed. That seems to me to be exaggerated, but it will certainly not be before the autumn.

You want to know about the camp. Well, it grows, is improved, is made more "comfortable," more hygienic, etc., etc.—also my position is a good one. I am "well regarded" and, hear this and be amazed, am the founder, director, and cashier of the camp bank. (So far my accounts have always balanced!!!) I am learning bookkeeping and (how strange)—think with gratitude of Scharf,[1] because after all he taught me to figure decimals to the extent that with some care I can figure the exchange without error. The day before yesterday Dr. Murmelstein paid a visit, was greatly celebrated, and, compared to the *glorious* English leaders of the camp (all Jews), appeared strange beyond all measure.

Many congratulations on your musical successes. How long will it be before I shall really have a *profession*. My analysis, about which you asked at one point, unfortunately had to be interrupted at a decisive moment in its last stage (?). I am sure that I will continue it. (Maybe in London.)

How much I look forward to us together in 40 years—
Heinz

1. Kohut's mathematics teacher at Döblinger Gymnasium.

Kitchener Camp, May 22, 1939 [original in German]
Siegmund Levarie
Chicago
Dear Siegmund,

Your birthday letter and in general the fact that you thought to write it as such gave me great pleasure—and yet was also no surprise. I, too, have recently thought often about when you have your birthday and why it was that until now we had never celebrated it [see below, May 5, 1980]. The reason lies deep and was, I think, no accident—it went along with many other things which changed only as we took indefinite leave from each other. It is remarkable how well we understand each other.

Today I was hit rather hard by terrible news which, to be sure, presents itself for the time being only as a possibility. The American government is supposed to be considering a change in the emigration regulations which would give preference to Jews still in Germany and impose on us a further waiting period of 10 months. Only after these 10 months will our normal waiting period begin—in my case about

3–4 months, so that altogether I would have to reckon on far over a year. Well, relaxation and tea-drinking becomes rather difficult under such circumstances.

Camp life itself makes me abundantly nervous and I fear that it will be rather difficult to get out of here. True, as I think I wrote you already, I am now employed as a physician, or, perhaps more accurately, as a medical assistant in the camp hospital, something which is naturally more agreeable to me than any other work. I am, however, quite worn out by the unbelievable uniformity of my days, which with all their fullness are fully fruitless.

But now I really have cried enough. It is nice and encouraging to hear that things are going as well for you as probably never before in your life and that everything is progressing for you toward a goal or at least in a direction.

Farewell, my dear fellow—the Chinese laundry bill was very nice—I accept it as a birthday present. Have you already unpacked my Goethe?

Heinz

June 2, 1946[1] [original in German]
Director [Vorstand] August Aichhorn
Vienna
Dear Mr. Director!

I had the great joy of hearing of you through Dr. Ruth Eissler, with whom I have been in analysis for more than three years: that you had survived the awful war years in relatively good shape; that Walter and Gustl came through it in spite of injuries; and that your wife and little Christl are well.[2] I have been informed about everything with the exception of Schniddi [sic; see below, July 21 and September 2, 1946], the black beast [Rabenvieh], who was always jumping onto my stomach and disrupting my free associations.

Now I must tell you a little bit about myself. As you probably still remember, I left Vienna in January [sic] 1939. I spent a year in England, first in a refugee camp near Dover, and then for about six weeks in London after I had contracted pneumonia in the camp. In London I lived with my mother's brother and in spite of the fact that the city was blacked out I got along well. At the end of February I sailed in an English convoy via Halifax to Boston and from there travelled by bus to Chicago, where my friend Siegmund was already waiting for me. At about the same time my mother left Austria and arrived in Chicago a couple of weeks after me. I soon found a position at a small hospital in Chicago, something that was absolutely necessary since I had almost no money. This lack of money has unfortunately become chronic with me. Although I have been employed for more than five years at the University of Chicago (my official title is Instructor in Neurology and Psychiatry) and have a salary of $3000 per annum, I have to pay for my analysis and that amounts to about $1200 a year so there's hardly anything left over. I became an American citizen only after the war and because of that (and also because I was teaching at a university) I was not drafted into the army. Last week I took my specialty boards in neurology from "The American Board of Neurology and Psychiatry" and I think I passed. Next year I will take the psychiatric portion. That reminds me that last Sunday I was at the Forty-Seventh Meeting of The American Psychoanalytic Association. The program: Paul Bergman, "Scolding as a Psychotherapeutic Technique"; discussed by Helen Ross; Emmanuel Windholz, "The Discharge Neurosis"; Ernst Simmel, "Alcoholism and Addiction"; Eri[k] H. Erikson, "Ego Development and Historical Change." As far as the gossip went it might have been old Vienna, because your name was mentioned a number of times, as well as by [Edmund] Bergler, Helen Ross, and others who took part in the program discussions.

I myself intend to take courses at the Institute here and to begin my analytic training as soon as I have finished my analysis. How long that will yet last I don't know—I don't think very long.

My mother, whom you have already gotten to know, is fine. About five years ago she opened a shop with some money she had managed to hide away and has had great success with it. Unfortunately, almost all of my relatives died in various concentration camps: a brother [Wilhelm Lampl] of my mother's and his small daughter, a brother of my father's along with his wife and son, a sister of my father's, another sister together with her husband, etc., etc. An aunt, an "Aryan," still lives in Vienna [see below, September 2, 1946], and then another cousin—even if almost all my dreams still take place in Vienna, at other times it seems like a foreign city to me. I also notice with some astonishment that it is no longer second nature for me to write in German and probably some of my sentences sound a little funny. In spite of all this, as paradoxical as it may sound, I will not deny that I have something like a chronic homesickness—but that is something with which one must come to terms.

Now enough for today. I hope that I will hear from you soon. Please write and tell me what you would like to have so that I don't send over things you don't need.

Cordial greetings to you and the whole family (Walter could write just once) from your

Heinz Kohut, M.D.

1. During the war years, Kohut's correspondence was limited by the interruption of mail service to Europe and by the fact that his friends in America were all in Chicago. He did carry on an extensive correspondence with Siegmund Levarie, who was in the army from December 1941 until February 1946, but these letters have not survived.

2. Aichhorn was one of only two psychoanalysts to remain in Vienna after the *Anschluss*. He did so in part because his son August ("Gustl") was a conservative Austrian nationalist who was imprisoned by the Nazis in Dachau for a time. From 1938 to 1944 Aichhorn supervised psychoanalytic training at the small Vienna branch of the German Institute for Psychological Research and Psychotherapy in Berlin. See Geoffrey Cocks, *Psychotherapy in the Third Reich: The Goring Institute* (New York, 1985), pp. 187, 288–89; and Wolfgang Huber, *Psychoanalyse in Österreich seit* 1933 (Vienna, 1977), pp. 56–68.

July 21, 1946 [from August Aichhorn; original in German]

Dear Dr. Kohut!

Your letter of June 2 sent on June 4 was a long time in coming in spite of being airmailed. I answer in haste so that you do not have to wait too long.

I am glad that you have been informed about everything, with the exception of Schnidi, "the *Rabenvieh* that was always jumping on your stomach and disrupting your free associations." Don't grumble about the poor fellow; in 1940 he had already left for the eternal hunting grounds. One fine summer day in the full vigor of youth during a walk, unnoticed by his companion, he ate something poisonous. After a few hours of heavy vomiting and intestinal bleeding he was dead. At the time we were so upset that we resolved never again to have a dog. A good thing since now what would we feed him?

I had heard about your stay in London. I also saw a few of your letters. You ended up with your friend Siegmund in Chicago. What happened to his parents? Could his father maintain his position in the Jewish Community for long and was he able to get out in time?

Did you have to retake your exams or did you get the hospital and university position with your Vienna diploma? It is not comprehensible to me how you and the other emigrants who had to leave without any money were able to rebuild an existence. What you write about your income are only numbers to me. It would be easier if you could compare this income with those in Vienna. Is $1200 for an analysis a normal amount? Is your specialty exam for neurology and psychiatry comparable to our specialist [*Facharzt*]?

I haven't heard any gossip as you did when you took part in the '47 APA Congress and heard my name mentioned. I did receive a lovely letter from Helen Ross. Bergmann [*sic*] had sent his congratulations on the reestablishment of the Psychoanalytic Society.[1] I haven't heard anything from [Ernst] Sim[m]el. The other analysts you mention in your letter I don't know, with the exception of Bergler.

In America may one begin analytic training only after the training analysis has ended? Here it has always been different, with training beginning toward the end of the training analysis.

I'm amazed by your mother—please give her my cordial greetings. It takes great courage and energy to start a business in a foreign land and to run it successfully. (Will she not take steps to get her possessions under the provisions of the restitution policy[?])

I hear all the time in letters from acquaintances and dear friends what National Socialism had done to their families. It is terrible.

You, dear doctor, probably can hardly imagine the conditions under which we had to live for so many years. One was never sure when one might be picked up by the Gestapo in the middle of the night. Anyone could make a spurious denunciation and one would be arrested without any legal proceedings and without knowing why and end up in the concentration camp; and then the daily threat of being killed in the ever larger air raids.

If your "chronic homesickness" were eventually to compel you to visit me on vacation, then such a return is not to be advised. We have become very poor and will remain so for a long time. Soon there will be so many doctors that there will be a medical proletariat. Presently there are 1200 university students signed up for the courses in medicine; that means that in five years at the latest there will be at least 800 more trained doctors. And add to that the other university cities and the smallness of Austria.

You certainly have not yet heard the latest about the Society: as an introduction to psychoanalysis we now have a ten-hour course behind us. There were 192 interested students who signed up and we divided them into four groups: first group, academics, lecturer Dr. [W.] Hollitscher; second group, university students, lecturer Dr. [Th.] Scharmann; third group, laypersons, lecturer [Lambert] Bolterauer; fourth group, initiates (those with some training already), lecturer, Aichhorn.

Dear doctor, you also want to know what I would like to have. Ruth and Kurt Eissler provide for us in such a generous and loving way that it would be a luxury to ask for anything from you. Your package, which Ruth Eissler said had been sent off in October, arrived a few weeks ago. I told her some time ago to send on my thanks and I repeat them again now.

Walter read your letter and was excited that you are awaiting a letter from him. Whether he will actually write soon, that I don't know. His enthusiasm is very quickly consumed by everyday matters, then after a few weeks heavy feelings of guilt set in and that takes the place of writing. It is so similar to someone who plays hooky from school on a beautiful summer day and doesn't go to school at all anymore precisely because he is a truant.

In conclusion, I and my wife thank you once more very much for your gift parcel, send you our and the dilatory Walter's greetings, and look forward to another letter from you soon.

Yours,

August Aichhorn

1. See Huber, *Psychoanalyse in Österreich*, pp. 71–85. Aichhorn died in 1949; see *Search*, 1:131–33.

September 2, 1946 [original in German]
Director August Aichhorn
Vienna

Dear Mr. Director,

Many thanks for your letter of July 21 which was in my hands by August 2. Naturally it gave me great joy and I have read it, or at least portions of it, to a large number of people who know your name (*Wayward Youth* [1925] by Ajkorn!).

Now to your letter: Poor Schnidi, he was very close to me—he must have often had to fulfill the role of brother to your patients and felt some ambivalent feelings directed on to him, but I, an only child, had more of a feeling of identification with him. However that may be: rest in peace!

Siegmund's parents remained in Vienna the entire time. His father was imprisoned by the Russian occupying forces because he was accused of collaborating with the Nazis. He was then set free and in the meantime came (together with his wife) to the United States.[1]

After my arrival in Chicago I had a year-long internship, that is, I had to live in (a not very good) hospital, was given free room and board along with $30 a month. At the end of the internship year I was allowed to take my State Board Examination and then received my license to practice in Illinois. At that time I got my first position at the

University (as "resident"), which was only slightly better than the internship. From then on every year I received better contracts. It is difficult to compare dollars with schillings—still it is easy to report that an income of $3000 is very little when one has to pay for an analysis from it. In general, one can say that here things that are produced by machines cost relatively little, for example, a new car (Chevrolet) about $1000, a book (novel) $1–$3, whereas handmade items are very expensive, for example, a hand-tailored suit $90–$100. I assume that the normal honorarium for an hour of analysis is $10, something which naturally I cannot afford.

The exam (American Board of Neurology and Psychiatry) has, as far as I can judge, no Austrian counterpart. Here as there every doctor can specialize in a chosen field and call himself a "specialist." In order to protect against incompetent "specialists," these exams have now been instituted, which are completely voluntary but which also bring with them distinct advantages when it comes to gaining university and public positions as well as posts in the army. (During the war one automatically became at least a major, especially if one had a specialty board.) In private practice as well a diploma, which here everyone hangs on the wall, is an advantage.

Here as in Vienna one can begin analytic training analysis. How that will work out in my case I don't know. A couple of years ago when I sought a training analysis at the Institute here I was turned down (Helen Ross wrote the letter, but probably had nothing to do with the rejection) and it was recommended that I first continue with my personal therapeutic analysis. On the advice of Dr. [Lionel] Blitzsten I contacted Dr. Ruth Eissler, with whom I have been in analysis for three years now. How all this will connect up with analytic training I don't yet know. Dr. Eissler is of the opinion that the Institute here which is under the direction of Franz Alexander has little to do with analysis in the Freudian sense—the people with whom I work at the hospital (for example, my superior, Dr. Henry Brosin) were trained at the Institute here and think that the European analysts who have come to America are unnecessarily traditional and conservative and reject progressive experimentation. It is simply impossible for me to come to any halfway reasonable conclusion. I think, however, that I myself, if I am given the opportunity, will decide to take courses at the Institute here.

Our possessions, so far as they could be traced (house, my mother's store), are under the stewardship of my aunt (Mrs. Ria Kohut . . .), who as a non-Jew survived the war. Whether we will get anything back I naturally don't yet know.[2]

This has become a somewhat disorganized letter and I hope you don't mind. I have simply answered your questions one after the other. I confess that I sometimes have the feeling that it is no longer so easy for me to write in German. I hope you will write again soon. You just don't know how happy that prospect makes me. Cordial greetings to you and to all friends,

Heinz Kohut, M.D.

1. See George E. Berkley, *Vienna and Its Jews: The Tragedy of Success, 1880s–1980s*, pp. 342–43.

2. Else Kohut received monetary compensation for her confiscated bank account and valuables, the emigration tax which ate up RM 22,402 of the RM 28,000 she received from the sale of the house, and the amount she paid the "Gildemeester" *Auswanderungs-Hilfsaktion* for assistance in obtaining emigration papers. See HF-Abg.F. 679/26: Österreichisches Staatsarchiv, Vienna.

October 12, 1946 [original in German]
Director August Aichorn
Vienna

Dear Mr. Director:

Many thanks for your letter of September 13 and the very clearly expressed opinions contained in it. It is naturally impossible for me to come to my own conclusions without first going through a series of intellectual conflicts. I also think that results to which one comes too easily are usually not durable and reliable. Nothing remains to me save to "muddle through" [*fortzuwurschteln*] and to complain in the spirit of [Austrian] Emperor Franz Joseph, "[N]othing is spared me!" Your advice, on the other hand, for me to bury myself in Freud's life work and only then to listen to others, I will follow, at least in broad outline. That will be made so much the easier for me insofar as at the Institute here there is (as far as I can tell) no tendency to belittle Freud's work. I have just started with courses, but I have to wait to begin my own analytic work until they get to know me better. Presently I am attending two series of lectures: (1) Freud's Papers on Technique with Dr. [Therese] Benedek, and (2) The Metapsychological Papers of Freud with Eduardo Weiss. Variations from "classical" analysis (= orthodox analysis) I have noticed only in Benedek's course, but even here only in the spirit of ideas which Freud himself had hinted at. For example, Dr. B. assigns great weight to the advantage of irregular analytic hours and is of the opinion that sometimes the analysis can make faster progress when one sees the patient less often. She sees great value in having a therapeutic plan and that one should not forget that Freud in his own work had to be the first to discover the results while we in many cases already have them. In other words, one should not go into every little resistance and every little symptom, but rather the underlying conflict [*"den Hauptkonflikt"*] "the principal dynamisms" [in English in the original] should be analyzed. This has led to the so-called formulas which are valid for different kinds of cases, for example, the formula for the "ulcer-personality" (people with stomach ulcers) goes roughly as follows: there are people who possess a particularly strong oral dependency but at the same time cannot allow themselves to show this dependency. There are generally successful, apparently thoroughly energetic businessmen or industrialists who spend their entire lives dreaming of one day being able to retire but who cannot bring themselves even to take a vacation and who see their regressive wishes fulfilled in their consequent illness and their care. The (psychosomatic) illnesses are not perceived as an hysterical symptom, rather it is assumed that over the years the unsatisfied dependency finally calls forth organic damage through the roundabout way of the vegetative nervous system (production of large amounts of stomach acid as a result of the constant expectation of being fed). The therapy in such cases lays particular weight on the previously described conflict. One avoids creating overly strong transference dependencies that the patient cannot endure and restricts oneself to bringing the patient to allow himself a moderate amount of dependency. It is maintained that such patients cannot bear orthodox analysis with its transference neurosis. It is also asserted that such therapy produces a change in the personality of the patient (not simply a removal of symptoms), since it provides for him through various means the experience that one can grant oneself some amount of dependency. Other cases are handled in a similar fashion; I have presented the example above because it is typical. The important points are clear: it is, in many cases, a turning away from the infantile neurosis that should be solved in the transference situation.

About me personally there is not much to report. Next year (from July 1, 1947, on) I will probably be working only in the psychiatric division (as "assistant professor"). That will bring with it a slight raise in pay ($3600 instead of $3000) that I can really use. In the meantime I will continue to work half the time in the neurology division, but I think the two spheres can scarcely be united without one or the other being harmed. I'm reading quite a bit, mostly Freud, but also some other psychiatric literature. Lately I have read all the technical works, then *The Interpretation of Dreams* [1900], "Mourning and Melancholia"

[1917], and some others. During the past year I read most of the case studies (Dora, the Wolf Man, the Rat Man, Hans) and before that the two volumes of lectures as well as *Beyond the Pleasure Principle* [1920], *Group Psychology and the Analysis of the Ego* [1921], *[The] Ego and [the] Id* [1923], and *The Future of an Illusion* [1927]. Of the important works I have not yet read the Schreber case, *Inhibition[s], Symptom[s] and Anxiety* [1926], and probably others. There is much that I have read just once that I have not digested. I own [Otto] Fenichel's last book (*The Psychoanalytic Theory of the Neuroses*),[1] but have not been able to bring myself to use it anymore than occasionally as a reference book. It is written like an encyclopedia and contains so much material that the minute I open it I lose all desire.

Now once again many thanks for your lovely letter—I hope I receive another one soon. Please write and tell me whether my German has suffered; sometimes it strikes me as quite tortured. By the way, the picture that I sent you is agreeable, but I prefer the pictures that you took of me.

Many cordial greetings,
Heinz Kohut, M.D.

1. The correct title is *The Psychoanalytic Theory of Neurosis* (1945); see below, March 7, 1947.

March 7, 1947 [original in German]
Director August Aichhorn
Vienna
Dear Mr. Director!

Cordial thanks for your letter of February 19 and for your sympathy over my accident.[1] Happily that is now all completely in the past and I am suffering no ill effects. The car unfortunately is not yet in such good shape as I am, but we have been promised that it too will be put right.

I was very interested in your reports about the rebuilding of the Vienna [Psychoanalytic] Association,[2] although I was not familiar with the old Association. The organization plan looks really very impressive—I proudly showed it to my colleagues at the hospital as if I had something to do with it. Who is Professor for Neurology and Psychiatry at the University now? Still [Otto] Pötzl?[3] I still remember exactly how I (during the time of my analysis with you) took exams from him and how he strutted around with a big [Nazi] party button. Oh well, it doesn't matter and he was probably not one of the worst.

As far as Mr. Kraulic goes, you are exactly right. He disputes everything, was never a Nazi, had only acted towards us out of love, etc. That he called my mother in the middle of the night and told her that I would end up in a concentration camp if she did not decide soon to "sell" him the house, that he naturally has forgotten.[4]

And how is the situation in Vienna? Please, write and tell me exactly what you need. You don't know what great joy it gives me to be able to send you something. It is now possible to send books as well and you certainly would have interest in some publications.

On the 24th of this month I will be away from Chicago for about three weeks. A friend (a former colleague at the University of Chicago) has invited me to Texas (Dallas) and I am very much looking forward to the trip. It is really the first long trip that I have undertaken in the U.S.A., apart from my original trip from Boston to Chicago by bus. We may also take a side trip into Mexico from Texas, but that is unlikely. Although it is still two weeks until then I am already close to having travel fever.

I am continuing my analytic hours: at the moment I am reading Fenichel's latest book, *The Psychoanalytic Theory of Neurosis*. There is an ungodly amount of material concentrated in the book and there are no trimmings (anecdotes, for example) that would ease the way for the reader—in spite of this I find it excellent as a teaching and reference tool. From the new German edition of Freud, which will comprise 18 volumes, I already have ten and naturally read diligently in them.

I hope to hear from you again soon and, please, don't forget to mention any wishes, whether for books or anything else.

With many cordial greetings to you and your family,

Yours,

Heinz

---

1. Kohut had suffered serious head injuries when, while driving his mother's car, he had been hit by a bus; see Kohut to Aichhorn, February 2, 1947. A passerby shed his coat to keep Kohut warm. Kohut later made an effort to thank the man by identifying him through photographs taken at the scene and obtained by Kohut.

2. See Huber, *Psychoanalyse in Österreich*, pp. 71–85.

3. See Cocks, *Psychotherapy in the Third Reich*, pp. 97, 98, 106.

4. See also Else Kohut to Finanzaut für den 19. Bezirk, February 15, 1939, HF-Abg.F. 679/27: Österreichisches Staatsarchiv, Vienna.

August 26, 1947 [original in German]
Director August Aichhorn
Vienna
Dear Mr. Director:

It has been a long time since we've written each other. From Dr. Ruth Eissler I learned to my sorrow that you had been ill and had the flu. I hope you have completely recovered in the meantime.

I am, as you will probably remember from my last letter, now solely in the psychiatric division at Billings Hospital. The work is very nice but still not exactly what I want to do. Not enough time for longer treatments and also cases which are not very amenable to treatment. I am continuing my work at the Institute here and about two months ago began my first control analysis. My supervising analyst is Dr. [Fritz] Möllenhoff, originally from Berlin, I think—anyway from Germany (see below, November 1960). To be honest, I am not very happy with the supervision. Up until now I have been able to see my supervising analyst only three times and that of course does not suffice for the vast quantity of material that piles up. Usually I can explain a couple of my patient's dreams—but that's all. I see my case five times a week. That is something very unusual at the Institute—most of the cases are seen only twice, or at most three times, and after awhile only once a week. It is argued that the results are better than what one can get with daily interviews. Naturally it is very difficult for me to be objective about all this, but it does seem to me that such treatments have very little to do with proper analysis.

The summer here was really terribly hot; and it is very humid at night so that one hardly ever feels well. I can't remember it ever being so hot in Vienna, but that may be due to the common tendency to idealize the past.

And how are things in Vienna? Are conditions any better? And how goes your newly founded Institute? I would very much like to hear from you again and have answers to these questions.

Not long ago I read *Wayward Youth* again and was very impressed. I have also diligently studied Anna Freud's *The Ego and the Mechanisms of Defense* [1936] and will shortly give a small presentation on it. At the moment I am reading Theodor Reik's *Masochism in Modern Man* [1941], which contains a series of brilliant observations and deliberations. Unfortunately one can't replace by reading everything one should learn in seminar, supervisions, etc.

That's all for today! Cordial greetings to you and your entire family.
Heinz

January 14, 1948 [original in German]
Professor August Aichhorn
Vienna
Dear Professor!

Thank you for your lovely Christmas wishes and for your letter of January 3. You said on December 20 that you had already been a long time without a letter from me. I unfortunately do not keep copies of my letters, but in spite of that I am completely sure that at least one, but probably two of my letters must have been lost. What should I tell you about myself? As before my work gives me great joy. I already have 140 hours with my first official control case and it appears to be moving forward slowly. It is a very difficult case; a very intelligent man who . . . [is a professional person] . . . ; has no particular neurotic symptoms that were a stimulus for treatment, rather he feels generally unsatisfied with his life. He fills the hours with complaints about his fate and with complaints against others who allegedly have treated him unjustly. Whenever I try to lead him toward fruitful considerations he becomes aggressive and feels himself treated unfairly by me. Behind all these defenses lies probably a deep feeling of guilt because of his prematurely deceased father and, despite his intellectuality, a superstitious ego that fears death and believes in the omnipotence of hostile wishes. I also have a second case in analytic treatment which I am having supervised unofficially by Paul Kramer. This case too, which I have seen around 120 times, is not simple. It is . . . [a woman] . . . who since her marriage . . . years ago suffers from severe abdominal cramps. She remains in bed for a week at a time, neglects her two children, and has become dependent on the immoderate use of sleeping pills which she uses in periods of depression. She has formed a very strong transference to me and had, in spite of great external difficulties, continued the treatment without interruption. . . . Her bodily pains are apparently no better, but her depressions have lessened. Besides these two cases I will soon be assigned another official control case. Friday and Saturday are filled with classes at the Institute. The other mornings I teach medical students. Recently I have also been writing on a work that I will perhaps finish in not too long a time. It has to do with thoughts I have had about the pleasure of listening to music. My friend Sigmund [sic], who is an assistant professor in the Music Department at the University, is helping me with some of the formulations and especially with the detailed knowledge.[1] I am enjoying this work very much.

Outside my work there is not much to report. I sometimes go to the theater or to concerts, read a lot, and play some sport. During the

summer I played a lot of tennis, now in winter I am playing badmin-
ton, which is very entertaining. And occasionally I play cards (bridge).
What I really miss is the social life, a circle of friends like I had in
Vienna. Of course I know a lot of people, but I can't say that I have
formed any truly warm relationships. Why that should be is hard to
say. Partly of course due to me, but also partly due to the circumstances, that is, the different cultural "background" and the lack of
school friends that one keeps throughout life and around which other
relationships group themselves.

Today it has gotten terribly cold here and I wonder if you have
enough heat in Vienna to keep the apartment warm. The little bit of
coal that I sent you could not have lasted long; but surely you have
received shipments from others. That you don't want to tell me what
you need most urgently makes me a little bit angry. Do it and without
the feeling that you are forcing me to send what you desire without
fail. If it should be too difficult for me, financially speaking, I will not
do it—that I promise you.

And now *auf Wiedersehen* or until we write again [*Wiederschreiben*]! I
am always so glad when I find an envelope of yours in my mail at the
hospital.

Heinz

My address: Heinz Kohut, M.D.
            950 East 59th Street
            Chicago 37, Illinois
            U.S.A.

1. *Search*, 1:135–58.

August 16[, 1948]
My dearest, sweetest Betty—you see there is no more caution and,
boy!, it's wonderful. I think of your sudden start when you saw me
through the car window and how quickly you came out and our last
few minutes together in the fishmarket smell and the crowds. This
begins to sound like a page from [James Joyce's] *Ulysses* [1917] which
I never finished although I liked it. I better get organized and tell you
what I have been doing all day. Well, right now it's 11:15 P.M. and I
am sitting at the desk in my office. After your train left (I hope you
got the idea that I was signalling the question whether you had the
"Bridge-book") I rushed back to the hospital and arranged a few practical matters (consultations and the like). Then I had a ½ hour discussion
with Dick Cook (one of the [Samuel] Weiss-boys, you know) and we

complained about the rest of the department, particularly [Henry] Brosin and [Nathaniel] Apter. Then I began to move furniture again, this time in my office where a new filing cabinett [sic] had arrived. I kept switching things around, filled and emptied the bookcase twice etc but finally arrived at a fairly satisfactory arrangement which was not easy because the room is small and there is a lot of "Möbel" [furniture] in it.

Afterwards I had dinner with Robert [Wadsworth] ("By the way, what *is* this girl's name?"—"It's B[etty]. M[eyer]. and you'd better remember it!") and a friend of his at a rather gaudy place on 63rd Street where the restrooms are marked "Dames" and "Sires." For some reason I chose scallops which I rarely order (perhaps because you are going to be near a lot of them soon [New Hampshire]) and they were really good. I returned the car to my mother who, of course, was in a tragic mood. Interestingly enough, she made almost the same remark that your mother made: she noticed that I love you a great deal which, I guess, implies on both sides the maternal fear that their darling children may not be loved enough by the other. Well, who knows? and "nitchewo!" ["nothing"]. This evening I spent working a little on the music paper.[1] I didn't achieve much except for two inserts: one on the reaction to extraneous sounds (train-noise in open air concerts, whispering of neighbors & so on), the other on the significance of the moments of silence just preceding the first sounds of music. I haven't started working on the bibliography yet and I keep putting it off because I dislike the task.

I am getting a little tired and think I'll enjoy going to bed, soon. Tomorrow is going to be a busy day—students, two analytic cases, the afternoon teaching at Cook County Hospital. Wednesday I'll meet Robert to finish discussing the paper. Perhaps I'll find time some evening to see the "Physician despite Himself"[2] at the 11th Street Theater.

Well, darling, my eyes won't stay open any longer. I send you all the love I have and a million and one kisses.

Heinz

1. Heinz Kohut and Siegmund Levarie, "On the Enjoyment of Listening to Music," *Psychoanalytic Quarterly* 19 (1950): 64–87; see above, January 14, 1948.
2. *The Physician in Spite of Himself*; Jean-Baptiste Molière, *Le médecin malgré lui* (1666).

1951–1963

"the old, youthful poet"

Carmel-by-the-Sea, September 10, 1951
Siegmund Levarie
Chicago
Dear Siegmund,
   Your letter (Vitznau [Switzerland], 3 September) reached us here
in California in an amazingly short time. It didn't need the enclosed
Edelweiss[1] to touch me considerably in various psychic locations. I
think I know what you are talking about although for obvious reasons I
am experiencing it only in the negative, in the form of a vague *Heimweh*
[homesickness] for Europe, its houses, mountains, streets—including
the ornaments that you talk about. I think it was quite characteristic
that you addressed your letter Everett Str. (*Strasse*) & not Everett St.
(street) which is quite a different thing. Well, I can hardly imagine
anymore what a living thing a *Strasse* can be. When you say that it is
not only *Kindheitserinnerungen* [childhood memories] you are assuredly
right and Norma's reactions (and Henry Adams') are proof enough.
Yet, it has something to do with *Kindheit* and longing for it and finding
it again, I am sure. The cliché that America is a land with little past,
and Europe with a lot of it has emotional significance. Only think:
America has no mythology, hardly any fairytales, etc. That may all
mean more to us than we realize. It may not be so for the old New-
England family—but even there, cf. Henry Adams who found himself
"at home" in Europe.[2]
   Well, enough tears shed. Anyway, we are spending the nicest vacation imaginable in a lovely spot. My mother was here for a week after
a memorable trip (Grand Canyon, etc.) and enjoyed herself a lot. Now
Betty's mother is with us. We have taken a number of car-trips up &
down the beautiful California coast, as well as into Carmel Valley, lie
on the beach, dip into swimming pools, and let the cold ocean-surf
wet our ankles (and higher, involuntarily). We have rented a small
house with open-fireplace (often needed) and lovely garden—and we
all have the wonderful bronze California tan on our bodies.
   The *Psychoanalytic Quart*[*erly*]. has sent me a book for review, André
Michel's *Psychanalyse de la Musique* [1951].[3] It contains a lot of good
stuff, mostly fragmentary—the main thesis (putting artistic, esp. musical thinking ahead of conceptual thinking; music as descriptive of not
yet discovered, or just created reality) seems a little obscure in an
adolescent way and is unnecessarily conceited. On the whole I enjoyed
reading it but haven't written my review, yet.
   We'll be back in Chicago on Sep. 20 and I'll start to work shortly
thereafter.

Thanks for your letter, it was fun reading it and we are looking forward to the verbal report, the exchange of memories to follow, etc. Love from all of us,

Betty and Heinz

1. A mountain flowering herb and symbol of Austria.
2. Henry Adams's autobiography, *The Education of Henry Adams* (1918), was a favorite of Kohut's.
3. *Search*, 1:167–70.

October 12, 1952
Dr. Kurt R. Eissler
New York[1]
Dear Dr. Eissler:

I remember that you showed some interest last December when I mentioned the topic of analytic investigation of music and I hope that you might want to look at the enclosed reprints. The reason for my letter is, however, a different one: I would like to report to you, as Secretary of the Freud Archives, Inc., on my one and only encounter with Freud. Whether the following information is of any value to the Archives I do not know and must leave to your judgment.[2]

I saw Freud on the day of his final departure from Vienna, in 1938. The information that he would be leaving, the Railway Station (Westbahnhof?), and the time of the train's departure came to me through Aichhorn with whom I was in analysis at that period. Aichhorn told me that Freud had requested that the fact and, at any rate, the details of his leaving be kept secret and that he didn't want any friends to come to the station. Aichhorn suggested, however, that there would be no harm in my going there if I kept myself in the background. A friend of mine and I arrived at the station about 15 minutes before the train was to leave. It was a beautiful, sunshiny day. The station was rather empty and there was no evidence of any surveillance by the police. We located Freud quickly as he was sitting at the window of his compartment, facing the rear of the train. We kept about ten steps back of Freud's part of the train and, therefore, could not see anyone else in the compartment. Next to Freud's window, on the station platform, stood a crying woman in simple dress (we assumed it was a maid of the Freud household) who was spoken to, apparently in an attempt to console her, by a lady of Freud's party (Anna Freud?). Freud's face was calm and, almost as if he were embarrassed by the emotional scene, he seemed to pay no attention to it. My friend recognized Professor Marburg, the Neurologist, in the same car. When the train began to move we walked up toward Freud and lifted our hats. Freud looked at us, took off his traveling cap, and waved to us.

Please give Ruth my best regards and thank her for her recent letter which I'll answer soon. I hope to see you both at the Midwinter meetings.

Cordially,

Heinz Kohut, M.D.

1. The Eisslers had moved to New York from Chicago in 1948; see Kohut to August Aichhorn, May 4, 1948.

2. There is no record in the Freud Archives at the Library of Congress of material donated by Kohut. On Eissler, see Janet Malcolm, *In the Freud Archives* (New York, 1985). See also below, Kohut to Alexandre Szombati, July 12, 1968; and *Search*, 2:665–66. Cf. the erroneous claim that Kohut "knew Sigmund Freud personally" in "One of a Diminishing Number," *Medical Tribune*, December 21, 1964, p. 8.

December 8, 1955

Dr. Kurt R. Eissler

New York

Dear Kurt,

I have read and very much enjoyed your "Notes on an Aspect of Goethe's Relationship to Music." The *Vorgeschmack* [foretaste] of the whole Goethe-book[1] that you are evidently working on makes me look forward to the finished product with real anticipation to the esthetic and scientific contribution that it will provide.

I do not feel equipped to pass judgment on the objective merits of your conclusions except that the primal scene screen memory is quite convincingly described. I have, on the other hand, for several years been exposed to comments by musician friends to the effect that Goethe's contribution to the field of music in the wider sense was considerable. This does not contradict your thesis as it refers to verbal secondary process productions concerning music. The comparison with the *Farbenlehre* [theory of colors], the creation of an independent theory, i.e., a theory complete in itself yet apart from the main body of knowledge of the "experts" of his time, is striking. (See: W. Heisenberg, *Philosophic Problems of Nuclear Science*, Pantheon, 1952, on Goethe and Newton. See: E. Levy, "Goethes musiktheoretische Anschauungen," *Schweizerische Musikzeitung*, October, 1952.)

With regard to your general statements on the "elusive" psychology of music on pages M19 and M20 I might mention the article I wrote with Levarie, "On the Enjoyment of Listening to Music" (Psa Qu. [*Psychoanalytic Quarterly*] 19, 1950.) On the relation to primary and secondary (verbal) processes and on the difference between the ecstatic and the secondary process listener (pp. 73 and 74), on controlled regression in music (p. 84), and the whole psychoeconomic theory presented in the article. See also the suggestion to differentiate primary and secondary musical processes in my review of Michel (Psa Qu. 21, 111, 1952). The whole problem of how the extraverbal medium of music relates to the controlled regression to preverbal psychological organizations will be contained in an essay I hope to present shortly. For another theory on doing work while there is music in the next room see Michel, e.g., *Annual Survey of Psychoanalysis*, vol. 2, page 699. Or better Michel's book, *Psychanalyse de la Musique*, Presses Universitaires de France, 1951, page 135. Please return the Levy reprint to me at your complete leisure. I enjoyed very much seeing you and Ruth.

With best regards,
Heinz Kohut, M.D.

1. K. R. Eissler, *Goethe: A Psychoanalytic Study*, 2 vols. (Detroit, 1963).

March 28, 1956
K. R. Eissler, M.D.
New York
Dear Kurt,

Thank you for your letter of March 26. Please tell Mr. Lambda that I am not interested in the Aichhorn bust. (As I wrote to you, I didn't think it was particularly good.)

Something else has several times occurred to me which I wanted to tell you although you are, undoubtedly, quite familiar with it. I remember reading quite a long time ago (probably in Eckermann but possibly in Goethe's letters or diaries) that Goethe hated people who wore glasses. I think I remember that this came up somewhere in connection with an Englishman who wanted to see Goethe or who actually had an audience with Goethe. I think this is interesting in the context of (1) Goethe's anger at Newton for forcing light through a prism, and (2) your thoughts concerning some "primal scene" complex which may well lead to conflicts about scoptophilic impulses. Undoubtedly, you know all this very well, and much better, but I thought that there is no harm in mentioning it to you in case you should not have come across it.[1]

We were sorry to hear that Ruth won't be in Chicago for the Annual Meetings. Is she still not feeling up to par? I am going to present a paper on the Psychology of Music on Saturday, April 28.

Thanks again, for thinking of me with respect to the Aichhorn sculpture. It will be nice to see you in Chicago. Best regards to Ruth.
Cordially yours,
Heinz Kohut, M.D.

1. Eissler makes no mention of eyeglasses in his book. See below, October 22, 1963; as well as Eissler letters of April 2, 1956 and October 2, 1963; and also *Conversations of Goethe with Eckermann and Soret*, trans. John Oxenford (London, 1875).

June 15, 1956
Dr. Gerhart Piers
The Institute for Psychoanalysis
Chicago
Dear Gerhart,
I have read your draft for a letter to Dr. Sara Bonnett, the Chairman of the Ad Hoc Committee of the American on the Detroit situation.[1] I should like to make the following remarks rather informally although I have thought about the situation at length, long before our recent discussion in staff.

I think that the Detroit situation is truly the business of all analysts. I don't want to seem to absolve, for example, the Sterbas and others from blame. I can neither blame nor absolve them because I don't know the situation, or at least only from vague hearsay. I am convinced, however, that what happened in Detroit in a malignant form is a potential disease of all of us.[2] The violence of the dissension, of mistrust, of argument, in analytic circles surpasses definitely what I have seen to happen in academic surroundings, and, I believe that the usual strivings for power, the wish to be right and to have the other fellow wrong, the projection of one's own delinquent impulses, etc., can only partially explain these phenomena when they occur in analysts who, I believe, on the whole are not unable to control their emotions and to see things in a reasonably realistic perspective. I also believe that the disease is unexplored at present and that some of the basic causes are not understood. Let me repeat, then, that under these circumstances the Detroit situation is our business. It becomes our business, especially for the sake of the younger or future generations of analysts (the Detroit students) to be truly a synthetic force, i.e., not in any way, be it ever so subtle, to exploit the situation by taking sides as would be natural against the Sterbas and their group and for [Morton] Barnett and his group. I would think it highly unfortunate if the "Geographical rule"[3] would lead to the result that Chicago appoints people from the Barnett group and New York and Boston people from the Sterba group as Training analysts.

To prevent misunderstandings: I am not against reasonable disagreements and reasonable "splits." But this is not the time for such events in Detroit as I see it. I think that the only way by which we can help the students to regain a basic confidence is by acting thoroughly controlled and reasonably. As I said before, their disease is ours, and as we fight theirs we fight it for our sake.

As far as the letter goes that you propose to write to Dr. Bonnett, I have no objections. I think that the idea proposed is practical and basically sound. It would be my suggestion, however, that some of the spirit of my letter to you could be incorporated into your communication to New York. How does the saying go? Every little bit helps! At least there is nothing to be lost.

Sincerely,
Heinz Kohut

1. In 1953 the Detroit-Cleveland Institute was disaccredited by the APA due to an "emotional atmosphere . . . detrimental to the conduct of satisfactory training in psychoanalysis" (*JAPA* 3 (1955): 725). The Detroit Psychoanalytic Society revoked the membership of two lay (non-M.D.) analysts, Editha Sterba and Fritz Redl (*JAPA* 2 (1954): 804–5). Editha's husband, Richard, was an M.D. and with his wife a founding member since 1940 of the Detroit Society. Training resumed in 1958 under the auspices of the Chicago and New York institutes. See John A. P. Millet, "Psychoanalysis in the United States," in *Psychoanalytic Pioneers*, ed. Franz Alexander et al. (New York 1966), pp. 562, 583.

2. In his inaugural address as president of the APA, Kohut would label "an excessive tendency toward dissension" as "our worst disease." See *Search*, 1:392.

3. The system whereby a training analyst "in relative isolation should be under the supervision of an institute." This is to prevent candidates from overidentifying with the analyst under whom they train. See Jacob Arlow, "Dilemmas in Psychoanalytic Education," *JAPA* 20 (1972): 555–66.

October 10, 1956
Dr. Douglas N. Buchanan
The University of Chicago Clinics
Dear Douglas,

I have learned that not only Bobs Roberts Hospital is being celebrated these days but that you too are marking your twenty-fifth anniversary at the Clinics and will be the center of the many expressions of admiration and affection that you deserve.

You know that my own interests have gradually but inexorably followed a course that has removed me from professional contact with you. I am glad though that I can think of a time, fifteen years ago, when you not only were my teacher in the rudiments of clinical neurology but also became my guide to that fascinating dreamworld at the fringe of poetry, the world of Alice and of the Carpenter.[1] I must confess, regretfully, that my knowledge of clinical neurology has become rusty; I can report to you, however, that my interest in Father William and in the Walrus has been unflagging, and that I remain ready at command ("First boy!") to recite "The Jabberwocky" to the teacher.

I know that you come from the sentimental land of professed unsentimentality where emerging emotion is quickly chased away, and where the art of understatement takes the place of rhapsody. Yet, I cannot spare you, at this one occasion, an expression of gratefulness for the help you gave me and the example that you were.

Ad multos annos!

Heinz Kohut, M.D.

1. According to Betty Kohut, Heinz claimed to have learned much of his English from reading *Alice in Wonderland*. See also January 31, 1967, below.

November 26, 1956
Dr. Bruno Walter
c/o The New York Philharmonic Society
New York

Dear Dr. Walter:

I am at the present time preparing a psychological study on Thomas Mann's *Death in Venice* which is to appear in the *Psychoanalytic Quarterly*,[1] and I am taking the liberty to ask you whether you have any information that you care to transmit to me or know of some published or unpublished material that would throw light on the relationship between Thomas Mann and Gustav Mahler.

You may know that Aschenbach, the principal figure of *Death in Venice*, resembles Gustav Mahler in various details (the first name, the description of the face, the mention of a Bohemian conductor as his ancestor). It is known that both Mahler and Mann had a direct relationship with Freud, and Reik reports and reprints a letter by Freud in which Mahler's single therapeutic session with Freud is mentioned (*The Haunting Melody*, page 343). There exist also rumors—how well founded, I do not know—that Mann was advised against analysis by Freud so as not to endanger his artistic creativity.

The statement in my paper that concerns these topics is as follows: " . . . the figure of . . . Mahler has been woven into the story. It would be attractive to speculate on the reasons that induced Thomas Mann to utilize so many of Mahler's features in the creation of his hero. Here it can only be pointed out that Gustav Mahler died in 1911, the year in which *Death in Venice* was composed. One is tempted, however, to assume deeper connections: either that there was a personal relationship between Mann and Mahler, or that a more intimate knowledge of Mahler's personality led the author to avail himself of external characteristics when a more profound similarity between Mahler and Aschenbach was to be implied. To establish the reasons for the special significance of Mahler's death would be an intriguing study. . . . "

I should be very grateful to you if you could give me any information about these relationships that you might have. Please, be assured that anything you might be able to tell me will be used only for inclusion in a scientific publication and, with your permission, will be transmitted to the Freud-Archives.

Respectfully yours,
Heinz Kohut, M.D.

1. *Search*, 1:107–30. Written in 1948 (see below, August 25, 1965), Kohut waited until 1957, after Mann's death, to publish this essay. See also Harry Slochower, "Thomas Mann's *Death in Venice*," *American Imago* 26 (1969): 99–122; and Kohut to Slochower, December 31, 1968, where Kohut observes that "the name Tavzio as it is expressly described in the Novella as 'Adgiu' with a long drawn out last vowel, made me think of a link with Thomas Mann's childhood in Lübeck and on the shores of the Baltic. If you try to pronounce it as indicated by the author with a soft 'dg' and a long 'oooo': don't you hear, as I do, the melancholy sound of a foghorn? I believe that here might be a truly unconscious link with a depressive childhood mood, concentrated into the sound that the child must have heard on many a foggy day or night. I had stated this connection in my original paper, but the editor found it far-fetched and objected."

January 1, 1957
Dr. Bruno Walter
Beverly Hills, California
Dear Doctor Walter:

Thank you ever so much for your letter of December 13 and for the careful attention that you gave to my questions. It was especially important for me to learn that Mann and Mahler had not been personally acquainted with each other.[1] Your letter also confirmed my assumption that the meeting between Mahler and Freud, in Holland in 1910, was their only one.

Again, many thanks for your kindness,
Sincerely yours,
Heinz Kohut, M.D.

1. Unfortunately, Walter, who knew both Mann and Mahler, was wrong about this and wrong as well about Mahler not inspiring Aschenbach. See Norman Lebrecht, *Mahler Remembered* (New York, 1987), pp. 310–11; see also George Pollock, "On Freud's Psychotherapy of Bruno Walter," *Annual of Psychoanalysis* 3 (1975): 287–95. Kohut reports Walter's conviction that Mann and Mahler were not acquainted, though he leaves the sentences quoted in his initial letter to Walter essentially unchanged. But Kohut also does not pursue the connection between Aschenbach and Mahler.

November 22, 1959
John Frosch, M.D.
Editor
Journal of the American Psychoanalytic Association
New York
Dear Jack:
Thank you for your inquiry about the purpose of my request to see the commentary of the editors concerning my paper on introspection.[1]

I must admit that I feel somewhat at a loss with regard to an answer. I have no motive other than my interest. The paper was discussed by a variety of people, both in Paris and in Chicago where I presented it at the celebration of the 20th Anniversary of the Institute. These discussions were extremely interesting to me. I believe that most people thought that I had made a contribution concerning a basic theoretical question. Others—I believe it was rather a small group—felt that I had narrowed the investigative basis of psychoanalysis by calling Introspection or Empathy an essential ingredient that must be employed even if different investigative methods are used. Although I feel quite sure that the objections were based on a misunderstanding I learned something even from those who proceeded on the basis of this misunderstanding. At any rate, I do not know that the topic with which I dealt is a difficult on[e] and it would seem to me that it would be valuable for me to get the opinions and commentary of those knowledgeable and thoughtful people which are on the Editorial Board. I hesitate to say all this because I am quite sure that you know it. I have no further use for the material, and do not mind negative opinions.

I hope I have given your question the right understanding. If you had something else in mind, please do not hesitate to ask me again.
Sincerely,
Heinz Kohut, M.D.

1. *Search*, 1:205–32. Kohut received the comments: see Kohut to Frosch, December 11, 1959.

July 5, 1960

Mr. Sydney J. Harris
Chicago Daily News
Dear Mr. Harris:

To my great surprise I found today in your article "Why Quitting Cigarets Is Difficult" a description of a psychiatrist who "devised a novel and (for him) effective way of quitting the cigaret habit." Now, undoubtedly—unless I have a double—I am the psychiatrist you are describing. Almost all the details of my method are correctly reported by you, and I am glad to learn that you consider it sound. May I, however, make a small but perhaps not unimportant correction? I never was faced with the decision whether to "taper off" or to "taper on," as you put it. *My* decision was whether I should "cut down" or "cut up"—naturally I decided for the latter. I have often wondered whether my pleasure in the pun was not an important motivation in the whole procedure.[1]

Sincerely yours,
Heinz Kohut, M.D.

1. The "shrewd psychological" idea was every year to add one cigarette to a daily quota so that there was something to anticipate; by the age of seventy, when the pleasure was worth the risk, he would be up to a pack a day. Kohut, in fact, eventually quit smoking and started exercising, which he enjoyed, in order to live longer. See below, March 19, 1977.

November 1960

THE LIFE OF FRITZ[1]
by H. Kohut

A case study in rhymes (with only sparing references to the superiority of Austrian culture).

When our Fritz was seven
He was a Prussian child.
He grew and grew, in height and years,
Up to young-manhood wild.

He emptied glass and stein and mug,
He duelled without fear.
The alcohol metabolized;
The *Schmisse*[2] are still here.

On Austria, without a doubt,
The Prussian grenadier

Looked down with six-foot-two contempt:
"And who is a Grillparzier?"[3]

But lo! an Austrian minstrel comes
The Prussian to relax;
He is no Meistersinger,[4]
His name is yet—Hanns Sachs.[5]

Analysis is soothing
In oedipusean crises;
But from life's chronic fever-ill
He's cured through Anna[6]-lysis.

Oh Aennchen (though not from Tharau)[7]
How you are pleasing him!
Away with sword and out the mug—
Life's cup you filled to the brim.

The cup it runneth over:
Two daughters and grandchildren four.
Past sorrows are vastly outbalanced;
You cannot ask for more.

— — —

Year follows year. The Prussian boy
Hears seventy-birthday chimes;
And custom, wish, and pride demand
To toast him now in rhymes.

But Austria's poet has to find
A word to rhyme with Fritz,
Else he'll be eating humble pie
(Or worse still—Koenig-grits.)[8]

Enough of puns! My pegasus
Is tired and wants to graze;
The poet's mind, you saw it well,
Has long been in a haze.

Thus will I quickly finish
Ere I lose all my wits
And, for this whole assembled crowd,
Will end the song by singing out:
"We love you dearly, Fritz!"

1. Fritz Moellenhof (1891–1981) was a psychoanalyst with a special interest in psychoanalysis and literature. Born in Solingen near Cologne, he left Germany in 1935, eventually settling in Peoria, Illinois, where he worked at a sanitarium and, beginning in the 1940s, was on the staff at the Chicago Institute for Psychoanalysis.

2. Duelling scars.

3. Franz Grillparzer (1791–1872), a Viennese dramatist and poet.

4. Singing poets of the fifteenth and sixteenth centuries in Germany.

5. Hanns Sachs of Berlin was Moellenhof's psychoanalyst, and Hans Sachs was the most famous of the Nuremberg *Meistersinger* who were the subject of Richard Wagner's opera, one of Kohut's early favorites. See below, August 3, 1968; and January 11, 1969.

6. Moellenhoff's wife.

7. "Ännchen [the diminutive of Anna] von Tharau" is a famous seventeenth-century poem and folksong celebrating the wedding of Annke, the daughter of the pastor of Tharau in East Prussia.

8. Königgratz (Sadowa), the battle that decided the Austro-Prussian war of 1866 in Prussia's favor.

December 12, 1960
The Christian Century
Chicago
Sir:

The following quotation may not apply directly to any of the arguments employed during the recent debate about the Oberammergau Passion Play[1]—yet, I feel certain that it is of interest, however one may wish to interpret it. It is taken from Alan Bullock's authoritative book *Hitler, A Study in Tyranny* (pp. 338–39 of the authorized abridgment; Bantam Books, New York: 1958. Original edition: Harper, 1953). Mr. Bullock states the following:

> One evening Hitler was discussing the need to warn the rising generation against what he called the "racial danger." On these grounds alone, he went on, he would permit the continuation of the Oberammergau Passion Play. "Nowhere has the Jewish danger in the case of the Roman Empire been so vividly depicted as in the representation of Pontius Pilate in the Oberammergau performance. His superiority as a Roman, both racially and intellectually, is so apparent that he stands like a rock amid the Near Eastern scum and swarm." In his recognition of the value of this drama for the enlightenment of the coming generation, Hitler added, he was a hundred percent Christian.

There seems to be little doubt that Bullock took his reference from the book *Hitler's Tischgespräch* [*Hitler's Table Talk*] by Paul Schmidt, Athenäum Verlag [1951].

Very truly yours,

Heinz Kohut, M.D.

Copy to Mr. Tom F. Driver

1. Tom F. Driver, "The Play That Carries a Plague," *Christian Century* 77 (1960): 1016–1018, 1475–77.

November 22, 1961
Maurice N. Walsh, M.D.
Beverly Hills, California
Dear Doctor Walsh:

Thank you for sending me a reprint of your paper on Aretino.[1] I read it with interest and found it both enjoyable and instructive. Two small questions occur to me: 1) why you include Schnitzler[2] among the satirists and 2) why you do not refer more directly to the Aichhorn–Anna Freud concept on "Identification with the Aggressor" in your study of the personality of the satirist. But those are small points, and the second one is perhaps unjustified since you refer to other authors (Reich, Brenman and Skinner)[3] in your context.

Since in my paper "Death in Venice" by Thomas Mann I made a hypothesis on the genetic context in which an artist's ironical attitude arises (especially pages 223 to 225), I am enclosing a reprint of this paper. While it is only distantly related to your topic it might still be of some interest to you.

I must say that I was slightly disturbed and chagrined by your letter. It seems to me that you feel that I have deprecated (in what you refer to as my "recent published opinions") the value of psychoanalytic studies of literary figures. I frankly do not know and understand what in my recent published opinions could give such an impression. Most likely you are referring to the "Beyond the Bounds of the Basic Rule" which appeared in the *Journal of the American Psychoanalytic Association* in July of 1960.[4] I did, however, not try in this article to depreciate efforts in applied psychoanalysis but to give a balanced account of their position in our field. I do hope that a perusal of this article, particularly its conclusions (pages 583 to 586) will convince you that I see a great deal of value in studies of this type.

Sincerely,
Heinz Kohut, M.D.

1. Maurice Walsh, "Some Character Aspects of the Satirist (Pietro Aretino)," *American Imago* 18 (1961): 235–62.
2. Arthur Schnitzler (1862–1931), Viennese dramatist and writer noted for his sharp portraits of Viennese society.
3. Annie Reich, "The Structure of the Grotesque—Comic Sublimation," *Bulletin of the Menninger Clinic* 12 (1940): 160–71; Margaret Brennan, "On Teasing and Being Teased: And the Problem of 'Moral Masochism,'" *The Psychoanalytic Study of the Child* 7 (1952): 264–86; and John Skinner, "Lewis Carroll's *Adventures in Wonderland*," *American Imago*

4 (1947): 3–31. A comprehensive guide to books and articles on psychoanalysis from its
origins until 1974 is *The Index of Psychoanalytic Writings*, ed. Alexander Grinstein, 14 vols.
(New York, 1956–75).
   4. *Search*, 1:275–303.

June 22, 1962
Dr. and Mrs. K. R. Eissler
New York
Dear Ruth and Kurt:
   How nice of you to send me such friendly notes of congratulations
at my having been nominated for President-Elect of the Association.
It's a little premature for me to worry about all the tasks that lie ahead
since I have not been elected yet and other candidates may still be
nominated. But, should I get elected, you know that I will give the
best I can to the cause of analysis; and (you need not worry, Kurt!) I
will not forget my friends.
   Thanks again for your good wishes.
   Fondly,
   Heinz Kohut, M.D.
   P.S. I phoned you on Sunday, June 10, when I was in New York
and hoped to drop in to see you but unfortunately could not reach
you.

October 15, 1962
Professor Hans Meyerhoff
Department of Philosophy
University of California, Los Angeles
Dear Professor Meyerhoff:
   Thank you so much for your most kind response to the Death-in-
Venice paper and for the admirable vistas which your letter opened
to me so generously. The idea that the artist is the symbol, paradigm,
or "model" of civilized man is dear to me, too. Perhaps the analyst
would stress him as the symbolic battleground not only of the struggle
between life and death, object love and creative withdrawal, but also
as a stage on which the freshness of childhood asserts its place most
creatively in the world of reason and restriction.
   Did I discern a reproach against psychoanalytic scientific dryness in
your dislike of the term "object-relations"? If so, a host of related
problems is stirred up which arises from the peculiar position of psy-

choanalysis between the natural sciences and the humanities. To be reductionistic without becoming irrelevant in a subject matter that includes the complexities of the whole man, is surely one of the great challenges which analysis faces. And your successes and failures in the field of applied analysis are more telling in this respect than the shortcomings of our nomenclature. I cannot resist sending you the reprint of yet another paper ["Beyond the Bounds of the Basic Rule"] which deals (more clearly than the present lines, for which you must forgive a busy practitioner) with the problem area on which your letter touched.

Again, many thanks for your valuable and generous reply.
Sincerely,
Heinz Kohut, M.D.

November 20, 1962
Martin Wangh, M.D.
New York
Dear Martin:
Thank you for sending me the reprint of your excellent essay on prejudice.[1] I read it with keen interest and found it scholarly, well reasoned, and well presented. Your balanced exposition of the mutual influence between the socio-economic-cultural and the endopsychic factors was particularly impressive. I congratulate you warmly on this fine achievement.

Some time ago I became interested in the possibility of differentiating varieties of prejudice and, after some study of the personalities of Hitler and Goebbels, thought that I could discern a walled-off psychotic form and a more phobic variety. Certainly Hitler's hypochondriacal, lonely, querulous early adult period from which he emerged with the fixed idea that the Jews had penetrated into the body of Germany and had to be eradicated differed from the much less fixed prejudice that characterized Goebbels's biography. I discussed these tentative thoughts once in the Chicago Society (*Bull. Phila. Assoc.*, 10, 156, 1960) but I did not follow them up.

We are looking forward to being with your wife and you in New York and to get to know both of you.
Sincerely,
Heinz Kohut, M.D.

1. Martin Wangh. "Psychoanalytische Betrachtungen zur Dynamik und Genese des Vorurteils, des Antisemitismus und des Nazismus," *Psyche* 16 (1962): 273–84. See also

Wangh, National Socialism and the Genocide of the Jews. A Psycho-Analytic Study of a Historical Event," *IJP* 45 (1964): 386–95. Wangh would later head a group on narcissism at the New York Psychoanalytic Institute: see Lester Schwartz to Kohut, November 24, 1971.

December 17, 1962
Robert J. Thurnblad
Department of Psychiatry
University of Chicago
Dear Doctor Thurnblad:
I was very touched by the farewell ceremony that the group of residents had arranged, and pleased with the lovely book that was presented to me. Despite the fact that I should be at home in the world of emotions, I found myself not quite capable of expressing the pleasure that I felt at your thoughtfulness. So let me say once more in writing what I tried to say in words: that I was very pleased to receive the expression of your appreciation and that I wish for you all to be good psychiatrists who will obtain continued gratification from the intellectual and emotional pleasure that comes with the deepening understanding of people and their problems.
Again my thanks and good wishes.
Sncerely,
Heinz Kohut, M.D.

January 17, 1963
The Reverend John F. Hayward
Meadville Theological School
Chicago
Dear Jack:
Thank you ever so much for sending a copy of your beautiful sermon on the Rose Window.[1] I can promise that it will not be just filed away but that it will be read and enjoyed, just as I enjoyed it when I heard it last November. I wished that I could reciprocate by sending you a work of similar inspiration and beauty, but, alas, it is the curse of the scientific mind that, in taking apart, he must destroy the wholeness of the whole, and what intellectual pleasure might be derived from the discovery of new parts and ingredients cannot make up for the loss incurred in the destruction of the whole. But so be it! One can

only strive for a scientific reductionism that does become irrelevant in a subject matter that includes the complexities of the whole man and of his art. And one may safely trust in the fact that the recognition of the ingredients has never prevented the truly creative from reassembling them in a new and beautiful order. Well, after all this preamble, thank you again for the Rose Window, and I hope that you will not judge too harshly the samples of my thoughts on the psychology of art and artists which I enclose for you.

Cordially,

Heinz Kohut, M.D.

1. A circular window common in medieval churches, especially in France.

January 23, 1963
Mr. Leo Nedelsky
University of Chicago
Dear Leo:

Thank you for your valuable critique of "The Psychoanalytic Curriculum."[1] Let me comment on your remarks. You imply that analysts cannot admit that they have something to learn from the educators. I can understand that my remarks (on page 162: "When analysts undertake these new assignments . . . good training in this specific skill for all of us.") must have angered you. And I confess that the phrase " . . . bow to the supposedly superior knowledge of . . . the non-analytic educator" does sound offensive. Yet, believe me, it is not meant that way. In order to grasp my full meaning here you would have to be acquainted with a certain trend in analysis to disregard our own, not inconsiderable knowledge about the motivations for learning and (through an isolated concentration of logic and method) to miss the unique opportunity to attempt to integrate our knowledge of psychic depth and psychic development with the methods and the psychology of learning and teaching. I have no doubt that the professional educator has more useful knowledge about learning and teaching than the analyst—but I don't want us to miss the opportunity "to integrate our experiences as organizers and teachers with the essential capacity of the analyst: to understand people and their problems in depth." I am not arguing, however, against our use of the help and advice of educators; I am, however, (and I have good reasons for it) arguing against our simply handing over our problems to experts outside our field. The paragraph in question must therefore be understood as a polemic against a trend within analysis—not as an attack on the professional educator for whom I have the fullest respect. In practice I believe that there will be an optimal time when we should (and will!) seek consultations with educators. Hopefully, however, these consultations will not be a taking of technical prescriptions but will be a mutually fruitful dialogue.

1. Objectives: I am not certain whether I understand the trend of your thoughts here. I assume, however, that the methods employed by us in this respect are so familiar to us that we did not spell them out in our discussions. Each student analyzes at least four cases under supervision and the supervisor is responsible for "teaching" the specific cycle (or imaginative listening, and of rigorous formulation of what has been perceived) of which you seem to speak. Then there are clinical seminars in which the teachers again, this time with a whole group, teach the mental attitudes that are specifically indicated in our work. Are you aware of the age of our students? They are usually in their mid thirties or older, which means that, unfortunately, much of our efforts are undertaken in order to produce "unlearning" in people who have already formed firm patterns of thought. It is one of the great problems in our profession that it requires both emotional flexibility (found mainly in young people) and sober self-possession (found mainly in the older).

2. Liberal Education: I, personally, agree warmly with you.[2] The difference in opinion that appears in the paper is due to the fact that I had to be the objective reporter of the whole spectrum of opinions. As far as I am concerned "applied analysis" should have a strategic and central position in the curriculum. Your remarks about the term "applied analysis" are also correct. Have you read my article "Beyond the Bounds of the Basic Rule"? The title, of course, was my way of avoiding the term "applied analysis" and to circumscribe the area by pointing to the methodological difference rather than to any essential difference in the subject matter.

3. Organization: Again, I agree with your comments. For purely practical reasons however (shortage of gifted teachers) I believe that any acceptable method with which a particular teacher is comfortable is all right at this time. I also agree with your remarks about "dogmatism." The only safeguard against it is inner freedom and courage. It is my conviction, however, that the "unwilling suspension of disbelief" is not harmful during the learning of a complex set of propositions, and I have often seen that the most dogmatic teachers are the ones that stress most loudly, in their verbal asides, that they are serv-

ing complete freedom of thought. That "the latest is easily equated with the best" may be correct but here I could only demonstrate my ideas by the use of concrete examples of development of psychoanalytic theory, and this letter would become quite an essay. A chapter in a forthcoming book on various schools of modern psychology (published by the University of Chicago) will, I hope, demonstrate my meaning in this respect.[3] I hope to be able to send you a reprint during this calendar year.

4. I wished I knew what you mean by a systematic analysis of the ways of correlating theory, practice and technique of "gimmicks." My own preference is the old-fashioned one of stressing the science over the profession, i.e., of teaching the barest minimum of "technique" in any systematic way and to trust that the understanding of principles combined with "experience" will lead the practitioner in the right direction. I admit that this attitude may be overly idealistic. Yet, since we do a great deal of practical-clinical teaching, technique is demonstrated by the clinical supervisor as clinical events demand it.

5. Evaluation: I fully agree with your remarks about questionnaires.[4]

I hope I understand your last remark correctly as a joke. What is implied in my statement is of course not that bad teaching is good for the students but that spoon-feeding methods (and over-concern with the preparing of the material so that the minimal work is demanded for the student to get by) does not in the long run satisfy the students themselves. In other words, that real learning is active study and active work by the student; and that the gratification from this work increase rather than decreases the pleasure of learning. In addition, of course, my joke was directed at the fact that the psychoanalytic educational effort is almost 100 percent paid for by the analysts themselves who teach with little or no financial compensation and pay sizable dues to their organizations in order to support their educational efforts.

And now thanks again for the attention which you gave to my article. I hope we will have a chance to continue our discussions verbally.

Cordially,

Heinz Kohut, M.D.

1. *Search*, 1:319–36.

2. In his letter of January 15, 1963, Nedelsky argued that psychoanalysis involve itself more with critical issues outside of its own aims.

3. Heinz Kohut and P. F. D. Seitz, "Concepts and Theories of Psychoanalysis,"

in *Concepts of Personality,* ed. J. M. Wepman and R. Heine (Chicago, 1963), pp. 113–41.

4. Nedelsky argues that open-ended questions fail to get at the respondent's assumptions.

January 24, 1963
Rudolph M. Loewenstein, M.D.
New York
Dear Doctor Loewenstein:

I wonder whether I could ask for your (private and informal) counsel in the following matter. As you may know I will be the Chairman of the Symposium on Fantasy at the Stockholm in July. I believe that you also have heard, through David Beres, the Chairman of the Program Committee of the International Psycho-Analytical Association, that there has developed a certain tension among those of the colleagues in the Paris Society about their participation in this Symposium and particularly apparently some feelings concerning the question whether Dr. Maurice Benassy, or Dr. D[aniel]. Lagache, is to represent the Paris Society on this panel. Judging from copies of the correspondence between Dr. Beres and the French colleagues which David Beres sent me, Dr. Francis Pasche as a Corresponding Member of the Program Committee of the International Psycho-Analytical Association, was somehow involved in the development of this sensitive situation, by asking Dr. Benassy to represent the Paris Society without notifying Dr. Beres who, in the meantime, had asked Dr. Lagache.

I understand, of course, at least up to a point, that such touchy situations have a way of developing, and I am not unduly worried about it. I wonder, however, whether from the background of your knowledge of the French colleagues, you could give me the benefit of your insights concerning these tensions. Do these people belong to different schools of psychoanalytic thought? And what are their basic differences? What personal and organizational factors have contributed to the touchiness that is emphasized by their reaction to this Symposium? It might be easier for you to reply to my inquiry than it is for me to formulate sensible questions. Please do not feel that I am asking for a detailed exposé—I would rather have a few highlights about the French situation (if you feel that you can share your knowledge with me) than a great number of details which would probably mean little to one like myself who is uninitiated.[1]

With best personal regards,
Cordially,
Heinz Kohut, M.D.

1. Lagache was head of a group not recognized by the IPA and was involved in a rivalry with the officially recognized French society, although there were no fundamental differences between them over psychoanalytic theory. See also below, September 22, 1965; and Lagache to Kohut, August 31, 1965. For Kohut's remarks to the Symposium on Fantasy, see *Search*, 1:375–85.

July 4, 1963

Dear Gustl,

Happy Fourth of July! The sun is shining here, some flags are out, and there is now and then the sound of a firecracker to be heard. This morning we played tennis which was great fun even though neither mom nor I played very well. Last night we went to the soccer game. It was a lovely evening, cool and clear—but the game was miserable. The Hungarian team beat the Polish team 1:0, and there was, of course, some excitement whether the Poles might even the score. The game, however, was not very spirited and the two clubs were quite second-rate. It was the poorest game that we have ever seen at Soldier Field. We decided that we would not go to another game this season, except perhaps to see the Austrian club. That game, however, takes place shortly before my going to Stockholm, and I might not have time for it, what with all the travel preparations.

Otherwise, there is not much to report. We miss you, of course, and think of you often and talk about you being in camp.[1] We both hope very much that, this year, the beginning of camp won't seem as bad as it seemed to you in years past; after all, you are getting to be an old hand at it now, and, in some ways, it must have seemed like a homecoming. We are looking forward to hearing from you. What are the activities that interest you most this year? Who are your friends? Are there any campers around from last year whom you like especially? Are you making any new friends? And so forth, and so on.

Do the "Kinderlieder" [children's songs] still hum through your mind at times? I am writing out "Summ', summ', summ'!" for you on a separate sheet of paper, including some kind of an English translation, so that you can at least know what you are humming in case the tune follows you around.

And now good-by, my boy. Be a good camper and a good sport. Don't show it too much if you are out of sorts or a little homesick but keep your chin up and your spirits high. Keep playing your best even if you are losing in the game; and keep on trying with any skill that you don't master: time, effort, and repetition can do a great deal. Don't forget: "Rome was not built in a day," and "masters don't fall from heaven." And remember that I am very proud of you even though I seem to do a lot of nagging sometimes.

Love,
Dad

1. Camp Kechuwa, Michigamme, Michigan

October 22, 1963
Kurt R. Eissler, M.D.
New York
   Dear Kurt:
   Many thanks for the reprint from *Psyche.*[1] I read it with deep emotions and admired your genius to take a dry professional problem as a starting point, ending up leading the reader to the ultimate questions of humanity. Of all your qualities I believe that your courage of the written word is the outstanding one and I think that essentially you are a moralist in the best sense of the word.
   I have also finished with Goethe. Reading it was an event; yet I feel hardly able at this time to respond to it articulately. As a cultural and a personal phenomenon alone I find your study of the greatest importance. I know nothing, of course, of your personal motivations but I cannot believe (the beautifully expressed reasons in your preface notwithstanding) that the wish to find a bridge to the German past with which we are so intimately connected was not a powerful motivation for devoting so many years to the intensive study of Germany's greatest son and to this greatest period of German cultural history. Let me say it differently: your work seems to me an attempt to heal a cultural rent, by going back to the time when there existed indeed a Germany that seemed to be a direct precursor of those ideals of cultural Europeanism, which we all cherished. To heal this rent is a personal task to which we all must take our individual positions; it is also a cultural task for those who remained physically "at home." Interestingly enough the reprint on the evaluation of the victims of persecution appears to me as an appeal in the same direction—even though there is no direct mention of the German classical period and of German humanism.
   From the more restricted point of view of psychoanalysis I believe that one of the greatest contributions you make lies in the definition of a problem by giving a concrete example. To put my meaning into a somewhat paradoxical form: your description of the Goethe–Charlotte von Stein relationships poses the question whether the ana-

lytic situation was an "invention" or a "discovery." In essence I believe most analysts treat the technical setting and the process of analysis as if they were an "invention," replaceable when a new invention makes the old machinery outmoded. But perhaps this is not so. The occurrence of spontaneous long-term relationships (outside of a quasi-technical setting such as between doctor and patient; priest and believer; master and disciple, etc.), for the preconscious purpose of solving an internal psychological task through structural rearrangements, seems to me to be a strong argument for the hypothesis that psychoanalysis has its precursor or analogue "in nature" and that the invented elements should be regarded as refinements added to the natural phenomenon.

There are innumerable details in your monumental study to which I now could address myself if I had only read the volumes with paper and pencil. I did not and so will helter skelter make a few remarks as my present memory carries them to me. There is hardly any place in your study where I did not gain something from your interpretations despite the fact that I may occasionally have felt that the constructions were not sufficiently founded empirically. My objection is not to such constructions per se, but perhaps I wished sometimes that they should be even more clearly pointed up more as creatively conceived possibilities than as solid interpretations. Take for example your interpretation concerning the drowning of the boys in *Wilhelm Meister* (Appendix V). Your line of thought with regard to homosexuality is instructive regardless of its specific correctness. But could one not also entertain the possibility that the episode relates to the guilt of having been the sole survivor among the siblings, the fear that they will pull him, too, down to death. That in fact five siblings had been born and had died by the time he was 12, I believe, and that the only other survivor, Cornelia, was also dead when he wrote the episode. Birth, death, and sex may all be linked in the contemplation of the attractive and destructive power of the water (for example, in "Das Wasser rauscht, das Wasser schwoll, etc,"),[2] and the twinship-homosexuality theme might relate to having to discover himself as the sole survivor. At any rate, the episode seems to me to be an example of an interpretation that might be seen from another point of view (or at least with a different dimension) than the one taken by you.

Concerning Goethe's "psychosis" I personally have no trouble with your use of the term and with the diagnosis. An encapsulated formation, even though highly pathological, is after all still the sign of active self-protective processes and I do not believe that we know enough of these things yet to shy away from your use of the term and to restrict it only to instances where the whole personality is manifestly involved in broad areas. I have one small question in connection with the psychosis theory. I wonder why you did not refer to Goethe's idiosyncrasy against eyeglasses in the context of the Newton problem. I mentioned it to you some years ago [December 8, 1955] and it was, of course, no surprise to me that you were fully familiar with this fact. Yet it seems to me that in his idiosyncrasy the irrationality was open and not covered up by the grandiose scientific rationalization of his "Farbenlehre."[3] I wonder why you deprived yourself of this argument.

I also have a few thoughts concerning your theoretical considerations on neutralization. We talked about it briefly in Stockholm and you may remember the point of view that I expressed then. At that time, however, I had not yet read Appendix U on the "Problem of the Transformation of Instinctual Energy." I must confess that after reading your chapter I have not changed my mind. Now that I disagree with your impression that the creative process is fed from strong instinctual sources which remain at times close to their origins. Yet I cannot see that your arguments militate against the *concept* of neutralization. Without it, how could you have expressed yourself as fully as you did concerning the *non*-neutralized energies which the genius uses during his creative spell? My disagreement, it seems to me, is partly due to the fact that you adduce a specific instance against the validity of the general concept that furnishes a framework even for your own argument. My disagreement is also related to the fact that you are accepting the occurrence of one extreme within a series as an argument against the (potential) occurrence of other points on the scale. I think this problem is related to the difficulty which I tried to point up in my closing remarks at the Fantasy Symposium in Stockholm concerning the difficulties with the use of continua. In view of the fact that I hope to have expressed my thoughts on that topic, clearly at that time, I will not pursue them now but enclose a copy of my remarks with this present letter.[4]

But now enough of these impressionistic remarks. A second reading will come some time (though not soon, I am afraid) and perhaps I can report other impressions based on deeper familiarity. Stockholm was a nice experience in many ways—not the least because it provided the chance to see you and talk with you. Your assumption that I went to Italy rests, unfortunately, on some error. Perhaps my post card from California made an Italian impression—I have no other explanation. I went straight back to Chicago from Stockholm and, two weeks later, went to California with Betty and Tom. I am spending a number of weekends in New York—but there is too much rush even to give you a ring. Before the December meetings I will spend a week in New York, and Betty will join me either on Thursday or Friday. But then there are all the obligations which I will take conscientiously for the next year and a half, and I do not know how much time there will be left for seeing friends. I do hope though that there will be a chance to get together even if only for part of an evening.

Warm regards to Ruth, and as usual, in friendly admiration the best to you,

Cordially,

Heinz Kohut, M.D.

1. K. R. Eissler, "Die Ermordung von wievieler seiner Kinder muss ein Mensch symptomfrei ertragen können, um eine normale Konstitution zu haben?" *Psyche* 17 (1963): 241–72.

2. "The water rushed, the water swelled"

3. *Zur Farbenlehre* (1810) was Goethe's theory of light which disputed that of Newton's.

4. *Search*, 1:379–85.

November 7, 1963
K. R. Eissler, M.D.
New York
Dear Kurt:

I am very grateful for your extensive reply. I feel, in general, in agreement with your remarks concerning the drowning episode. It is the nature of evidence and conviction in applied analysis that troubles me. I know that you present material aplenty to support your constructions and that your empathic finesse is outstanding. But there is something about a patient's quiet statement of recognition (or the dream subsequent to interpretation) which is not to be matched in applied analysis. I remember an experience years ago in a dream seminar held by Tom French concerning some dream material of one of my patients. He proved painstakingly with hundreds of details and a really great gift for matching and for the recognition of subtleties, what a certain dream sequence expressed. Everything seemed to fit—yet I know from later material that the interpretation was wrong.

With regard to the question of neutralized energy our differences may also partly be founded on a different conception of the "drives." I tend to abstract the concept of drives from experiences or extrapolate them from psychological experienced data. The various shades of neutralization appear to me as a helpful dimension of drive quality (analogous to the continuum Primary Hallucination—Thing Presentation—

Word Presentation) in which even the most drive-remote word presentation, as a unit within the context of the secondary processes, still contains a trace of libidinal sensuality (the *sound* of the word). Also could one not think of large quantities of neutralized drive in the service of some creative activity? There is still a difference between sexual passion and creative passion, between raging aggressive furor and the neutralized derivatives of aggression that lead to performance in the areas of separation, analysis, and formal delimitation. Perhaps the mode of creation of some geniuses are freaks of nature—perhaps Michelangelo's chisel-swinging hand was really nourished by unneutralized oral-sadistic libido that belongs to the early tooth. Even so. But I will think further about it and can see that conceptualization is possible in more than one way.

With regard to December, let me tell you that Betty and I are trying to keep Friday evening (12/6) free. It would be nice if we could indulge in the luxury of being with friends, but we know that this may depend on conditions that concern Ruth and you, and you should by no means disturb your own plans and arrangements for us. At any rate, we are looking forward to seeing Ruth and you at the meetings.

Cordially,

Heinz Kohut, M.D.

November 13, 1963
Gerhart Piers, M.D.
Chicago
Dear Gerhart:

This is a private communication concerning a matter which has been on my mind, off and on, for some time. It relates to a topic which you and I discussed in New York, informally, almost two years ago. Despite the time however which has passed, I feel sure that you remember our conversation. The topic is the assignment of candidates for their training analyses.[1] I expressed my feeling to you two years ago that our system was not right and that it should be re-evaluated. You agreed with me then and said that you would initiate steps to open this topic for review, asking me to do nothing further about it on my own initiative. I believe that I have some understanding for the fact that it may indeed be very difficult for you to open this subject matter for possible revision; I think, nevertheless, that I must mention it to you again. Since this is an informal communication (even though I prefer now initially to put down my ideas in writing) let me proceed and give you a few thoughts, helter-skelter, as they occur to me.

The mere fact that our way of handling the situation is, to my knowledge, unique should make us think about it and assess the advantages and disadvantages of our procedure in this area. Uniqueness, of course, does not mean either impropriety or lack of effectiveness. The recognition, however, that one is doing something that no one else is doing should be an incentive for a second look and for especially careful scrutiny. The assignment of candidates is obviously not an unimportant routine matter that can be passed up simply on the basis that there are no complaints and that everything appears to be working out all right. The training analysis is the most important single step among those by which the young psychiatrist moves toward the goal of becoming a psychoanalyst, and every detail which surrounds the training analysis is, therefore, of potential importance. If we leave the present situation undiscussed, we cannot, for example, even begin to probe the profoundly significant question whether it is better for the candidate to be assigned or to choose (even if choosing should mean the choice from a slate of names which is presented to him). The choice itself, even if the question of assignment could be disregarded, poses many problems. Assuming that the choice is handled by a person who is uniquely qualified by intelligence and intuition to make the best possible predictions or guesses, there are still disadvantages to such a narrow system. There is no gathering of experience by other people concerning the problems involved in making the choice. Despite striving for fairness and psychoanalytic propriety in all respects, predilections cannot but help play a role, e.g., some few favorite models of the selector would tend to get more of their share of the most promising candidates, etc. The long-range deleterious effects of such a possibility should not be underestimated. The formation of cliques and sub-schools of psychoanalysis in one location might be mentioned here as well as the possibility that an unspoken trend toward the perpetuation of one's own specific outlook on psychoanalysis may be supported in this way. The latter I would consider as a particularly touchy matter. Not that I believe that analysts do not have the right to speak up for what they think is correct and true; of course, they have that right and should use it in scientific meetings and, though to a much lesser extent and much more restrainedly, in their teaching. The assignment to a training analysis, however, is not the proper medium for such motivations.

I shall not emphasize the social or organization implications of our system of assigning candidates, and will here mention only one point. The Teacher Development Committee, the Education Committee, and the Staff cooperate in the appointment to the status of training analyst, a rank which is invested—inordinately so, in my opinion—with great prestige among analysts. The non-assignment of candidates, the rare assignment of candidates, or the assignment of the less promising candidates is capable however of transforming the rank of training analyst into a rather empty honor. The fact, by the way, that our present system permits us the advantage of a quiet, unofficial weeding out of training analysts who have become undesirable or whose work has deteriorated, etc., I consider only as a mixed blessing. True, it spares us many of the open dilemmas that plague other institutes; but I am firmly convinced that such conveniences and avoidances are never pure gains: the social working-through process of a more consciously faced (and shared) decision is, I am convinced, more wholesome in the long run.

But now I must put an end to this letter; it has grown longer than I had intended. Let me repeat only once more that this is a private communication, written in the hope that I can convince you that it is necessary to open this subject matter for debate and re-evaluation in any way that appears most conducive to real progress and the maintenance of good will.

Sincerely,
Heinz Kohut, M.D.

1. The training analysis is designed to provide the candidates with insight into their psychodynamics so that they can be as effective as possible in analyzing others. At the time, the Chicago Institute for Psychoanalysis assigned candidates to those of its members approved for such duty.

December 10, 1963 [from Phyllis Greenacre]
Dear Heinz,

Something happened to me with your introduction of me last Sunday.[1] I have tried to think what it was: I thought "I was greatly touched"—"No, I was moved"—and then it occurred to me that perhaps it was not so much one of these, as that I was gently and reassuringly solidified. It may surprise you that I should feel a need for solidification,—but in the milling and teeming (perhaps high powered) intellectual projects of present day psychoanalysis, I do not find a familiar foothold and had begun to feel outdated, and the only thing I could do was to go my own way stubbornly pursuing my own interests; and yet aware that to get out of the current stream is not only lonely but insidiously undermining, perhaps in any profession, but especially so in ours. And so the acceptance of my work and myself, so graciously expressed, was deeply heartwarming. Thank you for sending a reprint of "Concepts and Theories of Psychoanalysis."[2] I am especially glad to have it. It is still on my bed side table but I shall read it very soon. Against my better judgment I seem again to have gotten caught up in the relentless pressure of practice,—and most of my reading gets done between 3 and 5 in the morning. Just now I have been sleeping too well.

Best wishes and my deep appreciation.

Phyllis

1. At the APA annual meeting in New York; see Heinz Kohut, "Phyllis Greenacre: A Tribute," *JAPA* 12 (1964): 3–5. Greenacre was especially interested in early infantile origins of creativity. See Kohut's review of her book on Jonathan Swift and Lewis Carroll in *Search*, 1:275–303.

2. *Search*, 1:337–74.

December 27, 1963
Emanuel Windholz, M.D.
Chairman, the Committee on Honorary Membership
San Francisco

Dear Doctor Windholz:

I should like to propose Mr. Lionel Trilling for Honorary Membership in the Association. Before submitting the name of Mr. Trilling (who will be sixty years old in 1964) for the consideration of the Committee on Honorary Membership, I have pondered at length not only about the merits of the proposal but also about the objections that can be raised against it. In the following I will try to set down some of my thoughts.

Our By-laws state: "Any person who has made an outstanding contribution to the science of psychoanalysis shall be eligible for election as an Honorary Member." The phrase "contribution to the science of psychoanalysis" is the crucial one in this sentence and much depends on how it is interpreted. On the evidence of previous choices, I assume that the traditional interpretation has been a rather strict scientific-professional one; i.e., people were chosen (almost, but not quite, exclusively) who were themselves analysts and who had made scientific contributions to the science of psychoanalysis (the word "science," itself, being understood in a circumscribed sense, as the body of scientific psychoanalytic knowledge). If such an interpretation were to be given to the phrase in point, I would assume that Mr. Trilling would, a priori, not be acceptable. May I, however, earnestly raise the question (independent, here, of the specific qualifications of Mr. Trilling) whether such a restricted interpretation is warranted? To my mind it is not. I believe rather that it is proper for us to bestow Honorary Membership on persons who are not analysts and whose contributions are not primarily psychoanalytic, if they deserve our gratitude because they have promoted the acceptance of analysis in the larger matrix of society and have become significant interpreters of analytic insights to the broader community of the scholarly and the cultured.

Mr. Trilling is, in my estimate, deserving of the gratitude of psychoanalysts because he has made significant contributions in this last-mentioned context. As you know, Mr. Trilling is not a psychoanalyst but a respected and brilliant literary critic. Seen from the vantage point of a well-trained psychoanalyst, some of his commentaries on psychoanalysis are imperfect—I understand, for example, that his widely known [Freud Anniversary] lecture *Freud and the Crisis of Our Culture* [1955] was, for this reason, received with mixed feelings by a number of the analysts who heard it delivered. Having read the lecture in its final form (Beacon Press; Boston: 1955), I would personally not agree with the judgment that the presentation is lacking in wisdom or discrimination. I would rather emphasize that it is the very virtue of Mr. Trilling's approach that in his explorations he remains faithful to his own knowledge and skills, that he has not merged himself into our field and become a pseudo-analyst, but that he interprets it as a sophisticated and friendly representative of the wider culture. Doubts similar to those that can be raised with regard to Mr. Trilling's commentary on analysis could also be leveled against the significant analogous contributions that were made by Thomas Mann; yet, (occasional half-joking critical remarks notwithstanding) there is no doubt that Freud himself was deeply gratified by the support of this brilliant mind from beyond the borders of our field. While Mr. Trilling's literary stature does not measure up by comparison with Mann, I believe that, on the other hand, his spiritual relationship to analysis is much stronger and that his knowledge of analysis is ever so much more intimate than was Thomas Mann's.

Mr. Trilling has in fact devoted a good deal of hard work and imaginative thinking to our field. I heard him not long ago as a discussant of a paper on applied analysis in one of our national meetings and was deeply impressed by the way in which he, unlike other specialists in related fields, used his knowledge of cultural factors not to deride or oppose but to enrich the psychoanalytic approach to the literary figure under discussion. I have not studied the one-volume edition of Freud's biography by Jones and cannot say anything about the merits of Trilling's labors in this respect (except that a scholarly abbreviated edition is badly needed) but I have read the preface written by Mr. Trilling and found it dignified and inspiring.

Let me summarize my reflections by stating once more my conviction that, as a friend of analysis, Mr. Trilling has contributed importantly to the increasingly solid bonds that exist between psychoanalysis and the humanities, not only through the prestige which he carries in his own field but also by being a true mediator between his field and ours. By bestowing Honorary Membership on him I believe that we would add a further strand to the numerous existing ones by which psychoanalysis is woven into the intellectual and cultural fabric of modern society. I think, therefore, that it is proper for the Association to give recognition to a significant friend of psychoanalysis and that Mr. Trilling deserves to be honored by the Association.

Although I hope that my own arguments have expressed the merits of my proposal sufficiently to warrant a serious consideration of Mr. Trilling by the Committee on Honorary Membership, I will mention that I have (with due discretion) spoken to a few people whose judgment concerning the particular, relevant problems I value. Although one or two of those whom I approached for their opinion appeared (with some hesitations) inclined to view the proposal with disfavor (almost entirely on grounds that are concerned with uncertainties about Mr. Trilling's stature or personality) a decisive majority appeared keenly impressed by the validity of the suggestion and encouraged me strongly to pursue it. I have asked some of those who expressed themselves in favor to permit me to mention their names. If the Committee desires, I know that the following are willing to give a statement in support of the proposal: Drs. Greta Bibring, K. R. Eissler, Heinz Hartmann, and Helen V. McLean.[1]

Sincerely yours,
Heinz Kohut, M.D.

1. Trilling (1905-1975) was not made an Honorary Member of the Association.

December 29, 1963
Mrs. Jacqueline Kennedy
Washington, D.C.
Dear Mrs. Kennedy:

There is little chance that the enclosed tribute will be noticed by you amidst the overwhelming outpouring of feelings with which the world has tried to undo the evil deed. It is a message given to a small society of scientists in a comparatively unknown field of human endeavor. Yet perhaps some day when your son will page through the pages of past events and will attempt to construct for himself an image of his father's significance, this little message may serve him as an example of the many and varied influences which his father's actions have had.

Respectfully yours,

Heinz Kohut

ADDRESS OF THE PRESIDENT OF
THE CHICAGO PSYCHOANALYTIC SOCIETY
November 26, 1963[1]

Members of the Chicago Psychoanalytic Society:

After some reflection I have become persuaded that it is fitting for us to devote a few moments to the memory of President Kennedy. It is true that, as a scientific and professional society, we usually react to public events and to public figures only insofar as they have become the subjects of our scientific or professional interest: as psychoanalysts we are dedicated to deepening the understanding of the human mind, and to further this understanding is our major obligation to society. It is, therefore, through our scientific and clinical work that we are participating in the decisive struggle of mankind, the struggle for the dominance of reason and of self-control, and for the harnessing of the drives in the service of the creation of cultural achievements.

Our work, however, constitutes only one among the many forces engaged in the battles of civilization. We are the inheritors of what, I have no doubt, shall be recorded—if civilization will indeed survive—as one of the brightest victories of the human mind. Still, scientific heroism, even as great as Freud's, cannot arise, and its fruits cannot be maintained, without the support of brave men of action. President Kennedy, whatever anyone may think of this or that detail in his personality, his beliefs, his methods or his motivations, was, take it all in all, a courageous soldier for the ideals of reason and good will. And thus his death summons our respect for him as a gallant figure fighting for a cause that is also our own.

Let us remember him as he appeared in his best moments, with that youthfulness and enthusiasm that must be welded to the forces of rationality—as when he stood on that wind-swept day next to the old, youthful poet, in that first symbolic partnership of the man of culture and the man of action.[2]

1. The Chicago society sent a copy of this address to the APA on November 27 for possible dissemination or publication. There is no record of such, but see David Beres, "John F. Kennedy," *JAPA* 12 (1964): 401–4.
2. Kohut speaks of Kennedy's inauguration at which poet Robert Frost spoke.

1964–1965
"our worst disease"

March 13, 1964
Heinz Hartmann, M.D.[1]
New York
Dear Dr. Hartmann:

Rarely in my life have I felt as much enjoyment with the gift of a book as when I opened the package from the International Universities Press and found unexpectedly the handsome volume of your *Essays in Ego Psychology* [1964] with your generous personal inscription. I am, of course, familiar with almost all of the content of the volume; to be able now to go directly to the book instead of having to go to back issues of journals whenever I want to read one of the essays will be very pleasant indeed.

It might interest you to learn that a meeting of the Chicago Psychoanalytic Society was recently devoted to your *Ego Psychology and the Problem of Adaptation* [1958]. It was a very good and fruitful evening for all of us, and at least a glimpse of appreciation for the depth of your contribution to psychoanalysis even by the least sophisticated. I am enclosing a program of our meeting.

Thank you once more for your gift. What a profound satisfaction it must be for you to look at this volume of papers and to see before you the fruits of a lifetime of creative work and thought!

Cordially yours,
Heinz Kohut, M.D.

1. Heinz Hartmann pioneered psychoanalytic research into the ego and into narcissism, introducing the world "self" into the literature. He was a major source of inspiration for Kohut's work. See Elisabeth Young-Bruehl, *Creative Characters* (New York, 1991), pp. 131–34.

July 27, 1964 [original in German]
K. R. Eissler, M.D.
Hotel Kaiserin Elisabeth
Vienna
Dear Kurt!

I'm sorry that you weren't able to let me know what the plan is you have in mind for me and the International. I assume that you want to nominate me for an office in the International and that placing the lecture in a prominent position will serve to make me known among European and South American colleagues. Unfortunately I cannot contribute anything to this. I work here daily from early morning to late evening, can scarcely keep up with my correspondence, at the moment am involved in preparing all the new committee appointments, and will (although on the whole the work is rewarding) be very glad when my four-and-a-half-year tenure as a bureaucrat comes to an end. After May 1965, when my presidency of the American ends, I will devote myself to the research that I will present in New York in December 1965. I cannot at the same time prepare a paper for Amsterdam and moreover don't see how such a paper could be placed prominently since the major papers which have already been determined will be devoted to the Congress theme of obsessional neurosis. Even if I had prepared a paper (which will not be the case) I could lay claim only to a smaller forum.

Since I don't know what your intention is I naturally cannot say much more. For myself I could wish nothing better than peace and relaxation after the great exertions of the last few years. At the moment I harbor no ambitions for positions and prestige. Sometimes of course one has the feeling that one has to participate when all that is dear to one seems to be at stake. That can scarcely be considered the case now, at least not in the International.

Anyway, I think that the South American colleagues know me very well (I held a lecture in Mexico City during the first Pan-American Congress) and that many Europeans also know me very well (I was the Chairman of the Fantasy Symposium in Stockholm; my paper will appear in the International journal and in French in the French psycho-analytic review).

That's all for today. I'm sorry that I must disappoint you, but I know that you will understand my situation. Cordial greetings and the best wishes for a beautiful summer from your

Heinz Kohut

August 4, 1964
Dr. Anna Freud
London
Dear Dr. Freud:

Have you become used to the new form of address? I failed to congratulate you in Philadelphia at having been given the Honorary Degree [Jefferson Medical College], but this formality was hardly required. I did write a warm letter to Floyd Corneilson, thanking him for his share in bringing about this event. In all I behaved like a relative in a family affair: more identification than object relation.

As you had predicted, your letter was waiting for me when I returned to Chicago. You are very generous! What you had to say gave me great pleasure, and your approval was a welcome support amidst the inescapable insecurities under pressure to which we are all exposed. Strangely enough, it was not the discussion of the scientific contributions and other statements that I had sent to you but the very last, parting sentence of your letter which gave me the most food for thought. You sent me your best wishes for the presidency of the American Psychoanalytic Association, and expressed the hope that "this office permits opportunity for some revolutionary moves." My mind has returned to your statement time and again since I first read your letter.

I know, of course, the objectives which we hold in common: to fight against the conception of psychoanalysis as a "sub-specialty" of psychiatry; to counteract the tendency to replace the psychoanalytic methods which are appropriate to our subject matter with the inappropriate (and thus sterile) methods of academic psychology; and to strengthen the position of psychoanalysis as a broadly based human psychology with its own body of knowledge and methodology. Toward all these objectives, however, we can work without "revolutionary moves," and victories can be won either by achieving limited degrees of improvement affecting a comparatively large area within the social framework of American Psychoanalysis (such as the small improvements which have occurred in some of the larger American Institutes during the last decade) or by creating a significant psychoanalytic activity on a limited scale (such as the publication of *The Psychoanalytic Study of the Child*, the organization of the Center for Advanced Psychoanalytic Studies [at Princeton], and, within the framework of the American Psychoanalytic Association, the organization of scientific meetings in such a way that outstanding psychoanalysts occupy the important spots in the program and that good psychoanalytic papers are accepted in our Journal). But these are not revolutionary moves.

While I cannot be certain that the membership will agree to the establishment of a Forum for Scientific Child Psychology (open to all child analysts, whether they are lay analysts or have a medical degree), I assume that the vote will be in the affirmative. If so, a nice piece of progress will have been made and I will be pleased at the thought of having contributed to it.[1] But again: this is not a revolutionary move but only a shift of emphasis. We are also preparing a mail ballot to allow training analysts without medical degree to become regular active members of the Association. At present I am doubtful about the success of this proposition (it needs two-thirds majority since it involves a By-Law change), but even if it should be accepted it would not be a revolutionary move.[2]

The only move that could be called revolutionary, would be to abolish *in principle* (not as an exception) the medical and psychiatric requirements for membership (and thus automatically for students at our institutes); or, put it in another way, to approve the establishment of even a single institute which would train people without a medical degree and without psychiatric experience for a regular career as analysts (not as research candidates for a research career; this is, as you know, done now). Disregarding the question of the desirability of such a move, let me first discuss the question whether it could be achieved. I think that it could be done, i.e., with the right kind of leadership a secessionist movement could be started, something like the "Academy,"[3] except on the opposite end of the psychoanalytic spectrum. Up to one-fifth of the present membership of the Association might be willing to join such a splinter group (as individuals they could remain in the Association, just as at present many members of the Academy are also members of the Association) and they could (somewhat illegally) organize one or two institutes open to medical as well as to non-medical candidates. Chances are such institutes would soon have an almost exclusively non-medical student body, a result which is probably not desirable; my opposition to the revolutionary move rests, however, not on this possible drawback but on my anticipation of the following consequences: the best analytic teachers would be taken away from the established institutes; and the best and most firmly grounded psychoanalytic minds would be taken away from the meetings of the Association, with the result that the regular institutes and the regular meetings would deteriorate, would become analytic in name only, and would be taken over completely by "dynamic psychiatry." The established institutes would, however, continue to draw the major part of the gifted students and of the younger generation in general. (I have discussed an analogous problem concerning the topic of training analysis in a recent letter;[4] I am enclosing a copy of this letter for you; it may also serve as an example of the non-revolutionary daily spade work that some of us are engaged in and of which I have given you other samples in my preceding letter.)

As you can see, I am, at this time, disinclined to employ "revolutionary moves" but will instead, as I have done in the past, endeavor (a) to achieve slow changes in the broad field of American psychoanalysis, and (b) to establish limited foci of pure analysis within and without the framework of organized psychoanalysis in the United States.

My conviction that this non-revolutionary approach is the correct one is based on facts which I have only gradually learned to understand. I am aware, of course, of the true nature of the resistances against analysis. I have, nevertheless, come to hold the view that the attraction which analysis exerts on many potentially capable students in this country is intimately connected with specific, culturally determined, and thus pre-formed, sublimatory patterns; and I believe that these specific motivations help to explain both the comparatively widespread acceptance of psychoanalysis in this country as well as the specific ways in which it tends to be diluted and distorted (the scientific-psychiatric distortion; the interpersonal cure-through-love dilution; and all kinds of blends and amalgamations of the two).

Let me briefly tell you about the two major groups that participated in the initial growth of American psychoanalysis which took place before the great influx of European analysts to this country. While these two groups were propelled toward psychoanalysis by different cultural motivations, each of them separately, and both of them together, have basic cultural value systems which are different from that of the educationally and culturally secure core of European analysts to whom analysis provides (in non-individual cultural terms) a union of their interests in biology and in the humanities. It is, of course, well known that the influence exerted by the European group on the two groups of analysts which were already established in this country has been a very strong one. Yet, the picture cannot be understood fully from the point of view of the value system of the Europeans. But what constitutes the older core of analysts in the U.S., what are these two groups? The one, more numerous but not necessarily more influential group, is Eastern European Jewish, a generation or two removed from the ghetto, to whom the haven of American institutions (despite the prejudice and narrow-mindedness of a large part of the population) was liberation and for some of whom the rationality of a career in medicine and in psychiatry as a branch of medicine was the professional embodiment of a whole new world of freedom. The other group, numerically smaller but of great influence, is predominantly Anglo-Saxon, of that attractive branch of Protestantism that has replaced increasingly the belief in the dogma of orthodox Christianity with a tendency for missionary work, progressive social action, and social reform. This is a well-established minority on the American social scene; best known among them are the more mystical Quakers and the more rationalistic Universalists and Unitarians who received their baptism of fire during the Abolitionist period. It is the combination of these two groups and, with all their differences, their friendship (and often marriage, in the literal sense) which has up to very recently determined the direction of American psychoanalysis: a combination of a close tie to psychiatry with an emphasis on interpersonal healing, helping, and reforming.

It is my conviction that the best human material for psychoanalysis in the United States will continue to come from these two groups which, to some extent, counteract and complement each other. For both groups (although probably more for the first one) the tie to the recognized profession of medicine (and psychiatry) is a very strong and deep one. Institutes who would separate themselves from medicine and psychiatry would draw their student body largely from the second group with their tendency to non-scientific (or scientifically rationalized) healing through love, through interpersonal support, through education, through being a living example, and through offering a cure by identification. (An already existing example is the William Alanson White Institute in Washington, D.C., which is outside the American Psychoanalytic Association.) Thus, one predictable result would be an increase of existential psychiatry and existential analysis, analogous to the European pattern.

For the time being, I believe that the best hope for American psychoanalysis is a realistic acceptance of this strongly established balance of preferences; not to upset it with revolutionary moves, but to continue to exert a gradual influence by word and example (of which I have furnished some illustrations in my enclosures last time and today). I myself have, therefore, not entirely given up my University connections although I resisted a prestigeful offer which would have taken me away from analysis. I still give a weekly seminar to resident physicians in psychiatry, to stimulate their interest in the insights of psychoanalysis and to draw the best of them into psychoanalytic training.

I am sorry that this letter has expanded into a small essay, explaining little with many words. But I know that (if you find the time to let me have the benefit of your reactions) your clarity and courage will not fail to have its effect on me.

I hope that you are well and that you are enjoying a good summer. Please give my regards to Willie Hoffer, to the Sandlers [Anne-Marie and Joseph], and to Mrs. Burlingham[5] (who may remember me from Princeton).

Cordially yours,
Heinz Kohut, M.D.

1. The Forum for Child Analysis was not approved by the membership of the APA. American Psychoanalytic Association, Minutes of Executive Council, December 3, 1964, p. 6; *JAPA* 13 (1965): 449.

2. This proposal was not even submitted to the members of the APA for a vote.

American Psychoanalytic Association, Minutes of Executive Council, December 3, 1964, pp. 6–8. See Anna Freud to Kohut, March 7, 1965, below. In 1989, however, as a result of a class-action lawsuit, the APA agreed to set aside almost half of its training slots for nonmedical candidates with doctorates.

3. The Academy for Psychoanalysis was founded in Chicago in 1956 as a forum for ideas not necessarily acceptable to the APA but which were seen to build upon the biological and scientific foundations laid by Freud, particularly as interpreted by Franz Alexander. See *IJP* 45 (1964): 618–21.

4. Kohut to Paul Kramer, January 24, 1964; and to David Kairys, January 29, 1964.

5. Dorothy Burlingham was a child analyst and longtime companion of Anna Freud. See Michael John Burlingham, *The Last Tiffany: A Biography of Dorothy Tiffany Burlingham* (New York, 1989).

August 18, 1964
Dr. and Mrs. Alexander Mitscherlich
Heidelberg
Dear Mitscherlichs:

Thank you both for your various "Lebenszeichen" [signs of life], i.e., the post cards from Carmel and Yugoslavia, the *Monat* of May, 1964 [pp. 7–29], and the reprint about "Toleranz."[1] Betty and I enjoyed hearing from you, and I read the two articles in *Monat* [on the Holocaust] with all sorts of emotions and the reprint with great interest and profit.

I think that it is important and proper to point out that "Toleranz" is a positive ego-achievement of great complexity, and that it rests, like all great cultural achievements, on drive control and the adult capacity to tolerate frustration. To my mind the most awesome enemy of "Toleranz" is not aggression or hostility towards others per se but a core of unmodified narcissism and specific narcissistic fantasies that were defensively built up on the basis of infantile narcissistic traumata. It is the threat to these defensive narcissistic structures (and/or the promise of the fulfillment of the narcissistic fantasy) which accounts, I believe, for the severest degrees of intolerance, at least in the decisive incipient stages. Later developments may, of course, give full reign to unmodified sadism; but I consider these late stages to be non-specific.

In addition I think that it would be rewarding to study in detail the thinking processes employed in intolerance and, specifically, in prejudice. Despite the presence of often quite sophisticated rationalizations (for example, the vulgarized Darwinism to which you referred in Chicago) I believe that archaic thought processes are quite prominent. Among them is the often unrecognized archaism of a near-animistic, psychologizing interpretation of events, which is supported by the traditional religious concept of divine justice: namely, the person in trouble, the person who is weak, the person who is in the minority, etc., must be at fault, must be bad, unclean, immoral, etc. This conviction is a residue of infantile thinking which even science has a hard time overcoming. In historical sequences (just as is true in physics) the recognition of a Principle of Indeterminacy would be the expression of having overcome the infantile need to see any present state as *meaningfully* (or even as morally) connected with the preceding events.

I cannot resist adding one more consideration, although it is only very loosely connected with the topic of your chapter and was more stimulated by my perusal of the two articles in *Monat*. There is no question in my mind that a consciousness of the enormity of the crime must be achieved and maintained in Germany and that the preconscious guilt of the many who cooperated, or looked away and did not resist, must be made conscious. It is, however, of no avail, I am convinced, to act, on the social stage, like the analyst who over and over again confronts the ego of the patient with the unconscious drive demands and the unconscious guilt. If one tries to force people to carry such guilt without some promise of relief or some mitigation, all that can be achieved is pathological masochism in those who are susceptible to it or a re-enforcement of the only possible self-justification, namely that the victims were not human, that it was really a creditable and painful job to exterminate them (like vermin) etc. But what can one say to those multitudes who, as you are satisfied is the case (and I believe you!), carry a share of guilt for the events of the Nazi period? I don't believe that it is difficult for an analyst to find the right attitude, and I think that the right attitude is not a "technical gimmick" or a "therapeutic ruse" but that it is truthful. The guilt of the many is not only individual guilt, it is shared guilt; it is shared by all of humanity, probably even by the victims. It is true that the only thing that would have been meaningful during the Nazi period (and especially before it all happened) would have been deeds tantamount to heroism. Yet it is just this choice between heroism and guilt that must be brought home to people if humanity is to survive. One does not become a hero out of guilt alone. To confront people with their past sins has no chance of transforming them into the heroes of the future. If, however, the guilt is shown as a common fate, if people can see that they, themselves, were victims, too, (that the highest, most differentiated, most precious part of their own personalities had been killed), then that positive wish to unite again with the old ideal might be generated in people, to create in a few (and not so very many are needed; the others will follow) that heroism which inspires the will to survive in a sense that is more meaningful than biological survival.

Thank you once more for the thoughtfulness of sending these *Monat* [articles] and the reprint. We do hope to hear from you again some time. Our own vacation (in Carmel) will begin in about ten days and we can hardly wait for it. I am enclosing a copy of my Los Angeles Address as a little souvenir of your attendance at our Meetings. Cordial greetings to both of you from both of us, and auf Wiedersehen!

Sincerely,

Heinz Kohut, M.D.

1. See Alexander and Margarete Mitscherlich, *The Inability to Mourn: Principles of Collective Behavior* [1967], trans. Beverly Placzek (New York, 1975), pp. 223–34.

August 21, 1964

The Honorable Richard J. Daley

Mayor of Chicago

Dear Mr. Daley:

The recent unrest in Dixmoor and the occurrence of similar disturbances in other big cities has prompted me to share an idea with you which, despite its simplicity, may have some merit. The thought occurred to me that the availability of outdoor swimming facilities, installed by the City in the crowded sections of our town, would be a very valuable supplement to the already existing recreational facilities: the beaches, playgrounds, and the forest preserves.

The greatest tensions appear to occur during the hot summer months, especially in the evenings, and the age groups which appear to be involved predominantly are the adolescents and the young adults. For many of these people there are no recreational facilities available during the evening hours which would equal a cooling "dip" right in the neighborhood (without having to travel to and from the beaches), in a number of dispersed places which would "belong" to each neighborhood. Loud speakers could provide entertainment and news information in the earlier hours, there could be auxiliary recreational facilities around the swimming pool area, and the whole area could be well lighted and thus create an atmosphere of openness and lack of stealth.

Any effective implementation of such a program would, of course, be very expensive. Pilot studies in selected neighborhoods, however, could be carried out with limited funds and (since the problem that the project is to combat is shared by almost all big cities and since the results of the pilot study would be of value to all of them) cost sharing and/or federal assistance might be obtainable.[1]

Sincerely yours,

Heinz Kohut, M.D.

1. Kohut's letter was also passed on to Edward Marciniak, executive director of the Chicago Commission on Human Relations. There is no record of a reply from Daley or Marciniak. See "U.S. Vows Funds for Trouble Area Swimming Pools," *Chicago Sun-Times*, July 17, 1966. The mayor's office did send a representative to the banquet on June 2, 1973, honoring Kohut on the occasion of his sixtieth birthday (Ernest Wolf to Daley, May 5, 1973).

October 16, 1964

Victor Calef, M.D.

San Francisco

Dear Vic:

It was good to receive your letter and I am glad that you feel some kinship with my method of supervision. Frankly I believe that I have never lived up to very rigid principles in my supervision but that I have let myself by guided by my instinct concerning the best way of furthering the student's development. My primary and principal objective remains the teaching of clinical psychoanalysis, i.e., I listen and explain what is going on in the patient, the transference, the reactions to interpretations, and the patient's ego-reactions, beyond what the student himself has grasped. If I see blind spots, persistent faulty understanding, persistent interfering behavior, etc., I point them out, usually without much direct fuss about the student since I do not believe in calling up resistances that cannot be handled in the supervisory situation. If the student is still in analysis I might simply say that here seems to be something in need of understanding. Most of the time however this is not necessary since the material will get into the analysis by itself. If the student is not in analysis any more however and if I can clearly see that something (or something specific) is interfering from the side of the student's personality, I believe that I usually manage to draw the student's attention to it. The ways in which I do this vary from cautious allusions to direct confrontation, but always in a way that expresses my conviction that we are all exposed to unmanageable intrusions from the unconscious at times and that the student need not feel attacked or ostracized but should attempt to analyze the difficulty and, if necessary, get further personal analytic assistance with the problem.

All these problems deserve a more extensive discussion than I can afford at the present time. I hope we will have a chance to chat about the whole problem area when we will see each other in Princeton. You might by the way suggest the topic of supervision and of the supervisor's attitude to Sam Guttman. I believe that all members of our group have supervisory experience and that therefore a discussion should be quite interesting.

As an example of my way of supervising I am enclosing an old sample of one of my quarterly reports to the Education Committee of the Chicago Institute. For reasons of discretion I have removed the name of the student. Please keep it however confidential and return it to me. It is my only copy. As a further example of my supervisory activities you might also look up in the files of the Membership Committee the report that I wrote in June, 1961 on an applicant by the name of H——.

But I must close now. I am looking forward to seeing you either in Princeton or in New York and I hope that we can talk about these problems.

Cordially,
Heinz Kohut, M.D.

New York City, December 4, 1964
My dear Gustl,

Your letter to me was a very good one, and it gave me a great deal of pleasure. Your thoughts are quite well expressed and the form of your writing has improved tremendously.

I was interested in your reactions to Granny's paintings. They are indeed bright but I wonder whether they express happiness. Regardless—her painting keeps her active and satisfied, and it prevents her from growing old in mind and spirit, and so it's a very good thing for her.

Betty and I went to the opera last night and saw a wonderful performance of [Giuseppe Verdi's] *Falstaff*—a sheer delight in all respects from the beginning to the end [see below, January 11, 1969].

The weather is unfortunately terrible—it's raining, moist and cold, and it's lucky that all the meetings are right here in the hotel. Well, it won't be long now. In two days we are leaving and on Monday we will be back in Chicago and with you again.

Tovey's eyes worry me. I hope they will heal again as they did the first time. I wonder whether he injured the eye in the country or whether he scratched it because of their itchiness.

Glad to know that you are working hard. Keep it up and don't get discouraged even if your grades won't stay up or move up. It always takes quite a long time until one sees results in things of this kind.

See you soon, Gustl,

Love,

Dad

December 15, 1964

Merton M. Gill, M.D.

Professor of Psychiatry

State University of New York, Brooklyn

Dear Doctor Gill:

Your message of appreciation concerning my letter to the members of the Association[1] gave me great pleasure and I am glad to find that the thoughts that I expressed appear to strike a responsive chord in many of our colleagues. There is no question in my mind that analysis would be doomed if it should ever become near-exclusively a profession of therapists. Not everybody can be a creative discoverer of new truths in the dimly lit depths in which the analyst and his patients are searching; I believe nevertheless that every analyst must be patterned more after the model of the discoverer than after that of the technician. At any rate if analysts should ever cease to search for significant discoveries about the human mind with the aid of their unique investigative instrument, the profession itself would become diffused into dynamic psychiatry and would disappear.

I am enclosing a copy of my Los Angeles Address which pursue, on a somewhat different level, the same line of thought that I expressed in the letter to the members.[2] And now once more thank you for your friendly note, and cordial wishes for a good holiday and for 1965.

Sincerely,

Heinz Kohut, M.D.

1. *President's Newsletter*, 5, no. 1 (November 1964).
2. *Search*, 1:389–93.

December 21, 1964

Miss Maibelle Mohrherr

Chicago

Dear Maibelle:

Your question puzzles me. You ask: "Do you consider the statement 'men seek pleasure to avoid pain' a *fact*?" Do you want to know whether I think that the content of the statement is true? Or do you want to know whether, independent of its truth, the assertion concerns a "fact" or a "theory," "view," "opinion," "hypothesis," or the like? In either case one could write a lengthy treatise to answer your question.

In particular with regard to the first possibility, i.e., whether the assertion is true or correct, the answer depends on the level on which one wishes to examine the formulation. In terms of direct experience, the statement is undoubtedly erroneous: pleasure has positive quality of its own and is striven for, according to our direct experience, for its own sake. On the level of a system of psychological theory however which attempts to explain (i.e., beyond the direct experience) pain and pleasure in terms of tension increase and tension decrease, the statement may be said to be valid.

With regard to the other interpretation of your question, I can only say that it is extremely difficult to draw a line between "fact" and "theory." In everyday language, facts are considered aspects of reality that can be grasped with our senses; the statement in question relates to a complex relationship between such simple "facts." Yet one may well consider even such complexities as facts if one stresses their occurrence in time and space rather than our thinking about them.

Sincerely,
Heinz Kohut, M.D.
cc: Dr. Shapiro

February 10, 1965
Dr. Rainer Zitta
Oesterreichische Hochschulzeitung
Vienna
Dear Dr. Zitta:

Thank you for your inquiry of November 4, 1964.[1] You may find biographical details in the 1964–65 edition of *Who's Who in America* (p. 1123); also *Who's Who in Austria*, 5th edition, Intercontinental Book and Publishing Company, Ltd., Vienna, 1964 (Bohmann and Taylor, eds.). I am also enclosing a recent article about me in the *Medical Tribune* of December 21, 1964 [p. 8], as well as an interview in the *New York Times* of May 2, 1964 [29:8]. A popular article by a science writer in the *Chicago Daily News* of September 22, 1950, might also be of some service to you.[2] I also hope that the enclosed photograph will be satisfactory.

With regard to my writings however I find it much more difficult to know how to comply with your wishes. I might start by telling you that, like my specialty psychoanalysis, I have been standing with one foot in biology and with the other in the humanities. My interest (and my publications) have ranged from the purely biological approach (several papers on neuropathology) to the purely psychological-interpretative one (a number of papers on the psychological effects of music; a psychoanalytic investigation of *Death in Venice* by Thomas Mann; a paper on the methodology of so-called "Applied Analysis," etc.). All these papers are based on a scientifically disciplined method of "explaining" aesthetic phenomena by applying to them the cohesive concepts and the explanatory system of psychoanalytic depth psychology. It may be of some interest to state that, vastly different though the approaches to the psychoanalytic explanation of musical activity and of the effect of Thomas Mann's work are, my explanations lean in each instance heavily on what is known as the psychoeconomic factor. To state it more specifically: in both instances I have found that it is the intensity of early (i.e., premature) psychological (over-) stimulation which leads to certain artistic counter-measures: in the one instance (the psychological effects of music) to an abreaction of the tonal overstimulation (frightening noise) through the controlled musical experience of the mature psychic organization; in the other instance (Thomas Mann; the ironically detached artist) to a defense against the early overstimulation suffered by the child as an excited observer (the so-called "primal scene" experience) through the artistic detachment of the mature psychic organization of a talented writer.

In view of these predilections, it will not be surprising that basic theoretical questions concerning the nature of the methodology of psychoanalytic explanations have been very attractive to me. Three papers in this field express probably most clearly the conclusions which I have reached in these areas: (1) A paper "Introspection and Empathy" as the basic mode of observation used in psychoanalysis and on the way in which the use of this observational method influences the theories which psychoanalysis has evolved. (2) A paper (written in collaboration with Dr. P. F. D. Seitz) in which the "Concepts and Theories of Psychoanalysis" are systematically investigated from this point of view. And finally (3) a brief (but I believe concentrated) discussion on the nature of psychoanalytic explanations, entitled "Some Problems of a Metapsychological Formulation of Fantasy" in which I drew certain parallels between theory formation in physics and in (psychoanalytic) psychology. Finally I will mention also that, as the President of the American Psychoanalytic Association, I had the occasion to think and to write about the goals and ideals of organized psychoanalysis.

I hope that this summary may be of assistance to you. I am sorry that it had to be written in English in order to facilitate the job of typing it.

Sincerely yours,

Heinz Kohut, M.D.

1. "Oesterreichische Gelehrte im Ausland: Heinz Kohut, Chicago," *Oesterreichische Hochschulzeitung*, May 17, 1965, p. 10.

2. Arthur J. Snider, "Love of Music Laid to Fear of Noise," p. 18; *Search*, 1:135–58.

February 22, 1965

Dr. Alexander Mitscherlich

Heidelberg

Dear Doctor Mitscherlich:

Your long letter of December 17 was well worth waiting for and I hope the unavoidable delays in our correspondence (we are all much too busy!) will not set up that well-known emotional cycle (of guilt about not having answered yet, leading to increased unpleasure about confronting the unanswered letter and therefore more delay, leading to a further increase in guilt about not having answered) which has broken many a promising correspondence and relationship.

Right now I am up to my ears in work and cannot do justice to the thought-provoking content of your letter. I would particularly like to discuss with you the problems which are posed by the application of psychoanalytic insights on mass psychology. You have of course recognized my hunch (expressed not only in my last letter to you but also in the two recent communications to the members of our Association which I sent to you) that what belongs most privately to the individual, namely the (repressed?) narcissistic fantasy, might be one of the crucial specific factors in the social pathology of our age. I am too busy now with administrative duties to give sufficient thought to this problem, but I am planning to turn to it as soon as my official duties here will be over. As you may know, the Past President of the Association addresses the membership in the meeting following the end of his term of office. It is at the moment my plan to discuss some problems of narcissism as much as they lend themselves to specific scientific formulations with our present conceptual armamentarium and the empirical data obtained in the analytic situation.[1]

I cannot say much about your wish to find a director who will raise the Frankfurt Institute to the oedipal age of five. I can see no rational possibility for myself, despite many irrational attractions. Nor can I think of anyone else. But the idea is in my head and, if it activates anything useful or promising, I will let you know.

We are here very sad about the death of Max Gitelson. I still remember clearly the evening in his house when Betty and I met your wife and you for the first time. Although I do not know how well acquainted you were with him, you got no doubt a glimpse of his personality and recognized the strong influence which he exerted on the development of our science. I am enclosing a copy of the brief remarks about him which I presented in the framework of a memorial service held in Chicago shortly after he died.[2]

And now my good wishes and the hope to hear from you from time to time and perhaps to see you before long. I will be in Amsterdam for the Pre-Congress Conference on Psychoanalytic Training and for the Congress itself. I am however planning to return to the United States almost immediately after the Congress. Will I see you in Amsterdam? The best to your wife and you from Betty and me.

Cordially,

Heinz Kohut, M.D.

1. *Search*, 1:427–60.
2. "At the Memorial Service for Max Gitelson. February 14, 1965."

February 21, 1965 [from Anna Freud]

Dear Dr. Kohut,

I was so glad to have your letter and your very beautiful obituary for Max Gitelson.[1] I knew him very much less than you did and in spite of that my thoughts and feelings were almost identical with yours. I had pinned very many hopes for the future of analysis on him. Who will take his role now? Will you be the one?[2]

I did not realise that my father had ever written about his thoughts on the transience of people and things; or from where else did it come to you? It was one of the few points on which we disagreed. I always wanted all good experiences, including people, to be permanent and I took losses badly. He tried to teach me that possession of something good implies no claim to having it for ever. But even now, after so many years, I do not find it easy to be philosophical.

I look forward to seeing you in Amsterdam.

Yours sincerely,

Anna Freud

1. Anna Freud in fact refers to the eulogy for Gitelson given by Kohut in Chicago on February 14, 1965; see above, February 22.

2. On Anna Freud's early appreciation for Kohut, see Robert Coles, *Anna Freud: The Dream of Psychoanalysis* (Reading, Mass., 1992), p. 119.

March 2, 1965
Miss Anna Freud
London
Dear Miss Freud:

How generous you were again in your response to me! and I prize the fact that the thoughts and feelings about Max Gitelson that I had expressed in the obituary are shared by you.

You asked two questions. One I can answer easily; to reply to the other is more difficult.

The remarks in the obituary about which you inquire alluded to thoughts in your father's essay "On Transience," [1915] Volume XIV of the *Standard Edition,* specifically the reflections on page[s] 305 and 306. His line of thought remains metapsychologically incompletely worked out; but I am of the opinion that it is of great significance. I believe that these remarks in the paper "On Transience" and some conclusions which I derive from his paper on Humor [1928] give us a clue to the understanding of the metapsychology of the quality which we call wisdom. I hope to follow up this line of thought in a paper on varieties and transformations which I am planning to present next December.

Your other question, whether I will be the one to fill Max's role, I cannot answer directly. Whether one occupies a place of leadership depends on many factors. If, in the future, the circumstances should offer a position of responsibility to me and if I were convinced that I am needed (as I was when I accepted the office in the American), I would not refuse.

My office in the American will end in May. I am planning a final address on May 2 in which I will discuss once more the major problems of organized psychoanalysis, including the relative importance of the problem of lay analysis.[1] When I exchanged a few words with you in New York you mentioned that you might reply to my letter on this topic. Is there any hope that you might still give me your reactions? You must believe, however, when I say that, much as I wish to know your thoughts, I would rather do without them than to put any burden on you if you are under the pressure of other work.

And now: warm regards. I, too, am very much looking forward to seeing you in Amsterdam.

Sincerely,

Heinz Kohut, M.D.

1. *Search*, 1:395–403.

March 7, 1965 [from Anna Freud]

Dear Dr. Kohut,

You were quite right to remind me that I still owe you an answer in our former exchange of thought about lay analysis, and an explanation of what I mean by talking of "revolutionary moves." I shall try to be a little clearer about both points now.

In the meantime I had your letter of August 4 and I was very impressed with the contents. They are the clearest evidence of the thought which you have given to these matters instead of merely accepting the prevailing atmosphere and taking it for granted as so many other people do. I merely know the American scene as an outsider and in that position it is easy to misjudge matters. I try to be careful about that. Also I have quite a lot of opportunity to compare the American and English scene; nothing could be more different so far as the attitude to psychoanalysis, the advantages and disadvantages are concerned.

When I talked of "revolutionary moves," I had nothing as drastic in mind as the steps to which you refer and which would imply the breaking up of the A.P.A. Certainly not. I thought much more of a revolution in spirit which would then lead to the gradual steps and changes which you outline yourself. My thoughts in that direction were almost identical with those expressed by Max Gitelson in his talk to the A.P.A.[1] When I read this speech, I felt very excited. It seemed to me that Gitelson had taken a long round-about way and had arrived exactly at the view of psychoanalysis which my father, and we others with him, had always held. That somebody in his position could do this seemed almost a miracle.

Since your August letter, two promising moves in the attitude toward lay analysis have been defeated. I mean of course the questions of child analysts and of analytic lay teachers. This may mean no more than a delay, but anyway it shows clearly that the spirit which I call revolutionary is not there yet, or certainly not very wide-spread. Surely, there are many members in the A.P.A. who are content with developments as they are. We both know that there are many others also who are looking out for changes.

It would be quite wrong to say that I am first and foremost con-cerned with the question of lay analysts. For me the latter are only incidental to a bigger question, namely the expansion of analysis from too intensive concentration on psychiatry and medicine, i.e., therapy, to the applications in a whole variety of fields. I do not need to name these, you know them anyway. Lay analysts are important because they come from these fields and carry their interests with them when they become analysts, just as psychiatrists carry out their ana-lytic work in the spirit in which they have been trained. If candidates are recruited from many fields, analysis will in the final result reflect this and remain, or rather become again, a broad discipline. If the training previous to analysis is a uniform one, (as it is, with all other preparations excluded except medicine) this uniformity will spread also to the final result. I think it would be exactly the same if we admitted as candidates only teachers, or only psychologists, or only philosophers, etc. Perhaps it is argued by some people that the medical training is broad enough in itself to serve as a basis for analysis. But is this really true? Medical training is so exacting while it lasts, and so exclusive, that it leaves hardly a possibility for involvement with other matters.

If these are my arguments about the intake of candidates, I am even more concerned about the form of training which has become our standard throughout the whole I.P.A. It is true that we began analytic training as an evening affair, i.e., a part time training. In those begin-ning days this was a necessity, excusable because of our poverty and lack of resources. Still, the disadvantages were counteracted in the individual cases by the deep involvement of our candidates and their affective response to the analytic experience. But now, when poverty and lack of resources have disappeared, can we really justify the part time aspect of our training schemes? I have the possibility to compare the effect of part time and full time training since I work for the Insti-tute for Psychoanalysis here as well as for our own Hampstead train-ing, the former part time, the latter full time. What one can give in the full time training just does not compare with the other. On the other hand it compares very well with all other full time trainings of University standard, medical or otherwise, where the student lives in the atmosphere of the discipline in which he is trained, works with his teachers (apart from his personal analysis), shares in study and research, and, above all, has time to do so. My Institute students which I have at present in a clinical evening seminar, all arrive after at least 10 hours hospital work, and I often feel that the only thing important to them is to get home and to bed. I know that in America this varies from Institute to Institute, and in Chicago it may be much better than in many other places. But on the whole the fact remains, that we believe analysts can be trained additional to other work which has to be pursued at the same time. It seems of no advantage to me if this work is psychiatric, and therefore similar.

I have no doubt that this change to full time analytic training will come about some day, But do we really have to wait until analysis is taken up by the Universities? Cannot we bring it about on our own? In a modest way we have tried it out on the Hampstead Clinic, and really, it is not as difficult as it sounds, and it gives an Institute all the research assistants needed for intensive work.

Now you know what my revolutionary thoughts are. I shall be glad to know what you feel about them.

Yours sincerely,
Anna Freud

1. "On the Identity Crisis in American Psychoanalysis," *JAPA* 12 (1964): 451–76.

March 16, 1965
Medical News Limited
London
Dear Sir:

Medical News of February 12, 1965 contained a report by Dr. Henry A. Davidson called "Personal psychoanalysis as tax deductible expense." In this article Dr. Davidson concludes that it would be unlikely for an analyst in training to report to the authorities (i.e., the Internal Revenue Service) that he is suffering from a psychoneurosis. "Yet," Dr. Davidson continued, "the American Psychoanalytic Association has stated (in its 1962 *Journal*, in an article by Dr. H. Kohut) 'that the principal objective of a training analysis is therapeutic.'"

It is indeed difficult to weigh the various purposes of a complex enterprise such as psychoanalysis and to decide, within the framework set by experts in taxation, whether in a given instance therapeutic or educational objectives are paramount. My article did not attempt to define the objectives of training analysis from the point of view of taxation; it was however also not, as Dr. Davidson suspects, an admission to be made only "strictly within the family." The crux of the problem is the fact that education and therapy cannot be as neatly separated as tax officials would like. Judging by the phrase quoted from my 1962 article one could easily be led to assume that I, too, (and therefore, as Dr. Davidson concludes, "the American Psychoanalytic

Association") think of the training analysis either as therapy or as education. The full rendition, however, of even the single sentence from which Dr. Davidson quoted will clarify that I was not using the term therapy in its traditional narrow sense. I said: "We shared the universal conviction that the principal objective of the training analysis is therapeutic in that widest meaning of the word which comprehends not only the aims evoked by the term character analysis but refers also to the freeing of such faculties as psychological perceptivity and tolerance of uncertainty which are specifically required in analytic work."

Very truly yours,
Heinz Kohut, M.D.

April 7, 1965
Harry Slochower, Ph.D.
Editor-in-Chief, *American Imago*
New York
Dear Doctor Slochower:

Thank you for sending me a reprint of "Eros and the Trauma of Death,"[1] a fascinating and erudite little essay which I read quickly and with great pleasure. No, I don't think that I object here to the absence of clinical examples since, through appropriate quotations from the poets and philosophers you are supplying "living" material to an extent that satisfies my requirements.

The problem of death, death instinct, thanatos, etc., is exceedingly complex since people (Freud included) speak about these concepts on many different levels. The search for one's own death, for example, may refer to a psychological constellation which one carries in the depth of one's personality and may thus refer simply to a living out of a fate which one considers to be most intimately as one's own. (For example, to die in battle when one's father and grandfather, etc., have died a similar death.) Dying one's own death, however, may also mean the striving for a final (in practice unreachable) state in which all life has been spent and the organism returns to the original inorganic tensionless balance. All externally imposed death (through illness, through violence, etc.) is an undesirable artifact as seen from this point of view and the struggle for life, for self-preservation, is, as seen from this angle, only an attempt to attain the "natural" form of dying. Since fantasies attach themselves to psychological constructions on all levels, the issue becomes even more complicated. At any rate I think that many of the arguments between the optimists and the pessimists, between the anti-death-instinct and the pro-death-instinct group would resolve themselves if the level were defined on which they arrive at their formulations.

I personally think that one has to differentiate not only between (1) the level of psychological elaboration (where man knows nothing about death and covers his ignorance with specific fantasies) and (2) the level of opposing drives (Eros and Thanatos) but also, (3), on the second level, between the "living" conflict of Eros and Thanatos on the one hand and the increasingly autonomous structuralization of the ego, on the other hand, which is beyond life and death and may point into the direction of the attainment of permanence, of frozen form (i.e., as a fulfillment of the wish: "Könnt' ich zum Augenblicke sagen, verweile doch, du bist so schön").[2]

To philosophize in a letter is one thing; to participate in a symposium is quite another. Unfortunately I have to husband my energies and there are none available during this coming fall.

I am glad to hear that plans for the handling of the business affairs of *Imago* are proceeding in a favorable direction and I can well imagine that you would like nothing better than to be able to deal with the editorial work only.

Your final paragraph puzzled and amused me greatly: A bearded nephew. Unfortunately, it must all be an illusion. I do not have a nephew, let alone a bearded one; and while my sympathies are for any individual who can give a thoughtful discussion of "The Grand Inquisitor,"[3] I must set the record straight and tell that a nephewship must be either a misunderstanding, or a joke, or a hoax of some kind. I would be interested in finding out more about it.

With warm regards,
Sincerely,
Heinz Kohut, M.D.

1. *American Imago* 21 (1964): 11–22.
2. "Could I but say to the moment, stay, you are so beautiful" (Goethe, *Faust*).
3. Fyodor Dostoyevsky, *The Brothers Karamazov* [1879–80]. The Grand Inquisitor in the novel examines the human choice between freedom and happiness.

April 13, 1965
Dr. Joseph J. Sandler
London
Dear Joe:

Time seems to fly. Last September you sent me Abercrombie's book[1] which I had not yet read when I saw you early in December in New

York, but which I read shortly thereafter. So many events diverted my attention (recently, of course, the saddest one: Max Gitelson's death) that I did not find the leisure to give you my impressions concerning it. Now some time has already passed since I read it and some of the details are beginning to slip my mind.

I must admit that I was not very deeply impressed by the work. I found it rather pleasant and easy to read, and I was struck with how little psychic energy is needed to read about psychic processes which disregards the deeper motivations and deals with cognition only, complex as it might be in its own right. You asked me on the fly leaf whether I thought that Dr. Abercrombie's method should be applied to the teaching of psychoanalysis. I don't know how to answer this question. If you mean it in a concrete way (i.e., whether we should form groups that are left to themselves to puzzle over the definitions and methods of psychoanalytic judgment), then my answer would be in the negative. This kind of training and thinking should take place much earlier in life and it would seem to me that the disregard for content which is the essence of Abercrombie's experiment cannot very well be applied in our institutes. But perhaps a specific suggestion which I have made many times (and to no avail) might come closer to the meaning which you, too, might have intended by your question. I have suggested several times that we should get away from any attempt at "completeness" in our teaching and that we should teach by a "sample method." I am convinced that differences in basic philosophy about psychoanalysis are expressed in the argument which I always encounter when I express this point of view, even though I am not quite capable of stating these differences clearly. The trend in our institutes (for example, in Chicago) is the traditional one towards completeness. There should be many cases supervised, the theoretical areas should all be covered, the "technique" of analysis should be divided up according to the various "stages" of analysis, etc. My feeling has always been that this completeness and the concomitant stressing of the variety of phenomena which need to be learned, covers up a lack of understanding of the depth, and perhaps also a rationalized fear of this depth. I have no adolescent wish to exaggerate my position. I do not advocate that students should analyze only one case, in great detail; or one dream only; or demonstrate one theoretical concept in all its ramifications. I do think, however, that in the time at one's disposal one cannot cover everything equally well without becoming shallow, especially not in the way in which teaching proceeds (for example, in Chicago once every other week end), and that it would be better to let oneself go in the demonstration of a detail, be that now the comprehensive understanding of one case at a crucial point, or the comprehensive understanding of a single symptomatic act, or of a concept or theory. I have the strong feeling that teaching in depth rather than in extenso would go hand in hand with a return from a predominantly dynamic understanding of patients (with a sprinkling of socio-environmental etiology tossed into the salad) to the broader analytic-empathic grasp of patients. The latter includes the comprehension of earlier modes of experience (i.e., the genetic reconstruction of the crucial childhood experiences) and the acknowledgment of the importance of psycho-economic factors.

All this seems pretty far from discussing Abercrombie's book—but is it? Thank you once more for having sent it to me. I am very much looking forward to seeing you soon again.

Cordially,

Heinz Kohut, M.D.

1. Minnie Abercrombie, *The Anatomy of Judgment: An Investigation into the Processes of Perception and Reasoning* (New York, 1960).

May 26, 1965

Samuel D. Lipton, M.D.

Chicago

Dear Sam:

In your discussion last night of Tom French's paper you were completely correct in your emphasis on the interruption of the flow of material perpetrated by the "analyst" or "investigator." French, actually, is probably not the worst offender in this respect, perhaps because he uses also many other defences to ward off the impact of the material that emerges in the analytic situation. Although he dwells at length on the role of empathy and of fantasy, his basic stance is one of optimistic rationality which sees the human tragedy essentially as one of faulty problem solving, to be remedied by feeding the right information into the thinking machine. This attitude leads him to re-interpret every aspect of psychoanalysis in accordance with this basic view. Fantasies are to him precursors of rational planning; the id is an attenuated ego; and the psyche has no built-in propensity for conflict but suffers only from faulty solutions to the problems posed by its relationship with reality.

Within the limits of his view of the psychic world French is often impressively subtle and perceptive. Anything however that threatens the limits which he has set, is quickly pushed aside. It is here probably where he quickly interposes "interpretations" and forces the patient to stick with the problems of external reality instead of facing the emerging fantasies in the transference.

Sincerely,

Heinz Kohut, M.D.

June 5, 1965

K. R. Eissler, M.D.

New York

Dear Kurt:

The fact that the main part of the work for the Anna Freud Birthday Fund is to be done in the fall makes no essential difference regarding my decision. As I said earlier: I will not take on any substantial new responsibilities before the beginning of 1966. At present I have to wind up a number of Association affairs; then comes the trip to Amsterdam; in the fall (to September 20) Betty, Tom, and I will go west on our vacation. Not only will this be our last time together before Tom goes off to school it will also be the first comparatively undisturbed time that I will be able to spend with my family. What free time I have I must devote to the preparation of a paper which I am to present at the December meetings and for which I have a great deal of work to do since the Association has kept me away from many things for so long. I do hope, therefore, that you will forgive me for not acceding.

Are you underestimating the amount of time and energy that it would take to do a creditable job? Could a professional fund collecting agency help you? I noticed, for example, that (while my own contribution check has been cashed) I have received no follow-up thank-you note, encouraging me to persuade others to make contributions. Are printed forms through which to make contributions and return envelopes enclosed with the letters enlisting these contributions? Has the mail pouch of the A.P.A. been approached for a listing of the Anna Freud Drive as the Gitelson people have done? (I am enclosing a clipping in case you have overlooked it.)

As I told you over the phone: I am willing to speak at the gathering for the Fund in Amsterdam and will do my best to be properly persuasive. I am also willing to compose a personal letter, if you wish, which you may enclose with the decisive fall mailing—but not in an official position. My letter could begin with "I have been asked by the Anna

Freud Birthday Committee to support its drive for contributions and I
am gladly doing so . . . " etc.
    With my warm regards,
    Cordially,
    Heinz Kohut, M.D.

June 6, 1965
Siegmund Levarie
Brooklyn, New York
Dear Siegmund:
    My administrative duties are officially over but there has not yet
been a real respite because of left-over commitments, the turning to
long-postponed tasks, and some residual fatigue. All in all I do not
anticipate a decisive relaxation of the pressures that have been on me
until about the beginning of 1966.
    Your letter gave me great pleasure. I admire the philosophical bent
which appears to allow you to face the realities of change and ageing.
I am, unfortunately, not equally flexible and am driving myself at times
at a pace which is not quite appropriate for my age. But then, I suppose, we are all living out patterns that have been determined a long
time ago which fixed not only our aims in life but also the form in
which we pursue them.
    I will not flatter you with any technical opus. It may amuse you,
however, to get a glimpse of the style in which I have functioned as
one of the leaders of my profession in the recent past. I am, therefore,
enclosing copies of two addresses: one which I gave at the beginning
of my term as president, the other at the end.
    Give my warm greetings to Norma and Janet. Betty sends her love
to all.
    As ever,
    P.S. I am unimpressed by the performance of your typewriter. Just
look at this; not only umlaut signs but real umlauted letters: Ä, ä, Ö,
ö, Ü, ü. And a scharfes "s": ß Are you green with envy?

July 9, 1965
Harold A. Sofield, M.D.
President, The Chicago Medical Society
Dear Doctor Sofield:
    I should like to draw your attention to a book review on page 606
of the June 26 issue of *Chicago Medicine* which contains a number of

statements about psychoanalysis which go far beyond the limits of the customary interchange between colleagues and scientists.

The sweeping condemnations can hardly be answered since they are leveled against a field which bears no resemblance to psychoanalysis. After some fifteen years of a practice which is predominantly devoted to clinical psychoanalysis, I know not only that psychoanalysis is indeed of great value in the treatment of properly selected cases, but also that it has shortcomings and limitations which only further investigation will have a chance to remedy. The reviewer's references, however, to psychoanalysis as brain washing, to sex as the basis of its philosophy, to "dream book" authors, and the like, do not constitute scientific criticism but a kind of propaganda which, without regard to what analysis really is, describes it in terms which will make it appear obnoxious and contemptible.

Perhaps the most striking of all misunderstandings accepted by the reviewer is the belief that the analyst gives his patient "a few crumbs of comfort" through "brain washing" and does not allow him "to use what God-given mental faculties he possesses solving his own problems. . . . " No psychoanalyst would have any doubt about the fact that the very opposite is true. In essence the patient in analysis learns to face his inner and outer problems, and to solve them with his own powers. It is paradoxical that during a period when many physicians feel threatened by the forces of collectivism, a publication which represents organized medicine should attempt to belittle psychoanalysis which, by concentrating its attention on the individual and his conflicts and resources, remains one of the bulwarks of individualism in our culture.

Sincerely yours,
Heinz Kohut, M.D.
cc: Dr. H. Kenneth Scatliff, Editor, *Chicago Medicine*

August 25, 1965
John E. Gedo, M.D.
Chicago
Dear John:

I finally had a chance to read your Orpheus study, and I will now try to give you a few of my impressions and reactions. As has happened to me often in the past, I was struck from the beginning by the almost insuperable problem of defining the author's aims in analyzing a myth. I suppose that you went about it as have all analysts who undertook similar tasks: you approached the myth as you would the fantasy (or the artistic product) of an individual. We are not certain that such an analogy is proper but we are justified in hypothesizing that it is and, applying the methods which are appropriate to the individual, to assess whether the results fit into a broader or into a different context.

Your study does not go sufficiently far into a broader cultural context to buttress your thesis in this way but your explanation of the old myth fits with archaic material obtained from the analysis of patients with specific family constellations and fears from their childhood. It is indeed a pity, therefore, that you cannot share your detailed case material with the reader; it would go some way in giving support to your hypothesis. Could you not disguise the case material sufficiently without interfering with the essentials? I did this once in one of my papers ("Observations on the Psychological Functions of Musical Activity")[1] by adding carefully selected misleading details which allowed me to leave the essential material intact. I am mentioning this technique to you since most people attempt to disguise by omitting telling details.

At best, however, even if the case material is included, I believe that one can only give evidence for the unconscious relevance of a myth to certain emotional constellations present in modern man. To furnish this proof is not a negligible achievement, it falls short, however, of explaining either the psychological forces which led to the original genesis of the myth or of elucidating its meaning for the people for whom it was a living cultural possession.

I am not optimistic about the possibility of achieving reliable analytic explanations of this kind. While certain central fantasies may well reach back to the dawn of culture when a semblance of the family constellation first formed itself, psychoanalytic understanding should go beyond establishing such continuity. I do not wish to elaborate my doubts and hesitations any further at this point. You may know that I tried once before to spell out some of the tasks and difficulties of applied psychoanalysis in an essay "Beyond the Bounds of the Basic Rule." I do not, for example, share Helen McLean's optimism about the comparatively easy accessibility of the meaning of the Greek drama for modern man.[2] How was it possible (in a highly developed civilization!) to portray the deepest conflicts of man on the stage? Was it the fact that the plays were among kings and demigods and gods which provided a gap between the stage and the audience, and thus the possibility for tolerating these conflicts? Or were there other reasons which we cannot discern across the chronological and cultural distance which separates us from antiquity?

Concerning your own specific interpretation I will say only a little. It seems convincing within the limits I tried to indicate in the foregoing remarks. Yet the possibility of gross error cannot be excluded. It is striking how relative and timebound such interpretations are. At one time all such material was seen in its oedipal meaning; now it tends to be interpreted pre-oedipally. Is this simply a widening of our horizon, or are we projecting our newly found insights upon the mythological structures?

There is one dimension which I personally feel you neglected by concentrating so strongly upon the deep pre-oedipal fears: Orpheus is the symbol of art, specifically of music. There is something about the creative narcissism of some types of artists which requires distance from the object, especially from the heterosexual one. The total devotion to the work of art as an extension of the self (analogous to the narcissistic cathexis which the pregnant mother directs toward the fetus) may require the relinquishment of the developmentally later sexual involvement. Thus Orpheus may not only be seen as the prototype of the unconsolable widower but also as the prototype of the narcissistic artist who calms the wild beast of passion, and breathes life into inanimate matter through artistic creation, under the condition that he relinquish strong object cathexes in the reality that is outside of the world of his creations.

Many thanks for letting me read your manuscript. As you can see I found it very stimulating and enjoyed it greatly.

Sincerely,

Heinz Kohut, M.D.

1. *Search*, 1:233–53.
2. See Helen V. McLean, "Freud and Literature," *Saturday Review of Literature*, September 3, 1938, pp. 18–19. McLean conducted a seminar on psychoanalysis and literature at the Chicago institute at which in 1948 Kohut first presented his paper on Thomas Mann. See above, November 26, 1956.

September 24, 1965 [from John Gedo]
Dear Dr. Kohut,

I am writing to thank you for two things—the referral of _____ and your thought-provoking comments on the Orpheus.

. . . .

I am particularly grateful for your detailed comments on my paper because you have singled out some of the questions I have been most uncertain about. My original interest did not concern the myth at all; I was merely casting about for a good way of disguising the biographical data of my patient. He had a dream of descending to some underworld on the anniversary of his wife's death, and this gave me the idea that the mythical hero might provide such a disguise. In a sense I was not trying to write a paper within applied psychoanalysis. However, when I began to read about Orpheus I discovered that most versions and details of the myth are relatively so unfamiliar that I felt obliged to include an exposition of their content. I am afraid that this effort has skewed the contents of the study away from my original aims, and this is the indeterminancy in goals which you have accurately detected. What I eventually became fascinated with in the course of gestating the paper was the illumination of certain aspects of the clinical material by alternative versions of the myth. This experience may be too atypical, however, to have much interest for analysts in general. As to the relevance of the myth in its original cultural context, that is a theme far beyond my present competence to tackle.

I neglected the dimension of Orpheus as artist because my patient has poured his energies into being a therapist, hence the parallel in the myth was that of Orpheus' priestly functions. Once again, your comments have shown me that in trying to effect a compromise between case presentation and applied analysis I have fallen between two stools. Clearly, the paper has not reached full term, but I do not know as yet in which direction I shall let it develop.

Once again, many thanks for your invaluable help.

Sincerely,

John E. Gedo, M.D.

September 22, 1965
Dr. Daniel Lagache
Paris
Mon cher Lagache,

Your letter [August 31] was forwarded to me on my vacation and I had no chance to acknowledge it and to thank you for it until now, after returning to Chicago. There is no need at all to write to me in English. I do indeed read French without difficulty and, as a matter of fact, am always enjoying it.

Despite your caution and the need for confidentiality the information which you gave me was very helpful and I believe that your main message came through. Details would be interesting but they are probably dispensable. I wonder why there is this tendency to dictatorial aspirations among analysts. Is it essentially a question of unresolved narcissism? It has nothing to do primarily with the form of the institutions and societies since dictators within the framework of a democracy are still dictators even if they use different methods. But believe me: the problem is not unique for France but a general one even though the forms and the rationalizations might differ in various locations. There are undoubtedly other motivations involved (such as for material gain), but judging by my own observations these are not the strongest ones.

I do hope very much that sooner or later we will have the chance for a long chat. I am very glad that you seem to have recovered from your operation and happy to know that you will continue to exert your active wholesome influence on European psychoanalysis.

With my warmest regards,
Sincerely,
Heinz Kohut, M.D.

September 25, 1965
Dr. med. Paul Parin
Zurich
Dear Dr. and Mrs. Parin:

Returning from my California vacation I found to my surprise and great pleasure your book *Die Weissen denken zuviel*[1] [*White Men Think Too Much*] waiting for me. Thank you ever so much for it; I am looking forward to reading it as soon as my present commitments will give me the time.

Let me tell you also at this occasion how much I enjoyed making your acquaintance. I can still vividly remember our conversation in the Rijksmuseum [Amsterdam] and how, to both of your apparent entertainment, my old Viennese began to come bubbling out of me while I myself watched the phenomenon with amazement.

Such things are pleasant and it is good to make the acquaintance of colleagues all over the world during these International Congresses. It was for me of course especially meaningful to watch the slow return of psychoanalysis in Europe and in particular in the German-language areas.

I hope very much that we shall be able to keep in contact and to get to know what analysts around the world are thinking through a more personal medium than the official reports that are contained in the journals.

Just for a starter I will collect a few of my reprints and will send them to you. As you thumb through them you may get some idea of the problems with which I have been preoccupied over the years. At the present time I am working on a rather ambitious paper (tentatively

called "Forms and Transformations of Narcissism") which I will present at the Fall Meeting of the American Psychoanalytic Association
in December in New York.

And now once more my warm thanks for the book and the expression of the hope that our contact will be continuing.

Cordially,
Heinz Kohut, M.D.

1. Paul Parin, Fritz Morgenthaler, and Goldy Parin-Matthey, *Die Weissen denken zuviel: Psychoanalytische Untersuchungen bei den Dongon in Westafrika* (Zurich, 1963; Munich,
1972).

November 7, 1965
Victor H. Rosen, M.D.
New York
Dear Victor:

Rumors have it that you are engaged and that your fiancée was
formerly a long-term analysand of yours. I have, of course, no first-
hand information but, judging by the reliability of those who told me
about it, I assume that the story is true.[1]

Although I have come to know and like you during the year when
I was president, and although I gratefully remember the pleasant way
in which you expressed the thanks of the Association at the end of
my term of office, our acquaintance would not be close enough to
permit me to express my concern to you, were it not for the fact that
you are the President of our Association and that I am worried about
the effect which your contemplated action might have on the membership, and on our students and patients.

It may, of course, be maintained that after a well-conducted analysis
the patient has relinquished the infantile attachment to the analyst,
that self-analysis has dealt with the counter-transferences, and that
patient and analyst are therefore free to form a post-analytic relationship of any degree of intimacy, including marriage, just as is available
to any other man and woman. Yet, when the unusual step of marriage
to a former patient hinges on the answer to the question whether the
transferences and counter-transferences had been sufficiently resolved, one would not expect an analyst to come to a decision until
he has undertaken a renewed psychoanalytic investigation of his motivations.

If you were a private individual among analysts I would not have been impelled to write to you. But as the President of the Association you have become an example for and a representative of our science. As an individual I would grant you that it is courageous to go counter to established attitudes if one is convinced that one is right; and I have no doubt that you are convinced of it. But your personal conviction and your personal courage are not the issue at stake while you are the President. To many who hold the traditional views concerning the intensity and tenacity of the transference, your actions will imply a loosening of the basic ethical obligation of analysts: not to make use of their patients' emotional attachment for any purpose other than to enlarge their mastery over themselves through insight. Whether you are right or wrong with regard to your and your fiancée's personal life, therefore, your action while you are President could have deleterious consequences for analysis and could weaken the position of our science.

What is there to be done under the circumstances? Is there hope against hope that you might still consider a change in your plans and, as an example of an analyst's standards, first investigate your motives through further analysis? Could you postpone the final decision until some time after your term of office? Or would you consider giving over some or all of the functions of the presidency to Leo Rangell before the end of your term in order to allow you to be free of official pressures while you are thinking things through once more, and in order to lessen the impact of your private actions on analysis as a whole?

I cannot go further. I only want to assure you that there is no rancor in what I am saying. Despite my overriding concern for psychoanalysis, I wish you well as a person, as that friendly individual with the fine mind that I have come to like and to appreciate; and I truly hope for your happiness and inner balance. I wish I could say more, but I am afraid that you will feel that I have said too much already. With good wishes,

Yours,

Heinz Kohut, M.D.

1. Rosen, president of the APA 1965–66, married this patient in 1965, and that same year resigned his post as a training analyst at the New York institute. He committed suicide in 1973. See Janet Malcolm, *Psychoanalysis: The Impossible Profession* (New York, 1981), pp. 91–93; and Paul Roazen, "Freud's New York," *Virginia Quarterly Review* 58 (1982): 713. Rosen, however, remained active in the profession on the national and international level. There is considerable disagreement and confusion about what Rosen did and why as well as what the psychoanalytic establishment did or did not do, and should or should not have done. The medical examiner established that his death was

caused by an overdose of barbiturates but did not rule it a suicide (Connecticut Office of the Chief Medical Examiner, personal comunication, October 8, 1991), and it was not reported as such (*New York Times*, February 7, 1973). That it was a suicide was acknowledged by the family and known within the psychoanalytic community, although the connection between Rosen's death and the professional controversy over his marriage is disputed. Paul Roazen, personal communication, October 13, 1991; Janet Malcolm, personal communication, October 28, 1991; and Elise W. Snyder, personal communication, October 31, 1991. See also P. J. van der Leeuw to Kohut, November 21, 1965.

1966–1967

"the greatness of America . . .
is not so much depth but breadth"

January 4, 1966 [from Anna Freud]

Dear Dr. Kohut,

I left the reading of your paper on Narcissism [see above, September 25, 1965] for the peace of the Christmas holidays and I have just finished it to-day. I feel very excited about it since I do not only feel your argumentation very convincing but also I feel it to be one of the most beautiful analytic papers which I have read in recent years. I like the way in which you build on and widen existent knowledge. I think the differentiation of the two streams arising from primary narcissism (the narcissistic self and the idealised parent imago) is a most fortunate one; and the application of this thinking to creativity, empathy, sense of impermanence, humor and wisdom is fascinating to me, and also in the very best analytic tradition. There has been no analytic writing like this, really, for a very long time. How was the paper received by the audience? Did they feel as I do?

The differentiation between ideals and ambitions I found intriguing, but I could not make it as clear to myself as the other parts. Could you, perhaps, illustrate for me with a clinical example?

January 7, 1966

I did get as far as this when your letter of December 28th arrived here and was followed the day after by the letter of the President of the University of Chicago. I was surprised, and also pleased, and also upset by the offer of an honorary degree by the University. As matters stand, it is quite impossible for me to be in Chicago March 18th which is the date of the convocation. My plans for this spring have been made up almost a year ago. In March I have a string of lectures here in London (apart from patients and clinic events) and at the beginning of April I am due at the Menninger Clinic for a week. To be in Chicago the 18th March, back in London and back again in April for Topeka is, of course, out of the question; to stay over in the U.S. is equally impossible because of the commitments here.

I shall write to the President of the University and ask whether the honor can, perhaps, wait for a next convocation. I hope he will not be offended.

Yours sincerely,

Anna Freud

P.S. Thank you for all your very nice offers.

February 1, 1966
Miss Anna Freud
London
Dear Miss Freud:

Your letter was the best New Year's gift that I could have hoped for, and your generous approval sustains me in the resolve to pursue my work for analysis with all that I can bring to it. I am happy to tell you, in answer to your question, that my presentation was received warmly by the audience in New York and, afterwards, at a small luncheon which I had with Marianne [Kris] and her daughter, Dora and Heinz [Hartman], Lisje and Rudi [Loewenstein], and a few others.

Concerning your inquiry about the "ambitions-ideals" problem, I am afraid that my exposition (my paper is a condensation of certain parts of a very much larger manuscript on narcissism that I hope to develop in the future) became especially compressed and my argument must therefore have remained partly incomplete. Please forgive me for postponing an adequate reply to your question. The essence of my answer hinges on the issue that it is psychic location and genesis which allows for the essential differentiation between one's ideals (which have object qualities). The idealized object's ambitions, for example, may become one's ideals. On the other hand the ideals of a grandiose self belong to the nexus of ambitions. My larger manuscript contains extensive case material, including the case of a shame-prone man who seemed to have very high ideals but—after prolonged analysis—it turned out that these were not true ideals (i.e., not introjected after passing through an idealized parent imago) but the invented ideals of an early, defensively reinforced grandiose self concept, a fantasy figure which has a name that was an "improved" version of the patient's own name. As I said, I cannot, at this time, go into sufficient details but will do so at a later time when I can either send you some of the pages of the manuscript of the wider study or be more elaborate in a letter.

Since I knew about some of your other commitments I was not surprised to learn that you would not be able to come to Chicago for the spring convocation on March 18. According to my information your suggestion to postpone the bestowal of the degree until later (Fall of 1966? Spring of 1967?) can be expected to be acceptable to the University of Chicago since the celebration year extends until the Spring of 1967. I learned, in addition, through an announcement which Dr. Piers made at a meeting of the Chicago Institute, that you would spend several days at the Institute if you came to Chicago in

September, 1966, or March, 1967. But all this seems far away since I am looking forward to seeing you much sooner in Topeka where Betty and I are planning to go for the meeting of the American Association for Child Psychoanalysis. I hope to have the chance to talk with you there, especially since I would very much like to hear your reactions to the tentative plans which I (as chairman of the planning committee) have formed concerning the next Pre-Congress on Training in Copenhagen.

With warm regards,
Sincerely,
Heinz Kohut, M.D.

January 20, 1966
Dr. Angel Garma
Buenos Aires
Dear Doctor Garma:

Thank you for sending me a copy of your paper "Origins and Aims of Pan-American Psychoanalytic Congresses"[1] and for the accompanying letter. I read your paper with pleasure and, as you know, I fully share your wish to bring the analysts of North and South America closer together and to encourage an interchange of scientific opinions between the two groups. Both propositions which you make deserve in my opinion careful attention and I will do what I can to assist you in having them discussed and considered.

Since I am a member of the Editorial Board of the *Journal of the American Psychoanalytic Association*, I will mention at the next meeting of that Board how important it would be to undertake steps which would make the best of the psychoanalytic literature of South America available in English translations to North American analysts and analysts in other parts of the world. I know that not only the Latin American analysts but also many European analysts (especially the French) feel that the present communication is too much of a one-way street, i.e., that the Latin Americans and for example the French analysts read the English and American literature and are familiar with it but that the same does not hold true in the reverse. I know that the present leaders of the I.P.A. are quite familiar with this problem and in addition Dr. Valenstein and I have talked about it and have pondered ways and means to improve this situation. The Executive Committee and the Executive Council of the American Psychoanalytic Association might also wish to talk about this matter and to consider possible steps to improve this condition. At any rate I will send copies of this letter to Dr. Rosen, the President, and to Mrs. Helen Fischer, the Executive Secretary of the American Psychoanalytic Association.

Your idea of holding a Pre-Congress (before the meetings of the I.P.A.) in the United States has much to recommend itself and I hope that the Executive Committee of the American will discuss it. On the negative side it must not be forgotten that this would be the third Pre-Congress before the next meeting of the I.P.A. (the others are the Pre-Congress on Training in Copenhagen and the Pre-Congress in England) and that the Annual Meetings of the American Psychoanalytic Association take place in May which leads to a crowded schedule of meetings and makes especially great demands on the contributors to these Congresses. Nevertheless it might be maintained that the North-South American Pre-Congress has its own special purpose and that the various hardships are outweighed by the advantages. But these are things which the leadership of the American Psychoanalytic Association and of Copal [Comité Coordinador de las Organizaciones Psicoanalíticas de America Latina] will have to weigh and discuss.

As I said I will do what I can to bring about the consideration of these issues. I am looking forward to seeing you in Buenos Aires. With warm regards,

Sincerely,

Heinz Kohut, M.D.

cc: Dr. van der Leeuw; Dr. Rosen; Dr. Valenstein; Mrs. Fischer

1. See Angel Garma, "Early History of the Pan-American Psychoanalytic Congress," in *Psychoanalysis in the Americas: Contributions from the First Pan-American Congress for Psychoanalysis,* ed. Robert E. Litman (New York, 1966), pp. 3–8. See also Garma, "Primer Congreso Psicoanalítico Latino Americano," *Revista de Psicoanálisis* 13 (1956): 341–51.

January 27, 1966

K. R. Eissler, M.D.

New York

Dear Kurt:

I said that I would try to read the Hammett article and the exchange of letters between [Martin] Stein and Hammett.[1] Please forgive me for not really doing so. I skimmed Hammett's article and got angry at seeing the same old hostile distortions and the selected quotations from [Roy] Grinker et al. As to Stein's answer I really have no understanding for it. Many of his points are acceptable, but his politeness with Hammett, his always beginning with the statement that Hammett is right before shifting over to a more or less psychoanalytic viewpoint are hard to take. I have on occasions used techniques in debates that may superficially resemble what Stein is doing and I was for a moment misled. But what I am at times trying to do is to see the best in the opponent's argument *without distorting it* (somewhat after the inimitable dialogues in [Freud's] "The Problem of Lay Analysis" and, especially, in *The Future of an Illusion* [1927]), and the real respect that I try to muster for the opponent with whom I disagree has at times helped me to make somebody listen to my arguments[2]—but I am afraid this is not what Stein is doing.

The potential effect of the exchange of letters does not worry me too much and I do not think that it requires a public reply for external reasons. I myself feel also not motivated to hold up Stein's regretfully conciliatory reply to public scorn, expecially in view of the fact that on the whole I trust him and believe that he is working for the good of analysis. If you could write to him and, without attacking his character, point out the errors in his statements (most glaringly to me, the discussion of psychic determinism which completely misses the point that the very essence of psychoanalysis lies in raising conflict into the sphere of choice and decision), it could be all to the good but, knowing you, this would be a very hard direction for you to take, and so perhaps I should express only the hope that you simply do nothing. I will, at an opportune time, take up the correspondence verbally with Stein. As I stated in my previous letter to you, he displays a certain blind admiration for the socially acceptable and a striving for being acceptable himself which may have drawn him into the unwarranted politeness of these letters. As to your suspicion that he wants to be President of the Association, that is no doubt true and he will probably become President.[3] I do however not think that the tone of this correspondence with Hammett was influenced by his wish to become President; nor am I afraid that he will be a bad President, although I must confess that I see him in a less favorable light now since reading these letters.

Cordially,

Heinz Kohut, M.D.

1. Van Buren O. Hammett, "A Consideration of Psychoanalysis in Relation to Psychiatry Generally, circa 1965," *American Journal of Psychiatry* 122 (1965): 42–54; 122 (1966): 830–33. On Stein and Kohut, see below, August 28, 1969.
2. Eissler would later criticize Kohut for going too easy on Erich Heller's criticism of

psychoanalysis in the pages of *Critical Inquiry* in 1978. See Eissler to Kohut, April 27, 1978.

3. Stein did not become APA president.

February 7, 1966
John Frosch, M.D.
Editor, *JAPA*
New York
Dear Jack:

Please accept the expression of my sincere appreciation for the thought and effort which you put into your extensive letter of January 28. Since there is hardly anything in it with which I disagree, let me, before I mention the few points where there is perhaps a difference in emphasis, simply enumerate those points where we are in complete accord, namely (1) that the Editor must have freedom to decide on layouts, order of papers, etc.; (2) that the handling of my two addresses and the Association's Position Statement on psychiatric opinions in political matters was exactly as I think it should have been;[1] (3) that the policy of a blanket acceptance of plenary session papers should be re-examined.

Having expressed the area of complete agreement (which really includes almost everything), let me just add a point which you did not directly express but about which I assume that we think alike. If, with regard to the plenary session papers, the policy of blanket acceptance is to be changed, this change in policy should be announced, should not apply to papers already given and ready for publication, and should perhaps include an expression of the view that in most cases the plenary session paper is likely to be accepted by the *Journal*.

Now to a small area where my feelings appear to differ slightly from yours, although I assume that this difference is due only to the context in which you expressed yourself to me. From the way in which you wrote (probably because you felt that I needed reassurance) it sounds as if the acceptance of the Presidential Addresses and of the Position Statement contained a personal element, a Kohuting of the *Journal* as you humorously expressed yourself. I believe that these addresses should be looked at in this way: they were meant to provide a sense of cohesion for the Association despite the existence of disruptive forces. It was with this purpose in mind that I stressed our common goals and ideals and, in the second address, I attempted to raise to the highest level of discussion that I could reach those areas which had proved to be the breeding ground of serious strife and hostility among our members (reorganization; lay analysis; the section on child analysis). I tried to counteract disruption by emphasizing our common goal of supporting scientific progress. Thus, I do not believe that over-Kohuting or under-Kohuting is involved in the answer to the question whether these addresses should have been printed and how central a position should have been given to them; the issue was simply whether the publication was for the good of the Association.

The Position Statement, too, does not have much to do with me personally; it was signed by the President and the Secretary of the Association, and the Chairman of the Committee on Public Information. There were good reasons for incorporating it in our *Bulletin;* if a similar situation should again arise, our members might let themselves be guided by it in their future public expressions. In all three instances it was the Administrative Board of the *Journal* which, quite properly, took the responsibility for the decision that the material should be published.

As far as my "narcissism" paper is concerned, I can speak only as a private citizen and plead in my private behalf. Knowing that up to now the plenary session scientific papers given by former Presidents and others had appeared very promptly, I had without much thought simply assumed that my paper, too, would appear promptly. Since I will be presenting a paper this summer at the Second Pan-American Congress[2] which presupposes a familiarity with the paper I presented in December,[3] I would be very unhappy if my paper had, against my expectations, not appeared by then. Therefore, please, do not take it amiss when I plead my cause and express again the hope that you can find a way.

And now only my warm regards,

Cordially yours,

Heinz Kohut, M.D.

1. American Psychoanalytic Association, "A Statement on the Use of Psychiatric Opinions in the Political Realm by the American Psychoanalytic Association" (October 5, 1964), *JAPA* 13 (1965): 450–51. This statement condemned the use of psychiatric diagnoses of political figures during election campaigns and was prompted by a poll of psychiatrists on the psychological "unfitness" of Republican presidential candidate Barry Goldwater; see Warren Boroson, "What Psychiatrists Say about Goldwater," *Fact* 1, no. 5 (September–October, 1964): 24–27; and APA, minutes of Executive Council, December 3, 1964, p. 9. Both the American Psychiatric Association and the American Medical Assocation (which had provided *Fact* with the list of psychiatrists) condemned the poll, while Goldwater sued the magazine and won (*New York Times*, May 5, 1968). Cf. Kohut's

letter in *Christian Century* 81 (1964): 1306–7, in which he expresses opposition to Goldwater's extremism.

2. *Search*, 1:477–509: as revised and presented in New York in 1968.

3. "Forms and Transformations of Narcissism," *JAPA* 14 (1966): 243–72.

March 13, 1966
Gerhart Piers, M.D.
Chicago
Dear Gerhart:

In the minutes of the last meeting of the Committee on Training Analysts you are quoted as having said that you had recently been impressed by my lack of energy. My concern about this remark, even if it may not have been quite accurately transcribed, is sufficiently great that I feel I must not hide my reaction from you.

Despite (and probably because of) the fact that the substance of your statement is in error, your diagnosis does not bother me, except that I would find it unnecessarily burdensome to demonstrate that I am not suffering from a depletion of energy, and that I will, therefore, say only that I am working hard, that I am enjoying my activity, and that I have been feeling well. It is surprising, however, that you should hold the view that I am suffering from a lack of energy when I just recently, in the course of our discussion about my wish to take a "sabbatical" from committee work at the Institute, had told you in glowing terms of my involvement in my writing: that I could often hardly wait to get home because I wanted to set down my ideas; and that I wanted to concentrate on my writing without the distraction by the immediate demands made not only by time but also by the emotional excitement which is stirred up without fail in the intense atmosphere of committee rooms. You appeared to be pleased about my involvement and said with apparent warmth that you thought that I could here make a real contribution to psychoanalysis. My reaction when I read your remark was, therefore, one of surprise and anger: I felt it as an unfair blow and as a kind of attack which is expressed in the form of concern and objectivity against which one is left with no sensible defense.

In practical terms there is little to be done about such statements since even retractions do not usually result in an amelioration of the initial impression which has been created.

I must thus restrict myself to emphasizing again my concern about the fact of your remark: [W]hat does it mean, what are its implications, what does it portend? While I hope that it was only the outgrowth of a temporary feeling on your part and thus an ephemeral matter, I have no choice but to raise the issue openly, in accordance with the basic psychological code by which we live.[1]

Sincerely,

Heinz Kohut, M.D.

1. See Piers to Kohut, March 13, 1966.

May 16, 1966

Heinz Hartmann, M.D.

New York

Dear Heinz:

We all missed you in Atlantic City and you know, of course, that many of us felt that a celebration of [Anna Freud's] *The Ego and the Mechanisms of Defense* without your presence was only half a celebration. I was glad to get your approval of my South American efforts even though I do not believe that the Latins "saw the light" as you hoped—at least they did not admit it officially [see below, October 11, 1966]. Concerning your pro domo[1] aside: I would think that it's one of the fringe benefits of your broad influence on our theoretical outlook that we can deviate at times from focusing on the central ego-autonomy and speak of ego-dominance, not only in the sense of the rider *on* the horse rather than *off* the horse but also concerning different aspects of the control which he asserts while he is on the horse.[2]

You have, of course, grown beyond quotation in your special domain—I hope that you will agree with that. When speaking to analysts we do not mention the Oedipus complex and put Freud in parentheses; neither does one do it with ego autonomy and you—except in historical essays or to a non-analytic audience.[3]

Warm regards from Betty to Dora and you, and my usual fond greetings.

Sincerely,

Heinz Kohut, M.D.

1. In a letter to Kohut of April 16 acknowledging receipt of "Transference and Counter-Transference in the Analysis of Narcissistic Personalities," published under a different title in 1968 (see above, February 7, n. 2), Hartmann had indicated his prefer-

ence for "ego-autonomy" in place of "ego-dominance," but observed that this was just a defense of the domain of his own ideas ("pro domo"). See also below, May 5, 1970.

2. This refers to Freud's metaphor for the ego and the id, whereby the rider of reason (ego) attempts to control the horse of instinct (id).

3. Kohut would later be criticized for not adequately citing forerunners of his theory of narcissism and the self; see below, June 18, 1973. Upon Hartmann's death Kohut praised him for his "aristocratic turning away from the primacy of empiricism" (Kohut to Alexander Mitscherlich, May 18, 1970), an empiricism Kohut saw as having been a vital step away from "wild theorizing." He also felt that Hartmann's successors had fallen prey to sterile scholastic wrangling which had to be "softened" by a "reborn empiricism."

May 17, 1966
Jeanne Lampl-de Groot, M.D.
Amsterdam
Dear Doctor Lampl:

I trust that you have in the meantime received a copy of my narcissism paper. It's not the finished version but the later additions and corrections are not very important, especially in view of the fact that I am working on several aspects of the problem and have just finished a clinical paper ("Transference and Counter-Transference in the Analysis of Narcissistic Personalities") which I will present this summer at the 2nd Pan-American Congress in Buenos Aires. Your warm comments on my efforts are deeply meaningful and encouraging to me. I became actively stimulated to investigate the problems of narcissism not only by my clinical work and the study of the literature (including, of course, your own pioneering papers) but—*mirabile dictu* [wonderful to relate]!—by my organizational work, which brought home to me with undeniable impact how strong the motivating influence of narcissism is, especially on the social scene. A first draft of a larger manuscript on the topic is therefore also concerned with the psychological characteristics of "narcissistic rage" and especially its destructive influence on human affairs. But the days are short and the demands are many: When will I ever be able to work it all out for publication?

Thank you also for the friendly welcome which you extended to me as a member of the Program Committee of the I.P.A. I will contribute to its work to the best of my ability but must concentrate my major efforts in this area on the preparation of the Pre-Congress on training since I am chairing the Committee which plans and organizes it.

The road for psychoanalysis continues to be a hard one, and I am aware of the fact that our science is increasingly being diluted and falsified in many overt and subtle ways. Yet, despite many setbacks and disappointments, I am keeping active and am enjoying the battles, in the spirit of that lovely phrase in the Freud-Abraham correspondence: coraggio Casimiro![1]

With warm regards,

Cordially yours,

Heinz Kohut, M.D.

1. "Courage, Casimir!" A common salutation between Freud and Berlin psychoanalyst Karl Abraham, it stemmed from a mountain climbing experience of Abraham's and expressed courage in the face of adversity. See Sigmund Freud and Karl Abraham, *Briefe 1907–1926*, ed. Hilda C. Abraham and Ernst L. Freud (Frankfurt am Main, 1965), p. 145. Kohut had a lifelong love for mountains and hiking.

May 17, 1966

Prof. Dr. Alexander Mitscherlich

Heidelberg

Dear Friend,

Your letter reached me after my return from the meetings of the American Psychoanalytic Association in Atlantic City and, after the noises and the activities of the convention, gave me much food for quiet thought.

You are, I believe, comparing your disappointment in America and American psychoanalysis with the disappointment in the idealized father. As you know, this is a topic with which I am analytically preoccupied at the present time (I just sent off the manuscript of a paper on "Narcissistic Transferences" which deals with the idealizing transference and the therapeutic importance of optimally-fractionated disappointments) and I might, therefore, tend to give too much weight to this aspect of your remarks. But laying aside the individual part of your involvements: the greatness of America (including the development of psychoanalysis in this country) is not so much depth but breadth. Our conventions are filled with poor papers—but occasionally there is a good one; and now and then there is one that has a touch of originality. Yet the outstanding feature is, for better or worse, that so many people have a reasonable working knowledge of what our science is all about. Even though my own inclinations are not spontaneously directed toward the broad social scene, I am in the fullest agreement with you that psychoanalysis must remain more than a specific form of therapy. To me, that goes almost without saying. (Have you, in the meantime, received my little essay, "Beyond the Bounds of the Basic Rule"?) All in all, I am therefore not surprised to hear that the smaller group of analysts of the European continent is, in essence, just as far as the larger American group, even though the visible productivity which fills the journals comes still to a large degree from this side of the Atlantic.

Chances are that the disappointment which you felt after you returned from the U.S. will be followed by a more favorable appraisal; I am looking forward to a further exchange of views on the comparison between the technological decency (or is it cultural impoverishment?) of America, which suddenly finds itself in the father role, with the goal-directed idealism (or is it the dangerous haziness of rationalized mysticism?) of a Europe which has suddenly lost its status as a parent.

My summer plans are: a brief trip to the 2nd Pan-American Congress in Buenos Aires and Rio de Janeiro; then a stay in Carmel, ending with some lectures and seminars in Seattle. I will be away from Chicago for most of August and September.

Your visit, including Drs. [Lutz] Rosenkötter's and [Clemens] de Boor's, was a very enjoyable and meaningful one for me and I'm looking forward to maintaining contact not only on the personal but also on the scientific level. I am looking forward to your books, and I am touched by your remembering to send the sample page of the Modern Stamp Album.

My greetings to Drs. Rosenkötter and de Boor. Warm regards to your wife and the best from house to house.

Cordially,

Heinz Kohut, M.D.

June 4, 1966
Erhard Künzler, M.D.
Psyche
Heidelberg
Dear Dr. Künzler:

Please accept my warmest thanks for sending me the first issue of the twentieth year of *Psyche* with the new subtitle[1] which characterizes unmistakeably [sic] the future aim of your publication in the service of psychoanalytic research and development.

To us, outside of Germany, it is a welcome sign that psychoanalysis is again taking roots in German soil; that German research and psychological understanding is not shying away from the seemingly dangerous fields of unconscious mental phenomena; and that "the nation of poets and thinkers" will make its appropriate contribution to psychoanalysis which may well be characterized as the human activity which more than any other combines the rigor of scientific thinking with the psychological perceptivity that is usually associated with the mind of the poet.

My warmest good wishes to *Psyche* for a great future!

Sincerely Yours,

Heinz Kohut, M.D.

1. Founded by Alexander Mitscherlich as "A Journal for Depth Psychology in Research and Praxis," *Psyche* now had as its subtitle "Psychoanalysis and Its Applications"; see Geoffrey Cocks, "Repressing, Remembering, Working Through: German Psychiatry, Psychotherapy, Psychoanalysis, and the 'Missed Resistance' in the Third Reich," *Journal of Modern History* 64, suppl. (December 1992): S204–5.

September 28, 1966

Mr. John F. Hayward, Professor of Theology

Meadville Theological School

Chicago

Dear Jack:

Our meeting in the street gave me the chance to tell you how much I enjoyed your response to my narcissism paper. I should like to repeat here that your grasp of my ideas and your successful translation of them from the language of scientific psychology into that of poetical religion was not only a pleasure to me but also reassurance. That my thinking had meaning within the confines of my own science, of that I felt certain. But so long as one remains within one's conceptual frame of reference one wonders whether what one has been doing was not just the setting up of a complex tautology. Your ability to understand my thoughts and to move them from their specific operational and technological surroundings into a different cohesive ideological environment without loss of meaning gives me the hope that I have touched on something that has indeed broader validity.

The most important aspect of my scientific message was, as you understood well, that narcissism must not only be regarded as a forerunner of object love but that it, too, like object love itself, reaches from the gross, archaic, and primitive to the elaborate, developed, and sublime. In view of the fact that I suspect that it is the Judaeo-Christian value system of altruistic object love which made us disregard the potentialities of narcissism, it is particularly gratifying to me to see that you are able to find a place for the higher forms of narcissism within the system of a religious outlook on existence. It is my turn to thank you.

Warmly,

Heinz Kohut, M.D.

October 11, 1966

Miss Anna Freud

London

Dear Miss Freud:

Last night I checked out the last of my letters about the Pre-Congress (an information copy was sent to you, too) and can now turn to more pleasant activities. There is some enjoyment, however, in having this complex enterprise taking shape and seeing it fitting into the larger context of our science. In my letter I tried to give a glimpse of broader perspectives to the recipients, many of whom feel outside the mainstream of the development of psychoanalysis. To give to analysts a sense of their participation in a science which constitutes a significant step forward in Man's cultural development is, as I have always held, among the most important tasks of the leaders of our organization—a conviction which has enabled me to take with equanimity some of the setbacks which are unavoidable in organizational work.

I wish that I could give you my South American impressions with the same security and broad perspective. Much of South America is officially "Kleinian," yet I have a feeling of cautious optimism about the future. It is based on seeing the heart-warming enthusiasm which the younger generation appears to have for psychoanalysis; on the repeated experience that there is great eagerness to learn and that there seem to be no rigid defenses against our ideas; and, finally, that there is willingness toward the open discussion of clinical material and of the analytic process.

Is my optimism ill-founded? Perhaps. The South Americans were certainly on their best behavior with us and may not have shown their ambivalence. I found it useless to confront our opposing systems of thought head-on; that leads only to their recitation of the gospel according to Klein and gets nowhere.[1] I have, however, patiently stuck to other, more effective methods. When, in discussing clinical material, mention is made (it appears to happen less and less!) of the patient's evidently having swallowed the analyst as the bad breast who was now eating him up from the inside, or analogous formulations within the depressive or paranoid "position," I reply in two ways. I say that I don't know anything about these fantasies and, while I see little evidence for them, can neither rule them out nor deny that they may occasionally be harbored by patients. What interests me, however, is not standardized fantasies which supposedly underlie a patient's depressed or anxious mood but the specific context in which the mood arose. Are you the bad breast, I ask the analyst, because you were late to the appointment last time, or because you announced that you would go on vacation, or because you gave an interpretation which the patient didn't like? If so, let us concentrate on what it means to the patient in terms of the present and the past that someone goes away, that someone is late, that someone says something that hurt his feelings. If you always concentrate on a standard reaction, the patient soon learns that your reference to the standard fantasy is just a complex way of telling him that he is depressed or anxious. Assume, I tell them, that we other analysts would treat Freud's remarks about the prototypical anxiety (that the form of its manifestations is correlated with the first great tension state, the passage through the birth canal) in the same way that you treat the supposedly existing standard fantasies underlying depressive and anxious moods. Suppose we would tell our patients (every time when we believe that they are anxious) not that they are anxious but that they have fantasies of being enclosed in a narrow dark space, that they are trying to catch a breath but can't, that they want to get out into the open, etc., in short that they are repeating the process through the birth canal. Our patients would soon realize that with these complexities we are simply telling them that they are anxious, and that is the only thing they will hear.

The other approach that I have been using is the stressing of the structural point of view and, especially, of the structural model of the mind. When they tell me for example that the analyst works always with his "countertransference," I do not directly contradict but ask them to fit this assertion into the structural model of the mind, with the result that we get soon into a discussion of the complexities and varieties of psychological activities as describable with the aid of the structural model. And we end up discussing the many ways in which an analyst "responds" to his patients.

Aside from the irrationality and the stereotypical nature of the specific nature of the creed of the Kleinians—I have often predicted that they will finally die out because of the sheer boredom which their formulations must cause them—I have often been repelled by the fact that their analyses are characterized by a heavy atmosphere of guilt, reproach, and expiation which struck me as even more harmful than the theoretical views which are correlated to this atmosphere. It made me rather optimistic that I did not get the impression that this was the predominant mood in which analyses are conducted in the Latin American countries. (I have noticed, however, that some of the "reformed" Kleinians continue this "depressive" attitude in their analyses, even though the reproaches about the fantasies of the "bad" baby-patient are replaced by a holding up to the patient their adult "badness" with an emphasis on their "lack of integrity," their "corruption," and the like.) So much for today about South America!

A few days ago during an informal evening with a number of our students, I found myself talking with them about the "ideal institute." Granted the necessity of making compromises, I said, and, at least in this country, the need to train psychiatrists in the skills of analyzing, could there not be in a country as large and wealthy as the U.S.A., room for *one* institute whose methods and goals would transcend those of the standard training institutions. Since I know that this topic is dear to your heart, it occurred to me that you might like to talk about it while you are here in Chicago. The thought occurred to me in a specific context. Among the activities of the Chicago Institute is a meeting on scientific topics which takes place once a week after lunch. Dr. Piers approached me a few days ago and told me that you would be attending one of the post-luncheon Wednesday conferences. He said that he was doubtful about the program for this session, was considering a discussion of the "Adult Profile," but wondered whether instead of that I would be willing to present some of my work on one of the aspects of the topic of narcissism which he knows I am working on. After some reflection I decided that none of the unpublished parts of my work on narcissism would at this time lend themselves for the loosely knitted discussion format of these meetings. But the thought occurred to me that "The Ideal Institute" might be a nice topic and one about which you might wish to lead off by giving your ideas free reign in this informal setting. Would you want to have this opportunity to talk about your views on psychoanalytic education, on "The Ideal Institute—A Utopia?" Since, for a number of reasons, you might not wish to discuss this topic during your visit here, I have not mentioned it to Dr. Piers or to anyone else. But I do know that, if you should want to, it could easily be arranged instead of the "Adult Profile" (or of some other, as yet undetermined, topic). Please let me know about it so that other arrangements can be made in case you prefer not to treat this topic or to have the burden of this additional task.

It will amuse you to learn that I found no need to exert my tactful pressure with regard to the tendency to involve you in a string of dinner parties. On my arrival I found among my mail a copy of a reply by Dr. Piers to a letter from Helen Ross in which she obviously had already expressed herself clearly about the issue.

Concerning your stay with us, please do realize how much genuine pleasure it will be for us to make your stay comfortable. As Betty wrote to you, we hope that you will feel at home here and that, for example, you will feel as free to ask your friends over as if you were in your own house in London. I hope that I can convince you that you are giving us pleasure (and not work or hardship) if you tell us in all respects what you would like us to do for you. We are quite centrally located for your purposes: Marianne [Kris], for example, will be nearby and she is looking forward to consider our place as one to come and go to at her leisure. The same should hold true for all the other friends whom you wish to be included.

One further thought occurred to Betty and me, there is a house in the country, not very far from Chicago, which belongs to the family and is available to us as a quiet retreat, e.g., during the weekend of December 17–18. Would you be interested in that as a respite from city life in a lovely wooded area[?] No luxury but comfortable and quiet with surroundings which allow pleasant non-strenuous walks in the woods? No need at all to decide on it, or to consider it now, but you might like it with a few books and a friend or two. It can be easily arranged without special notice.

Well that really has become a long letter—and I haven't even told about the lucky coincidence that, as Marianne mentioned to us a few days ago, your no-egg preference happens to be *my* dietary habit as well: so you can see, as I wrote to you some years ago [August 4, 1964], it's again a case of "identification" and therefore no trouble at all.

Carmel was as lovely as ever and the squirrels are just as lively and strong as when you knew them. Only one squirrel this summer seemed to be feeble. We watched him sitting in our garden on a big fir tree, seemingly very old and with a shaky limb. Betty took pity on him and, every morning and evening, put out some peanuts next to the bird feeder and provided fresh water. You can reconstruct the rest of the story from the poem which we composed afterwards.

> "There was a scrawny old squirrel who lived in a
>   tree,
> His paw had a tremor, he could hardly see.
> But peanuts and water have cured his disease:

He now chases the blue jays and is getting
   obese."

With warmest regards from Betty and Tom,
Sincerely,
Heinz Kohut, M.D.

1. Some Kleinians sought to harmonize Kohut's approach with their own: see Su-
sanna Isaacs Elmhirst to Kohut, January 10, 1979.

October 25, 1966 [from Anna Freud]
Dear Dr. Kohut,
   Thank you for your letter of October 11th. I think your idea of the
"Ideal Institute" is excellent and I will enjoy talking about it. It would
be especially nice if we could have an open discussion about it, up-
holding various points of view about training, its consequences for the
later work of psychoanalysts, etc. Anyway, I am all for your suggesting
it to Dr. Piers and I think the topic could make a good evening.[1]
   I have only just remembered that I need a H-1 Visa for my visit to
Chicago and I have written to Dr. Piers about it. I hope that he will
not mind too much to be burdened with the task of getting it from
Washington. My visitor's visa to the U.S. does not cover professional
engagements.
   I was very interested, of course, in what you said about South
American analysis. I cannot help being pessimistic about any discussion with Kleinians. We have had too many failures here in this respect.[2] I do not know what the fascination of theory is for those who
hold it, but it seems very rare that somebody abandons the streamlined
simplicity of it for the metapsychological complications. Probably what
it needs is a new personal analysis. (But the Kleinians say the same
with regard to us, which means that the whole discussion never arrives anywhere.) Still, it is good and necessary to make them aware
that their point of view is not the only one in existence.
   December is coming very near.
   Yours sincerely,
   Anna Freud

1. See Elisabeth Young-Bruehl, *Anna Freud: A Biography* (New York, 1988), pp.
382–83.
2. During the 1930s followers of Melanie Klein, who stressed the genesis and analysis
of mental conflict during the first months and years of life, established a strong position
in the British Psycho-Analytical Society and came into conflict with emigré analysts from
Central Europe. During the war, in a compromise over training, two groups were

formed: the "A Group" (Kleinian) and the "B Group" (Freudian). Over time, a middle group of "Independents" came to hold the balance of power and to attract increasing numbers of candidates. Anna Freud headed the separate and classically Freudian Hampstead Child Therapy Clinic. See Edward Glover, "Psychoanalysis in Britain," in *Psychoanalytic Pioneers*, pp. 538–42.

October 24, 1966
K. R. Eissler, M.D.
New York
Dear Kurt:

It was good to have you here, and your lecture was very impressive to anyone who has any sense. One afterthought to our dicussion at the Moellenhofs' about [Pablo] Picasso. To me your differentiation between genius and talent is exquisitely illustrated by a comparison between let us say [Eduard] Manet (and others of his caliber) and Picasso. Manet refines our perception of the world, its people and their emotions—Picasso must, restlessly, create new visual worlds, one after the other, each of them for me cohesive, complete and expressing meanings and feelings in a new and original synthesis after a deep dissolution and regression had torn the world asunder. You will, of course, say that the argument goes around the question whether Picasso actually achieved that, whether his is not a playful reshuffling of external forms, etc. To enter into that is too large a task for me but, at least, I thought I could explain better than at a party the direction in which my response to Picasso's work is going.

Betty joins me in sending warm regards to Ruth and you.

Cordially,
Heinz Kohut, M.D.

October 28, 1966
Miss Anna Freud
London
Dear Miss Freud:

I am glad that you like the idea of a session: "The Ideal Institute—A Utopia?"; I told Dr. Piers about it and appropriate arrangements will be made. I am very much looking forward to this session—it should be an exciting occasion.

Concerning the Kleinians and what to do about them (i.e., whether it's worth any effort), I can only add to my previous remarks that some time after the death[1] of a pathological leader the followers feel suddenly unprotected and become amenable to rational argument; and that particularly one or the other of the younger group on a comparatively "isolated" continent such as South America may be more open to reasonable argument, especially if it follows the building up of some emotional attachment. There are, in addition, a number of non-Kleinians in South America to whom our presence is a tremendous support and encouragement. Be all that as it may, I for one have the feeling that I must at least have tried. If nothing else, I will have learned something and will have sharpened my insights concerning the meaning of socially established resistances—just as the spark which led me into my narcissism studies came originally from certain experiences in the organizational field.

I reminded Dr. Piers about the H-1 visa and he assured me that everything will be taken care of.

One last question: some of your friends from New York may well wish to be in Chicago during the weekend of the Honorary Degree (perhaps the Hartmanns, the Eisslers, certainly Marianne Kris, and perhaps others). Would you want them to come to Chicago and should we then try to provide convocation tickets for them? Would you want to have them over for a simple afternoon tea (or [Austrian dialect] *Jause*) after the convocation, or for a simple supper on that evening? On Saturday, I understand from Frances Hannett, you will be at her house for dinner—do you want it that way?

And now, as you say "December is coming very near" and we are very much looking forward to your visit.

Sincerely,

Heinz Kohut, M.D.

1. Melanie Klein had died in 1960. See Phyllis Grosskurth, *Melanie Klein: Her World and Her Work* (New York, 1986); Janet Sayers, *Mothers of Psychoanalysis: Helene Deutsch, Karen Horney, Anna Freud, and Melanie Klein* (New York, 1991); and the scathing memoir by Klein's daughter, Nini Herman, *My Kleinian Home* (New York, 1989).

October 26, 1966
John E. Gedo, M.D.
Chicago
Dear John:

I just finished a quick perusal of your [Sándor] Ferenczi study for *Psyche*[1] and will give you my impression now since I might not find the time for a more careful reading in the near future.

Your review is excellent and it gives me great satisfaction that I thought of you when the project first presented itself.

Your's is a youthful review—as it should be—and some of the older generation among analysts will read with amazement that Ferenczi is now "generally remembered for [his] inconclusive technical experiments," etc. Yet, chances are your statement is correct at this time as far as the younger group is concerned. Your retrospective discovery of hints (and more than hints) in Ferenczi's work of what later came to fruition in the development of analysis, is very valuable and I think that you have found a balanced attitude toward his flights of fancy and toward his later restlessness. That his gifts were second only to Freud, with that I will agree—yet, taking an overall view, I think that [Karl] Abraham's early emphasis on the pre-oedipal stages of the libido were more truly original and independent of Freud than Ferenczi's early hunches about archaic ego mechanisms (which were much more in tune with themes which Freud had already elaborated to some extent). Nevertheless to me the "Stages of the Development of the Sense of Reality" is Ferenczi's greatest contribution and, if I had to add something to your historically balanced description of Ferenczi's position in the history of analysis, I would say that Abraham and Ferenczi complemented each other (the one on the drive side, the other on the ego side) in extending our knowledge (beyond what Freud had discovered) into the pre-oedipal realms.

Your concluding statements are well worth thinking about. For clarity's sake, I would suggest that you improve your communication around the thoughts expressed in one sentence on page 24, eight lines from the bottom: "None the less, I feel that Ferenczi's accomplishments have most to teach us about the very process of creativity. . . ." etc. That Ferenczi's works might be the raw material for an investigation of the creative processes in analysts, may be true and we may "learn" a great deal by studying them. We might also loosely say that they are "teaching" us something. Nevertheless this kind of teaching and learning is not to be put into an analogy with the intentional teaching of his "accomplishments." In other words, the value of your speculations about Ferenczi's creativity for which you use Ferenczi's writings as source material must not be compared with the value of Ferenczi's writings insofar as they form part of the body of psychoanalytic literature.

And now once more the expression of my great pleasure in your work and many warm wishes for a fine future as a contributor to our science.

Cordially,
Heinz Kohut, M.D.

1. John E. Gedo, "Noch einmal der 'gelehrte Säugling,'" *Psyche* 22 (1968): 301–19. Sandor Ferenczi was a member of Freud's early circle who later opted for a mode of analysis that involved the type of personal interaction between analyst and analysand prohibited by orthodox practice.

October 26, 1966
Dr. Carlos Whiting d'Andurain
Santiago
Dear Carlos:

Your letter gave me the greatest pleasure and many thanks also for the photographs. I like especially the one in which the two of us are sitting side by side since it reminds me of our nice excursion from Rio, and my wife and son think that the large picture of me is among the best that have been taken recently.

You make a trip to Chile sound so attractive but, unfortunately, the distance is very great and time and money, these inexorable messengers of the reality principle, will not allow themselves to be disregarded easily.

I thought of your scientific position the other day when I read a manuscript by [Charles] Socarides on homosexuality.[1] He stresses pre-oedipal factors and sees the overt homosexuality as a defence against the dreaded regression to the undifferentiated state of primary union with the mother which is the dangerous point of fixation in these people. As you know, I consider these formulations as essentially correct but not specific since similar fixations (and the concomitant fears of regression) can be seen in a very large number of our patients. I feel certain that, on deeper psychological levels (i.e., levels that are harder to reach psychoanalytically than the mother fixation) there is in many instances the dread of the archaic father image, a dread that could not be worked through in childhood (and thus could not end in a healthy identification with the father) because the father's actual weakness (or his absence, or his death) interfered with the gradual decathexis of the admired archaic father imago and thus healthy identification. In other words because the father was realistically weak (depreciated by the mother) the *gradual* process of disillusionment was disturbed and did not permit the gradual replacement (by identification) inside the child's own psyche of those qualities (the father's greatness, power, perfection) that were relinquished in reality. I tried to spell out these important processes of psychological structure formation in the papers of which I sent you reprints (I hope you have received them!), namely in "Concepts and Theories of Psychoanalysis," especially pp. 137/8, and in "Forms and Transformations of Narcissism" (*Journal American Psychoanalytic Association* 14, 243, 1966; especially pp. 247–49).

At the present time I am quite busy with the preparation of the next Pre-Congress on Training in Copenhagen in the Summer of 1967—you may have seen the letter which I, as the Chairman of the Committee responsible for the Pre-Congress, wrote recently to all the training institutions. I hope very much that Chile will be represented and, in particular, that you will be the representative so that I can see you again.

In ten days I will go to Frankfurt, Germany, for a weekend, to participate in a two-day workshop of German analysts and German language European analysts. I understand that one day will be devoted to the discussion of the paper which I gave in Buenos Aires.

Well, I hope that you will not have too many difficulties with this letter. I could understand your letter a little, just reading it by myself, and luckily I have a friend who speaks Spanish very well (he works for the United Nations as an educational consultant for Latin America and travels extensively in Central and South America) and with his help I was able to grasp the full meaning of all that you wrote me.

Warmest greetings to you and to your family.

Cordially,

Heinz Kohut, M.D.

1. *The Preoedipal Origin and Psychoanalytic Therapy of Sexual Perversions* (New York, 1988).

December 2, 1966

Miss Anna Freud

London

Dear Miss Freud:

It is very good to hear your brother Ernst is doing well; that's really splendid.

Your brother Oliver and his wife are intending to come to Chicago (despite a recent tooth extraction: Oliver; and a swollen ankle: his wife). We have made reservations for them at a nearby hotel (Hotel Windemere), they will be with us for dinner on Friday and will be invited by Frances Gitelson for dinner on Saturday.

As you can see from the enclosed copy of my letter [of December 2] to Dr. [Daniel] Freedman [Chair, University of Chicago Department of Psychiatry], I spoke with Mr. Clemen[t] Stone and found him very warm and friendly. His address is . . . in case you want to drop him a note. The move was Kurt Eissler's idea, the lie (I said that you had mentioned it to me and that you had wondered whether he would like to attend) is my responsibility.[1]

Yes, I will of course suggest that the Eisslers be invited to attend the Saturday activities (A.M. Child Therapy Program and P.M. C[ommittee on].I[nstitutional].T[raining and].C[ontinuing].E[ducation]).

Concerning your being "very handy about washing up," etc., I must disappoint you slightly. We have an electric dishwasher and it is *my* prerogative to turn the knob to the ON position. I might, however, let myself be persuaded to let you do that once in a while.

Sincerely,

Heinz Kohut, M.D.

1. Stone was the son of the multimillionaire Chicago insurance tycoon and Republican party benefactor who once gave $25,000 to the Hampstead Clinic; the psychoanalysts hoped to stimulate him to give again. See Eissler to Kohut, November 26, 1966.

December 6, 1966
Miss Anna Freud
London
Dear Miss Freud:

Your letter of November 30 arrived today, December 6. The annual overburdening of the postal services before Christmas had begun and my reply will most likely not reach you anymore in London. I am therefore sending this letter c/o Marianne Kris in N.Y. with copy to you in London. Our (your) telephone number in Chicago is *MU*seum 4-1884; all that is needed to reach us (you)—unless someone wants to dial directly via Area Code 312—is to tell the Long-Distance operator my name and Chicago.

Apropos your discussion of the auxiliary id I looked through your schedule again, found it demanding but feasible if (and that is the decisive word!) you will remain strong and oppose any further commitments. Betty will be your companion during all your activities at the University (she was officially given this assignment by the University) and she will say "NO" for you and keep people from engaging you in long after-the-session discussions, invitations, etc., and will in all ways try to protect you from undue strain if you will let her.

I am glad that you are looking forward to the *Play of Daniel*[1]—we all do, too. I have taken enough tickets to allow Marianne, Mrs. Burlingham and Mrs. [Mary Burlingham] Schmiderer to join us if they wish.

Now about the letter from Dr. Gelman. Here is already a good test of your determination. I think that you should not accept. Theoretically there might be time for such a "tea," in practice it would add a burden. The members of this "Forum" will all be able to get to hear you etc. during your activities at the Institute and the Society. The group it-self—well, I would rather discuss this with you verbally than in writ-ing. All I can say is that most of them were violently opposed to the inclusion of the Assoc. for Child Psychoanalysis in the A. Psa A.; many of them hold views in the theory and practice of child analysis with which you would hardly find yourself in sympathy. Still, these are the child analysts of Chicago such as they are, many of them are decent people, and I would not have argued against the meeting on "ideologi-cal" grounds. Yet, adding the strain of your other commitments, this is indeed how I argue: I think that you should say no.

The snow has disappeared, it is quite warm now; as a matter of fact I would rather have it a bit colder and clearer. But the weather is unpredictable and one can only hope that it will be all right for your arrival.

Daniel, by the way, was indeed a great interpreter of dreams, al-though perhaps not as widely known for this capacity as Joseph.

Warm regards,

Sincerely,

Heinz Kohut, M.D.

1. *The Play of Daniel: A Thirteenth-Century Musical Drama,* ed. Noah Greenberg (New York, 1959).

January 31, 1967

Mr. William Benton

Chairman, *Encyclopedia Britannica*

New York

Dear Senator Benton:

Thank you for your generous and candid response to my articles. Your doubts about the validity of the psychological formulations which I distilled from *Death in Venice* will be shared by many, and you ex-pressed them well and in a kind and balanced tone. It is true, of course, that it is never possible to arrive, from the study of a work of art, at psychological conclusions which carry the same degree of conviction as that which we derive from our work with a patient. I am aware of the difficulties of "Applied Analysis" and I tried to express and define them in my article "Beyond the Bounds of the Basic Rule."

Yet, I do not think that we should deprive ourselves of these speculations. Thomas Mann, for example, did not intentionally and consciously contrive to portray the specific personality structure that I
discussed in my essay. But he and many others of the very finest
artists are able—from the depths of their own personality!—to arrive
at depth psychologically valid constructions which are indeed worthy
of a psychologist's investigation. Does such an investigation spoil our
pleasure in the artistic product? I do not think so; as a matter of fact
it has been my experience that a searching psychological scrutiny en-
ables me to enjoy and admire the formal artistic perfection of a work
of art even more. I wish that you would put my experience to the test
by reading *Death in Venice* once more, now that you have seen at least
one psychologist's views on it.

Many thanks for the clipping concerning the Miller-Alice[1] which I
read with great interest. I wonder whether it will be performed on any
station accessible to me.

With my friendly greetings and again my gratitude for your generous response to my efforts.

Sincerely,

Heinz Kohut, M.D.

1. This was a British television production of *Alice in Wonderland* directed by Jonathan
Miller; see above, October 10, 1956.

February 6, 1967

Miss Anna Freud

London

Dear Miss Freud:

The enclosed "Beilage" [special section] to the Sunday edition of
Chicago's second newspaper, the *Sun-Times*,[1] will undoubtedly bring
back many memories. You are receiving it through the courtesy of
Tom who ran up and down many floors in several wings of our building until he found a copy in a back hall.

Although undertaken under the auspices of the publicity agent of
the Institute—that photographer was not a "friendly" student after
all!—the result is not too bad. At least some of the photos are very nice
and the overall tone of the report attempts to be friendly to analysis on
a sentimental level that is acceptable to the "public."

My own reactions are hard to define. Mainly, I am trying to close
myself off from all such things because the "image making" is truly a
frightening phenomenon. Before they know it people believe what the

hired publicity men say about them and their work, it becomes the publicity agent who ends up dominating those who are employing them, and no "Besen, Besen, sei's gewesen"[2] can stop the undermining of goals and values: "appearance" carries the day.

But still, some of the photos are lovely, and since you do not have to live with the shortcomings of the American scene, I hope that you can enjoy the article with amusement about the distortions but without serious misgivings.

Sincerely,

Heinz Kohut, M.D.

P.S. Did you read my friend Henry v. Witzleben's essay "Goethe und Freud" (he told me that he sent you a copy)? Though uneven, I found it on the whole very enjoyable and moving [see below, January 11, 1969].

1. Arthur Shay, "Anna Freud in Chicago," *Midwest Magazine*, February 5, 1967, pp. 4–8.

2. "Broom, broom, be as you were"; a reference to *Der Zauberlehrling* (1797), a ballad by Goethe about unforeseen consequences that was the basis for *The Sorcerer's Apprentice* (1897) by composer Paul Dukas.

February 19, 1967 [from Anna Freud]

Dear Heinz Kohut,

Thank you for your two letters of January 31st and February 6th. I waited with my answer until I should be able to announce that the transcript of the "Ideal Institute" has arrived. This happened now two days ago, and I can begin to work on it as soon as I have a little leisure time. As usual I was horrified to see how nonsensical the spoken word impresses one if it is put on paper. I wish very much that tape-recording had never been invented.

Thank you also for sending me the copy of the Chicago newspaper. Tell Tom that I appreciate very much the trouble which he took for me. (By the way, did he get my second book? But do not urge him to write, I do not want to become a nuisance to him!) Do not tell him my reactions to it which are easy to define, since they are not at all ambivalent but purely negative. I hate the whole publicity business. I cannot understand how the Institute can permit a reporter to be present in a seminar. The whole thing is such a mixture of incorrectness and sentimentality that one can only find it revolting. I ought to be used to these things by now, but I am not. The only thing one can do is to retire into obscurity.

I did read the "Goethe and Freud" essay and I liked it very much.

Just yesterday I brought it to my brother (who is still in bed) to cheer him up a bit.

Yes, of course, I did receive your photos which just crossed with the ones I sent. I like them very much, and I liked showing them to my friends here.

The story of the snow in Chicago which was in the papers here made me realise how lucky I was. Just think, if we had never made it from South Dorchester Avenue to the Institute!

Dr. Harold Boverman of the University Department will come to London to our Clinic for the Summer Term. I am glad of that since he was the man I liked best there. Is there anything more you can tell me about him, apart from what I know of my short contact?

I like to think of the coming Easter holiday, but it is slow in coming. Sometimes I feel disinclined to work, or rather inclined to work at something in peace and privacy. That is not so easy. A great deal is going on in the Clinic. Have I told you already that there is some chance of our acquiring a third house in the street? The decision from the Borough Council is supposed to arrive next week.

Paula [Fichtl][1] and Coco [see below, July 5] are well, but Dorothy Burlingham is in bed, recovering from a severe influenza.

My love to Betty, Tom and Tovey [see below, July 5],

Yours sincerely,

Anna Freud

1. The Freud family's longtime housekeeper.

March 5, 1967

Miss Anna Freud

London

Dear Miss Freud:

Your letter made me feel a little guilty. I should have known that the man who took pictures of you (and whose face I did not recognize as one of the students) was a newspaper reporter hired by the Institute. Of course, I suspected something of that sort (and mentioned it to you), but I did not pursue it vigorously enough and pushed it out of my mind by telling myself that it was probably a paid photographer who took pictures for the Institute *Bulletin* or some other "home" use. In retrospect I know now, of course, why I fooled myself about that. Acknowledging to myself that it was a reporter working for the public relations agent of the Institute would have necessitated an open clash with the Institute administration and, as you know, my whole situation with the Institute is difficult enough as it is. My opposition concerns, of course, not just such a symptom as is this kind of publicity seeking,[1] but a whole underlying attitude which sees the Institute as an expanding "empire" in which efforts to be widely known and to exert a broad influence outweigh quiet learning and the kind of research pursuits that are central to analysis but have little popular appeal. The whole story has a funny side, too. The Department of Psychiatry at the University of Chicago is enraged about the publicity which the Institute got out of your visit, while they did not. And, ironically, they appear to be blaming me as the culprit. Since I had stood firmly for a no-publicity policy with them (as I did, of course, also in innumerable talks with the administration of the Institute), they think that I must have double-crossed them since, after all, I must have known what the Institute was up to. (I know that these things are said about me, but since no-one has yet said them to me to my face there is little I can do about it—nor do I really care.

Yes, Tom received *War and Children*.[2] He has been mighty pleased and proud about the gift, and he has been reading it systematically alone and with Betty. Since he is planning on writing to you again soon I will not anticipate his message to you. He is also planning to send you a series of photos which he took for you when we were having all that snow.

About Dr. B. I cannot tell you anything, except that, after some hesitations he has now been accepted by the Institute as a candidate.

I am up to my ears in work—too much of it. I have therefore not been able to make the progress with my narcissism paper that I had hoped for. I think, nevertheless, that in a few weeks I will send you a long draft (such as it will be) since I am very eager to have views on it.

We are all sorry to learn that your brother's recovery is slow and also that Mrs. Burlingham has been ill. But her illness is, we hope, by now a thing of the past. Paul Kramer, by the way, is in Bethesda, Md., in the hospital of the N[ational].I[nstitutes of].H[ealth]. He had an artificial valve inserted in his heart (he is only the fifth person who has had this operation after a "coronary"). I spoke with his wife in the evening after the operation (on Friday, March 3) and she appeared to be optimistic. But it's going to be rough sledding.

How nice to hear that you may be acquiring a third house for the Clinic. You had told me about it before and I am eager to learn what the Borough Council will decide. Can't a Commander of the Empire give a command?[3]

Yesterday we spoke with Marianne. She will not join us in Salzburg as we had hoped but she may well be with us in Switzerland toward the end of August. (We are in the process of renting a simple house in the Lower-Engadine, in the Chur-Klosters region.)

And now: love to all of you from all of us. Betty will write soon, and Tom—well, maybe.

Sincerely,

Heinz Kohut, M.D.

1. See George Pollock to Ruth Rashman, November 17, 1978, concerning *People* magazine's projected article on Kohut and the possibility of mentioning the Chicago institute and its work. See also below, Kohut to Giovanna Breu, November 25, 1978.

2. Anna Freud and Dorothy T. Burlingham, *War and Children* (New York, 1943), a study of the effects of separation from parents in children evacuated from urban areas during World War II. The nurseries directed by Freud and Burlingham were funded by the Foster Parents' Plan for War Children, which in 1936 began its work on behalf of children subjected to bombardments during the Spanish Civil War.

3. A reference to one of Anna Freud's many honors, this one from the British government. On May 8, 1967, as a result of nomination by Kohut, she was made an Honorary Member of the American Psychiatric Association. See Walter E. Barton to Kohut, May 17, 1967.

March 10, 1967
Mr. Robert Sussman
Boston

Dear Mr. Sussman:

Yes, I remember of course that I spoke with you briefly in December; and I will be glad to chat with you if you feel that I can be helpful. There should be no difficulty about getting together during the days which you mention (April 7 to 10, plus perhaps one or two extra days) and I will note the fact that you will be in Chicago on my calendar. Please let me know how much time you want me to reserve for you and how you propose to meet with me: we could get together either in my office or at my home, whichever way you prefer.

You asked for advice concerning other analysts in the Chicago area who might be helpful to you. I would suggest Dr. Therese Benedek, Dr. Thomas French, and perhaps Dr. Edoardo Weiss of the older group. If you are interested in talking with a gifted younger member of the profession (How does analysis look to a rather recent graduate?), I would suggest Dr. John Gedo who is well informed and articulate.

If I understood you correctly, you are also asking my opinion whether you should interview people who have become broadly estranged from psychoanalysis as most of us would define the field, i.e., people who either stress an eclectic approach (which includes shock treatment, drug therapy, social psychiatry, dynamic psychiatry, etc.) or who emphasize one of the other of these areas in opposition to analysis proper. I do not believe that the decision whether to interview such people or not depends on the question whether these interviews would supply something of historical interest, or whether the issues would be clarified or confused. The decision rests rather on the way in which you define the purpose of your examination. By interviewing such people you will be scrutinizing views which are not only at a great distance from what most of us consider to be analysis, but which are also widely divergent from each other (the purely "organicist" approach, for example, versus the approach of the social or community psychiatrists).

The result will be that the area of analysis proper will be reduced to a comparatively narrow band in the broader spectrum which you are examining, and the significant variations and changes in the central area (the relative emphasis on ego-psychology, for example, or the relative emphasis on pre-oedipal stages of development) will look like minute nuances when seen within the broad field of your interest. If indeed you wish to use such a wide-angle camera for your picture then you will undoubtedly have to include men who are representative of broadly differing positions among those to be interviewed.

Let me close by telling you again that I am very willing to be of assistance to you if I can and that I hope to hear from you concerning the details of the meeting that you are envisaging.

Sincerely yours,

Heinz Kohut, M.D.

P.S. I am enclosing a few reprints that may be of aid to you in your preparations. I would very much appreciate receiving a copy of any writing about analysis by you that has already been published or that you can otherwise make available to me.

March 22, 1967
Dr. James E. Kleeman
Bethany, Connecticut
Dear Dr. Kleeman:

Many thanks for your letter concerning the peek-a-boo game to which I referred during my seminar in New Haven in January, 1966. The peek-a-boo game has for many years been one of my favorite examples when pointing out not only how optimal frustration leads to gradual tension tolerance, but also, specifically, how the mother can during this game dose the just tolerable frustration, letting herself be guided by the expression on the child's face which she watches empathically. I have often said jokingly that the decisive spots in the peek-a-boo game are the spaces between the mother's fingers, i.e., her peeking at the child's expression between her fingers. This game (and the way it serves to build up tension tolerance) is similar to what Sanford Gifford described in his paper on the sleep cycle, i.e., how the child's sleep pattern gradually adapts itself to the mother's needs.

I was touched by your thoughtfulness in first asking for my permission before sending me your manuscript. Although you are guessing correctly when you assume that I do not have much spare time, I shall be very glad to read your paper and I am looking forward to your sending it to me. I hope that I do not have to read and return it immediately upon receiving it. And thank you also for the fairness and integrity with which you are acknowledging the stimulation which I apparently gave you for this specific aspect of your work.

With warm regards,
Sincerely,
Heinz Kohut, M.D.

March 28, 1967
Dr. Fidias R. Cesio
Buenos Aires
Dear Doctor Cesio:

Your letter gave me great pleasure and ever since I received it I have been waiting for a period of leisure so that I could finally give to my reply the time and attention which your communication deserves. Unfortunately, the required period of leisure has not materialized and, I am afraid, it will not come until after this summer, when my responsibilities as the Chairman of the Pre-Congress will be over. Since I do not want to wait any longer, however, I am writing to you only briefly at this time and hope that you will understand my situation and will excuse me.

Up to a point I believe that I followed your way of thinking and, up to a point, it seems quite true that some of our thoughts are parallel. But there are, of course, terminological obstacles and, in addition, I tend to rely—much more than you—on the analyst's use of the autonomous aspects of his ego in his responses to the patient. (Have you ever seen Freud's remark about counter-transference in his letter to [Ludwig] Binswanger of February 20, 1913? [See below, September 27, 1967.]) Empathic resonance belongs to the autonomous equipment of the personality; counter-transference, however, I consider in essence to be a hindrance (except insofar as it leads to a piece of successful self-analysis). The crux of our differences lies probably in the analysis of what I call the Twinship Transference. According to my experience, a correct analysis of the Twinship Transference leads to the gradual emergence of grandiose fantasies from childhood, and it is the taming of this childhood grandiosity and its ideas being fitted into the realistic, adult personality which is the most important curative factor.

I sincerely hope that there will be an opportunity to continue our discussion. I enjoyed our encounter in Buenos Aires and I have no doubt that, after bridging some terminological and conceptual differences, we should be well on the road toward a meaningful communication. Will I see you in Copenhagen this summer? I hope so.

Warm regards and many thanks for your very nice and instructive letter, written in excellent English (I wished that I could reciprocate by writing in Spanish!).

Very sincerely yours,

Heinz Kohut, M.D.

April 8, 1967

Mr. Robert Sussman

The Palmer House

Chicago

Dear Mr. Sussman:

I read your review[1] with the greatest pleasure—the pleasure was shared by my wife to whom I read the article—and I want to tell you how grateful I am to you for your levelheaded, convincing, and beautifully presented statement. It really leaves nothing to be desired, and it makes me now look forward with anticipatory enjoyment to your History of Psychoanalysis since the Death of Freud.[2]

I also enjoyed the interview and have the impression that we came to terms about a number of issues even though I know, of course, that what I said and felt will soon submerge in the totality of memories that will be formed in your mind after you are done with the many interviews and readings which you are undertaking in preparation for your study. Among the several afterthoughts concerning unfinished topics taken up in our discussion—do you know what the Zeigarnik experiment demonstrated?[3]—there is only one that I would like to pursue because here I know not only that I remained incomplete but also why it happened. When you asked me about my work about narcissism I was less clear than I could have been in response to your attempt to find out how much there was basically new in my contribution. The reason for my incompleteness was that I was concentrating to some extent on trying to find out how much you, a layman, had understood about my highly technical topic, and it was only gradually that I began to recognize that you had indeed understood a good deal. Now, to give you belatedly the answer that I failed to give you during our discussion: my contribution is, in a nutshell, that I am not only demonstrating (as has been done before in many different ways) the existence of narcissism as an early developmental stage of which traces may still be noticeable later—in the form of pathological personality features, fixations, and impediments to adaptation—but that narcissism has its own development and that it leads from the primitive to the complex and advanced. I am demonstrating, I believe, that there is not only a development from narcissism to object love, but also from lower forms of narcissism to higher forms. And, finally, that in psychoanalytic therapy progress must be measured not primarily in terms of how much the narcissism of narcissistic personalities has been changed into object love but also, and foremost, how much archaic forms of narcissism have become remobilized and reintegrated and have been transformed into such useful attributes of a healthier personality organization as are ideals, self-esteem, humor, creativity, wisdom in the contemplation of one's shortcomings and limits, etc. Does that answer your question better?

And now let me again tell you that I enjoyed our meeting, thank you once more very warmly for your splendid book review, and give you my good wishes for success in your present endeavor.

Sincerely,

Heinz Kohut, M.D.

1. Robert Sussman Stewart, "Posthumous Analysis," *New York Times Book Review*, January 29, 1967, pp. 3, 42. This was a review of Sigmund Freud and William C. Bullitt, *Thomas Woodrow Wilson: A Psychological Study* (New York, 1967).

2. This work, which was to be serialized first in *The New Yorker*, has never appeared; see Sussman to Kohut, March 3, 1967.

3. The "Zeigarnik effect," named for a Russian student of German psychologist Kurt Lewin, demonstrates that interrupted tasks are remembered better than completed ones. See Blyuma Zeigarnik, *The Pathology of Thinking*, trans. Basil Haigh (New York, 1965); and Kohut, *The Analysis of the Self*, pp. 315–16.

May 1, 1967
James A. Kleeman, M.D.
Bethany, Connecticut
Dear Doctor Kleeman:
Although I am pressed for time just now before the Association meeting (and other deadlines), I would like to give you in the following my impressions of your paper in "The Peek-A-Boo Game."

1. I found the reading of the paper quite taxing (especially the perusal of the long series of Observations demand a good deal of concentration), but also very rewarding.

2. Would not the reader's task be easier if, preceding the Observations, a brief outline were presented, anticipating the major lines of development which are illustrated and can be traced in the series of Observations?

3. From my point of view the essential difference between active and passive aspects of the game must not be overemphasized. There are differences, to be sure, but in the infant the psychological differences between "active" and "passive" as encountered in the game are not as great as analogous differences would be in older children or adults. The infant observes the mother and considers her as part of his own ego (self?). This concept is an illusion only from the standpoint of an unempathic adult observer. In (psychological) reality the empathic mother is indeed fulfilling ego functions, is a part of the child's psychological equipment: the response of her hand is approximately identical with the response of the child's own hands as regards the child's desire for tension and relief from tension. If the mother is grossly unempathic, however, the infant experiences her as traumatic and defends himself against perceiving her by primitive means, i.e., he shuts her out of his active psychological organization.

4. Is there a basic form of the Peek-A-Boo in which the first moment of the appearance of the mother's face is experienced as (just a trifle) traumatic and is accompanied (as a playful, active expression of this minimal trauma) by the sound "boo," meant to frighten the child, if ever so little? If this is the case (as I believe it is), that would be significant because it would emphasize that the psycho-economic aspects of the game is the most important one. It would underline the fact that the sudden emergence of the face is in itself traumatic because the child is unable to master the visual stimulation through immediate recognition. The momentary trauma, however, heightens the pleasure of the then immediately following recognition. The cognitive mastery is blissful because it renders the apprehensive, anxious tension unnecessary.

5. Are you familiar with my papers on the enjoyment of music? My psychoanalytic musical theory deals with just such phenomena and since games are the precursors of art, the peek-a-boo game may well be constructed in just this way, taking into account that the tension tolerance of infants is very low and that, in order to give enjoyment, the trauma must be of very short ("boo") duration. I am enclosing two reprints regarding my musical theory.

And now warm regards and many thanks for letting me see your fine study. Will I have a chance to talk with you in Detroit?

Cordially yours,
Heinz Kohut, M.D.

May 4, 1967
Raymond Prince, M.D.
McGill University
Montreal
Dear Doctor Prince:

Thank you for your kind letter of April 15 and for your interest in my paper on narcissism. The investigation of "mystical states" is somewhat peripheral to my focus of attention, but I can see well that the concept of a "cosmic narcissism" might be helpful in this context. Actually I do not know how I could amplify at this moment what I said in my paper. My main point was: (1) that there exists an original psychological union with the empathic mother out of which the self concept emerges gradually as the child matures; (2) that, towards the end of life, some individuals may achieve a revival of this primordial psychological state in a new and creative form, i.e., since (in view of the certainty of death) the illusion of the eternal existence of the self cannot be maintained, the loving investment of the self concept (the cathexis of the self with narcissistic libido) is given up and the instinctual energies which invested the self are now turned toward the surrounding reality (cosmic narcissism) and toward the ideals which one cherishes. This shift from the self to one's values and ideals, and to the world as a whole, is in its most perfect form not a mystical experience but a sad and realistic goodbye to oneself. Are you a musical person, Doctor Prince? If so I believe you will understand when I tell you that the end of Beethoven's piano sonata opus 111 is the most perfect artistic expression of this detachment from oneself in the face of the end of life.

Sincerely,
Heinz Kohut, M.D.

May 16, 1967
Martin Grotjahn, M.D.
Beverly Hills, California
Dear Martin:

People generally tend to adapt to the way in which others see them. Your perception of me as "The Scholar," which you transmitted to me in such a friendly fashion on our walk from the Detroit Art Institute, prompts me to prove to you that you were right—and here is the result. It concerns, of course, [Rembrandt's painting] "The Visitation" [1640]. The reference is Luke 1, 34 to 64, especially 39 to 44. Mary has been told by the Angel that she will have a baby; and when she protests "How shall this be, seeing I know not a man?", the Angel tells her that everything is possible under God. Has not, says the Angel, Mary's cousin Elizabeth "conceived a son in her old age"? Then Mary goes to visit her aged cousin and the cousin's aged husband, Zacharias, and "The Visitation" is the moment of their encounter. The old woman, in an advanced stage of pregnancy, the young woman in her early pregnancy, and the touching moment when, at the point of their encounter, the baby of the old woman (later: John the Baptist) senses the presence of the Christ child and leaps for joy in the womb.

It was good being with you in Detroit and I am looking forward to seeing you soon again. Will you be in Copenhagen? My best to Etelka!
   Cordially,
   Heinz Kohut, M.D.

July 5, 1967
To: Coco (Poodle. Owner of Dorothy Burlingham, Paula Fichtl,[1] Anna
       Freud).
From: Tovey (Pug. Owner of Betty, Heinz, and Tom Kohut).
Dear Coco:

Please forgive me for addressing you by your first name without having even made your personal acquaintance. But, first of all, I do not know your last name and, secondly, I am an American dog and we Americans believe in using first names quickly. I have a family of people, however, (and I hear the same is true for yours) who are quite reserved in this respect and, once they are fully grown, don't like to call others by their first names even if they like each other well. I cannot really understand why this should be so but I think that something that accounts for this behavior must have happened to them while they were puppies in Europe.

My three people, by the way, have been talking a lot about your people recently and they can't say enough about all the nice things that they have been getting from them. They got very sweet letters from your Anna, Dorothy, and Paula. My Tom also got an inscribed book from your Anna with which he is terribly pleased. And my Betty got a handsome collar (also from your Anna) and she, too, is terribly pleased with it and proud about it (you know how people are!). I personally think that the collar is rather flimsy and could hardly hold a leash (at least not the way I can strain) but it's probably meant more for decoration. I must say I was myself very happy to see all the nice photographs that arrived here today, particularly, of course, because there was a picture of you among them which I liked very much.

But now I think this is enough for a first letter. Will I ever hear from you?

Sincerely yours,

Tovey.

1. See Paula Fichtl to Kohut, June 7, 1969; and below, January 25, 1968.

August 27, 1967 [from Anna Freud]

Dear Dr. Kohut,

Thank you for your letter of August 15th and for the two pages which I inserted in their right place in your paper.[1] I hope that you do not mind too much that I did not return your paper to Switzerland as I had promised. I meant to do so. But then I got very much involved in reading it, and in discussing the contents also with Marianne, who wanted to read it also. In this way, it became rather late and now Marianne and I have decided that it is much safer not to send it to Switzerland any more, but to give it to her to take back to New York from where she will send it to you. I hope that this is all right with you.

I read it carefully once more from beginning to end and I had many thoughts about it. I could probably give a better account of these in a talk with you; but since this cannot happen now, I shall put on paper the essentials, leaving many minor points aside, especially where what you say connects with experiences and clinical material of my own.

About the *main idea* first: I think it is a good and important one. It answers the question why the transference neuroses are easier to treat analytically than the other mental disturbances and it shows at the same time how the field can be widened and where the treatment of the so-called narcissistic disorders branches off from it and how it is related to it. It also shows the impasses into which treatment runs if the narcissistic phenomena are treated on a par with the transference neurosis symptomatology.

About the question whether what you describe should go under the *name of transference:* here I, personally, would worry very much less than you do. I was in a similar quandary when I had to write about transference in child analysis in my book, and I made a different decision. I thought that using the person of the analyst for the revival of old and repressed object relationships is merely one of the uses to which he can be put in treatment. With children he is also used as a real person; as a person different from the parents; as the representative of the patient's id; as an auxiliary ego; as an externalised superego; as a need-satisfying object, etc. All these uses are open to analysis and useful for interpretation (except perhaps the "real person") so long as one does not confuse them with transferred object relationships, i.e., with what we usually call transference. It seems to me that you say very much the same: that in your cases the patient uses the analyst not for the revival of object-directed strivings, but for inclusion in a libidinal (i.e., narcissistic) state to which he has regressed or at which he has become arrested. You may call that transference; or you may call it a sub-specialty of transference, as I did; or you may give it another name. This does not matter, really, so long as it is understood that the phenomenon is not produced by cathecting the analyst with object-libido. We might ask, of course, whether it would be right to say that the analyst in these cases is "cathected" with narcissistic libido. This is tempting, but somehow it does not seem an exact description to me. Rather than being cathected, the analyst is drawn (according to the term used by Hoffer) into the patient's "narcissistic milieu." Cathexis as a term refers to states when the differentiation between self and object has been made already and is secure; which is not the kind of state which you have in mind.

I asked myself whether I had caught all the main *points of your argument.* I repeat them here, for you to judge whether I understood you right.

You go back in the pathogenesis of your patients to the various stages which precede object-relatedness. *Auto-erotism,* as the most primitive, cannot be shared with anybody, and for this reason cannot be "transferred," i.e., relived with the analyst; regression to it also means withdrawal from the analyst.

Then comes the phase of *integrated narcissism* in which self and object are one, which is normally interfered with by experience with reality and which the individual tries to regain by idealising either the self or the object. Here I would like to register an objection to your terminology: you speak of the "narcissistic self" and the "idealised object." But is not the process the same in both instances? And would it therefore not be simpler to speak of the "idealised self" and the "idealised object"? I do not see why not. What I have against the term "narcissistic self" is very simple; the self can only be cathected with narcissistic libido, there is no other possibility. To speak of a narcissistic self does therefore to me not give the extreme meaning which you have in mind and which corresponds with the "idealised object."

For both representations, or externalisations, of idealised self and idealised object, you describe the person of the analyst as being very useful to the patient. You call them "the idealising transference" and the "mirror or twinship transference." In fact, they are both idealisations, both representing parts of the patient's own self. Since the two attempts at regaining the state of primary narcissism are rather different, naturally also their re-appearance in analysis, i.e., the way in which the anlayst is exploited for their representation, is different.

Have I understood it right, so far?

If I have understood it right, then I do not quite agree with what you say about the Counter-transference. You feel that the analyst's difficulty arises in part from his own narcissistic difficulties which are aroused by the type of relationship which the patient has established. I do not see that this assumption is really necessary. It seems to me that the other part, which you also describe, is quite sufficient to explain the analyst's negative response, boredom, etc. We are never "bored" by true transference manifestations, whether they are negative or positive, libidinal or aggression. Whatever we may feel about it, we feel spoken to, i.e., contacted by the patient; our danger is the opposite: we are too tempted to respond and have to keep this impulse in check. But where we are used by the patient to represent part of himself, we are not "addressed," "spoken to," and no answer which we give would be either welcome or natural. We are not a partner but a pawn in a game. To me this is quite sufficient to explain the analyst's reaction.

About the *technical question:* you describe very well how different interpretation has to proceed and how necessary it is to let the narcissistic relationship (or use of the analyst) develop first. I asked myself why this is really so, and I came up with the following answer which may be correct or not:

The narcissistic transference (I follow you here in calling it by that name) is not the revival of an old striving and of repressed events in object-relatedness but the revival or the up-to-date expression of a *libidinal state* of affairs. Such a state (*ein Zustand*) does not lend itself to interpretation, it just *is*. What can be interpreted are then the traumatic events which fixated the patient to that state or which made him re-gress to it. The *state* has to be developed with the analyst's quiet con-nivance; the *events* can and have to be interpreted.

About one of your *clinical examples:* you may remember when we talked in Copenhagen that I mentioned one of your clinical examples by which I was puzzled. I can make this more explicit now. It is the patient's story on p. 10.

A minor objection first: you say there that "the father took the son to his factory at an early age, explaining the business to him and even asking for the son's opinion in various business matters." This makes one expect a child of, at least, school age. But on p. 11 you make it quite clear that this happened before the age of 3½ which does not make sense. No father can ask for a child's opinion on business matters at that age. This is confusing.

But now the major objection: I do not think that this story fits your theoretical exposition since here the disturbance which occurs is defi-nitely not one in the realm of narcissism but in the realm of object-relationship. What is interfered with too early, i.e., before the proper time for internalisation into the super-ego, is the object-relationship to the father, not the primary identification with him. If at age 3, the boy would still not have made the differentiation between his own self and that of the father, he would have been very abnormal already, which he evidently was not. Or did I miss the evidence that this child's relationship to his father at this age was not the oedipal admiration for the big father which would normally have led to an internalised super-ego, but the remnants of the "idealised object" of a much earlier level?

In contrast the clinical example on p. 104 is extremely convincing.

That is, really, all for the moment. I do not know whether it is any help. But, at least, it shows you that I was very much concerned with your thoughts.

Yours sincerely,
Anna Freud

1. "Transference and Counter-Transference in the Narcissistic Disorder"; see Kohut to Anna Freud, January 19, 1967.

September 27, 1967
Miss Anna Freud
London
Dear Miss Freud:

We came back to Chicago on September after two glorious weeks in Rome which formed the end of an altogether enjoyable and instructive long vacation. Since I wanted to respond quickly to your letter of August 27 which I found on my return, I dictated a draft of a letter to you soon after our arrival while I was still suffering from the sleep disturbances which seem to be an unavoidable result of the abrupt time change from Europe to America. A week has passed since I dictated the draft of this letter. I am not only seeing my patients but I have also begun to work again on my paper, concentrating in particular on a long introduction to the chapter on the Idealizing Transference. I believe that this introduction will be the best response to a number of the most important points in your letter and I will therefore in today's reply not strive for completeness covering those topics with which I shall be dealing in the parts of the paper on which I am now working. I will send you the new pages as soon as they are reasonably presentable. Please do, therefore, consider today's reply only as an introduction to the material I hope to send you soon.

But now let me reply to those points in your letter that will not be primarily covered by the new sections of my paper.

(1) You asked me a number of times whether you have followed my line of thought. The answer is an unqualified yes everywhere.

(2) Concerning the term transference and the fact that I seem to "worry" about it excessively. I feel very clear about what I mean by transference and have stated my preference in the paper "Introspection, Empathy, and Psychoanalysis" (pp. 471/2) and in the paper (with Seitz) "Concepts and Theories of Psychoanalysis" (pp. 120ff.) I know, however, that the non-metapsychological use of the terms transference and counter-transference is now ubiquitous and ingrained and that direct arguments against such habits tend to remain fruitless. Instead, I was using a quasi-Socratic "pedagogical" method of stating the arguments pro and con; and of not making a decision about terminology, but of leading the reader to a decision on the basis of the thoughts

that I offered. Did I go too far by unqualifiedly using the terms transference and countertransference once I am done with the general discussion? I don't think so since the question concerning a definition of transference is not the major focus of this work. (I am postponing until later in this letter my response to your objection concerning my term "countertransferences" in the treatment of narcissistic disorders.)

(3) Now concerning your objection to the term "narcissistic self." I believe that your objection is valid and since I am convinced by your argument I will change the term. I do not, however, want to use the term "idealized self" since idealization implies to me a small, transitional step toward object cathexis. What I have been calling the "narcissistic self" is grandiose and exhibitionistic and has rudimentary subject qualities, while the idealized object to which the child has given over his original narcissism and of which he is in awe has rudimentary object qualities, even in its archaic form. To call the successor of the purified pleasure ego (which up to now I called the narcissistic self) the "exhibitionistic self" or the "gradiose-exhibitionistic self" would thus come closer to my meaning—but the first term is of a misleading "pars-pro-toto" incompleteness, and the second one is long and clumsy. At the moment I am inclined to call it the "grandiose self" and use this term instead of the former "narcissistic self" in contrast to the "idealized object." What do you think?

(4) Now to a number of important related topics which will, however, be treated more extensively in the new pages of the manuscript which I hope to be able to send you soon.

Like you I believe that the earliest states are not recoverable in analysis in the way in which, e.g., oedipal transference fantasies are. (Your mode of describing these conditions on p. 4 of your letter is a very felicitous one and, if you have no objections, I should like to quote your remarks about a libidinal state—*ein Zustand*—not lending itself to interpretation as do the traumatic events which led to (a fixation on or regression to) the libidinal state in question. Patients cannot remember these states and can only reinstate them in analysis, not only because they occur in the pre-verbal period, but also because the secondary processes (and especially our language) are altogether incapable of formulating and expressing these experiences. Under these circumstances the patient tends to use the description of later experiences in order to communicate something about the earlier one. (The analyst, in his *theoretical* formulations, must of course not follow the patient here, as did Melanie Klein.) Such a tendency manifests itself with particular clarity in case where there are indeed later analogous repetitions of the earlier experience which is by no means a rare occurrence. The clinical history on p. 10 to which you rightly objected in the form in which you unfortunately encountered it will actually be particularly suitable to show what I have in mind. But before I go into these details let me first briefly explain that I had hastily added that history from memory to the paper before it was typed, mainly so that it would remind me to write a more extensive introduction to the chapter on the idealising transference supported by case material. I did, however, not have the time to work on this part of the paper before the Pre-Congress, which accounts for the misleading aspects of the report. The patient had indeed "remembered"—in the context of an analogous present reality situation—that the father had taken him into the business, at the age of three and one-half—and had "consulted" him about business decisions. And we reconstructed the admiration which he had for his father and the traumatic disappointment when the father became suddenly powerless. The main point, however, is that the "memory" regarding age three and one-half is the telescoped focus of several later events as well as, I feel certain, of a much earlier pre-verbal one. The times of the later successive repetition of the cycle of admiration for and disappointment in the idealized father can be ascertained with reasonable certainty since political events allow a fairly exact dating. The family had originally been established in _____ when the first breakdown of the admired father image occurred. (Czechoslovakia, as used in the paper, is a disguise.) Then they fled to _____ where a re-building of the business took place. The father was again admired and became again helpless. Finally they escaped to the U.S.A. where the old traumatic experience was again re-lived: at first the father seemed potent and powerful, but he could not adjust to the demands of the U.S.A., gave up the attempt of being a success, and retreated. Older than these repeated traumatic disappointments in the father must have been (unremembered and only reinstated) certain traumata in a much earlier relationship with the mother which we reconstructed from the patient's behavior in analysis and deduced from his description of his mother who is a seemingly calm and quiet person (in contrast to the openly overemotional father) but who tends to disintegrate with terrible anxiety and unintelligible (schizoid) excitement when she is exposed to pressure. Thus the case, when presented in greater detail, demonstrates the "telescoping" of memories in two directions: (a) the use of later events to substitute for earlier ones (the father undoubtedly used the son later for advice; from what I learned about him, however, it is also not inconceivable that he might have played into the son's fantasies, even at three and one-half, by treating him as a "business partner"); and (b) the use of a later experience to express an earlier one which itself cannot be remembered (i.e., the use of the relationship with the father to express the earlier vicissitudes of narcissism in the relationship with the mother).

And now to my main point. I think that it is fruitful (and correct) to view libidinal development not only in terms of progress from lower to higher forms of narcissism. The development of narcissism, in particular, in that specific direction which I designate as the "idealized object" does therefore not cease when the end of the original archaic narcissistic position has been reached in which the differentiation of "I" from "you" does not exist or is yet very tentative. For this reason I see the archaic idealizing transference (arising from archaic idealized "objects") and the increasingly higher (pre-oedipal) forms of idealizing transference (arising from later idealizations up to the oedipal period) as (a) the beginning, (b) the developmental way-stations, and (c) the end point of a cohesive developmental stream in the realm of narcissism. During the later phases cognition differentiates clearly between "I" and "you," and the object is more and more understood as separate, becomes highly differentiated in many respects, and the emotional responses to the objects become more and more refined, mature, etc. Side by side, however, with the development of object love the narcissistic idealization continues. The (re-)internalizations tell the story in the obverse. In the realm of superego formation, for example (but there are also other, earlier internalizations) the abandonment of the oedipal object cathexes leads to the formation of introjects and to the endopsychic continuation of the old object relationship. The superego thus continues internally the parental prohibitions, punishment, withdrawal or giving of love, setting of standards, praise for good behavior and good intentions, etc., i.e., it is the successor of the former relationship to objects that were cathected with object libido (and aggression). The massive internalization is of course the inevitable outcome of the frustrated oedipal passion and of the oedipal conflict in the realm of object love and object aggression. Parallel with these internalizations in the realm of object cathexes occur the re-internalizations in the realm of narcissism. The child's disillusionment with the adult (successive smaller waves of such experiences of pre-oedipally; massive ones oedipally) leads to a re-internalization of the original narcissism which, after an archaic beginning in which separate object imagoes did not exist, had become amalgamated to object love and object aggression. Thus, two dimensions of the superego can be differentiated: its contents and functions (which are the heir of the child's object cathected attachments) and its exalted stature—its omniscience, powerfulness, and the unique position of its values, standards, and functions, whatever their form and content—(which is the heir of the child's pre-oedipal and oedipal idealizations). This is what I meant when I said in my previous paper that the successful lie (which reveals to the child that the adult is not omniscient) leads to a re-internalization of the narcissistic demands for a continuation of omniscience of the superego. In the progression from the original narcissism, through the archaic idealized object, via higher forms of idealization, to the final idealization of the superego ("the ego ideal"), the narcissism may become tamed, refined (neutralized) *by the passage through the object* and is also influenced by the actual behavior and by the emotional responses of the overestimated object. (Some of these thoughts are also contained in a number of paragraphs which I wrote earlier this summer, of which I am enclosing a xeroxed copy.) Just as the harshness of the superego, however, is to some extent uninfluenced by the parents' actual behavior (or even paradoxically heightened by their kindness), so also is the trend toward the absolutarian perfection of the superego (its idealization; its "ego ideal" dimension) to some extent independent of the parents' behavior and may—an analogous paradox!—be occasionally heightened by a parent's traumatic "modesty" that frustrates the child's phase-appropriate need to glorify the parent. Under such circumstances the "modesty" of the parent is out of step with the child's need at a certain stage, i.e., it corresponds to what I described as the analogous failures of analysts toward their patients' needs in the chapters on countertransference.

The foregoing considerations need not be expanded any further to support my final contention, namely, that the developmental stream of narcissism called the "idealized parent imago" can be interfered with (leading to fixations and developmental arrests) at any point from its early inception, when the archaic object is still almost merged with the self, to the point, just before its final re-internalization, when it is amalgamated with the experience of a highly differentiated (pre-oedipal) object. At this point I should say a few more words about the fact that certain aspects of all pre-oedipal objects distinguish them in essence from all post-oedipal objects. The distinguishing feature is supplied by the fact that pre-oedipal objects are precursors of permanent psychological structure while the post-oedipal ones are not (or not to that extent). Interference with gradual (or phase appropriate) re-internalization of the pre-oedipal object leads to a fixation on it and a need for it as substitute for psychological structure. Thus the seeming object hunger for, and yet the easy replaceability of, such "objects." In the case described on pp. 10ff. of my paper the traumatic disappointment in the father (prepared by earlier disappointments in the mother, expressed through memories of later disappointments in the father) led to the insufficient idealization of the superego and, in consequence of his fixation on the archaic idealized object, to an eternal search for external ideal figures to replace the specific inner void.

(5) Finally a few words about countertransference. What you mentioned about the explanation of the analyst's boredom in the framework of the absence of object libidinal demands I fully agree with and, as you say, referred to it in my paper. As you suggest, this might often be a sufficient explanation of the analyst's withdrawal. I feel reasonably certain, however, that occasionally there is also observable a fear of regression aroused by the archaic relationship, which induces the analyst to build up a wall of "rationality"—an attitude in other words to which one would have some right to refer loosely as countertransference since it is the repetition of an old state (or a defense against it). Be the foregoing as it may: I feel certain about the countertransference nature (again in the above sense) of analysts' embarrassed withdrawal from being idealized. I have observed this phenomenon many times and feel sure that it is due to a retreat motivated by narcissistic tensions about the threatening break-through of grandiose fantasies that had remained unanalyzed in the analyst's training analysis. (This formulation is the analogue in the narcissistic realm to your father's remarks about countertransference in the object-libidinal realm in his letter of Binswanger of 20 February, 1913.)[1]

* * * *

I believe that I should say no more at this point and only tell you how deeply grateful I am to you for having spent such care on my thoughts, for having spelled out your reactions so clearly and helpfully, and altogether for being so kind to me. We often think of you and talk about you, and every time one of us gets a line from you it is a little holiday for the family. With gratitude and affection,

Sincerely,

Heinz Kohut, M.D.

P.S. I spoke with Marianne who told me that you had discussed my work with her and that you had read to her parts of your letter to me. When I told her that I was writing to you, she expressed interest in reading my response. I am therefore enclosing a copy which you may send her if you wish.

1. Ludwig Binswanger, *Sigmund Freud: Reminiscences of a Friendship*, trans. Norbert Guterman (New York, 1957), pp. 50–53.

October 27, 1967
Therese Benedek
Chicago
Dear Therese:

For some time now I have been owing you a response to your note about my opening address at the Pre-Congress Conference on Training in Copenhagen.[1]

Since this presentation was the beginning of the conference, it was my intention not to give answers but to point up problem areas, to circumscribe them, and to outline the different directions into which the search for answers to the various questions could be moving.

I did not discuss the differentiation of social psychology from psychoanalytic psychology in my address, but would still like to clarify my outlook.

1. I do not imply a value judgment by the term social psychology; in particular I do not use it as a pejorative term, i.e., as something that is of lesser value than psychoanalytic psychology.

2. Social psychology and psychoanalytic psychology cannot be differentiated by the subject matter that is being investigated ("intrapsychic processes" as against "the psychoanalytic situation," etc.), but by the method of observation, by the theoretical background which organizes our observational attitude, and by the theoretical framework within which we formulate the results of our observations. Since I have attempted to make the differentiation a number of times (especially in my paper on "Introspection," etc.; but also, for example, quite recently, in my paper on narcissism: see the discussion on page 245) I will not spell out my reasoning again but rather refer you to these previous statements.

3. A final remark: psychoanalysis should continue to use theoretical formulations on several levels: close to the empathically observed facts (whether they concern one person, two people, or a crowd) and at a greater distance from them. The former needs no special encouragement since it is in line with the natural inclination of most people in our field. The latter, however (i.e., psychoanalytic metapsychology in the strict sense of the word) does need support, since—in addition to the gift of empathic observation—it requires the disciplined, hard

earned capacity for abstract thinking and for the translation of observational data into theoretical symbols.

With my affectionate regards,
Cordially,
Heinz Kohut, M.D.

1. *Search*, 1:461–75.

November 3, 1967
Miss Anna Freud
London
Dear Miss Freud:

I am sending you, enclosed, the introduction to the chapter on the Idealizing Transference which I announced to you in my previous letter about a month ago. I had hoped that I would also be able to send you the revision of the unfortunate case history but, with the December meetings coming up, and with a number of deadlines around the corner, I do not see how I can manage to devote myself to that in the near future. I believe, however, that the introduction can be read by itself and that the case history which I am now planning to write up rather extensively will not seem too disconnected when I send it to you at a later date.

In addition to pursuing the narcissism studies which—in keeping with my own theories about creativity; but these moods are experienced quite naively—I consider at times to constitute a substantial contribution to our field, while at other times I feel desperate about their worthlessness, I am working (as chairman of an Association committee) on problems of psychoanalytic research, in particular on the question of what one could do, in practical and not so practical ways, to encourage and support creativeness in the central areas of psychoanalysis.[1] This is an intensely interesting topic and I believe that I and my committee which includes [Seymour] Lustman, [Peter] Neubauer, Douglas Bond, [Russell] Anderson, and Gedo, have had some exciting ideas about it. We are planning to show the reports of our first two meetings (the third will be held in December) to a number of selected creative people in our field and to ask them for their reaction. You are on the list and will, I hope, get a copy of the reports of our deliberation in the not too distant future. I hope that you will read them and give us the benefit of your thoughts, but I do not want to put you under any obligation—I trust that you know that I mean what I say. If you have no time to react to it, please don't force yourself to give a reply.

And if you have no time to read our reports, please don't burden yourself with them but put them aside.

We are all settled down to our routines. Tom is working hard and consistently this year—he is especially enjoying a course on Melville which is given on a high level of scholarliness and by a teacher who, I believe, combines enough similarities with the father and yet enough striking differences from him to make him a fine object of idealization for an adolescent. We all hope to hear from you some time if only a line to tell us how you are. Give our best to Dorothy B. The enclosed stamps are, of course, for Paula, and Tom sends a special greeting to Coco.

Sincerely yours,

Heinz Kohut, M.D.

1. *Search*, 2:589–614; see also *JAPA* 17 (1969): 1180.

December 10, 1967 [from Anna Freud]

Dear Heinz Kohut,

You may think that it took me a long time to answer your letter and enclosure of November 3rd. The reason is very simple. Times here were not only extremely full of work but also troubled by personal matters. Dr. Hoffer's death shook us all. My brother Ernst is no better than before. Our Dr. [Josephine] Stross in the Clinic as well as our Dr. [Liselotte] Frankl have been ill for a long time. The N[ational].I[nstitutes of].M[ental].H[ealth]. in Washington left the Clinic in anxiety about renewal of grant[s] for many months. And so on. There was more than usual to fill one's mind.

At the moment we are snowed in. The snowfall is by no means as bad as yours last year. But England reacts to a few inches already with a complete disruption of traffic everywhere. There are hundreds of vehicles štalled on the roads. We were lucky not to be caught in it. But inability to move also makes for additional time at the typewriter.

I was quite delighted with your photographs which came already. I think the pictures are excellent, without exception. Difficult to say which is the better likeness, Betty, or Tom, or Marianne, or the mountains. Thank you very much! And thank you very much for the welcome pencils. As you know, I am addicted to pencils and can never have enough.

I sent a small present to Tom by mail which, I hope, will arrive. Betty's jacket [knitted by Anna Freud] will be taken by messenger to New York and will come from there. I hope it will fit. If not, please return!

And now to your letter. I would be most interested to read reports on research in psychoanalysis. It might give me ideas for the Clinic. Also I wonder very much what you recommend and whether you succeed in keeping it really "analytical." Please, do not hesitate to send something.

Now comes the most important part of your sendings: "The Idealising Transference."

1. THE IDEALISING TRANSFERENCE.

I read the chapter carefully, more than once, and I agree that it is very much clearer than before. I had no difficulty this time to follow your exact meaning, which is after all not too complicated. What emerges much clearer now is the relationship of the narcissistic processes to the object related ones, and also of the earlier to the later events. Especially the overlaying of early experience with later experience comes out very well.

On the other hand, there is still the need to read certain passages twice, and experience says that many readers will not trouble to do that. My feeling is that this is entirely due to the *Einschachtelungen* [insertions], sometimes in brackets, sometimes in dashes, and sometimes in footnotes. They break the flow of thought, instead of emphasizing it, as you mean them to do. If these passages were spelled out fully in the text, it would make it much easier for the reader.

On p. 9 you say quite rightly that the reliability of empathy declines where the observed is dissimilar to the observer. That sounds very true. But in the case of the first year of life, is it really the dissimilarity of the infant from the adult? Is it not above all the absence of speech? Wherever speech is absent, we are kept guessing, also where the observed object is similar to us. That is really the reason why child analysis is so often unreliable. The child expresses itself too much in action, in symbols, etc., and then our interpretations go wild.

On p. 9b you quote me. I think it would avoid misunderstandings if you preceded the quotation by the words "In these cases . . ." People might think that I do not believe in proper transference altogether otherwise.

I find it very convincing that the original narcissistic relationship to the parental objects leave their traces in the later object-relationship and can be revived again, together with them, or in isolation. I wonder whether it would not be worthwhile to follow this more closely into the concept of "falling in love." The present analytic explanation considers this phenomenon exclusively from the quantitative point of view: i.e., too much libido is concentrated on the object, also those amounts which, by rights, should remain fixed to the self. If you go from there to the *quality* of the libido, the explanation would run, that the normal object-libido in these instances carries with it the narcissistic admixtures, so that the object one is in love with acquires the status of an archaic idealized object.

Or, is that included in your thinking anyway?

Loss of object in early times, traumatic disappointment in the maternal or parental object: I have to add here that recently I acquired a mistrust of these concepts which are in such wide use now. The terms seem to imply that there were real events in the external world and I think only too often that this is not true. That what exerts an influence are purely internal fluctuations of cathexis. There are, of course, no undisturbed relationships, especially not in childhood where the demands on the object are so unrealistic.

I am thinking here of two of my own patients, both homosexual before their analysis, both narcissistic personalities, one of them besides an addict, the other an obsessional neurosis. Both of them had devoted mothers who never wavered in their attention to them. Both had siblings, and were themselves the youngest, which means that the presence of the siblings was a given and immutable fact from the beginning, not a traumatic event. In spite of this, they acted as if they had been deserted at some time by the mother, and the addiction quite obviously had to make up for this. What the analysis showed was an inordinate jealousy of the siblings which turned every attention paid to them by the mother into a traumatic experience. Would you call this a disappointment or loss of the object? In reality it is an inordinate demand with disastrous consequences. Is it a special oversensitiveness and shakiness of object-relationship, i.e., a failure of frustration tolerance in this respect? Whatever it is, I believe it should not be confused with a real life experience such as death, separation, neglect, etc. Is it perhaps a narcissistic quality in the object relationship which turns every slight into a deadly insult?

These are just some of my thoughts which accompanied the reading. They are not worth very much, but you will take them for what they are: signs of interest in what you are producing.

I look forward very much to the case history.

Yours very sincerely,

Anna Freud

1968–1970

"Such means of political pressure as hungerstrikes and conscientious-objector status are foreign to me."

January 4, 1968
Miss Anna Freud
London
Dear Miss Freud,

You are so kind! The cufflinks for Tom, the beautiful sweater for Betty, the lovely photographs (especially the priceless shot of Coco and you) and above all your very helpful comments concerning my efforts!

What you have to say is of very great help to me. I have found hardly anything with which I disagree, but I do gain a great deal from your remarks because they point up to me where I have not been clear, where I have been ambiguous, and where I have failed to follow a line of thought to its conclusion. This is not an easy essay (mono-graph?) to write. The concentrated preoccupation with regressed states after a day of analytic work is often hard on men, and I believe that some of the lack of clarity of certain statements is more an outgrowth of inner conflicts than of an intellectual failing. Be that as it may: I would also be happy if I had more time for this work. Occasionally it may take me several hours to catch on again to a line of thought that I had meant to pursue, and there are, of course, not so many hours available. I am nevertheless hopeful that I am making a contribution concerning an area which has not been systematically integrated with the mainstream of psychoanalytic thought. I do know that my insights have been of great practical help to a number of analysts who are coming to me for regular consultation—supervision with suitable cases—and I am even toying with the idea of following up the clinical monograph with a case book composed of the cohesive presentation of three analytic cases treated by three different analysts under my intensive supervision. But that is for the future![1]

I will not try to "reply" to the details of your commentary at this time. I am enclosing the case history which follows directly the part on which you commented, and some of your comments will, I believe, find a "reply" in this case presentation. I can only say that in one form or another I shall be responding to your comments (in the most recent letter, in your earlier letter, and, I hope, in a future one) in the work itself; but I will also try to react to specific points that you have been raising after you have had a chance to look at the case without which some issues must still have remained incomplete.

We are very sorry that so many things have been going wrong with your surroundings in London but perhaps by now these are mostly things of the past. I hope so. Please tell Dorothy that the little paper knife is a wonderful object; just right to be held and admired and cherished. It is lovely.

A little while ago we had a long-distance telephone conversation with Marianne who is just getting over the flu. Her voice was low and slightly hoarse, she still does a good deal of coughing, but she seemed cheerful and as happy to talk with us as we were happy to talk with her. In February I will be in Frankfurt at the Sigmund Freud Institut for three days, and then go from there to the New York Institute for a one-day colloquium on narcissism. I trust that I will see Marianne at that time.

And now warmest regards to you from all of us, and once more my gratitude for your interest which, apart from the circumscribed valuable advice that it provides, is of great emotional assistance to me.

Sincerely,

Heinz Kohut, M.D.

1. *The Psychology of the Self: A Casebook*, ed. Arnold Goldberg (New York, 1978).

January 25, 196[8] [from Anna Freud]

Dear Dr. Kohut,

Just before your letter came, I had one from Dr. Piers enclosing a proposal from the University of Chicago Press to publish a record of the various Institute events during my stay in bookform, revised from the various transcripts. My opinion, which I wrote to Dr. Piers, was negative, as I suppose yours would be also. To publish the "Ideal Institute" talk now would be premature. The various discussions were wholly based on clinical material (who would want to read it all?) and were not sufficiently thought through for publication. On the whole, informal discussions are not the proper basis for publications. I hope therefore that the whole idea will be dropped. On the other hand, I told Dr. Piers that I am very willing to revise transcriptions for internal Institute use. What I had in mind there was especially to hurry up the transcriptions of the "Ideal Institute" so as to insert the footnote as you suggest it and as I had planned it already. Can you do anything to urge the appearance of the transcript? So far, I had occasion only in a letter to Mrs. Gitelson to stress that point. She had remarked especially on this "selection problem" in a letter to me, and I answered that this was a point taken over from you from my correspondence with you.

I look forward to your paper on Transference and Counter-Transference, in whichever form and state of completion it arrives.

Do you realise that, with the Pre-Congress time added, we shall be in Copenhagen [a] full 10 days? I ordered my room, feeling that it was a terribly long time, too long for a Congress. I hear from Marianne Kris that she will be travelling with you and your family on the Continent afterwards.

Paula was delighted with the stamps and sends many thanks. Coco is very well. He feels he owes Tovey a letter. He has not decided yet whether to write by paw or whether, by rights, there should be nice type-writers, electric or not, for dogs.

My brother Ernst is still not as well as he should be and sometimes very discouraged since he feels that he makes no visible progress. We all worry about him, but there is very little one can do to help. He is by nature so active, that the enforced inactivity together with his tiredness is especially hard to bear for him.

The Clinic had an exciting week with 5 people from the N.I.M.H. in Washington coming for the site-visit. It went off surprisingly well and none of my gloomy predictions based on earlier experience came true this time. The inspecting visitors were very friendly, very positive and very interested. We hope that they will recommend our application. Then, of course, comes the next step which is financial, and this may depend on the state and the expenses of the Vietnam war. I am all for ending that.

We also have the excitement of having been offered another house in Maresfield Gardens which we should love to acquire to ease our congestion. The money is available from last year's "birthday fund." What we are waiting for is formal permission from the Borough Council to use the premises for Clinic purposes (in a residential area). This may not be given, or given too late. It is like a game of chance.

Excuse the various typing mistakes. Even on an electric machine it is not easy to perform perfectly. I send greetings to the Olympia.

I have sent Tom another book (very impressed by his letter) and I send my greetings to Betty.

The Easter holidays still seem very far away.

Very sincerely yours,

Anna Freud

February 6, 1968
Mr. John F. Hayward
Meadville Theological School
Chicago
Dear Jack:

I read your letter a number of times and my contact with your concerns increased at each reading. Your problems and doubts are mine also, and I have no simple solution to offer to the question which you imply. But perhaps a re-phrasing of the dilemma. Could it not be that we are not moving to a "stark rationalism and existentialism of the coming era," not to a "thoroughly secular society" but toward an as yet unfathomable new stable synthesis of the human depths and surface? and could it not be that the stark rationalism of which we sometimes think as our future as well as the nostalgic return to the values of yesterday are just oscillations of the historical moment as we are moving toward the yet unknown territory of a new durable solution? Of course, I don't know whether this is so, but if humanity still has sufficient powers of life, then a cultural genius, one step ahead [of] the rest of humanity, will come forth with a new balance of deeply founded values and goals, and life will go on. What I spoke about at the dinner table (the psychological analysis of the failure of the Weimar Republic)[1] was the analysis of a small historical wave. Such attempts are not unimportant because they allow us to understand certain principles (the same holds true for the insights gained in the analysis of one individual) but they do not take into account the successful cultural mutation in which a whole set of new values establishes a new psychosocial balance and gives a new viable meaning to life which lasts not for the historical moment but for a long period—just as did Jewish monotheism and Christian ethics during the past few thousand years.

It was good of you to tell us of your enjoyment of the dinner party. We enjoyed it, too, of course, and despite the fact that I am harboring a not inconsiderable streak of the ascetic, I consider the rejection of the enjoyment of the senses as blasphemy. Yet, to receive not only thanks for food and company but as deeply felt and thoughtful a response as your letter is truly the best a host can wish for.

Warm good wishes from Betty and me and the expression of the hope that our contact will not cease despite your move to Carbondale.

Cordially yours,

Heinz Kohut, M.D.

1. The government of Germany from the end of the First World War to the rise of Hitler to power in 1933.

February 15, 1968

Dr. Myriam G. dos Santos

Rio de Janeiro

Dear Dr. dos Santos:

What can I say to you, how can I express to you the feelings which the news of Julio's death evoked in me. My eyes were moist as I read your letter and I remembered ever so vividly the lovely evening that I was allowed to spend at your home with Julio and you and in the company of Drs. Besouchet and Carlos Whiting. I remember the sleeping child in its crib upstairs, the older one who stayed with us for a while, the dinner, the servants' singing, and a general feeling of peace and contentment which surrounded us. I remember the contrast between Julio's quiet and proud seriousness and your lively happiness, and how one could sense the complementary nature of the two of you and how much he and you and the children were forming a unit. And all this is now broken up and he has to live on as a memory, through the work he has done, and through you and his children.

You are very brave and that is not only very admirable but also very lucky. You are not trying to escape from the pain but you are keeping it alive and you are struggling with it as you must until you can again devote all of your life forces and all your strengths to the world, and especially to your children. I have no doubt that your vitality will enable you to surmount the inner and outer difficulties with which Julio's death is facing you; everything in the tone of your letter points to the fact that you are one of those unusual people who can turn into victory the severest blow that can be imagined. The demands of your children, the birth of your next child, and the demands of life in general will call forth the very forces which are so abundantly your own and, gradually, a new balance will establish itself. And even though the loss can never be replaced, life will be full and meaningful again for you.

My wife and I send you and your children our warmest good wishes. Do send me Julio's biography and let us know about further developments.

With affectionate greetings,
Yours,
Heinz Kohut, M.D.

March 12, 1968
Professor Alexander Mitscherlich
Frankfurt/Main
Dear Alexander:

Back in Chicago (and almost re-adjusted after the two time changes) I am remembering with warm pleasure my work at the Sigmund Freud Institute and the splendid hours that I had with Margarete and you. You are outstanding hosts and it was great to be with you; I am worried only that you spent so much money on entertaining me. But I will admit that I enjoyed every moment.

I read your address about peace and human aggression and found it to be a sound and dignified statement.[1] As you undoubtedly realize I would expand your conceptions in one more direction. The prolonged infantile state required by the extended immaturity of the human young leads not only to the intensification of early object relations and thus to fixations in the realm of object love and object aggression, but also to a great internal elaboration of the infantile self and thus to fixations in the realm of narcissism. The elaboration of the self leads not only to a strong unconscious focus containing an almost ineradicable sense of the uniqueness of the self and an unrealistic overestimation of its value, but also to the persistent tendency to experience the mere otherness of others as offensive. The human animal is thus burdened with the tendency to react with narcissistic rage to this mere otherness of others, i.e., in particular to the fact that others do not obey him unconditionally as do his thoughts, his limbs, and his actions. Although these attitudes may be more or less overlayered by the realistic acceptance of our own relativity (in humor, acceptance of transience, wisdom, etc.) these achievements are hard to come by and are reliably obtained by only a few.

But you must by now have had your fill of Kohut about narcissism and I will not elaborate further. Once more my warmest thanks to you and Margarete, and greetings to all my colleagues.

Cordially,

Heinz Kohut, M.D.

1. "Die Idee des Friedens und die menschliche Aggressivität" (January 26, 1968), in Mitscherlich, *Die Idee des Friedens und die menschliche Aggressivität: Vier Versuche* (Frankfurt/Main, 1969), pp. 105–37.

March 19, 1968

Miss Anna Freud

London

Dear Miss Freud:

First, concerning the "permission to quote." I am assuming you intend to quote from statements made by me (either in my letter to [Douglas] Bond or during the discussions as recorded) and not from a report of the Committee itself [see above, November 3, 1967].[1] Although you might assume that a particular statement contained in such a report was written by me, it would still have to be considered as a statement by the Committee (with me as just its spokesman)[2] and the permission to quote would then probably have to be obtained from the Association under whose auspices the Committee is functioning.

Second, your request that I define "the *fringe area* of psychoanalysis, in contrast to the *core*." For the following reasons I do not think that one should give such a definition. The "core" should be defined (and, if necessary, redefined); the various areas which surround the cores in all directions, however, can be followed in a centrifugal direction without a clear border. In other words, we encounter the age-old problem of the continuum and are running the danger of being pedantic if we exclude areas close to the center and absurd if we include areas that are too far away. (You will remember your father's splendid simile in *The Ego and the Id* [1923], *Standard Edition*, [vol.] 19, p. 16, n. [gradations of light do not mean there is no darkness].) The whole area outside the core is, as I once defined it in the title of an essay on applied analysis, "Beyond the Bounds of the Basic Rule." Every time we are asking ourselves whether a scientific or therapeutic activity belongs to analysis we should (pre-consciously) have the core in mind and consider the essence of the core as we assess the relevance of the applied in the periphery. But I am afraid that there are no definitions that can reliably assist us here; each judgment must be separate, and each time the essence should be invoked (yet not directly applied). An analyst's insightful interpretation of one turn of a phrase of a poet, for example, might enrich analysis and should, therefore, be counted as belonging to analysis. Or, during clinical psychoanalysis consider for example an action as seemingly unanalytical as an analyst's phone call to a patient to communicate an addition to an insight obtained during the session; or, as another example, the seemingly unanalytic indulgence of speculating with the patient about some possible condition during the childhood of the patient's parents. Such actions, if handled by an analyst who has achieved technical mastery, may not only be fully compatible with the basic analytic principles, but might be decisive aids on the road to the ultimate goal of analysis: an increased mastery of the ego which is based on the expansion of its realm. Yet, on the other hand, there are examples of activities that externally look ever so much more like "the core," both in research and in therapy, but are yet not analysis. There is the couch, there is the basic rule, and there is even attention to transference and resistance. And yet, either because the analyst has undergone a personality change since

he became an analyst, or because the whole system in which he was
brought up analytically taught only an external compliance with the
appearance of "the core," or for other reasons, everything that happens is off center. In a number of instances of this kind the fault
appears to me to lie in the fact that the analytic method is applied in
order to prove a pre-formed essentially unanalytic hypothesis, i.e., a
hypothesis which deals with concepts that fit into the cognitive realm
of social psychology or clinical medicine but is foreign to the cognitive
approach which characterizes psychoanalysis. Thus I suspect that research enterprises ordered around a hypothesis concerning the effects
of specific gross external events in early life lead us away from the
core of analysis even though the investigative method itself remains
analytic. And the same holds true for the use of analysis in the investigation of psychosomatic disease entities. I believe in other words that
unless hypothesis formation itself is analytic, and was inspired by
analytic work and modes of thought, the work instituted to investigate
the correctness of the hypothesis, be its method ever so analytic, will
yet not produce an analytically valid result. (It probably goes without
saying that, in general, the method itself will in the long run tend to
deviate subtly or grossly from the classical model, and that for instance
such elements as quantified opinion polls about recorded material will
be added to support the insights obtained in the basic clinical situation.)

But one could go on forever. My real preference is to avoid a definition of the "fringe" or the "periphery"; to stick to attempts to define
the "core"; and to be liberal yet thoughtful in judging the distance
from the center. If I had to commit myself on a definition, then I would
reluctantly say that every accretion to knowledge should be considered
as belonging to analysis as a science that has been obtained (observed
and formulated) on the basis of introspective or empathic psychological activities by someone whose outlook on the psychological field has
been shaped by the grasp of the ordering principles of metapsychology
(the dynamic, economic, genetic, and topographic-structural points of
view).[3] In general I would expect the observer and the formulator to
have remained in touch with the "core" experience, whatever his
fringe application might be. I also believe strongly that we should not
deny that the raw data with which we are dealing are already complex
psychological configurations which, however, can be directly observed
on the basis of the fact that the experiences of the observer are similar
to those of the observed. But here I am probably introducing a side
issue. In the introductory chapter of my paper on introspection, and,

especially, in the paragraph which overlaps pp. 854–55 in my "Autonomy and Integration," I have addressed myself to some aspects of the problem on which you wanted my opinion.

Sincerely yours,

Heinz Kohut, M.D.

1. Anna Freud was to give the New York Psychoanalytic Society's Freud Lecture; see John Leo, "Youth Said to See Analysis as Passé," *New York Times*, April 17, 1968.

2. Kohut subsequently endured criticism that he had appropriated the ideas of the committee members in his report. See Gerhart Piers to Albert Solnit, April 15, 1971; and Kohut to Solnit, April 19, 1971.

3. Freud's five conceptualizations of the mental apparatus: topographical (1892), i.e., unconscious/preconscious/conscious; economic (1900), or quantitative notion of sexual energy (libido) and its vectors (cathexis); genetic (1905); or historical and evolutionary view of the origin and development of mental states; dynamic (1923), the conflict of energies in terms of psychological content; and the structural (1926) theory of opposing psychic systems of ego, id, and superego.

April 5, 1968 [from Anna Freud]

Dear Heinz and Betty Kohut,

Thank you so much for the surprise of the absolutely magnificent azaleas. It makes me feel as if I were at least a Hollywood star. You should see how beautiful it looks in my apartment here.

Congratulations for Tom! I hope he will enjoy Oberlin. You will miss him at home, I am sure.

Many thanks for the letters of March 19th and 24th.

I was very glad to have the answer to the "core and fringe areas." I had hopes that it would be that way. Especially the sentence about "metapsychological thinking" coincides wholly with the idea on which my paper is based: that what is getting lost gradually in present-day analysis is the ability to think metapsychologically which does not mean "theoretically, divorced from clinical material," but means to look at clinical data from all the 4 or 5 metapsychological aspects simultaneously and to relate them to each other, especially with regard to their relevance for the dynamic functions of the ego in therapy. You call that "creative," and so do others. But is it not really a "creative act"?

Many greetings,

Yours,

Anna Freud

April 10, 1968
Miss Anna Freud
New Haven, Connecticut
Dear Miss Freud:

It was good to talk to you and to receive your letter. I am glad that the azaleas made you feel as if you were "at least a Hollywood star" and that they look nice in your apartment.

I was not surprised to learn about our essential agreement concerning the "core and the fringe" of psychoanalysis. Your doubt about the correctness of my reference to the analyst's insights as minor creative acts, however, is important and I will give further thought to the topic. The simple application of the metapsychological points of view, and even relating them to each other as you say, would not be "creative." But the fact that the analyst's Unconscious is an active participant in his task, that there is "even-hovering attention" rather than focussed attention, and perhaps your reference to the fact that the analyst looks at the clinical data "from all the 4 or 5 metapsychological aspects *simultaneously*" (my underlining) makes me wonder whether "creative" is not the right term after all. I have more a mode of cognition in mind here than a value judgment.

But be that as it may: I have a request. May I show our interchange concerning the fringe areas to the members of the Committee on Scientific Activities? If you allow me to do so I will, of course, delete everything from the correspondence that does not belong strictly to this topic.

Betty and I will be going to New York next Tuesday and will attend your lecture. We will then stay in New York for the rest of the week, go to New Haven Friday evening, and will return to Chicago after your Sunday lecture. We are very much looking forward to seeing you and Dorothy soon.

Sincerely,
Heinz Kohut, M.D.

May 5, 1968 [from Anna Freud]
Dear Heinz Kohut,

I came home again last night, with six days of very good holiday in Puerto Rico making a very nice lazy contrast to the busy time that had gone before. I was sorry that there was not some free time to have a talk when we met.

I am writing about something special to-day. I had a telephone conversation with Jeanne Lampl to-day to ask her about the Congress papers which had come in in the meantime. I wanted to know whether you had announced your new study of the analysis of narcissism. She said that you had not. May I urge you very much to do it? I am afraid that there will be very few good contributions and I have the feeling that yours is really new and very much needed.

Give my love to the family. To-morrow work begins again.

Yours sincerely,

Anna Freud

June 1, 1968 [from Anna Freud]

Dear Heinz Kohut,

Thank you for your letter of May 26th. I think I ought to explain in greater detail what I meant with my letter about a Congress paper on your ideas about Narcissism.

Certainly, it would not mean repeating a letter [sic] which you have given already. As you know, what is wanted for the next Congress is something quite different. What they have in mind is more in the nature of a statement what alterations or additions to the existing theories the author considers as beneficial and why. In your case that would mean a statement [regarding] which parts of a patient's mind have up to now escaped therapy by virtue of not belonging to the realm of object relationship but to the narcissistic core; what steps you think should be taken to include them; in which form they will appear in treatment and in the transference; what abnormalities can then be included in therapy, etc. I thought that probably you could extract all this from your paper, as you had written it, and prepare it in this form.

My real reason for urging you was, and is, that I am sure that many worthless innovations will be presented and that it is terribly important to have some valuable ones included.

I am still catching up on work missed here during April!

Love to Betty and Tom,

Yours sincerely,

Anna Freud

June 11, 1968

Miss Anna Freud

London

Dear Miss Freud:

The purpose of this letter is twofold. First, it has the most pleasant task of carrying to you our congratulations regarding the honor bestowed on you by Yale University. We read the account in the *New York Times* [June 11], including brief summaries of the citations to the recipients of honorary degrees, and concluded that it must have been an exceptionally dignified and impressive occasion.

I feel miserable having now to turn to the second message, namely that I have decided not to present my narcissism studies at the [IPA] congress in Rome. To give you my reasons in detail would be cumbersome but, whatever their shortcomings, I can say that my decision was not arrived at lightly. I weighed the obligation to contribute to the success of the next congress against what I owe to myself, to my work, and perhaps also, if my work has merit, to analysis as a whole. I am not able to produce a meaningful twenty-minute summary of my complex, interrelated formulations with their interweaving of theory and practice; I think it would be wrong to spend the time that I had set aside for moving on with the monograph on writing yet another abbreviated version for prepublication in the *International Journal* (5000 to 7000 words are asked for, i.e., about two-thirds of the length of my recent Freud Lecture on the same topic ["The Psychoanalytic Study of Narcissistic Personality Disorders"]; and finally—a secondary consideration—I do not believe that the presentation of my approach to a form such as has been designed for the Rome congress is either conducive to making the audience understand what I am after nor is it likely to provide the kind of informed criticism that would give me optimal stimulation to bringing my work to a conclusion.

I am very concerned about the possibility that you will not consider my reasons to be valid. They are, after all, to some extent personal ones, i.e., bound up with the slowness with which I work, the amount of time consumed in the preparation of even routine condensations, and the specific need to seek that type of understanding critical attitude toward my work that is helpful to me, and to avoid rejections after only superficial acquaintance with my approach that tend to be a hindrance to me.

The only way in which I can at the moment see myself presenting my ideas at a congress would be in the setting of a workshop, with a limited number of participants whom (prior to the publication of my monograph) I would expect that they have studied my two papers. Two analysts who have treated cases of narcissistic personality disturbance under my intensive supervision could present their cases, and I could comment, answer questions, and engage in a free discussion with the participants. Such workshops concerning ongoing research have been held for some years at the meetings of the A. Psa Assn under the chairmanship of the leading investigator involved in the research under discussion ([Joan] Fleming, to give one example, has chaired workshops on the analysis of "parent-loss cases"). Perhaps at some future international congress such a workshop could be organized—it may not fit in the context of the organization of the forthcoming one. I know that the two analysts whom I supervised would be willing to cooperate.

And now warm greetings from all of us. Tom, to add a bit of good news, who is graduating from highschool this week, has found a summer job as a counselor in a school for disturbed latency children. He is very excited about this, his first, job and a bit afraid of the awesome responsibility. He will be in charge of nine children at the school in Wisconsin.

Sincerely,
Heinz Kohut, M.D.

June 18, 1968[1]
Honorable Everett M. Dirksen
United States Senate
Washington, D.C.
Dear Senator Dirksen:

Although I am in general not inclined to write letters to members of the United States Congress and trust that our elected representatives will be appropriately guided by their own insight and conscience I feel prompted to let you know that I am dismayed by the organized campaign against the enactment of laws to control the use and sale of firearms. I strongly believe that such laws should be instituted and that the arguments are spurious which claim that free men will be deprived of their right to be armed and sportsmen deprived of their pleasure in hunting. I understand that the argument is being advanced that laws to control the sale of firearms and to license their use are just a first step and that one should fight against such first steps in order to forestall later ones. With this logic any legislation could be barred. Any proper step could be opposed on the grounds that it is just preparing a subsequent improper one, and there is no rule or regulation that could not be opposed on such grounds. If an unjustly restrictive law should be proposed, it should be fought; but a good law cannot be fought because it might be the forerunner of a bad one.

There are many arguments in favor of strict gun control, quite independent of the recent assassinations which have brought this matter into the forefront of public consciousness.[2] To be brief: human society must protect the rights and security of all individuals, and thus it is obliged to see to it that potentially dangerous instruments, whatever their other use might be, should be handled with care and should be handled by people who know their use and can be trusted with their use. An automobile is certainly an instrument that serves transportation, pleasure, etc. Yet its use has potential dangers and there are therefore laws and regulations that attempt to ensure that only persons who can be trusted as drivers should receive a license. Before a certain age the driving of cars is not permitted. After a certain age there have to be regular examinations of the driver. Certain physical and mental defects exclude a person from the right to drive a car. And finally: the driver must be insured in order to be able to take care of the damage that he might inflict on others' health, life, or property. The same considerations that apply to the drivers of cars apply also, and with at least equal propriety, to those who wish to use firearms. The buying of firearms should be a responsible act and the buyer should know that he is buying an instrument the use of which involves great responsibilities. Guns should be sold only to people who are (1) physically healthy insofar as it relates to the appropriate use of guns (proper eyesight, for example); (2) emotionally stable; (3) skilled in the use of the weapon which they are buying. I believe strongly that the license to buy a gun and to own a gun should be given only after the buyer passes an examination in which he proves that he is aware of the dangers and that he knows how to use the weapon. Finally, as we mentioned before, there should be compulsory insurance for damages that the owner of a gun might inflict.

Whatever the details of a future legislation on the control of the sale and use of firearms, may I urge you strongly not to be influenced by the arguments of those who are either financially interested in the free sale of guns or by those for whom the possession of arms means something else than simply the ownership of a sensible instrument for a sportsman's enjoyment or of a measure of security under rare, specific circumstances.

Sincerely yours,

Heinz Kohut, M.D.

1. This letter also went to Senator Charles Percy and Congressman Barrett O'Hara. There is no record of replies to these letters.

2. Martin Luther King had been shot in April, Robert Kennedy in June. See also above, December 29, 1963.

June 18, 1968
Robert G. Page, M.D.
President, The Quadrangle Club
Chicago
Dear Bob:

I am writing this letter to you to express my sadness and concern about a small, but I think not insignificant experience which I had in the Quadrangle Club a few weeks ago.

For some time now it has become a cherished tradition between my son and me to go out once or twice a year for a stag dinner either at the Quadrangle Club or elsewhere and to end the evening with a leisurely father-son game of billiards at the Club. We did so again a few weeks ago, but after I had received the three billiard balls I was to my dismay informed by the young man at the desk that my son, being under twenty-one, was not allowed to play with me but could only watch me. When I protested that after all we had played many times before without anyone objecting, that my son was eighteen, and that he would go to college in the fall, that he was registered with the Selective Service System, etc., I was told in a friendly but firm manner, that there was nothing that the man in charge could do since he was only following instructions and that the instructions had been given him by the Manager, who, he understood, was acting in accordance with a recent decision by the Board of Directors. We complied of course without any further protest, and the evening, which had begun so pleasantly, ended on this note of disappointment.

A few days later I asked to talk with the General Manager of the Quadrangle Club. In our telephone conversation Mr. Fulop, in a most cordial yet firm manner, stated again what I had been told by the man at the desk, namely that the Board of Directors of the Club had recently decided that only members of the Club and their adult guests were allowed to use the billiard tables, that "children" would have to be excluded. When I said that my son was in his nineteenth year, Mr. Fulop explained that the age limit was twenty-one.

Since I still felt a good deal of disappointment about the rule and had not given up hope that something could be done about it, I asked Mr. Fulop about the reasons for this measure. Mr. Fulop gave me a number of them: (a) that groups of young people had done serious damage to the felt with their cues and had left marks on the tables by putting their soft drink glasses on them; (b) that the tables should be reserved for "serious players" and that they should not be used for children's games, as it were; (c) that there were only two tables and that they should be kept free for the use of the serious players in the

Club. I tried to object to some of these reasons but must admit that
Mr. Fulop had friendly but cogent replies in each case. When I said
that irresponsible behavior by a group of youngsters should not lead
to the exclusion of others who behaved responsibly, Mr. Fulop said
that one could not devise rules that take such differences into account
and that, unfortunately, the innocent had to suffer for those who behaved improperly. When I said that, after all, the Club was completely
empty when we were there, that we were not keeping any of the
"serious players" from playing, and that I as a member of the Club
was of course taking full responsibility for any damage that my son or
I would cause, Mr. Fulop answered that actual competition for the
tables at any given moment was not the issue but that, in principle,
the tables were for "serious players." To the statement that I would, of
course, be responsible for any damage, Mr. Fulop replied that damage
would often appear as late as two weeks after the felt had been weakened and that even with the best of intentions to shoulder the responsibility the fact of the damage inflicted on the table would simply not
be apparent at the time.

I will not go into any further details about my friendly and informative conversation with Mr. Fulop since, though on a much higher
echelon of responsibility, Mr. Fulop again was simply implementing
a decision of the Board of Directors and was only doing his duty by
defending it.

I must admit however that my doubts about the appropriateness of
this policy has not been put to rest. Must one really in a club such as
ours have steadfastly applied rules of this type in which the responsible and careful are punished for the transgressions of the irresponsible
and careless? Must one really consider as "a child" a young man in
his nineteenth year (registered with the Draft and going to college) for
the purposes of excluding him from the use of a billiard table, especially when he is the guest of his father? Is there not a way of setting
up a policy in such a manner that its implementation is enforced when
it is really indicated but not when even the most superficial scrutiny
will tell the observer that the reasons for which it was instituted do
not apply? There can be no question, I believe, about the fact—even
disregarding my grey hair—that I am a serious and responsible and
adult member of the Club, and that this was not going to be a wild
party of "children" who would damage the tables and mess up the
premises. Could there not be some greater kindness, some greater
concern for the varieties and nuances of human behavior, and the
responses that are appropriate to them in the policies and rules of a
private club in a university community? We are after all not members

of a military establishment, tend, in general, not to be rigid disciplinarians, but—whether we work in the humanities or in the biological sciences—have all learned to respect the individual and to pay attention to the specific details of the circumstances in which we respond to him.

But I will resist philosophical speculation. I am afraid that you may think the length of this epistle quite disproportionate to the tiny event which prompted it. But if you think yourself into the situation that I confronted and if you realize that I let quite a few weeks pass before responding to it with this letter, you might understand better what motivates me. I hope very much that the Board of Directors will be able to modify the present policy so that my son and I can again end our stag evening once or twice a year by playing a game of billiards, before he reaches the ripe old age of twenty-one.

Cordially yours,

Heinz Kohut, M.D.

June 23, 1968 [from Anna Freud]

Dear Dr. Kohut,

Thank you for your letter of June 11th and for your congratulations. The ceremony in Yale University was very nice indeed. It was the first time that I experienced it happening in the open, on an enormous campus, filled with the students, and their families behind them. It reminded me above all of the last act of the Meistersingers and I have the feeling that whoever devised it, must have had something of the kind in mind. I walked in a procession all round the campus, suitably disguised in cap and gown! Following it, I also attended the smaller ceremony in the Law School where I had to give a short speech. BOAC was surprised at the speed at which I flew back and forth.

And now about you. I feel gratified that you took my urging so seriously, but still I do not want you to have a bad conscience about not following it. Only one oneself can decide these matters as I know only too well. I suppose I underestimated the amount of work that a presentation at the Congress would mean for you. It seemed so easy (as things do from a distance) to show up the blocking of analyses by the narcissistic core and to show the advantages of entering into these and to create a "narcissistic transference," an event which was thought to be not feasible before. But you are probably right that people would not be impressed if it were put in these simple terms and that to explain it from the beginning is a complex task. If you feel that it is better to withhold the subject until full presentation is possible and that the risk of being misunderstood is too great, I accept that. Anyway, I want you to feel that I am with you.

Please, tell Tom that I am delighted about his summer job and that I look forward to hearing about his experiences later.

With many greetings to the whole family,

yours sincerely,

Anna Freud

July 5, 1968

Miss Anna Freud

London

Dear Miss Freud:

How perceptive you are, and how kind. Yes, in view of your urging, I had felt bad about my decision not to present my narcissistic studies in Rome, and I was very relieved when I read your warm and friendly letter. I have in the meantime accepted the chairmanship of one of the symposia in Rome.[1] Since the topic is "The Self" I should be able to put some of my new insights to good use. My Freud Lecture [in New York] will in the meantime have appeared in print[2] (did you receive the manuscript?) and people might have become more familiar with my thoughts and experiences.

The distractions from scientific work are unfortunately still great and the pressure on me to return to positions of organizational leadership is mounting. A group of New York friends (especially the Eisslers) have been alarmed about the potentially deleterious influence of the leading personalities in the American Psychoanalytic scene, and they are doing everything they can to persuade me to be a candidate for the presidency of the I.P.A., to follow [Jaap] van der Leuuw. I had thought that my decision was made and my mind sealed, and I believe that external pressure alone could not move me. Although once I am in a position of leadership, I enjoy my activities, am a responsible and conscientious administrator, and, what is much more important, am able to translate my ideals into suitable form which strengthens those who support analysis in our increasingly broad and diffuse ranks. I have hardly any drive at this time to strive for such a position and am prompted almost exclusively by a sense of duty. I am afraid that there is indeed the danger that the trend toward the integration of analysis with general psychiatry is in the process of being revived. Neither [Jacob] Arlow nor [Charles] Brenner have ever forgotten their defeat nor have they forgiven those who brought it about. Brenner, for example, in his parting speech as President of the American Psychoanalytic

Association lined up all the guns of his black-or-white logic, irony, and sarcasm against such non-threatening enemies as are the para-psychologists, and against such serious enemies (but not in the United States!) as are the Kleinians.[3] And, lo and behold!, who found himself suddenly in the same company of fuzzy-headed obfuscators? No other than I, because I had stressed the fact that since analysis is dealing with complex psychological configurations which are observed with the aid of empathy and introspection, it differed in essentials of methodology from the other biological and behavioral sciences.

I have learned long ago not to waste my anger in quarrels and I will not react to the provocation, especially in view of the fact that it was couched in a seemingly balanced and mild phraseology. Perhaps the final report of the Committee on Scientific Activities will give me a chance to discuss the question where and how analysis is similar to the other sciences and where and how the subject matter forces us to create our own methodology and our own system of theoretical formulations.

The real issue however is not a small one. It is the necessity of having to continue the watchful efforts on behalf of analysis on two, seemingly opposite, fronts: (a) against the foggy fantasies and the un-scientific mode of thinking of the id psychologists who see the psycho-logical world populated by depressed and paranoid babies; and (b) against those who are using the insights of ego psychology not in order to enrich their understanding of the interplay between the irra-tional and the rational aspects of the human mind, and of the more or less successful taming of the irrational in the service of the rational, but who have replaced the access to the understanding of the human mind in depth which your father opened to us by a preoccupation with the activities of the surface.

I know, of course, that one cannot help but be influenced by one's dominant experiences, and I know that you in England (and in a differ-ent form on the Continent: existential analysis, for example) had to confront those who disregard the powers of the ego. In America, as you also know, the opposite holds true. The in and of itself laudable interest in "technique," methodology, and theoretical systematizing, leads here often to a renewed surface behaviorism and considerations of professional acceptability, of merging with other disciplines (rather than a dialogue with them) are strong forces which endanger the sur-vival of analysis.

This has become a long communication; but these reflections are a background to the fact that people whose views I value highly have expressed deep concern and that I am urged to become a candidate for a four-year position which would seriously curtail the continuation of my scientific work. For the time being, I have stalled and said that I would see after my September vacation what progress I have been able to make with the monograph on which I am working.

And now only once more my gratitude for your understanding: it meant a great deal to me.

Warmly yours,

Heinz Kohut, M.D.

1. *Search*, 2:577–88.
2. *The Psychoanalytic Study of the Child* 23 (1968): 86–113; *Search*, 1:477–509.
3. Charles Brenner, "Psychoanalysis and Science," *JAPA* 16 (1968): 675–96. Cf. Kohut to Brenner, July 18, 1968: "I found your final scientific contribution at the Plenary Session in Boston a worthy ending of your year as President. I felt strongly that the whole audience was fully attentive throughout your address, that everyone enjoyed your clear and logical presentation and profited greatly from it." Kohut, however, penned a reply which he did not publish: see *Search*, 3:83–101. The "defeat" to which Kohut refers was the failure of the APA between 1958 and 1960 to approve by two-thirds majority a proposal to have psychoanalysis enrolled as a subspecialty of psychiatry by the American Board of Psychiatry and Neurology; see *JAPA* 8 (1960): 336–40. Brenner (personal communication, February 11, 1992) says that the proposal was neither his nor Arlow's, while Arlow (personal communication, February 15, 1992) says that, as APA president-elect in 1960–61, he was most concerned about the potential for a split within the organization. See also below, February 16, 1969.

July 12, 1968

Miss Anna Freud

London

Dear Miss Freud:

My eyes are always on the next analytic generation who will have to continue our work, and I am trying to identify the all-too-few who show unusual gifts and who promise to become significant contributors to analysis in the future. You know what a difficult task this is and how easily and how often one does get misled. Once in a while however one thinks that one has recognized genuine talent in a young analyst and feels stimulated to do what one can to further his professional and scientific development. In Chicago there are unfortunately very few people who show such promise. One of them is I believe Dr. John Gedo, a comparatively young analyst (he became a member of the American Psychoanalytic Association just about five years ago) who, because of his uncompromising and original thinking, has become increasingly disengaged from the local structure around the Institute and has turned toward private research pursuits. In view of my high opinion of his scientific potential I have supported him to the best of my ability. When I was President of the American Psychoanalytic Association I appointed him to one of the scientific committees, he has been serving as Secretary to the Committee on Scientific Activities, has worked with me on the regional workshop on narcissism, etc. Yet, I have wondered whether something more could be done for him and the thought occurred to me that it would be a particularly wholesome experience for him to spend some time with you, see the Hampstead Clinic at work, and get a chance to become stimulated by your mode of thinking and by your research methods. I asked Dr. Gedo whether such an idea would be of interest to him, and he responded with immediate warm enthusiasm. His time and resources are limited, but he thought that he could consider spending from four to six weeks in London in the late spring or early summer of 1969, supporting himself (though with some difficulty) for such a stay. Do you think that this idea is realistic and that it has merit? In order to familiarize you with the intellectual level and the analytic sophistication of this young analyst I am enclosing reprints of two of his small contributions which have just appeared. (You might be interested to know that he originally wanted to become a historian before he entered medical school to become an analyst.) If you want to see others of his writings, you can easily have access to them since all of them appeared, I believe, in the *Journal of the American Psychoanalytic Association.*

With my warmest regards,

Sincerely,

Heinz Kohut, M.D.

July 12, 1968

Mr. Alexandre Szombati

Brussels, Switzerland [*sic*]

Dear Mr. Szombati:

I am afraid that you will be disappointed with the meagre contribution that I can make to the important subject ["Professor Freud must be saved"] that you are investigating. Here are the facts that I remember. It must have been some day late in May, 1938, when Aichhorn with whom I was in analysis at that time mentioned to me that Freud was going to leave Vienna in about a week. He said that Freud's departure was being kept as quiet as possible and that he himself would therefore not go to the railroad station. Since I had never seen Freud and this was probably my last opportunity for it, he wondered whether I would like to go to the station on that day.

On the day of Freud's departure [Saturday, June 4] I went indeed to the station, accompanied by a close friend (Mr. Franz Krämer,[1] a musician, now with the Canadian Broadcasting Company in Montreal). It was a beautiful day, sunshine, agreeable temperature. The station was almost empty when we came and remained that way. We walked alongside the train (the then still elegant Orient Express) and had no trouble spotting Freud who was sitting at the window of his compartment. I remember a crying woman (a maid?) being consoled by another woman (Anna Freud?) and, in the compartment in front of Freud my friend (who was the son of a well known Viennese ophthalmologist) recognized the neurologist Professor Marburg, a lifelong denigrator of Freud who was leaving Vienna on the same train.

My friend and I kept a respectful distance a few steps behind Freud's compartment. When the train began to move, however, we stepped forward. I took off my hat and waved goodbye and Freud, noticing us, tipped his traveling cap in acknowledgement of our greeting.

Not long afterwards, perhaps on the following day, we heard over Radio Strasbourg (it was, of course, a severely punishable offense to listen to foreign broadcasts) that Freud had arrived safely in Paris and that he had been greeted there by, among others, the United States Ambassador Bullitt.[2]

This is, I am afraid, all I can contribute. With good wishes for success with your study—

Sincerely yours,

Heinz Kohut, M.D.

1. The friend mentioned in "The Two Analyses of Mr. Z.," *Search*, 4:397.
2. See Walter C. Langer and Sanford Gifford, "An American Analyst in Vienna during the *Anschluss*, 1936–38," *Journal of the History of the Behavioral Sciences* 14 (1978): 37–54. See also above, October 12, 1952.

July 12, 1968
Dr. Peter B. Neubauer
New York
Dear Peter:

Thank you for the copy of your introductory remarks.[1] Ruth Eissler is quite correct: I was in analysis with Aichhorn in Vienna. When Freud left Vienna Aichhorn told me about it and, apart from a friend who accompanied me, I was to my knowledge the only person to see

Freud off. When the train started to move I took off my hat and Freud tipped his traveling cap to me.

Do you know the small volume of Aichhorn's papers, edited by O[tto]. Fleischmann, P[aul]. Kramer and H[elen]. Ross?[2] Look at the frontispiece photo: it is placed in the wrong direction since Aichhorn is in reality lying on a couch. The photo was taken at the end of my analysis with him. He said: "I have seen you lying on this couch for a long time; it is time you saw me lying on it." Then he called one of his sons, an amateur photographer who took the picture which I then got as a souvenir. I put it at the disposal of the editors of the Aichhorn volume.

Cordially yours,

Heinz Kohut, M.D.

1. See above, February 7, 1966, n.2.
2. *Delinquency and Child Guidance* (New York, 1965).

July 31, 1968
Prof. Dr. Alexander Mitscherlich
Frankfurt/Main
Dear Alexander:
Your warm letter, so filled with serious reflections, was worth waiting for, and I would rather get one such in a year than any number of the politely worded, empty, obligatory notes which all too often seem to come my way. I don't believe for one minute, of course, that you will keep to your decision to retire from your endeavors to change the state of society through active participation—be that now in the traditional political sphere; through goal setting and value delineating publications; or through a strategic display of *Zivilcourage* which sustains and inspires the faltering others by providing them with an object of identification during a fear-arousing emergency. That you can do all this—or should I say: must do all this?—while yet preserving your ability to return to your study and there to resist the seductive, yet misleading approaches of the quantifying and simplifying neopositivism is truly not only a feather in your cap but gives you a very special position in the intricate web of modern psychology. I agree though that the future is gloomy and uncertain—not only in the mass-societies with their trend toward the de-differentiation of the individual, but even within the psychoanalytic microcosm which should be the bastion of attentiveness toward the complex psychological configurations which are the simple raw data of our empathic observation.

And like you, but in the small realm of analysis, I tend to despair when I see the unthinking simplifications of quantifications which enter our field, and I tend to retreat from open scientific polemics and organizational influence toward the position that only meaningful new contributions will really make a difference and that all the quarrel and fighting is a waste of time and energy. Yet, like you, though in my small arena, I cannot quite retire fully to my books and attempt at original work, but tend to mix it with organizational participation where it seems to me to be most strategic at any given period. Right now, for example, I am nearing the end of some years of work as Chairman of a Committee on Scientific Activities in which many of the basic questions about analytic research and analytic researchers, about high level productivity and true creativity in our field, have been asked, and for which even some fascinating hypotheses have been enunciated. Where will it all lead? I don't know. But at least these thoughts will be presented, will become available, and will stimulate others and encourage them to remain faithful to empathic observation and human concern in their assessment of human problems, instead of abusing the espousal of traditional scientific methodologies in the service of resistance to remaining on the road to new depth psychological insights.

Although this has become a very one-sided response to the many stimulating aspects of your letter, I must not go on and respond to all of your thoughts at this time. Only a response to your wish that I review Kuiper's book.[1] I am certainly looking forward to receiving it, but I am afraid that the chance of my reviewing it is not good. I have worked very hard in recent months just to clear my desk of all subsidiary obligations, so that I can finally turn again to my manuscript and move it forward. This work, in addition to the final report of the Committee on Scientific Activities of the American Psychoanalytic Association will completely fill the time that I can devote to non-clinical pursuits. I have, however, already thought of at least one way in which I could be helpful. The *Journal of the American Psychoanalytic Association* does not review individual books, but has a Book Section devoted to topical surveys. I will suggest to the *Journal* that such a Book Section be devoted to psychoanalytically oriented textbooks of psychiatry, primers, etc., such as Redlich and Freedman's book,[2] Kuiper's book and others of similar persuasion. For the rest I will certainly have a look at Kuiper's work before I give you my final reaction. Since you would like an American to review it I might make a suggestion or two if I can think of a suitable person.

Among the few organizational activities in which I am still interested is one which occupies a special place in my mind: it is the idea of instituting *continuing* international study groups about problems of psychoanalytic education. A first group might perhaps be organized under my chairmanship at the time of the Rome Congress. It would be concerned with selection for training, the topic of the preceding Pre-Congress. Two or three good people in the United States have already informally expressed their interest and willingness to work with such a group and I would (informally) like to know whether Margarete would be interested in participating in such an enterprise. There should, of course, be no publicity about this possibility at this point, and all I want to have is a preliminary response of possible participants. Please ask your wife to let me know at her leisure.

And now warm regards to both of you from all of us. Have a fine summer of work and rest.

In continuing affection,

Your,

Heinz Kohut, M.D.

P.S. I recently had the occasion to read a very fine statement which Senator [J. William] Fulbright, Chairman of our Foreign Relations Committee, made about a half a year ago.[3] Betty ordered a few copies of this speech and I will send you one as soon as we get them. Tom, by the way, is working as a counsellor in a summer camp for disturbed children from slum areas. He is an enthusiastic fan of Senator [Eugene] McCarthy for President and has devoted many hours of faithful work in this hopeless but by no means useless cause. He even—*mirabile dictu!*—got up in the early morning hours to canvas for McCarthy from door to door during the primary elections in neighboring Indiana.

HK

1. Pieter C. Kuiper, *Die seelischen Krankheiten des Menschen*, trans. Clemens de Boor (Bern, 1968).

2. Daniel X. Freedman and Fritz C. Redlich, *The Theory and Practice of Psychiatry* (New York, 1966). See also below, February 26, 1971.

3. Possibly "The Price of Empire: Traditional Values," *Vital Speeches* 33 (1967): 678–82; see also "The United States and 'Responsibilities of Power,' " *New York Times*, January 27, 1968; and see below, March 4 and April 7, 1980.

August 3, 1968

Metropolitan Opera

New York

Gentlemen:

I know that big enterprises cannot usually pay attention to individual questions and request, and I fear that this letter will receive a routine answer referring me to the fact that rules and regulations are necessary, and that exceptions cannot be made. Yet, since there is no harm in trying, I will try.

When I was a boy in Vienna my father introduced me to the opera by taking me to *Die Meistersinger*. I have never forgotten that evening and, although my tastes have changed, the magic of opera has never ceased to affect me deeply. When my son was a little boy I used to tell him about my first performance of *Meistersinger* and told him that some day I, too, would take him to hear it. Years passed, but there never was a performance of *Meistersinger* in Chicago where we live. This year my son will be in his first year of College and, as luck would have it, his Christmas vacation and my being for a brief professional stay in New York coincide. Thus, if I can obtain two tickets for *Meistersinger*, I could finally keep my promise and take him to hear it.

That would indeed be great—but I am afraid that it will all come to naught if I cannot get tickets. The performance in question is the one on *Saturday, December 21*. I know, of course, that I can write for two tickets, enclose a check for the amount of $27.00 and a stamped, self-addressed envelope, go to the Chicago Post Office on Saturday night, October 26, wait until midnight and then drop the letter into the box, air-mail, special delivery, at 12:01 A.M. on Sunday, October 27. I will do all this just as I outlined it. But will that bring me the two tickets? I am afraid of hazily imagined hordes of semi-professional and professional ticket getters who will drop their requests on October 27 at 12:01, too, and being in New York, will beat me with the greatest of ease. Or is there anything else that can be done to improve my chances? [See below, January 4, 1969.]

Very sincerely yours,
Heinz Kohut, M.D.

August 9, 1968
The Editor
The New York Times
Dear Sir:

The article by John Leo in the Sunday *Times* of August 4, is a more representative sample of the foibles of our day than the confused and contradictory image of the state of psychoanalysis that it portrays.[1] The essay consists of statements made by psychoanalysts; yet Mr. Leo had to choose a few sentences from each of his conversations and fit them together to make a whole—much as an artist might pick stones for a mosaic. Thus, for example, it was Mr. Leo who selected a particular respondent as his lead-off man and who picked as the challenge to face the claim that analysis is "as moribund and irrelevant as the Liberal party in England."

How characteristic for our time that such a tenet is offered to the reader as the leading statement of this survey! It by-passes any assessment of the intrinsic value of analysis, this new development in man's age-old search for self-understanding, and discards the whole science as insignificant because it is seen as weak and socially powerless. I would not even judge a political movement by these standards. The subtle influence of the ideals of the Liberal party in England, for example, might well have a more salutary long term effect on an eventual achievement of social balance in that country than the noisy battles of the Labor party and the Conservatives. But how much less relevant is it to judge a science by the current influence that it wields and by its popularity. What evaluative significance can be derived from a statement concerning what so-and-so thinks of analysis—for or against? Of value only are specific arguments which bear on the question whether the results of analytic investigation describe with approximate correctness the segment of reality with which the science deals; or which bear on the question whether these findings are useful in the service of certain practical applications such as—and foremost—in psychotherapy.

The ups and downs of the faddish acceptance of a flattened or distorted image of psychoanalysis might be of some interest to the social scientist who studies the vicissitudes of cultural fashions, but they tell us next to nothing either about the value of psychoanalysis or about its potentialities. The popularity of psychoanalysis, or even the mere degree of its acceptance, is not a criterion for the evaluation of this science which should command our respect. Instead we should consider the problem why analysis is not fully integrated into our culture, especially in those decisive areas of the social and political sciences which deal with the formulation of the aims and means of social and political action. This is indeed a crucial question, and one would give a great deal to know more about the answer to it.

Some analysts are naturally inclined to blame a recalcitrant antipsychological environment for the isolation in which their science finds itself, and they can marshall some cogent reasons for their view. But that analysis itself is partly responsible (if one wishes to speak in moralistic terms)—of that there is also no doubt. It must be admitted that analysis has not yet been able to provide the relevant insights that could guide society in its attempts to gain mastery over its historical destiny. Yet this failure must be assessed against the background of the fact that (considering the revolutionary character of its endeavor: the systematic exploration of man's inner life) psychoanalysis is a very young science. And it is to its credit that it refuses to apply its at present insufficient insights prematurely to the field of social and political action, i.e., to the shaping of the historical future, and that it continues to concentrate its efforts on its basic investigations of the psychological forces of man.

The time is probably not far off, however, when new discoveries will enable the analytic researcher to make significant contributions to the theory of social psychology and of its practical application. In the meantime—though powerless on the social scene like the Liberal party in England—it might yet aid society more importantly by the cumulative effect of individual therapeutic (i.e., socially small-scale) victories in man's struggles to gain mastery over himself and his destiny than some other endeavors which are favored by the opinion polls.

Sincerely,

Heinz Kohut, M.D.

Copy: Mr. John Leo

1. "Psychoanalysis Reaches a Crossroad," *New York Times*, August 4, 1968.

August 15, 1968
Mr. Kalman Seigel, Letters Editor
The New York Times
Dear Mr. Seigel:

Today I received your communication informing me that you will be unable to publish the letter which I sent to you on August 9 concerning Mr. Leo's article on psychoanalysis contained in the Sunday *Times* of August 4. Your message aroused a number of unpleasant feelings in me, notwithstanding the conciliatory tone of your general explanations.

The fact remains that a long and prominently displayed essay about psychoanalysis left the reader with a distinctly negative impression of this important science and that it seems to me, therefore, that my (I am convinced: reasoned and dispassionate) attempt to put some weight on the scale to rectify the imbalance was deserving of a better treatment than it has so far received by the *Times*.

I have no doubt that you, as a professional newspaperman, have access to, and made use of, the standard sources of information about your correspondents (such as *Who's Who in America, American Men of Science*, and even the "morgue" of your own paper: see the *New York Times* of May 2, 1964) that enable you to know that I am an acceptable correspondent. To mention only a couple of facts: I was the president of the American Psychoanalytic Association in 1964/5 and I am a Vice-president of the International Psychoanalytic Association. Thus it would again seem to me that my effort deserved a better response than your reply. It even occurred to me to wonder whether you had read my careful letter. But since I have no evidence in support of such a possibility I dismissed it and assume that my critique did not impress you sufficiently. In such matters of taste and judgment there is, of course, hardly room for fruitful arguments and, therefore, there is no appeal.

But when it comes to the undoubted fact that in your reply you do not even address me by name but are clearly shaking things off with a form letter that can apply to any letter writer, whatever he writes and whoever he is, then I believe that I can say that this procedure is not worthy of a department of the greatest newspaper in the Western world. O tempora, o mores!

Sincerely yours,
Heinz Kohut, M.D.
cc.: Mr. H. F. Bancroft
    Mr. D. Schwarz; A. Psa. Assn.

October 1, 1968
Margaret S. Mahler, M.D.
New York
Dear Margaret:

Congratulations on the birth of your book![1] In my monograph which, I hope, is near completion, I have occasion to refer to the complementarity of our views [*Analysis of the Self*, pp. 218–20]. We are digging tunnels from different directions into the same area of the mountain and our findings, while not identical, are analogous and will tend to support and complement each other. I am glad that you are interested in my work. I will send you a selection of reprints under separate cover.

Cordially,

Heinz Kohut, M.D.

1. *On Human Symbiosis and the Vicissitudes of Individuation* (New York, 1968).

November 17, 1968

My dear Gustl,

My thoughts have returned time and again to our brief talk last night. It won't be long until you are home, and we will then be able to talk things over. But some things can be expressed more thoughtfully in writing, and, also, I feel a little sense of urgency; thus this letter.

You told us that you, and another twenty students out of two thousand, have joined the anti-Navy recruiter protestors in a sympathy hungerstrike. You had also mentioned several times that you might fight your draft classification and become a conscientious objector. I conclude, therefore, that you are beginning to think of yourself as belonging (or that you are considering the idea that you will perhaps belong in the future) to a small group of activist protestors on your campus who feel that the social and political system of our society is intolerable and that one must take personal risks even for the small chance of changing it.

I will not enter into the substance of the opposition to our system of government and the specific policies which it pursues at this time: its shortcomings are glaring, the injustices are appalling, and it might well be that the war is not only immoral but foolish.[1] But I also know that the complexity of social events is staggering, and that other social and political systems (such as the Soviet system and that of the new left in China) have brought with them such gruesome side effects in suffering and loss of freedom that hardly any long term gain, be it ever so favorable, can justify the sacrifices.

But I am not against your struggling for convictions and values, am glad that you are questioning the existing values, and that you are searching. I am also not blind to the fact that there are times when one must throw caution to the winds, must take risks, and fight for one's life or one's values or both. My motivation for this letter, however, is to express to you the conviction that one must undertake extreme acts of courage only under exceptional circumstances. I think one should be ready to consider undertaking them, but should realize, too, that, in most people's lives, study, hard work, and the pursuit of long term goals by quiet means is the most decent, satisfactory, and valuable contribution. There are, of course, the professional revolutionaries: people to whom, for whatever reason, rebellion and risk-taking have become a way of life. These are sometimes admirable people (such as Dr. [Benjamin] Spock in this country, or Bertrand Russell in England, or [Pyotr] Grigorenko in Russia—I enclose a clipping about him from the *New York Times*),[2] but most of us must realize that we are not made that way, that our personalities could not sustain their kind of life, and that we must make our contribution by other means. For us the heroic deed—if we should ever be called upon to prove ourselves in this extreme way, which is not likely—must be the rare exception. It must then be undertaken with open eyes and with the full awareness of the extent of the risk involved. I don't believe that one should drift into heroism.

And here is where I have arrived at the central purpose of this letter. Please don't throw away your chances for a productive and happy future on the basis of an impulse, or even on the basis of a presently held strong conviction. To be a militant on campus does entail risks which may be greater than you allow yourself to know. Those on the other side of the fence do not see good will and idealism in their opponents, but only rebellion and obstructionism. Many of them are as fully convinced of the righteousness of their cause as you are of yours. And if those in opposition to them use provocative methods, they feel justified in suppressing them ruthlessly. I believe that you should think long and hard before committing yourself to extreme causes and, especially, to extreme means of furthering them. Such means of political pressure as hungerstrikes and conscientious-objector status are foreign to me [cf. below, December 25, 1971]. I argue, I try to convince, I fight to the best of my ability for seeing reason, tolerance, and patience prevail in this troubled world—but the stance of openly displayed martyrdom does not attract me.

Well, Gustl, that's as much as I will allow myself to tell you at this time. I want you to have a full, happy and productive life, and I want to do what I can to prevent anything from happening to you that could block your future.

Love,
Dad

1. In a letter to his son on August 29, Kohut expresses outrage over the actions of both protestors and police in the riots accompanying the Democratic National Convention in Chicago and worries that all of it will only help Nixon. On October 1 he sent

Tom two issues of *I.F. Stone's Weekly* "which will undoubtedly pour fuel on the fire of your alarmed pessimism about the state of the nation."
    2. "Dissident Soviet Voice," *New York Times*, November 16, 1968.

November 24, 1968 [from Anna Freud]
Dear Dr. Kohut,
    It is high time for me to answer your letter from Carmel and to-day I have a special reason for not hesitating any longer. Dr. van der Leeuw was in London over this weekend and we had long talks about the international analytic situation, the future of psychoanalysis (about which we are both worried) and the next Presidency for the International.
    You know probably very well how the matter stands. There are three possible candidates: you, Rangell and Arlow. Van der Leeuw and I and a good many people of whom we know want very definitely you,—in case you are ready to stand. We feel that we have to know as soon as possible to which decision you have come yourself. If you have decided to stand, it is not too early to begin to work for a positive outcome. I promised van der Leeuw to urge you towards a decision since this is really needed.
    On the other hand, I want to assure you that I have also every sympathy and understanding for your arguments against it. It is perfectly true that the Presidency interferes with one's scientific work. It is equally true that the Presidency, as it is now, is an administrative post and that in scientific disputes one's hands are tied. But it strikes me that there is one saving feature. A good President cannot undo the harm which is now being done to analysis in innumerable subtle and not so subtle ways; but at least he himself can stand for the right direction and influence others to join him. Van der Leeuw has done this certainly during his four years.
    It would be quite wrong for me to try to influence you since this is a matter you can decide only for yourself. But I want to say that this is the right time for a decision now and that you should let your friends know.
    I wonder why I am so specially pessimistic about the analytic movement at the present moment. Perhaps it is only that I see things clearer than I used to. But when you have to watch psychiatry, psychology, existentialism and Kleinianism all pulling away from analysis, you begin to wonder where all this is leading to.
    I hope that you, Betty and Tom are well. The term here is very busy

and I am looking forward to the Christmas holidays. I think we are going to have between two and three weeks in the quiet of Ireland.

Yours very sincerely,

Anna Freud

December 3, 1968

Miss Anna Freud

London

Dear Miss Freud,

I am willing to be nominated for the presidency of the International. There is no need to burden you with the soul searching which preceded my decision. I will only mention that I believe that I can have my monograph nearly in shape by this summer and I hope that even as president I should be able to put the remaining topics (on narcissistic rage; on the socio-psychological implications of my theoretical formulations) at least into preliminary papers. My other work will be wound up, too. I just finished an extensive draft of the final report of the Committee of Scientific Activities. If the American can be persuaded to follow up on it (that decision could hardly come sooner than a year from now), they can well do without me and my direct involvement.

Your letter moved me deeply. I am grateful that you put no pressure on me—yet, in thinking the situation over, I felt that I should try to get elected. When I, some years ago, made up my mind to become involved in the American, I was prompted by deep concerns for the future of psychoanalysis in the U.S.A. I could see things brewing (there was an active team under the leadership of Dr. Bandler at work at the time)[1] that no one else saw as clearly, and I knew that I had a chance to prevent the worst. As you say, a "President cannot undo the harm which is now being done to analysis," but "he can stand for the right direction and influence others to join him." I feel very uneasy—increasingly so—about the two most popular candidates. If analysis were not in danger there would probably be little harm in having either one of them since their influence would be countered by the resistance of the rank and file. As it is, strong positive efforts in the right direction must be made, not only in order to preserve the International as an instrument of analysis but, and foremost, to cement the bond between those of the members (they are in the minority) who understand and love our science.

It will be a hard battle though to get me elected. In a triple race the Kleinians will first vote for Rangell and then, if Rangell gets the lowest number of votes, they will switch over to Arlow. A respectable number of Americans will, of course, vote for me, and so will many of the Europeans (in Holland, Germany, Switzerland). But I fear that I am little known in England, France, and Italy. It must not be forgotten that the congresses are largely attended by psychoanalytic tourists whose single vote carries as much weight as yours and mine. I promised to let the Eisslers know as soon as I had decided (they urged me strongly to declare my willingness last summer and fall) and they will be of help among the inner circle in New York.

Much changed in the outlook for the I.P.A. when the Executive Council decided, in the name of democracy, to ask the nominating committee to prepare two slates of nominees instead of one. Had we stuck with one slate of official nominees the clearcut endorsement and expression of trust would have greatly benefited the official nominee(s) regardless of how many others would then still be nominated by petition, as long as the official nominee is somebody who is held in esteem by the membership. But these tactical considerations, important though they are, are now of no more value since the step taken last time cannot be undone without arousing suspicion. Anyway, I know that you, Van der Leeuw, and many others will do what can be done by word of mouth and correspondence and by other strategic statements to increase my chances for election. I know that I will give all that I have to give in leadership and devotion should I get elected.

Very sincerely yours,
Heinz Kohut, M.D.

1. Bernard Bandler was President of the APA during 1959–60. As president he was concerned about psychoanalytic training and its relationship to an ongoing decline in the number of candidates. See Bandler, "The American Psychoanalytic Association," *JAPA* 8 (1960): 389–406; and Edith Kurzweil, *The Freudians: A Comparative Perspective* (New Haven, 1989), pp. 208–9.

January 4, 1969
Miss Anna Freud
London
Dear Miss Freud:

I was so glad to receive your warm letter which arrived while I was in New York for the meetings: it confirmed my conviction that my decision to allow myself to be nominated was the right one. Marianne who had me for dinner despite her painful hip was also very encouraging and the Eisslers, too, are most supportive.

I am of course moved by your pessimism about analysis—realistic as some of your misgivings undoubtedly are, I cannot quite share them. Barring a war or a political holocaust which would do away with Western civilization as we know it, I believe that analysis will not only survive but become ever more strong and influential, notwithstanding the attacks and the defections. It is over and over again amazing and reassuring to me to see how many people are still working quietly, thoughtfully, and effectively in our science and I for one believe, as you know, that it will in the long run not be broad acceptance but creative discovery supported by solid productivity which will be decisive.

It makes me sad though, that you feel that your efforts are not arousing a sufficient response. You are so much part of an external ego ideal for so many analysts that there may be a counterforce which prevents them from showing their high regard in appropriate actions—and, of course, there is ambivalence in most toward all that is great and admired. It is foolish at this time to give thought to what I might do, should I become the leader of the I.P.A.—but the question occurred to me whether a future Congress program (or a series of them) might not be entitled *"Foci of Psychoanalytic Thought,"* beginning with your work at Hampstead (perhaps Dr. [Seymour] Lustman as chairman of the program), followed by a Congress on ego psychology, etc. Let me know some time what you think of the idea.

I am sending along two enclosures. One a communication which I sent to the *New York Times* (it was not published [see above, August 9 and 15, 1968]) which expresses some of the thoughts transmitted to you earlier in the letter. The other a draft for the final report of the Committee on Scientific Activities. It is too long and too chatty but that was the easiest way for me to prepare this draft. It will be much tightened and there will be some changes of substance in response to the reactions of the members of my committee. Since it is long you might not want to spend the time to read it all. But since I am referring to you in this (to me important) document which will I hope get wide distribution, I would like you to check page 13 and tell me whether I rendered the spirit of your views correctly.

Tom began his Christmas vacation by joining me in New York. We had a delightful father-son weekend: at the meetings, the *Play of Daniel* in a New York church, and in the opera (*Die Meistersinger*). Now he is here with us until approximately January 6 when he will return to Oberlin. Betty is nearly recovered from a slight attack of sciatica and the whole family is well and happy. We all send you our affection. Warm greetings to Dorothy. And a good 1969 to you!

Sincerely,

Heinz Kohut, M.D.

January 11, 1969 [original in German]
Henry D. von Witzleben, M.D.
Palo Alto, California

Dear Henry!

I'm sorry that my long silence upset you. It wasn't illness that caused the delay in my reply, but overwork. Thus I was not able to turn to your essay.[1] It reached me shortly before I left for the East (first a couple of days in Princeton, then over a week in New York); then came the busy holidays, and then all the many put off and waiting tasks that had to be addressed. Tom came to New York and flew with me to Chicago; and the couple of free hours I had I naturally dedicated to him.

But now to your essay! I liked it very much and it made a great and wonderful impression on me. You know of course that I deal with similar questions in the last part of my first narcissism essay and that we certainly agree on many things. Differences in terminology do sometimes obscure the parallels between our views. You write for example a great deal about irony, similar to what I have to say about humor. The example of Freud's that I quote ("Well, the week's beginning nicely!" as the condemned man is led [on Monday] to his execution)[2] fits well into your context on page 26.

The strength of your essay lies not in its (often very cleverly and well expressed) details, but in the overall impression that it makes. I hope that it will be translated for the English reading public. When a couple of (unimportant) psychoanalytic inaccuracies are rectified your work will be a very important contribution to the psychological understanding of aging.

The inaccuracies—and the ones I have in mind are in comparison to the extraordinarily successful whole only trifles!—are to be found primarily on pages 11 through 13. The following are the ones I remember from a single reading of your essay.

Insufficient distinction between "ego" as a functional system and "self" as those psychical configurations that [Erik] Erikson (in my view in a popularizing-superficial way) designates as identity.[3] The self and the ego constitute specific developments and mutually influence one another. A strong, cohesive self (well stocked with narcissistic libido) improves in a general way the ego functions; conversely, the consciousness of well realized ego functions contributes to the libidinal cathexis of the self (to enhanced self-esteem). Perhaps you can think through your remarks (page 13) about "ego-cathexis" more precisely. Your observation about regression in old age (page 12) also is not clear to me. The idea of a "regression as a defense against stimulation" that you mention later (page 15) is enlightening to me, although the term "regression" does not seem to me to be the right one. The expositions on page 12 could be improved if you keep in mind that a regression can either affect all the structural elements of the psyche (ego, id, and superego) or only some, and that it is important to grasp which of the psychical localities regress more and which less. You show that very well later on when you speak of the greater tolerance of the superego toward the creative ego later in life. But here as before: Is the term "regression" really the right one?

These are all of little importance. What I really want to add to your line of thought is the notion of conflict. You juxtapose the absurdities of denying old age and the value of its acceptance. But the tragic conflict of combating the aging process can also have its grandeur—or its pettiness.

A short time ago an insight came to me that I will share with you in this context. I compared two operas that concern themselves with the problem of the aging man: Wagner's *Die Meistersinger* [1867] and Verdi's *Falstaff* [1893], and I discovered how differently the leading characters and their conflicts are portrayed in these two operas. In *Die Meistersinger* the conflict is largely confined to Sachs; it leads in him to noble renunciation; he leaves Eva to her youth. Beckmesser, on the other hand, apparently knows nothing of this tragic conflict, he denies his age and wants to take the bride home. The contrast between the two is given some depth through the fact that Sachs preserves his artistic productivity while Beckmesser fails miserably in this respect. The people as representative of a general standard of value honor Sachs, but they mock Beckmesser and beat him.[4] You can see how the attitude of good aging and bad aging are divided schematically into two people. Fine! But how different, deeper, and more beautiful in *Falstaff*—Shakespeare's creation and Verdi's genial understanding of this conception (you know of course that Verdi completed this greatest of all his creations in old age). Here we have the full spectrum of human conflict united in *one* tragic figure, in one tragicomic hero. Here is no abstract ideal solution of the human tragedy, but the man who carries both sides within himself: the old man who tries to deny his years, who chases women, loses all perspective on himself and, justly, not only is subjected to general derision but (just like Beckmesser) is publicly beaten. But here it is the same man (unlike Beckmesser who in the last scene simply runs off and, completely dishonored, disappears) who when he has apparently hit the low point of dishonor suddenly finds his true worth. He recognizes his torturers behind their masks, causes them to feel the meanness of their anonymous atrocities of righteousness; he renounces, and grants youth their right to the fulfillment of sexual love; and he closes the opera with the deepest ironic realization: the unreality of reality, the theatricality of past life. *Tutto nel mondo è burla*—the jest, the joke is the only thing that counts in this world—is that so far from Goethe's *Alles Vergängliche ist nur ein Gleichnis?*[5]

You ask about the translation of my essay. I sent it to Frankfurt with an accompanying letter in which I referred to you and to Moellenhoff as helpers. Frau Hügel (the editor, not the translator) wrote: "Thanks for the effort that you and your friends put into the corrections. We are full of admiration for your splendid feeling for the language. With these corrections the German version has gained much in clarity," etc.

And now only my warmest greetings, also from Betty to Ilse. And all the best for the new year from us both.

Cordially yours,

Heinz Kohut, M.D.

1. "Goethe und Freud," *Studium Generale* 19 (1966): 606–27; see also *Search*, 1:171–76.

2. See *Search*, 1:456; and Sigmund Freud, "Humour," in *The Standard Edition of the Complete Psychological Works of Sigmund Freud*, ed. and trans. James Strachey (London, 1961), 21:161–62.

3. On Kohut's early enthusiasm for Erikson, see Paul Roazen, *Encountering Freud: The Politics and Histories of Psychoanalysis* (New Brunswick, N.J., 1990), p. 222.

4. See Peter Gay, "For Beckmesser: Eduard Hanslick, Victim and Prophet," in Gay, *Freud, Jews and Other Germans: Masters and Victims in Modernist Culture* (New York, 1978), pp. 257–77; and see also below, Gay to Kohut, June 22, 1980.

5. "What is destructible / Is but a parable"; *Faust, Part II*.

January 28, 1969

Dr. A. Kagan

International Universities Press

New York

Dear Dr. Kagan:

You will remember our discussion during the last dinner of the Editorial Board of the *Journal* in December, and our subsequent telephone conversation. I had mentioned to you my idea of an anthology

Illustrations

Heinz Kohut, age eighteen months, October 1914

With Felix and Else, 1917

Playing chess with Siegmund Löwenherz (left) in Brittany, 1929

Döblinger Gymnasium graduating class, 1932

First Row, *left to right* (teachers and female students):
Gertrude Kaluza, Elisabeth Freund, Bruno Watzl, Franz Hartel,
Director Karl Goll, Alfred Scharf, Oskar Weidinger, Alois Hornung,
Ignaz Purkarthofer, Ferdinand Komarek, Dora Petschenka, Elisabeth Seiberl.

Second Row:
Heinz Kohut, Erwin Asriel, Thomas Brunner, Karl Stephan Strauss,
Siegmund Löwenherz, Ernst Baschny, Hans Komarek, Friedrich Kail,
Roland Krug, Georg Kalmar, Ergen Krasny, Walther Bunzl.

Third Row:
Herbert Schall, Herbert Eckstein, Heinz Granichstädten, Adam Wandruszka,
Hans Hauke, Michael Conrad-Billroth, Franz Sykora, Kurt Steiner, Hans Salzer,
Georg Geyerhahn, Wolfgang Gröbl, Edwin Vyslouzil, Friedrich Schönberg.

Not pictured: Walter Neudörfer and Friedrich Wolf.

With August Aichhorn, 1930s

With Aid Station staff at Kitchener Camp, England, 1939
(HK is sixth from left)

In office at Billings Hospital, Chicago, 1942

With Betty and Tom in Carmel, 1954

At Institute for Psychoanalysis, Chicago, 1950s

With Mrs. Grinberg, Dr. P. J. Van der Leeuw, and Dr. Leon Grinberg,
second Pan-American Congress, Buenos Aires, 1966

With Anna Freud, Topeka, 1966

With Carlo Schmid and Alexander and Margarete Mitscherlich,
Frankfurt, 1969

With Tovey, early 1970s

With Betty and Tom's wife Susan at St. Antönien, 1973

Finishing *How Does Analysis Cure?* Carmel, 1981

of polemical articles, letters, etc., by psychoanalysts, and you apparently found the idea worth pursuing. Such a volume might contain certain parts of essays and letters by Freud, some striking articles by Robert Waelder, K. R. Eissler, and others; letters to newspapers and periodicals by Arlow, by myself, and others, etc. A preface should attempt to summarize the attitude of psychoanalysts toward their innumerable detractors, e.g., how the usual tendency to non-reply is grounded (a) on Freud's expressed predilection for non-reply and (b) on the professional habit of looking for psychological explanations rather than to engage in argumentation. The volume might have a title such as *Psychoanalysts Speak Back*, or the like.

As I mentioned to you I do not feel able to shoulder the burden of collecting the material for such an anthology myself, but I told you that I would consider the undertaking if I found a collaborator with sufficient skill and energy for the job. I asked Dr. John E. Gedo whether he would be willing to collaborate with me in this venture and he decided that he would.

I am thus letting you know that Dr. Gedo and I will soon get together to formulate our plans. We will let you know details as soon as we have become clear about them.

In the meantime, however, we would like to hear from you: (1) whether you are continuing your support of the plan, and (2) whether you can give us any advice and guidelines about the legal and practical problems of such a collection.

I am looking forward to hearing from you.

With best personal regards,

Sincerely yours,

Heinz Kohut, M.D.[1]

1. This volume never appeared. According to Gedo, Kohut lost interest in the project and Gedo himself was not particularly disposed toward polemics. John E. Gedo, personal communication, October 3, 1991.

February 4, 1969

Dear Tom,

Your phone call this evening made mom and me sit with gloomy faces over our T.P. [Tea Party] worrying about your future, about your anger, and about your seemingly headlong run into activities which we feel sure you would regret later on. I also have a certain helpless feeling about arguing with you. Your mind seems so closed, so absolutely convinced that the issue of the Navy recruiter is worth the enormous risk that you seem to be willing to take. I know all the arguments that you can put against what I am saying—and yet I also know that these arguments will seem to you like nothing a few years hence. If you really start out on a path by which you will get expelled from the college, have to face the draft, and then get involved in draft-bucking moves, etc., all normal growth is impeded, all the efforts that you and mom and I put into this normal further development are thwarted, and you will wake up and face the stark realities of having given in to an overgrown idea of your single-handed importance and responsibility. Where is your sense of proportion? Where is your fine sense of humor?

All this may of course make you more angry, but I can't see how I can avoid telling it to you. You are young and are just making the first steps toward independence. You get impatient when I mention to you the great difficulties of the next steps in maturation: commitment to hard work; adjustment to girls; greater wisdom in judging the merits of the issues that you are facing. You are veering back and forth between high-minded self-sacrificing idealism and devotion for great causes on the one hand and, on the other hand, self-indulgence in front of the television and in raiding the ice-box. In that way you are like I was and as every normal adolescent seems to be (Miss Freud was the first one to describe this state. You can read up on it: it's the last chapter in her book *The Ego and the Mechanisms of Defense*—the greatest contribution she ever made)—but there are differences in the degree of swings that young people permit themselves.

We are deeply concerned, Gustl, and we hope and pray that you will contain yourself and will not take steps, during your first year in college and nineteen years old, that might ruin the many great possibilities that life can offer to you later on (including later courageous steps that go against the stream of what society wants, if at a later and more settled stage of your life you should decide that the goal is worth the risk).

But enough! Think mainly of yourself in what you are deciding, but think also of your parents who would so much like to guide you toward control, reason, and some understanding of people whose opinions differ from yours.

All my love (and mom's)

February 5, 1969
Dear Tom:
Yesterday's letter was written late at night when I was tired and under the direct impact of you[r] phone call. Frankly, I have not been

able to think of much else since then and have had a hard time concentrating on the work with my patients. Today we also received a communication from Oberlin College spelling out the position of the administration which, as you know, is: (1) Peaceful demonstrations and peaceful picketing are encouraged; (2) Coercive interference with the right of students to talk with armed forces representatives if they wish to do so will not be tolerated, and offenders will be expelled from the college.

I have no doubt that the college administration means what it says, and, much as it may hurt your feelings, I cannot see what else they could do. There is room for argument, of course, about the merits of the case, but the college could not survive if a group of students were permitted to take the law into their own hands and use force to make their view prevail. The point of view of the administration that the armed forces representatives simply give the students an opportunity to choose between the different services since they have to enter the service anyway might be a debatable one, but within the campus itself, it allows for a freedom of choice (i.e., students may stay away; may make propaganda about others' staying away, etc.) while coercive picketing which prevents others from entering, or sit-ins, or the like, do not allow a choice.

So much about the merits of the case which at any rate strikes me as a subtle and difficult disagreement between two sets of ethic. Beyond that, however, all that I wrote to you yesterday still stands. I am racking my brains to figure out why you have become so intolerant and so single-minded about this issue, why you have replaced thoughtfulness with absolute certainty that you are right, and that, therefore, everything goes, and why you contemplate an action that could destroy your future and all our hopes for you.

I don't know the answer. Have we failed in making clear to you what the world is really like? Always just persuading and just getting angry, but never really letting you feel the consequences? I don't think so—at any rate we could not have been otherwise, and children do learn the difference between the discipline at home and the harsh realities of life even without punitive attitudes from the side of their parents. I wondered, too, whether the thought of being a radical, an activist, etc., might not contribute at this time to your self-esteem, to defining yourself as an individual. This would be very understandable. I know how angry you get when waiters wonder about your age, and I still remember vividly my own feelings of uncertainty about myself during the analogous period of my own life. But one has to suffer through such transitional periods—they don't last forever. And hard as it seems: an honest suffering is better than a quick solution of being a revolutionary and activist. I don't mean that one should avoid a stand—but within reason. The enormous inflation of the issue by you (I cannot speak about the others whom I don't know) which might drive you to activities that could have disastrous consequences for you goes far beyond the understandable need to assert yourself against the liberal values of free speech and a democratic society ruled by laws and constitutional rights.

I would not tell you the full truth if I would hide from you how badly I feel personally. Today I reconciled my monthly account and a glance at my last check for your tuition told me that I am spending about two full months of hard work every year just in order to earn the money needed for your tuition. That I am mentioning this may sound cheap to you—but the thought adds to my feelings. It's not just the money—that is really only a symbol—but it does mean that we and you are in all this together. It's not only your hard work that's getting you through school, but also our contribution. Usually one does not think about that (and I hardly ever do, except with pleasure). But when I consider the possibility that you might risk throwing all this away in order to make one subtle point of ethics, I do get angry and upset.

For goodness sake, Gustl, don't do such a foolish thing! I wondered whether you might wish to talk things over with a psychoanalytic colleague of mine (Dr. Brian Bird in Cleveland, for example), but I don't urge you to do that at this time. If you, yourself want help with clarifying your motivations, however, let me know and I shall be glad to assist you in making an appointment with Dr. Bird. And, of course, you can arrange it on your own if you prefer.

What more can I say? Again: to hope that your angry outlook on the world which sees all authority as evil and mean will not prevail, but that you will work with increasing pleasure on learning about what goes on, deepen your understanding of the variety of experiences that life has to offer, so that you can be happy and satisfied. Mom and I don't have to tell you how much our own peace of mind and enjoyment of life will depend on that. It takes little to destroy—but that power is spurious. Please be constructive!

February 10, 1969 [from Anna Freud]
Dear Heinz Kohut,

Thank you and Betty very much for your sympathy on the occasion of Oliver [Freud]'s death. It was a very sad experience. I flew there, even though I knew that I would be too late, probably, which I was. But I felt that somebody ought to be there, also because of Henny's state. She is confused, in a bad organic state, in a Nursing Home. I know that you will not be surprised. You saw it coming on when she was in Chicago.

If this had not happened, I would have written this letter one or two weeks earlier. I hasten to do it now. Please, keep the contents "private and confidential." I do not find it easy to write it, and the whole situation is very much on my mind and worries me.

The facts are as follows: before my trip to the U.S. I had an upsetting letter from van der Leeuw, he himself being very upset. At the meeting of the two Sponsoring Committees he had met a number of the representatives of the European Societies and had found to his surprise that they have all made up their minds to vote for Rangell as the next President. I do not know why, neither does he, but it seems an indisputable fact. This throws all our expectations into confusion. Van der Leeuw and I both know that you will encounter heavy opposition in the U.S. from supporters of Arlow and Rangell, but we had been confident that you would have the European votes. If they go another way, it is almost certain that you will be defeated, in spite of van der Leeuw, me, Marianne Kris, the Eisslers, etc. And I do not think that it is a good thing to offer oneself for defeat. In this case, it would be better not to stand; also in this case, my advice to you (even if "unspoken" advice) was bad advice. You will have to forgive me for that and you will have to think that I was guided by my wishes.

Perhaps it is simply that the time for preparation was not long enough and that you should have appeared on the election platform very much earlier, perhaps even before the last Congress. However that may be, this is how the matter stands now.

When I was in New York for one night, I had a talk with Marianne, and Dr. Eissler and I told them a bit about van der Leeuw's experiences. They were equally upset. They also thought that it was important for you to know before coming to New York shortly.

Again, please do not take this letter as advice. It may be that you want to fight the election, whether it leads to a positive or a negative result. If this is so, we, as your friends and supporters, shall do our best. But it also may be, that you decide now not to stand, and also in this case, we shall be with you.

That is really all. Do let me know how you feel about it.

Perhaps my pessimism about the future of the I.P.A. is not so unfounded? According to van der Leeuw, a President's job now is an administrative one, with very little influence on scientific matters. He regrets that, naturally, after all the efforts which he has put into it. But, if this is so, who looks after the scientific future of psychoanalysis?

Yours sincerely,

Anna Freud

February 16, 1969

Miss Anna Freud

London

Dear Miss Freud:

I had no trouble making up my mind after I received your letter, and I agree with you that it is not a good thing to offer oneself for defeat. I phoned the Eisslers and informed them about the fact that I was withdrawing from the race and gave them the reasons for it (I simply assumed that the "private and confidential" which you mentioned applied to everyone with the exception of the Eisslers and Marianne). I have not spoken to Marianne yet but told the Eisslers that they could talk to her. I will, however, probably phone her today, Sunday, and tell her about it personally.

With regard to my private life and my scientific work this development is a blessing. But—with all the feeling of relief—I will not deny that the disappointment was great. On the lesser side there were waves of hurt pride and anger, and, in particular, feelings of resentment that the very group that should have understood best what choice to make did not even seem to consider me.[1] Harder to settle internally is the turning away from the plans about the future of the I.P.A. that had begun to form in my mind. But here, too, I am making progress. After one disturbed night I am again sleeping soundly—and that is a good sign that I am well on the road to finding my balance.

As far as the I.P.A. is concerned it is hard to make a prediction. I do not believe that my present personal involvement interferes with the objectivity of my judgement. By comparison with Arlow, Rangell is the lesser evil: for the simple reason that he is the weaker person—more guided by needs for personal success and without strong convictions. I have serious scientific disagreements with the Arlow-Brenner approach.[2] How important a danger to analysis their work constitutes, however, I cannot evaluate. The older generation and those already established in their analytic thinking will probably remain unimpressed. But the younger generation, particularly those under their direct influence in New York, might well be led astray. Rangell's writings, on the other hand, seem on the face of it perfectly harmless. I find them polished, intelligent, very nicely put, but completely unoriginal. He is beloved by the South-Americans, has some friends in the U.S.A. (but many will prefer him to Arlow—most of those who would have voted for me will now vote for Rangell, i.e., against Arlow), and now, surprisingly enough, he has the leaders of the European psychoanalytic community on his side. If he gets elected—as you know, he barely made it for Vice-President in Copenhagen. He got the lowest number of votes of those elected; as a matter of fact he got in by the margin of a single vote!—he will probably do quite well as a peace-maker and compromiser. And strong pressures that would test his stamina and his devotion to analysis are not likely to arise.

And now I do wish to tell you, how much your letter meant to me. You have nothing to blame yourself for—on the contrary, you did what you had to do and you did it well. The behavior of large groups follows laws which we do not know. Things might very well have worked out differently, and there was no way of testing the situation without having at least gone as far as we did. My major efforts can now be devoted to my scientific goals, and—after I will have been done with my reaction to the present disappointment—I will now have a chance for a fruitful period of work.

Sincerely,
Heinz Kohut, M.D.

1. Kohut here refers to the Europeans who, he felt, should have understood the value of his opposition to the American analytic emphasis upon medicine and technique in contrast to Freud's broader cultural and philosophical interests.

2. On Brenner's "austere" approach to the analyst-analysand relationship in contrast to the "humanistic-empathic" position held by Kohut and others, see Malcolm, *The Impossible Profession*, pp. 44–46; and above, July 5, 1968.

March 3, 1969
Dr. Roy W. Menninger, President
The Menninger Foundation
Topeka, Kansas
Dear Dr. Menninger:

Please excuse the delay of my reply to your letter. It arrived while I was away from Chicago, and, in addition, I wanted the quiet of a weekend to think things over to be sure in my own mind that I had made the right choice.

After careful thought I concluded that I must decline your invitation. I did not arrive easily at this decision. I am aware of the varied and profound professional gratifications which a directorship at one of the great mental institutions in the world would bring to me. And I am fully conscious of the honor which you have done me by asking me to consider filling this key position at the hub of the whole Menninger Foundation.

Yet, to put it in a nutshell, it comes at the wrong moment in the curve of my life. For a number of years I have been engaged in a specific research [project?] which not only has been deeply satisfying to me but which has also already brought confirming approval to maintain my hope that I will be able to contribute to the widening of the scope of depth-psychological knowledge and the enlargement of the area of treatable psychopathology. Be that as it may, I am deeply committed to my present work, expect that it will have to be pursued for years to come, and know that it requires an optimum of concentration.

To unsettle myself at such a time, to undertake responsibilities which require not only a great deal of readjustment but also the devotion of much of my energies to organizing and administrative activities would run counter to my most cherished inner contentment. It is thus with a real sense of loss, yet at the same time with deep conviction of choosing the right path that I am declining the great opportunity which your message offered to me.

I am wishing the very best to the Menninger Foundation and to you. I trust that you will find a devoted and capable colleague who is able to accept the invitation with which you honored me.

Sincerely yours,

Heinz Kohut, M.D.

March 7, 1969
Dr. Fritz Morgenthaler
Zurich
Dear Dr. Morgenthaler:

Thank you for sending me the *Bulletin* which contains your article "Psychoanalytic Training Today."[1] I read your remarks (and Mitscherlich's Commentary) with interest and care, and should like to give you my reactions to your thoughts.

The proposal itself strikes me as very good and I like your courage of stating it straightforwardly. Mitscherlich's support adds further depth and historical perspective to your suggestion. From a practical point of view I would personally support at least an experimental implementation of your plan, i.e., not the kind of immediate sweeping reform which replaces an authoritarian approach by its exact opposite (which then often turns out to be just a new form of authoritarianism) but that gradual testing of new possibilities which will teach us the advantages as well as the disadvantages and pitfalls of the new philosophy. There are, after all, a good many problems connected with the outlook on educational policy which you are suggesting. My major worry concerns the possibility that the deeper conflict between the generations—which will, of course, not be abolished by a change in the external form—might become more intractable if the traditional stage for confronting it is removed. An older generation which *imposes* freedom, participation, equality, etc., on a younger one may be more subtly and stiflingly authoritarian than an older generation which honestly fights with the younger one—and faces its inevitable defeat. Do you know the play *Tango* [1964] by [Slawomir] Mrozek? (I saw it in a very competent performance in Frankfurt, last year.) Nowhere have I seen a more poignant rendition of the problems of a younger generation whose freedom became imposed on it by generations of liberals. It should give us food for thought that the most authority-fighting of the younger generation are the children of the most liberal parents, eternally in search of causes and of tyrannies to rebel against, etc.

I know what one could reply to the foregoing considerations but, as analysts, it behooves us to keep in mind that the subtle interplay of psychic forces that create balances and imbalances is in general not done justice to by gross external manipulation, but by an ever-deepening search. And, please, don't forget that I am saying all this after agreeing with you that your proposal should indeed be cautiously implemented.

That really is all I have to say regarding the substance of your article. It still seems hard for me to understand why you thought your opinions would make me want to reconsider my invitation to you to join the study commission on the selection of applicants. Nothing indeed could be further from my mind! I may, of course, not fully agree with some of your conclusions. I do not believe, for example, that the anal reaction formations and the active-passive conflicts play as uniformly the central role as you ascribe to them. But, if anything, it is the very variety of opinions, creatively expressed and presented, that I am looking for in the work of our study group, and not boring conformity and traditionalism.

Perhaps you know me well enough by now to realize that I see the major issue of life not in the terms of the outcome of the struggle for dominance, but in the terms of the outcome of the struggle to maintain active creativeness. Creativeness, however, depends in the last analysis on the ability to be in touch with the playful child deep in the personality, and thus on the ability to maintain the freshness of the child's encounter with the world. All mature creativity, however,— even inside of committees—depends on our capacity to encourage the growth of that inner freedom.

Please let me hear without delay that you are willing to join our group.

Cordially yours,

Heinz Kohut, M.D.

P.S. Please send the enclosed copy of this letter to Alexander Mitscherlich if you wish.

HK

1. See *IJP* 49 (1968): 748; and Fritz Morgenthaler, "Introduction to Panel on Disturbances of Male and Female Identity as Met with in Psychoanalytic Practice," *IJP* 50 (1969): 109–12.

March 11, 1969

Sydney E. Pulver, M.D.

Philadelphia

Dear Dr. Pulver:

Today I received a copy of your paper "Narcissism: [T]he Term and the Concept" from Dr. Wangh, the Chairman of the Program Committee in the Association who asked whether I would be willing to discuss it at the Annual Meeting. For a number of reasons, but especially in view of the fact that I have many other commitments, I will have to decline. I will return the paper to the Program Committee for the assignment of a different discussant.

I glanced at your essay, however, and noted that you are critical of me—and others—because I use the term narcissism in the restricted sense of self-esteem; later you object to the differentiation between "good" and "bad" narcissism which is "used by such authors as Kohut and Waelder." I myself am not aware of having simplified the problems of narcissism in the way for which you appear to blame me (you quote my paper "Forms and Transformations of Narcissism") but I was pleased to see that the solution which you "find most satisfying is the re-conceptualization of narcissism found in the Glossary." It is not without a slight sense of amusement that I must tell you that the narcissism entry in the *Glossary of the American Psychoanalytic Association* was written by me.

I am also enclosing a copy of my most recent paper on narcissism and hope that it will contribute to change your judgment about my views on this topic.

Sincerely yours,
Heinz Kohut, M.D.

April 6, 1969
Miss Anna Freud
London
Dear Miss Freud,

Yes, I knew about your illness from Marianne who conveyed to me the message that you had wanted to write to me but that you were not feeling well. I am so glad to know that you have now recovered from this nasty siege and that you will have the tonic of the Irish surroundings to restore you completely.

Concerning the I.P.A. I do not think that we should withdraw our interest from it—whoever the next president will be. I will do my best not to react in hurt withdrawal but to support analysis even in the unwieldy organization that the I.P.A. has now become. My personal reactions to Vander Leeuw's report about the attitude of the European training committees which prompted us to give up the race has largely subsided and I know more and more what a personal and scientific benefit accrued to me by this development. The only thing that still stirs me up from time to time is the arrival of expressions of support which I am still receiving from various quarters. I had, unfortunately, already started my "campaign" before I received your fateful message, i.e., I had written more than a hundred personal notes to people in all parts of the world who would, as I had reason to believe, support my candidacy in Rome. Since I had, of course, nowhere mentioned my candidacy directly there is no need (and really no possibility) to take anything back now—these things will quickly take care of themselves now by word of mouth. But from the replies which I received I got some very interesting impressions. The entrenched, institute-bound leaders seem to have been least responsive to me (in Europe and South-America, especially noticeable in France and Great Britain), perhaps because they have the (correct) impression that I would be a force that is opposed to the progressive institutionalization and professionalization of psychoanalytic learning. There seems to be a large group, on the other hand, which sees in me the representative of something that is in danger of getting lost in the institutionalized and professionalized analysis of the present; and it is, in particular, the fact that I received many enthusiastic messages about my last paper which gives me heart to hope that my efforts are not in vain. Well, somewhere I must be an incorrigible optimist—perhaps because I, too [like Sigmund Freud], am the firstborn child of a young mother.

The manuscript of my book is now nearing completion, and the first eight copies have been read by a selected group of young analysts, i.e., by people who are in their first decade of independent work after graduation from institutes. Some of their responses moved me more deeply than anything that I have experienced in my professional life. I don't doubt that these responses are an unrealistic overvaluation of the importance of my work—yet, the mere fact that I am able to generate this type of enthusiasm for the struggle with analytic insights in a group of analysts who promise to be the significant contributors of the future gives me no end of pleasure. I have decided, by the way, not to burden you by sending you my manuscript at this time since you would undoubtedly feel obligated to read it at a period when you are in the midst of editing your collected works and need every minute of your time and must husband your energies. But do drop us a line just to say hello some time.

Warm regards to Dorothy and fond greetings from all of us (including Tom who is home for an Easter visit).

Sincerely,

Heinz Kohut, M.D.

April 10, 1969

Dear Tom,

I don't know what to make of today's phone call which ended abruptly by your hanging up on us. Things have certainly come to a fine pass. You believe that you have the right to indulge in this type of impulsive, disrespectful, offensive behavior which completely disregards our feelings because we did not back you up, as you called it, when you tell us that you want to participate in a sit-in or a strike, as an immediate action against a dictatorial move by Mr. [Oberlin President Robert K.] Carr.

The two things seem to me very similar. No doubt you have the right to be upset about Mr. Carr and want to do something about it. But I think that what you want to do is nothing short of a declaration of war and is very similar to the way wars start on the bigger international scene, too. Each party is convinced that they are right, neither one will back down, and the process of escalation starts and goes on until a point of no return is reached. No doubt you were disappointed that I did not see things your way—but that does not give you the right to hang up on me. No doubt you are concerned about the faculty decision not to have student representation if disciplinary procedures are instituted against students—but that does not make it wise to start a chain of actions which drives the other side into a corner from which there is no escape, i.e., where there is only the choice either to fight or to suffer a humiliating defeat. Wars are avoided by working for justified goals in such a way that the adversary has at least a chance to save face, to be persuaded. If you hang up on me, if the students "hang up" on Mr. Carr and on the majority of the Oberlin faculty, then you have, by necessity, a war. Many issues can be enlarged into appearing to be a matter of utmost concern, of deepest principle, etc. But when one looks at the variety of causes that students everywhere seem to be fighting for, one gets the impression that the students are spoiling for a fight, whatever the justification.

I don't know what more to say. Each of the causes you feel are worth risking your career for (and the secondary issues of loyalty to your comrades which must be added, too) can be presented by you in such a way that one runs out of arguments against you. And yet, I am deeply convinced that there is something exaggerated here. Mr. Carr may be ill advised, imprudent, unjust. He should be wiser, more tolerant, more conciliatory. Would it help if he had all these good qualities? I am by no means sure that it would. When I see your intolerance about my counter-arguments, the inability to take it when I don't agree with you about your proposed actions which seem disproportionate to the provocation, I get the impression that you and your friends will accept nothing except having things totally the way you see them and to have them so without any delay. All I can do is to plead with you for a bit of prudence, wisdom, and thus the espousal of more conciliatory attitudes which do not hopelessly divide things into all good versus all bad. Such attitudes would be fully compatible with real courage and courageous action when, after much soul-searching, an issue is indeed important enough to take risks.

I hope that you will not hang up on us again!

Dad

June 6, 1969
Dr. René Spitz[1]
Department of Psychiatry
University of Colorado Medical Center
Dear René:

What a generous, marvellous letter! Such praise, and from a man
of your surpassing stature, is all that I could ever wish for as a response
to my efforts, and I feel thoroughly rewarded.

The question concerning the self as an object of introspective perception (what I call by the traditional term, the imago of the self rather
than by the term "representation" of the self which has come into
vogue recently) versus the self as a "center of identifiable function"
(see Levin, *Int. J. Psa.* 50, 41–51, 1969; p. 43), I will perhaps take up
in Rome in fulfilling my assignment as the discussant of Levin's paper
[see above, July 5, 1968]. At any rate, I have given some thought to
this question which leads into all sorts of basic problems concerning
concept formation in our introspective-empathic-explanatory metapsychology. My main efforts, however,—as you probably know from
Janice Norton—are now devoted toward putting the finishing touches
on a monograph about narcissistic transferences. The second reprint
which I sent to you is an abstract and preview of this book. I hope
that my future contributions will not disappoint you.

Once more, my deep gratitude for the generosity of your approval.
Warmly,
Heinz Kohut, M.D.

1. René Spitz was a pioneer in research into the emotional lives of young infants.
See his *The First Year of Life* (New York, 1965).

April 11, 1969 [original in German]
Herrn Dr. Tilman [*sic*] Moser
Frankfurt/Main-Rödelheim
Dear Mr. Moser!

Since it is my responsibility to report on the plenary session discussion of Douglas Levin's essay for the *International Journal of Psychoanalysis*, I would like to ask you to send me a short summary of your
remarks concerning the slighting of the social role of psychoanalysis
in general and in Douglas Levin's work in particular.

I read your article about the Rome Congress in the *F[rankfurter]
A[llgemeine] Z[eitung]*[1] that my friend Mitscherlich sent me with mixed
feelings. Much of what you say is certainly correct (for example, I find

your critique of Erikson right on the mark—only he is not so popular among American analysts as you assume) and your descriptions are attractive and—I too certainly don't hate a rogue—very amusing. But a couple of your pet themes I would have presented in a more balanced way.

I don't know if you know my work and to which of the three classes of analysts you describe you would consign me. But it seems to me that your description of your opponents is distorted and caricatured and thus does not allow for a response. If an orthodox analyst doesn't really know that there are psychological processes outside of the Oedipus complex—on this you principally and rightly quote the exasperated [Ralph] Greenson—, if he really doesn't know that the actual personality traits of the analyst are grasped by the patient, that he really feels that he has understood the world when he really believes that historical movements arise merely from early childhood conflicts, then your polemic is correct. But are there such analysts? And even if one could find a couple such oddballs who hold such views, do they represent a real danger to psychoanalytic science?

I saw things quite differently. In contrast to you I was impressed in the plenary session that Mitscherlich chaired by how applause greeted speaker after speaker who took a position against the investigation of psychological motives that were bound up with historical events. I cannot understand this rejection of the psychology of the individual and it distresses me that the old fascination with the study of the depths of the human soul seems to be slowly disappearing. Many of the speakers, and the applause that followed them, reminded me of the complaints that Freud had to endure (in the early days of analysis), to wit, that with such investigations he was degrading what was most sacred about human beings. At that time it was family, religion, the innocence of childhood; today it seems to be the idea of our brave younger generation that we analysts should stop fouling the air with our research. If an analytic researcher should demonstrate anal fixations in Rembrandt, does that mean that he questions his greatness as a painter? Not at all! On the contrary, it is fascinating for the analyst to study how, for example, pregenital elements dovetail with genius, the changes they undergo, how they contribute to restraints on developing abilities, and the like. We are quite far from constructing sure links between childhood experiences and great creations or actions (I tried not so long ago to show that in the case of Churchill; perhaps you saw the essay of mine on narcissism that appeared in *Psyche* in 1966)—but simply to make fun of our tentative steps in this direction seems to me to be unjustified.

I wouldn't be writing you all this, my dear Mr. Moser, if I didn't detect in your report the intelligence and earnestness of deep conviction (and naturally also in your contribution to the discussion to which I as moderator had to respond) and I hope that you don't mind that I wanted to demonstrate to you how the same events that you described in your way can be seen quite differently. And, please, send me the summary of your discussion remarks.

With best regards,

Yours truly,

Heinz Kohut, M.D.

P.S. I enclose a copy of this letter with the request that you send it on to Professor Mitscherlich. Since this letter is to you, I don't want to commit the now common bad habit of sending a copy to a mutual acquaintance without your permission.

1. Tilmann Moser, "Das Konzil der Freudianer," *Frankfurter Allgemeine Zeitung*, August 6, 1969. See also below, September 9, 1969; and May 11, 1970.

Carmel, September 9, 1969

Miss Anna Freud

Walberswick, Suffolk

Dear Miss Freud!

Your letter followed me to Berkeley where I spent a week by myself, preparing for an address which I will give on October 12 in Frankfurt at the occasion of Alexander Mitscherlich's receiving the *Friedenspreis* [German Booksellers Association Peace Prize]. It's a major occasion— on a Sunday morning over European television, in the presence of the German Federal President, etc.—and I wanted to do it justice. The speech is finished and I trust that it will be appropriate and that it will further the cause of analysis.[1]

From Moser, the fellow who wrote this nasty[2] article about the Congress in the *Frankfurter Allgemeine Zeitung*, I got a very nice—even moving—reply, including a second article by him on the Congress (also in the *FAZ*)[3] and a copy of a broadcast about the Congress which he had given. Both were ever so much friendlier toward analysis—the broadcast, by the way, contained the best brief summary of my work on narcissism that I have ever encountered. In his letter to me he explained the first nasty article partly on the basis of journalistic necessity; he said that unless he attacked at first, the readers would brush him off as another one of the true believers and no one would bother to read the second (positively toned) installment. He had given a copy

of my letter to him to Alexander Mitscherlich, and Mitscherlich wrote to me that Moser had been deeply impressed by my letter and that it had given him much food for thought [see below, August 14, 1971].

I am sorry that you should feel guilty about my reaction to the presidency affair. There is no reason for that whatever! My reaction is based on a complex background that I do not feel up to explaining in writing. I hope that there will be some day an opportunity to explain it to you. Now, I am unambivalently relieved that I am not burdened with this chore. But in Rome I did feel upset because of the great pressure exerted on me by so many people (especially Europeans— with the exception of [William] Gillespie, Sandler, and [Adam] Limentani) who were disappointed and reproachful.

I sent the *FAZ* article about the Berlin experiment to Jay Katz and suggested that he get in touch with Gerhar[d] Maetze in Berlin.[4]

Marianne is here. She arrived on a wheelchair from the plane, but after a good long sleep she awoke fresh and active, and has been up and around and is clearly enjoying herself. She told us that you had injured your finger quite badly and had been in a lot of pain. What a pity! I do hope that it is fully mended and that the Irish countryside will help to restore you to your full vigor. How nice it would be if you too could be here and join us in front of the fireplace after dinner.

Warmest regards to Dorothy, and my fondest to you!

Sincerely,

Heinz Kohut, M.D.

1. *Search*, 2:563–76. Kohut convinced *JAPA* to publish both his address and Mitscherlich's: see Kohut to Frosch, October 8, 1969. In 1976 Mitscherlich was made an honorary member of the APA.
2. Kohut here echoes Anna Freud's judgment in a letter to Kohut of August 27, 1969.
3. Tilmann Moser, "Nutzen and Schrecken der Angst," *Frankfurter Allgemeine Zeitung*, August 13, 1969.
4. Tilmann Moser, "Psychoanalyse für Richter und Staatsanwälte," *Frankfurter Allgemeine Zeitung*, July 8, 1969. Jay Katz is professor of law and psychiatry at Yale. The article concerned courses in psychoanalysis for judges and lawyers at the Berlin Psychoanalytic Institute.

Carmel, September 23, 1969

Mr. M. Masud R. Khan

London

Dear Masud:

This is the last week of a rather late vacation in California. Off and on the thought of dropping you a line had crossed my mind, but a

number of deadline tasks interfered. Another reason for the postponement is probably my hesitation in view of the fact that I really can't formulate clearly what it is that I want to achieve with this message.

It is motivated by the anger that I felt directed against me during the business meeting of the IPA—from you and from others—and which I am still at a loss to understand fully.

The idea to begin organizing international study groups came to me some years ago, and I kept pursuing it since I thought that here was a road toward the building of meaningful bridges between analysts across the world. This seems to me to be a very worthwhile goal which, as you may know, I have also tried to further by organizing a set-up in the *Journal* of the A. Psa. A. which will attempt to place before the American reader translations of psychoanalytic writings from language-areas other than the [E]nglish one.

Your criticism was directed at the choice of the participants. Now, it is true that I did not choose the Europeans at all (I did make suggestions concerning the Americans)—as a matter of fact I had not even heard the names of some of them. But since this is a very specialized area of competence and since Vander Leeuw is familiar with the European scene, in particular with the educational efforts, I saw little sense in not following his choices. On the whole, I think that these choices were good. I think that one must evaluate them against the background of the fact that this is a first step in a new direction. And I think that it was wise not to burden it with the kind of theoretical ego-psychologists which form the leading group in the U.S.A. (but there are a few in England also) or with those who are committed to the theoretical position of Melanie Klein, or—worse still!—with representatives of both these groups. It seems to me that it is best to strive, on the whole, for people who, like myself, have an open mind about those who have either committed themselves to the empathic immersion into the earliest states of mind (the Kleinians) or about those who see autonomous ego functions as the goal of maturation and as the measure of normalcy. We could undoubtedly have had better choices, but what is needed now is not perfection of choice but a quiet atmosphere in which to work, and a slow expansion of the experiment into other areas and with different types of participants.

When I return to Chicago I will send you a copy of the Report of the Committee on Scientific Activities of the A. Psa. Assn. which I presented recently[1]—it will perhaps give you a better idea about the kinds of goals which I pursue than you have now and will, I hope,

allow you to judge me and my intentions less harshly than you seemed to do in Rome.

With warm personal greetings,
Sincerely,
Heinz Kohut, M.D.

1. *JAPA* 17 (1969): 1180.

February 7, 1970
The New York Times
New York
Gentlemen:

I would like to share with you the following disquieting reflexion about Mr. [Harold] Carswell.

If Mr. Carswell had said that he had to struggle hard to free himself from his old prejudices but that he had now arrived at hard-earned new convictions, I would not hold his former opinions [with regard to segregation] against him.

But there is no evidence of inner struggle.

On the contrary, it seems that Mr. Carswell forms, expresses, discards, and disclaims important convictions depending on his immediate goals and ambitions.

Such adaptability is specifically disqualifying for a judge in the highest court of the United States.

Sincerely yours,
Heinz Kohut, M.D.

March 1970
To Helen Ross[1] on her eightieth birthday
Dear Helen:

To survey your varied and rich life from the present vantage point of eighty years must be deeply satisfying to you. It seems to us—to Betty who has known you well since her early adolescence as a camper and counselor at Ketchuwa, and to me who has known you for twenty-five years—that the emphasis of all your interests and activities was always with the young: understanding them, helping them, guiding them. And as you subtly steered Betty from her staid Milwaukee surroundings toward Vienna and analysis (and where would I be without that happy direction which her life took then, long before I knew her?), so you must have influenced hundreds of others by your example, your intelligence and, at last but not least, your charm.

To me, Helen—who was not one of your former camp-children; and, especially, to me as a man—you have always been a spot of bright femininity that provided relief from the all-too puritanical and largely drab society of psychoanalysts. Even in those worst times, up on 57th street, my memory sees your lovely face surrounded with rays of sunshine breaking through the windows of the Central Office, and it has done away with all the ugly nonsense of jealousy, backbiting, and intrigue to which you responded with elegance, silence, and alas, also with the temporary loss of your smile. But the nasty and sad aspects of that period we can now safely forget. What remains and what counts, is the solid product: that enduring brain-child which sprang from your cooperation with Bert, the volume on Education, which in its perceptive elegance, tells more about the essentials of the educational scene in psychoanalytic America than all the statistics collected by the committees of the Association.

Today then we can discard the petty stuff and think of the substance of your life; and we know that you, too, surrounded by your friends, are doing the same. We will think of that youthfulness which will never cease emanating from you, and of that restoring zest which you infuse into those who are lucky enough to be near you.

Dear Helen, we thank you for what you have been, and for what you are and will be. With our love and gratitude take our best wishes for many more good years.

Betty and Heinz

1. Helen Ross was Betty Kohut's mentor and a pioneer of psychoanalytic social work in America; see also Bertram Lewin and Helen Ross, *Psychoanalytic Education in the United States* (New York, 1960).

May 5, 1970
Ernest Wolf, M.D.
Chicago
Dear Ernie,

I had intended to go to your lecture[1] but was in the last minute prevented from doing so. This was clearly my loss. I was finally able to read your paper and found it beautifully written and very stimulating. You may realize, of course, that you are treating one of the basic questions of modern analysis when you talk about the amalgamation of art and science. In metapsychological terms the same question may be raised through a definition of the difference between "ego autonomy" and "ego dominance." Are we dealing with "the rider off the horse" (ego autonomy) or "the rider on the horse" (ego dominance)? I have always maintained—and I think that you are taking the same basic position in your essay—that many great achievements are not the result of "autonomous" ego activities but depend on the management of prerational (id-) pressures by the exertions of a strong and gifted ego. [See above, May 16, 1966.] This relationship between ego and id is indeed what you are demonstrating with regard to Freud's genius. Many thanks for this convincing investigation of Freud's adolescence.

Warm regards and best wishes for many more contributions of equally high quality.

Sincerely,

Heinz Kohut, M.D.

1. John E. Gedo and Ernest Wolf, "Die Ichthyosaurusbriefe," *Psyche* 24 (1970): 785–97.

May 11, 1970 [original in German]

Prof. Dr. A. Mitscherlich

Frankfurt/Main

Dear Alexander,

1) Here is the laudation in its English version, a piece that by and large strikes me as quite good [see above, September 9, 1969]. What do you think?

2) [Lutz] Rosenkötter has declared himself willing—"sight unseen"!—to take on the translation of my book. He will probably contact you after he has read the manuscript.

3) I hope that the book will be noteworthy not only in terms of its scope but also its content. I hope very much that you will give me your impressions.

4) A visit in St. Antönien would please us very much. Let's hope that it works out! . . .

5) I received a short note from Carlo Schmid on New Year's, half-officially as Vice-President of the German Parliament. He wrote: "Meeting you was the best thing about the days in Frankfurt. You will not misunderstand me when I tell you that it pleased me to meet in you that Germany about which Germans can be proud—but they did

not realize it." This letter moved me very much [see below, July 17, 1971].

6) Conditions in America are very complicated, but terrible things bring out the best reactions. At Tom's college the students and faculty joined together to suspend all academic activities, including final exams, when Nixon announced the invasion of Cambodia and the Ohio National Guard shot four students [at Kent State University]. In place of regular courses there were discussion groups and the like whose aim it was to bolster the influence of students and colleges on public opinion and political decision making. Last weekend Tom and many other students went to Washington to demonstrate against the war. You've certainly followed all this in the papers. The student demonstrations seem to have had a significant impact. [Interior Secretary Walter] Hickel's letter to Nixon, the naming of a college president as mediator between the students and the President, the strong insistence that the troops be withdrawn from Cambodia soon, shows the strength of the influence of the protesting groups. One naturally should not overestimate that influence. Nixon is a sly politician, whose strength is like that of a good boxer "to roll with the punch." He wins time and waits until the storm blows over. On the other hand I am unfortunately convinced that the present reactionary regime has a broad basis of support among reactionary groups in the populace who more than anything else fear the Negroes, who are disposed against intellectuals, and fear communism like the devil. But that has been the case for a long time and alone does not justify pessimism. The strength of the protesting groups also must not be underestimated.

In spite of our concern about Tom we are also very proud of him and his involvement with issues of peace and social justice. Our involvement is restricted mainly to letters and telegrams to our senators and congressmen. This type of influence is not senseless over here. The defeat of two reactionary candidates for Supreme Court Justice [Clement Haynesworth and Harold Carswell] is to some degree to be credited to this type of political activity.[1]

Many warm greetings from Betty and me to you both. Let us hear from you soon!

Cordially yours,

Heinz Kohut, M.D.

---

1. See Alexander Mitscherlich, "Introduction to Panel on Protest and Revolution," *IJP* 50 (1969): 103–8; William Braden, "Symbolic Issues in Watergate Told," *Chicago Sun-Times*, June 8, 1973; and above, August 11, 1969, and February 7, 1970.

Berlin, October 8, 1970

Dear Tom,

You probably got the postcard which I sent to you yesterday but it was so brief—and I have a little time now—that I want to tell you a little about my experiences here.

I have by now been in Berlin for almost four days and it really has been quite interesting. The flight over, in a Jumbo-jet, was less than pleasant, despite the fact that I had 4 seats at my disposal and could sleep rather well for about 3 hours. I changed planes in Frankfurt and flew through the "air-corridor" to Berlin-Tempelhof, an airport which is quite close to the center of the city and which is rather impressive in the massiveness of its buildings.[1] I was awfully air-sick on arrival and it took me nearly 24 h[ours] to get completely over it.

Berlin which was almost completely destroyed during the war consists of new buildings and broad, straight streets & boulevards— somewhat like American cities—only some variety, more life in the streets, more outdoor cafes and restaurants, etc. On the first forenoon I took the S-Bahn (an elevated electric train) into East-Berlin, crossed the Spree [River] and saw the wire-fences and security measures (broad, empty spaces behind fences) to prevent flight from East to West Berlin. I got off the train at the Station Bahnhof Charlottenburg[2] (as far as the train goes) in order to get a theater ticket for the next evening. Since I didn't leave the platform I didn't need a passport. There was a Kiosk (an enclosed stand) where tickets were sold—and I got one. But already I felt the eery feeling of being in a police state— people were looking around before talking, soldiers walked about with cameras to take pictures of people, lots of propaganda material was lying around everywhere about fascism, imperialism, anti-Israel pamphlets, praise of the DDR (Deutsche Demokratische Republik), etc.

The next day the Mitscherlichs & I went to East Berlin. Again the same eery atmosphere. Passport control, checking of my face— especially comparing the shape of the ear with the ear in the photo. I had to declare how much money I had. Had to buy 5 marks of the DDR, etc. The streets in E. Berlin were dark—the same contrast as in Chicago when one enters the Negro slum section. The theater was brightly lit, small, rather nice. But poorly aired out and the people were not allowed in to sit down until 10 minutes before the beginning of the show.

The show itself and the actors & the whole performance was excellent and gripping. It was an unknown (a fragment) play by B[ertolt]. Brecht, *Bädenmeister Meinungen* (or something like that)[3]—a play about the suffering of the workers during the time of great unemployment—

all clearly trying to show that there is only one kind of cause for human suffering—the economic one—and that all human motivation is secondary to the motivation of economic acquisitiveness. It was really beautifully performed and one was taken along with almost frightening speed. One forgot all reasoning & began to believe the doctrine. Yet I sighed a deep sigh of relief when we were back again—and could talk without fear and had the feeling that one was not exposed to being watched, to being arrested, etc.

I did some sightseeing—saw the Brandenburger Tor [1788–1791], the Reichstagbuilding [1884–1894], the bombed-out Gedächtniskirche [Kaiser Wilhelm Memorial Church, 1891–1895], the Zoo—and I enjoyed long walks in the large park, called "Tiergarten" in the lovely fall weather. I climbed up the "Siegessäule" [Victory Column, 1873] & had a fine view.

Today I visited a magnificent museum in Dahlem—will go back tomorrow because it has so many wonderful paintings (including Delatour[4] which I have not seen yet).

My public speech at the Free University went well—tomorrow I give another lecture. I am enjoying the company of the Mitscherlichs, saw deBoor and Rosenkötter. The day after tomorrow, Saturday AM I'll fly back via Frankfurt to Chicago on a Jumbojet of the Lufthansa.

I trust you are fine and enjoying your life and work. So-long, Gustl

Love,
Dad

1. Architect Ernst Sagebiel; completed 1937.
2. Kohut means Friedrichstrasse.
3. *Das Badener Lehrstück vom Einverständnis* (1929).
4. Georges de la Tour (1593–1652).

December 26, 1970
Leo Rangell, M.D.
President, The International Psychoanalytic Association
Los Angeles
Dear Leo:

During my recent visit in Berlin I had occasion to see clear evidence of the hostile activities of "Neo-Analysis," in particular of (1) the psychoanalytic school of Schultz-Hencke,[1] (2) the communistic psychological schools, and (3) Dr. [Günter] Ammon and his "Deutsche Akademie für Psychoanalyse" (German Academy for Psychoanalysis). I also heard the complaint that some of the members of the IPA (Masud Khan, for example) are co-operating with Dr. Ammon. Dr. G. Maetze (who undertook the enormous job of organizing the Berlin celebrations)[2] wondered in a recent letter to me whether the International Psychoanalytic Association could not undertake steps to interfere with such misalliances. It would strike me as worthwhile to investigate this situation further, perhaps by writing to Maetze and [Hans-Joachim] Bannach in Berlin, or better yet, by consulting with Alexander Mitscherlich regarding this matter.[3]

With warm personal regards,

Sincerely yours, Heinz Kohut, M.D.

cc/Frances Gitelson;

Alexander Mitscherlich.

1. A member of the German Institute for Psychological Research and Psychotherapy from 1936 to 1945, Harald Schultz-Hencke had evolved his own school of thought called "neo-analysis" centered on "inhibition" (*Hemmung*) in place of Freudian sexual conflict. See Cocks, *Psychotherapy in the Third Reich*, pp. 62–65, 232–35; see also Helmut Thomä, "Some Remarks on Psychoanalysis in Germany," *IJP* 50 (1969): 683–92.

2. Kohut participated in the program marking the fiftieth anniversary of the founding in Berlin in 1920 of the first institute for psychoanalysis (the second was founded in Vienna in 1922). See Heinz Kohut, "Ist das Studium des menschlichen Innenlebens heute noch relevant?" in *Psychoanalyse in Berlin: Beiträge zur Geschichte, Theorie und Praxis*, ed. Gerhard Maetze (Meisenheim, 1971), pp. 79–96; Kohut to Annelise Thimme, January 17, 1972; see below, July 17, 1971; the essay ("Psychoanalysis in a Troubled World") based on this address in *Search*, 2:511–46; and the excerpt, "Unterwegs zu einem neuen inneren Gleichgewicht," *Die Presse*, July 31–August 1, 1971, published on the occasion of the IPA Congress in Vienna.

3. Mitscherlich advised Kohut not to bother with the provincial Berlin situation, noting that since Ammon was not a member of the IPA nothing could be done about him; Mitscherlich to Kohut, February 10, 1971.

1971–1973

*"I have heard from many sides that
my book is very hard to read."*

February 26, 1971
Daniel X. Freedman, M.D.
Chair, Department of Psychiatry
University of Chicago
Dear Dan:

The other day, after an odd persisting pain in one of my ribs, I phoned _____ and asked if he could have a look at me. He said: Come over! and saw me fifteen minutes later, examined me thoroughly, then went upstairs to the X-ray Department with me, introduced me to one of the staff and went back to his clinic. X-rays were taken, the x-ray man showed me the x-ray which was normal. I went downstairs; and I decided that I had pulled an intercostal muscle. And so it was—the pain is now gone and the whole affair is forgotten. But while I waited to be x-rayed and afterwards while the film was processed I had an idea for a research project that I want to share with you.

One could entitle the project à la Kafka as "The Trial" or "The Castle." To be specific: What happens psychologically to the individual when he is caught by the machine of the big institution, when he is being processed? I think Billings Hospital would be a splendid field for a group in the Department of Psychiatry to study this question. The anxious patient in the system of the clinical process. How does he react? What are his vague fears? At what key points and through what key maneuvers could one alleviate them? The fear of one's ultimate destructibility (did I perhaps have metastases in my rib?); outbursts of angry rebellion (perhaps argumentativeness in the clinical process), the sinking back into becoming passive, identifying with the powers which surround you. All this can be investigated as extensively and as deeply as the researchers' imagination and creativeness will permit. Dreams of patients could be gathered who are in individual therapy while they are exposed to such experiences. The testimony of gifted writers ([Leo] Tolstoi, "The Death of Ivan Ilych" [1884]; Kafka; [Alexander] Solzhenitsyn: The Cancer Ward [1966]) could be added. Interviews could be conducted and self-observation practiced by the research team. All this could lead to important practical results not only for the more human and effective running of a big hospital but also for mass processing in non-medical settings. I was lucky: I was "at home at Billings"; "the professor" who took care of me was a former student of mine; I was favored by personal introduction and an easing of my way in every detail. And yet, I felt somewhere, under the pressure of vague anxiety, a variety of reactions which are otherwise foreign to me. I began to behave in an ingratiating way with the personnel. I felt ready to argue and complain. A short wait seemed endlessly long. I acted in a haughty fashion with fellow patients in the waiting room ("I am not one of you!", I probably wanted to say). Imagine what the average patient must experience![1]

This is not a research project that I could or would undertake at this point in my career—But what do you think? Does it strike you as worthwhile? [See below, September 2, 1973.]

Sincerely,

Heinz Kohut, M.D.

1. See also below, Kohut to Eissler, April 18, 1974. Siegmund Levarie recalls that when Kohut was diagnosed with a particularly malignant form of cancer he felt the doctor inadvertently communicated his own anxiety to Kohut. See below, December 25, 1971.

April 8, 1971

Mr. Richard M. Nixon

The White House

Dear Mr. Nixon,

To experience pity for Lt. [William] Calley is surely a good and humane attitude, and so is an understanding for the fact that under the pressure of war a man's shaky self control may give way and lead him to murder. These are considerations on the side of leniency and thus to a sentence of imprisonment rather than to the death penalty. But to make a hero of the man, to condone his misdeed, to interfere with the punishment, these are moves which add to the disgrace which this man has brought to our country. It will only be understood as an expression of contempt for the value of the lives of helpless men, women and children who are not Americans.

In our opinion there should be no interference at this point with the legal punishment, however strong the outcry of misguided popular opinion.[1]

Yours very truly,

Dr. and Mrs. Heinz Kohut

1. Lt. William Calley was convicted on March 29 of murdering Vietnamese civilians at My Lai and was sentenced on March 31 to life imprisonment. Reacting to public outcry, President Nixon ordered Calley released from prison to his quarters to await review of his conviction. See *The Nixon Presidential Press Conferences* (New York, 1978), pp. 165, 168–69, 178.

June 4, 1971
Joseph Lifschutz, M.D.
Orinda, California
Dear Doctor Lifschutz:

I just returned from two weeks in Europe where I discussed the topic of narcissism in general and of the narcissistic personality disorders in particular. Please forgive me for not answering your two interesting questions in great detail at this point, especially since I hope that my book will clarify my ideas better than I could do in San Francisco during the limited time that was at my disposal.

Your first question, in particular, you will find treated in some detail early in the monograph, i.e., in chapter one. As you will see there, I differentiate sharply between the psychoses and the borderline states [between neurosis and psychosis], on the one hand, and the narcissistic personality disorders, on the other. The psychoses and borderline states have their fixation points prior to the establishment of a cohesive self. In the overt psychotic the self is fragmented (either with or without overt psychotic substitution formations); in the schizoid personality the self is not fragmented, but because of the danger of regression to irreversible fragmentation of the self the individual distances himself from people in order to avoid wounds to his narcissism which might lead to the dreaded regression. I believe that what one usually calls borderline cases are people with covert psychoses. On the whole this is a catch-all term, based on symptomatology only. In general I do not consider the term to be very helpful.

With regard to the therapy of (1) the psychoses and borderline states, (2) the schizoid personality, and (3) the narcissistic personality disorders you will find my opinions expressed also in the first chapter of my book. Psychoses (borderline states) and schizoid personalities should be treated psychotherapeutically but not psychoanalytically, i.e., the nucleus of their psychopathology should not enter the transference. Narcissistic personality disorders on the other hand should be treated psychoanalytically, i.e., the nucleus of their disorders (the vulnerable but not permanently fragmented self) should enter into a narcissistic transference.

The difference between [Otto] Kernberg's and my approaches you will also surely understand more clearly after you have read my book. The major distinguishing points are, I believe, my emphasis on the developmental line of narcissism from archaic to mature forms and my sharp differentiation between archaic (pre-structural) objects, psychic structure, and (post-structural) objects which are cathected with object-instinctual cathexis.

I am afraid that all this is terribly condensed but I am confident that my book will help. Please feel free to write me again if you find that these questions are not fully answered in the monograph.

At the end I would like to tell you how happy I was with your friendly letter and what a good feeling it was altogether to spend this nice day with you all in San Francisco.

Cordially yours,

Heinz Kohut, M.D.

P.S. Please consult the on the whole excellent index of my book which was in the main prepared by Lottie Newman. Such entries as "borderline cases, definition, p. 18" or "object and self-object" pp. 50–52, will quickly lead you to the topics of your interest.

HK

July 17, 1971 [original in German]
Prof. Dr. Carlo Schmid
Bundeshaus
Bonn

Dear Herr Professor,

Many thanks for the talk on [Albrecht] Dürer,[1] which I studied with great enjoyment and from which I learned a great deal and received much stimulation (for example, the remarkable analogy between the two basic positions of the "self" which I have described in my book, *The Analysis of the Self*, which I hope will soon appear in German translation from Suhrkamp, and the principal spiritual attitudes of the Middle Ages and the Renaissance as you so admirably described them in your essay). And how much I admire your great erudition! The effortless mastery with which you sprinkle the text with the appropriate Latin quotations and portray the scholastic thinkers—by comparison people like us can only hang our everyday heads in shame.

You mention that in spite of the shortness of our meeting[2] I think of you again and again. Yes, but why? I sense the answer, but will not spell it out. Why do I travel again and again to Germany and subject myself to the rigors of these quick trips? In order to give one or another lecture, to take part in short seminars, to give a couple of courses for interested German colleagues? Perhaps you can detect the answer if you find the time to leaf through my Berlin address.[3] What are the bridges one wants to build? What sort of old identities which—in spite of everything!—at bottom wish to prolong themselves and to make themselves heard? You once wrote that you had met in me a Germany of which the Germans could be proud [see above, May 11,

1970]. It is precisely for the sake of this principle that I have written you again.

But I know how busy you are and I beg you sincerely not to feel obligated to further correspondence. Even without letters my affection will maintain itself.

Cordially yours,
Heinz Kohut, M.D.

1. Remarks on the occasion of a December 1970 ceremony at Dürer's grave to inaugurate the celebrations marking the five-hundredth anniversary in 1971 of the artist's birth; see Jane Campbell Hutchinson, *Albrecht Dürer: A Biography* (Princeton, N.J., 1990), p. 202.

2. At the ceremony in Frankfurt in 1969 honoring Alexander Mitscherlich, Schmid participated as president of the West German Parliament.

3. "Ist das Studium des menschlichen Innenlebens heute noch relevant?" [see above, December 26, 1970]. Kohut directs his remarks here to an audience of university students. At one point he speaks of how fortunate it would have been for "my own generation" to have been able to follow a charismatic personality committed to humane ends in opposition to "the most destructive mass leader of our time" (pp. 90–91). Kohut clearly means a German leader, since in many of his other works he speaks admiringly of Churchill's role in rallying the British and others to defy Hitler. More generally, this address highlights the "dialectical other" within psychoanalysis (pp. 79, 90), a theme congruent with Kohut's own personal sense of belonging to two worlds, that of his native Austria and of his adopted homeland, the United States.

August 14, 1971
Miss Anna Freud
London
Dear Miss Freud:

I trust that you have recovered from the strains of Vienna.[1] It was good to see you and to hear your splendid address. The hour that you devoted to Betty and me at Berggasse 19 [Sigmund Freud's home and office] was for us both the highlight of the trip.

That my wish to take you to Sluka[2] remained unfulfilled was however a disappointment, I must admit. It has several roots. But one is easily talked about. On your last day in Chicago you voiced the wish for a big chocolate sundae and we were planning on it. But somehow we never got to it. Since then I have always had the feeling that something was unfinished, and Sluka—still as wonderful as it was when I was a child—would have been just the spot for the needed completion. Well, some things must remain unfulfilled—at least I remembered the Peregrini Kipferln [a type of roll] and must be satisfied with the fact that the memory seemed to give you pleasure. (An example of the sublimation of orality?)

I am enclosing a copy of a review of your address in the *F.A.Z.*[3] which a German acquaintance sent to me. You remember the author? He used to write very hostile reviews about analysis and you remarked on them with dismay [see above, August 13, 27, and September 9, 1969]. Some years ago I wrote to him and took him to task [see above, August 11, 1969]. He is now on the way of becoming an analyst (though still quite conflicted about it), has attached himself to me with great intensity, and will be coming to the U.S.A. in the fall just to be able to discuss his professional and scientific future with me for a week. He has an interesting and promising mind. At any rate—and for the time being—this Saul has become a Paul.

Now only good wishes for a fine summer with the right mixture of enjoyable work and rest. After finishing *The Analysis of the Self* I am now turning to new work on group psychology and aggression. A month in Carmel . . . will I hope give me the necessary leisure to prepare the Brill lecture[4] for November which I will use as a launching pad for some new formulations.

Betty sends her love (also to Dorothy) and so do I.

Warmly,

Heinz Kohut, M.D.

1. On the IPA Congress in Vienna, see Tilmann Moser, "Was ist Aggression?" *Frankfurter Allgemeine Zeitung*, August 2, 1971.

2. One of Kohut's favorite cafes in Vienna.

3. Tilmann Moser, "Scholastiker und Praktiker," *Frankfurter Allgemeine Zeiting*, August 3, 1971.

4. *Search*, 2:615–58. A. A. Brill was an early American exponent of psychoanalysis.

August 23, 1971 [from Anna Freud]

Dear Heinz Kohut,

Thank you for the letter and for the clipping. I was very interested in the latter and the report was by far the best and most understanding that had appeared about the Congress and about my paper. Most reviewers only tried to catch some point which could be used for some sensation and that always makes me angry. But you can be proud of your convert.

About Sluka: I am sorry too to have missed the repetition of very nice experiences there. On the other hand, I remember as one of my father's convictions that it is never good, on any occasion, to fulfil *all one's wishes*, that it is better to have some unfulfilled. I can add to that from experience that pleasure always goes by the board if there are duties to be paid attention to, and there were many duties in Vienna.

In the meantime, I have read your C.E.A. report[1] and I was struck by the many complications of the task. It is a difficult subject and like all predictions a precarious one. I am curious what the final results will be.

By the way: could one have predicted [Otto] Rank's turning from analysis proper or [Sandor] Ferenczi's later decline? I think one could have foreseen [Karl] Abraham's steadiness or [Carl] Jung's later defection.

I have not yet read the book which I have for the peace of Ireland which comes now. The time here was a bit hectic.

I love Carmel from memory. I hope that you will have a good time there.

All the best to you, Betty and Tom.

Yours,

Anna Freud

1. Commission on the Evaluation of Applicants (IPA); *Search*, 1:461–75. See below, September 13, 1973.

Carmel, September 12, 1971

My dear Gustl,

Enclosed your allowance for the month of September, beginning with September 5. I hope that you are feeling increasingly settled and that you will get your bed soon and like it. It's nice that you are making yourself comfortable. Shame on you, though, that you thought Kohut was a fullback[1]—that was, of course, Popovich—and he played for an Austrian Club, "our" club, the Amateure which later became "Austria" and originally (before my time but during my father's time) had been the "Cricketers." There was a fine right wing of the Amateure, little "Cutti" (his full name was "Moracutti" but everybody called him "Cutti"). But Kohut was a left wing who for years played in the Hungarian national team. He was, of course, a "lefty." The Amateure had by the way two great players of Hungarian descent during my time: Kalman Conrad (a splendid center forward, or right forward intermediate) and Jenö Konrad, an outstanding strategist, the center halfback. I wonder whether your hungarian [*sic*] professor knows of them.

This weekend we had guests—first Henry von Witzleben and Ilse on Friday and Saturday; then today for lunch a colleague from Sausalito and his wife. They are all reading my book but apparently are making only slow progress with it. The S[an].F[rancisco]. Institute will have a workshop to study it.

I am working a little now—every day a bit of writing in my NY lecture for Nov. 30.[2] Progress is slow but steady. Only I am afraid I am doing so much tidying up of past work that I can't quite get to the new topics that I am eager to tackle. We'll see how it works out.

Enclosed I am forwarding your bank statement which was sent after us from 5805 Dorchester. Let us hear from you. Love to you from your Dad

The best to Sue and to all your friends.

---

1. For some years Tom had been playing soccer competitively.
2. *Search*, 2:615–58.

December 25, 1971
Anna Freud
London
Dear Miss Freud,

I want to respond to your messages and to tell you how much your warm participation means to us. Tom's C.O. [conscientious objector] classification is, of course, a great thing. As far as my health is concerned I feel quite relieved now, keep my fingers crossed for the future, but am—I think realistically—optimistic.

Yes, the Brill lecture went well. An acquaintance who could not attend it wrote to me that his first patient the next day, a training analysand, has said that it had made him proud that he was becoming a psychoanalyst. That made me feel good, too. What is even more important, I am in the swing of work (it never stopped, even while I was in the hospital expecting the worst) and I hope to move forward beyond the limits which I set myself in *The Analysis of the Self*. My work plans are an antidote to the guilt feelings which I experienced about withdrawing from the Freud Lecture in Vienna [1972], a step which I took with great reluctance.[1]

And how are you? We know that Paula Fichtl's accident and operation have been very taxing to you, but we also hear that things are gradually settling down again. " . . . carefree,—if there is such a thing," you say. Of course, there is not, and one learns not to expect it.

The best wishes for 1972 from Betty, Tom and from your
Heinz Kohut, M.D.

1. Kohut's lymphoma was diagnosed in the fall of 1971 and contributed, among other things, to his decision not to accept the Freud Lecture invitation. See Kohut to Frederick J. Hacker, December 7, 1971; see also Kohut to George Pollock, November 14, 1971; and Kohut to Siegmund Levarie, May 9, 1972.

January 26, 1972 [from Ernest Wolf]

Dear Heinz,

Just a brief note to let you know that your presentation today to the Institute was even more stimulating to me than the Brill lecture. Perhaps this is due to the changes you made, perhaps I felt more relaxed. Also I liked your reception by the staff better today than last week, there was less laudation of style and more coming to grips with the real issues.

My own thoughts wandered to the topic of narcissistic rage and group phenomena. Could it be that the current excesses in anti-technological sentiments, in so far as they are irrational and extol an impossible return to a never-having-existed pre-industrial idyll, could these be the expression of a narcissistic grudge about the lost omnipotence of Man (as idealized self-object) vis-à-vis the increasingly sophisticated machine? There have been recurring waves of Luddite sentiment. In 1811 there were bloody riots and they have been diagnosed, traditionally, as protests against material deprivations and unemployment. I think a different interpretation, along the lines that you suggested today, would be more to the point. In this connection it is interesting to note that the leader, a "General Ludd," was an *imaginary* person, who was thus suitable to represent omnipotence without danger of disappointment in him. These speculations become even more fascinating when I read (in the *Encyclopaedia Britannica*) tonight that the name Ludd was derived from a person of weak intellect, called Ned Ludd, who was the butt of the boys of the village (1779). On one occasion Ludd pursued one of his tormentors into a home where there were two of the frames used in stocking manufacture, and not being able to catch the boy, vented his rage on the frames.[1] It seems obvious to me that regardless of the correctness of my speculations your ideas about narcissistic rage open up a new interpretation of history.

Another line of thought wonders about the recurrent waves of anti-intellectualism, especially when they degenerate into irrational attempts to recover the lost omnipotence through group preoccupations with magic, such as spiritualism, astrology, or as a contemporary equivalent, predicting economic fortunes by reading the tea-leaves of the financial pages.

Well, I better stop. Needless to say, I was greatly stimulated and excited.

Cordially,

Ernie

1. On the various origins of the term, see Robert Reid, *Land of Lost Content: The Luddite Revolt, 1812* (London, 1986), p. 73.

February 15, 1972 [original in German]
Tilmann Moser
Frankfurt/Main
Dear Tilmann,

We enjoyed your letter very much, although it could not replace the visitor that we have all come to love. Your sharp, quick opinions, your powers of observation, your humor and your happy disposition all gave us great pleasure and we missed you noticeably a few days after you left. But we will see you again and that comforts us.

What you wrote about Washington and New York was impressive. I wouldn't say that I have no use for family therapy. And I can certainly understand what you like about it. But analysis is something completely different; and deep, new insights into men—and into *humanity*—will, I believe, not come from the observation of groups. I can't say exactly where the difference lies. Your analyst supposes that my particular attitude toward analysis is bound up with my love for art. This may be true, but I have no real understanding of such a relationship within me. I am aware of the differences between the tempo of insight into oneself and that of the explanation of what one has observed. But I can't say now what these differences mean. One can quickly comprehend a family scene. And one can quickly and informatively report on it when one is so gifted as you are. How different with analytic insights!

A short time ago I heard a report from a female colleague who wanted my advice about the handling of a case of anorexia nervosa. For her entire life the patient had strong secret dependencies on chemical substances (e.g., saccharine) which, it gradually dawned on me, represented for her an idealized distillate of nourishment. Something edible but that had scarcely any substance. Something that in considerable dilution produces a sweet taste but that is not sugar. This seemed to me similar to a magic love potion, to a witches' brew. A magical concentration of the edible—a symbol of an early oral maternal reality, but not the reality itself. When one now takes into account that as a small child the patient had a psychotic mother who then died; that after the death of the mother she had in her place a black housekeeper who also soon died (from breast cancer!)—then one begins to understand that the little girl was searching for the essence of maternal nourishment over which she could have control. A maternal nourishment that would not confront her suddenly in a psychotic-senseless way and that would not be unempathically taken away in death.

How long it takes for one to make even a little progress in understanding such a situation— in contrast to the speed and relative certainty with which superficial family relationships can be understood.

Or an example from my ongoing analytic practice. Yesterday a patient reported to me a dream that remained mysterious to us both. About three men who engaged in a remarkable ritual. On the roof of a tall building, blindfolded, they marched along a beam—slavishly following a religious rule. They had to count their steps, but they all miscounted and fell one after another to their deaths. Nothing occurred to the patient concerning the dream—at least nothing that was in any way helpful to us. He spoke of anxiety about premature heart disease and also about the wish to take a week of vacation in the next month. But we couldn't get any further—I remained without a clue. But today the puzzle of the dream solved itself with satisfying certainty. We realized that it had to do with his ritualizing attitude toward work and toward life as a whole. That his intention to take a vacation aroused in him anxiety and guilt feelings of the strongest kind. It turned out that he had never taken time off to relax. It turned out that he was afraid to give up his ritualized conscientiousness, because he sensed in himself the danger of losing all his values and becoming delinquent. I could show that beautifully piece by piece. The three men in the dream, for example, who fell from the roof, were acquaintances from the National Guard who always went to church in order to escape duty rather than out of true religious conviction. The whole National Guard here, naturally, is not an internally accepted inner authority for everyone, but only a external force toward which one acts like the delinquent does toward generally accepted norms. The patient's brother is in jail. He sarcastically rejects all the values of the majority—just like the parents who are shameless swindlers a) because as immigrants they had to get ahead and b) because the values to which they had to conform were those of an oppressive majority which

represented hostile and not internalizable values. The interpretation
of the dream led us to all the foregoing, but especially to the understanding of the whole compulsive work—and lifestyle of the patient.
He had to work like a machine, could not allow himself any freedom,
could not undertake anything spontaneously and joyfully, since he is
always in danger of having all his values collapse and leave him to
delinquency (like an addiction) just like his brother. When one makes
such progress in an analysis, when one can work through everything
slowly (probably in the transference, in the attitude toward analytic
"work"), then one has really brought the patient a nice bit of the way
forward—also his family, for example, his two little sons.

I don't think that insights into family quarrels, as enlightening as
they may be, can lead to such deep understanding and to such potentially lasting effect. The exploration of family dynamics certainly has a
place in therapy and research. But I also fear that these quick and
convincing insights can lead us away from the analytic work that takes
us into the depths. I come again to the slow tempo with which I
began. The long not-being-able-to-understand is often the necessary
precondition for a deeper understanding. And the satisfaction with
the quick successes of family therapy, etc. can easily lead to the result
that the work which can really lead to new insights will no longer be
undertaken.

Maybe you are smiling now. Such a not-being-able-to-understand
can naturally become the excuse for the mystical-poetic that leads to
play, remains unfruitful, is socially irresponsible; that it can be used
as an excuse for ignoring the concrete suffering of men. I can still
recall well the Beethoven-playing White Russian general in [Sergei]
Eisenstein's [Battleship] Potemkin [1925] who, without interrupting his
piano-playing, confirms the death sentences against the revolutionaries. But one cannot forget that with analytic insights people are
helped—and, as I hope, as well beyond the bounds of individual
therapy.

What you wrote about New York and the Eisslers moved us
deeply—but you certainly have not seen the larger whole. There is
much positive there that becomes visible only gradually.

Almost every evening we play one of the Beethoven trios and enjoy
it very much. But even without this lovely gift that you left behind
here as a remembrance we would not forget you. Write again soon.
My wife sends her warmest greetings.

Most cordially, your
Heinz Kohut, M.D.

March 9, 1972 [original in German]
Dr. Erhard Künzler
Munich
Dear Mr. Künzler,

Your letter has again given me great joy and I will answer it immediately.

First to your question regarding your problem child, "how long is it sensible to continue with such a case," especially when the financial position of the patient is a bad one. Now, I'm no Delphic Oracle and I can't give you anything more than a personal point of view. The deepest impulse for me under such circumstances is an unquenchable curiosity coupled with endless (or should I say timeless) patience. As long as I feel the unresolved excitement within me that I will yet come upon the tracks of the patient's secret, that I will understand better what he lacks on the deepest level (genetically and/or dynamically), then I can keep the analysis going even when money is tight. The wish to help is not enough for *me* under such circumstances. When I feel, however, that I can no longer endure the bother and I have the impression that the patient can get along for a while without me, then I let the patient go, permit him to remain in contact with me (occasional telephone calls, letters, occasional visits), and express the hope that later we can again take up an intensive analysis. That sets a goal and maintains hope.

What you wrote about the reading of my book I found very important. I have heard from many sides that my book is very hard to read. Other colleagues, however, assure me that it is not hard, rather that it is clearly and beautifully written. Your self-insights indicate that the difficulties in some cases are the unresolved narcissistic problems of the reader which are then projected onto the formulations of my book.

You have certainly misunderstood the matter of the "five departure groups." I did say that there are various groupings of analysts—for example, five, or ten, or fifteen; it depends on how one draws the lines—and that one must determine to which group each training candidate belongs. Then one must try to predict whether this person can make his way to becoming *that* type of analyst. How many such types there are I don't know. But I think that it is possible to isolate some major types. (In connection to Freud 1916c ["Some Character-Types Met with in Psycho-Analytic Work"] I spoke jokingly about "Some Character-Types Met with among Analysts." Cf. *Standard Edition,* 14.) Naturally I could write much more about this topic, but will put that off since I will send you (though not with this letter) relevant works:

a) my lecture "The Evaluation of Applicants for Psychoanalytic Training" (*Int. Journal of Psychoanalysis* 49, 1968, part 4; especially the part
which begins on page 551 and ends at the bottom of page 552); and
b) the "Report of the Study Commission for the Evaluation of Applicants" that I submitted last summer in Vienna to the Executive Council
of the IPA.

I regret that I cannot come to Europe at the present time. But I am
up to my ears in work and don't want to be interrupted by travel. The
Rococo churches of which you write make it even more difficult to
withstand the desire to travel—but postponed is not cancelled.

Cordial greetings on your wife and your children. I hope to hear
from you again soon. Please also greet Frau Dr. [Ingeborg] Zimmer-
man for me.

Yours,

Heinz Kohut, M.D.

March 13, 1972
Mr. Jeffrey Urist, Research Intern
University of Michigan Medical Center
Ann Arbor
Dear Mr. Urist:

I think that your research project[1] is fascinating; I have, however,
next to nothing to contribute. I do not use projective tests and have
no empirical knowledge concerning the question whether such tests
would be helpful in the (differential) diagnosis of various narcissistic
disorders.

One thought occurs to me: Would the study of manifest dreams
give you leads concerning the crucial images and stories which you
might expect to find in the projective tests of people with narcissistic
disorders? People and their twins; people seeing themselves in a mirror; people flying; people admiring some symbol of greatness or
strength—these might be such possible images and contents. Then I
would be on the lookout for the cohesion or fragmentation of these
figures.

All in all, clearly a project worth pursuing, with the possibility of
finding something new. If you want to follow my suggestion you
might do well not only to survey the dreams recorded in my own
various contributions to the subject but you might also write to others
who have worked with me and are familiar with the analysis of narcissistic personalities. These names come to mind: Dr. Michael F. Basch,
Dr. John E. Gedo, Dr. Arnold Goldberg, Drs. Paul H. and Anna

Ornstein (Cincinnati), Drs. Paul H. and Marian Tolpin, and Dr. Janice Norton (Denver).

I would be interested in learning about the progress of your work.

Best wishes,

Sincerely,

Heinz Kohut, M.D.

1. Jeffrey Urist, "The Rorschach Test as a Multidimensional Measure of Object Relations" (Ph.D. diss., University of Michigan, 1973).

March 21, 1972

Dr. phil. Tilmann Moser

Frankfurt/Main

Dear Tilmann:

Please forgive me for writing to you in English today but the opportunity of not having to do my own typing is irresistible. I read your letter several times with various emotions, and I chuckled over your lovely book review. But now I have settled down to thinking that you are right and that I should not argue with you any further about the different merits of family therapy and group observation, on the one hand, and individual therapy and depth psychological observation, on the other hand. I will trust your judgment and believe you when you say that much can be learned from the detailed study of groups and, especially, that much can be achieved therapeutically in this setting and that work on the application of analytic insights, "Beyond the Bounds of the Basic Rule," must be done.

My hesitation, I feel sure, is not due to fear of deviationism or, more general, to the fear of the new. (There is much to be said for a certain kind of conservatism in analysis, by the way—but I will not burden the present letter with this difficult topic.) I think that my stress on analysis over family therapy is connected with the fact that my primary motivation is discovery and insight, not therapy—or, to be more exact, therapy through insight not therapy per se. I like people—am happy when I can help them, unhappy (sometimes very unhappy!) when I cannot. But my real love is new understanding. The looking at not yet meaningful patterns is endlessly fascinating to me—surpassed only by the attraction of looking at patterns that are understandable and make sense but when, if one is able to discard the manifest meaning, one opens oneself to new questions and the possibility of new answers. I have created a private fairy tale for myself. Of Newton holding the apple in his hand, releasing it from his grasp and,

as the apple moves away from his hand, downwards, asking himself
in amazement: why didn't it stay? The question about the speed with
which conclusions are reached (the rapidity with which understanding
is achieved) sounded to you like a reproach about superficiality. But
what I wanted to ask was whether there exist different thinking processes and different classes of discovery and understanding. I did not
want to differentiate between microscopic and macroscopic observations; and I did not have in mind a judgmental comparison between
careful observation and sloppiness. I'm inclined to think, however,
that the mental activities which lead to understanding in the realm of,
e.g., group- and family-processes are different from those that lead to
insight in the analytic situation. Am I wrong here? I do not know with
certainty because I have not puzzled with endless time and timeless
expectation over family situations as I have over denouements in the
area of the single soul. If I am right, however, then it will be worth
paying attention to the consequences which in your case the shift from
one to the other mental attitude will bring about. If you spend half a
working day as a group and family therapist and the other half as
an analyst—will this be mutually helpful or will one form of activity
gradually tend to crowd out the other?

I cannot end this letter without giving voice to a complaint—and a
legitimate one it is. Here was this Moser with us in Chicago for a
week, opening himself up in natural intimacy and getting the same
treatment from all of us. And now he mentions casually that he's going
to get married soon. Now what kind of business is this? Where was
the detailed account, the shared excitement, the photograph? Or was
America so intense an experience that it could temporarily cover even
the mental presence of the future wife?

Warm regards and good wishes from all of us and especially from
your
   Heinz Kohut, M.D.

March 27, 1972
Vann Spruiell, M.D.
New Orleans
Dear Dr. Spruiell:
   Your friendly letter gave me great pleasure and, of course, I have
no hesitation to let you see the manuscript containing my recent
"Thoughts on Narcissism and Narcissistic Rage."
   I will not be in Dallas [for the Spring APA Meetings] and there will
therefore unfortunately be no opportunity to meet you. But I will

surely be in New York for the Fall Meetings and hope that you will try to get in touch with me then.

Your approval of my efforts to establish the importance of research goals in analysis is very welcome to me. But please don't lose heart! I have learned from long experience that organizational changes are not easily brought about and that the road to ultimate victories requires a few preliminary defeats. The work of the Ad Hoc Committee on Scientific Activities was always mainly educational and I believe that we have achieved something in this respect despite the fact that no Council on Scientific Activities was instituted.

Congratulations on your plan to spend a year at the Hampstead Clinic and on your stamina in carrying it through without external support. The research atmosphere around Anna Freud is truly a great inspiration for anyone who can participate in it for any length of time and I am sure you will not regret the sacrifices that this enterprise requires of your family and you.

Let me once more express the hope that we will get to know one another personally.

Sincerely,

Heinz Kohut, M.D.

P.S. You may keep the enclosed manuscript—but it is, of course, not meant for further distribution.

April 4, 1972
Mrs. Fay Sawyier
Chicago
Dear Fay:

Thank you for your note concerning my discussion of Roy Schafer's presentation. I had meant to say that we should avoid setting up a total, well-rounded theoretical system; i.e., that we should avoid a system that would correspond to the total explanation of the universe with the aid of an intentionalistic god. I wondered whether Schafer was not perhaps introducing such a "god" when he suggests that we make the person and his actions the center of a new psychoanalytic theory.[1] I said that psychoanalysis should stick with part theories and with explanatory and communicative devices of all kinds; in particular that we should not be afraid of being evocative through the use of analogies if these analogies help us to grasp one another's meaning. When I say that we are pushed by our ambitions and led by our ideals (or that we experience our ambitions as coming from below and our ideals as being above us) I am not, at that moment, setting up a theory;

I am rather making first steps toward pointing out important differences between mental contents which had formerly been considered as being very similar. The child "looks up" to the admired powerful adult (the later experiences of the internalized ideal still has traces of the early experience); the child wishes himself to grow up, he imagines that he lifts himself up, i.e., he has flying fantasies, etc. (the later experiences of his ambitious wishes still bear traces of this movement from below). I don't think we need be hypochondriacal about such modes of expressing ourselves but that we should preserve the freedom of speaking colorfully and strongly. The physicists are not afraid. Or do they get their fingers rapped because they speak of a "wave" theory of light, or use condensed models of moving particles rather than always carefully speaking of shifting energic fields?

So long,

Heinz Kohut, M.D.

1. Roy Schafer, "Action: Its Place in Psychoanalytic Interpretation and Theory," *Annual of Psychoanalysis* 1 (1973): 159–76.

April 18, 1972
Dr. Erhard Künzler
Munich
Dear Dr. Künzler:

Please forgive me for replying in English. But I am pressed for time and the advantage of having my letter typed outweighs my misgivings at burdening you with a communication in English.

Some comments concerning the topic of "curing" versus "understanding."

With regard to the specific question, how long one should go on with a patient. If the treatment *must* go on, then our therapeutic responsibility to the patient is paramount, whatever we feel, i.e., we will be guided by our superego code as therapists. But when there is a choice, my answer is in essence that we can go on profitably so long as the therapist's psyche is engaged *in depth*. Whatever that depth may be: whether it is the deep wish to cure, to heal, to rescue; or the wish to see, to learn, to discover. Ego dominance over the deep wish and the participation of the depth are both necessary. In my old formulation (see in this context, Kohut and Seitz, "Concepts and Theories of Psychoanalysis," in particular the model on page 136) it is the "area of progressive neutralization" which has to be engaged.

Your contrast between understanding and explaining, on the one hand, and "helping," on the other hand, is hard for me to grasp. True enough, some formulations, interpretations, and reconstructions may *not* help the patient. But then I would assume these formulations, etc., are either in error, or have not been worked through long enough, or are incomplete. Curative explanations lead to the accretion of psychic structure, i.e., to the patient's increasing ability to handle his object-libidinal and narcissistic needs. In your previous letter (2 March 1972) you described how you cured an inhibition (to read my book) through insight—you also mentioned that you had first given yourself an erroneous explanation ("The English is too difficult!") which had left you stranded. More broadly speaking: the analyst's empathy with the psychological situation leads to the patient's empathy with himself. It keeps the pathogenic psychological conflicts and tensions openly mobilized which, in turn, leads to the acquisition of new psychological functions to handle the tensions in more satisfactory ways.

You talk about the interpersonal tensions in the surroundings in which you grew up. Surely here, too—and in the larger historical arena—the insights of depth psychology (understanding and explaining) should prove to be helpful. At any rate, nothing else has been helpful so far. As you may know, I am working on the application of my formulations concerning narcissism to group behavior, to the behavior of Man in history. (First hints concerning this work are contained in my latest paper, "Thoughts on Narcissism and Narcissistic Rage," which will appear in *Psyche* in translation. Lutz Rosenkötter has the manuscript.)

Enough for today. There is nothing in your letter which strikes me as provocative in any way. On the contrary, all your comments are very apropos and would deserve a much more extensive discussion than I am able to give. I would have liked in particular to take up the large topic of the analyst's empathy as a tool and as a curative factor in analysis, but it is my intention to write about this topic in the not too distant future and to put down my thoughts on this subject matter more carefully than I could do at this point.

Your architectural discoveries keep me excited; I tell my wife about them; and I have little doubt that the day will come when we will appear and say: "Künzler, please start your car!"

Warm regards,
Cordially,
Heinz Kohut, M.D.

[original handwritten in German] *P.S.* Now quickly a couple more words in German so that it doesn't sound so cold and foreign. I hope I have expressed myself clearly enough. The most important is 1) that deep layers in the analyst must be engaged as well if he wants to treat a difficult patient; and 2) that empathy, the "feeling-oneself-into-another," from the first to the last moment of our lives is the barrier that protectively divides us from the lifeless, cold inorganic world (death, psychosis).

May 9, 1972
K. R. Eissler, M.D.
New York
Dear Kurt:

I was touched about your phone call and sorry I missed it. I was in particular moved by the fact that it was a dream that had reminded you of my birthday—an occasion which the scare of last fall has lent a significance which takes it out of the humdrum of a taken-for-granted recurrence. I will try to dream of you but I am doubtful about my ability in this respect. With me, as with the rest of us, one has to be satisfied if the primary process [the unconscious] gives us an occasional useful hint and one must not aspire to reverse the direction of the chain of command.

Warm regards,
Yours,
Heinz Kohut, M.D.

November 3, 1972
Arnold Goldberg, M.D.
Chicago
Dear Arnie:

I just read your presentation during an otherwise uneventful I[lli-nois].C[entral]. ride downtown. It's excellent and I have no suggestions.[1] Your clinical presentation especially was somehow very reassuring to me. If *you* could translate my writings into practice, so can others. (You had of course also my oral presentations—that might make a difference. But still. . . .) Naturally we will chat about that panel in Princeton. If the tension in the Chicago Society is in any way a measure, you might as well prepare yourself for some attacks. But I have not yet heard of anything that would be difficult to deal with.

(The latest: I am unmasked as a Sullivanian. That pleases me, because I took care of that nicely already in a favorite footnote in my old paper on Introspection.[2] Anyway: you are courageous, and you are young.
Affectionately,
Heinz Kohut, M.D.

1. See Arnold Goldberg, "On the Prognosis and Treatment of Narcissism," *JAPA* 22 (1974): 243–54; presented to the APA in New York in December 1972. Cf. Otto Kernberg, "Contrasting Viewpoints Regarding the Nature and Psychoanalytic Treatment of Narcissistic Personalities: A Preliminary Communication," *JAPA* 22 (1974): 255–67.
2. *Search*, 1:218–19, n.4. Kohut argues that his notion of empathy is distinct from Harry Stack Sullivan's observations concerning *interpersonal* relations.

March 3, 1973 [original in German]
Dachshund Solms-Rödelheim[1]
Vienna
Dear young dachshund,

I'm an old *Mops* [pug] and, generally speaking, no longer have any contact with the younger generation, but I did want to write to you today. Namely, I learned from my Heinz that your Wilhelm, in spite of the great distance took part "in spirit" (can you comprehend that?) in a scientific meeting that was organized for my Heinz in June here in Chicago. Now I must say that I really didn't understand this affair. I cannot, for example, understand why such a fuss is made over the simple fact that my Heinz has gotten a little older. Anyone can get older. (I'm already almost fourteen years old; in dog's years that's much older than Heinz. But that doesn't attract anyone's attention.) But I think one shouldn't try to understand everything. Only one thing is certain—and you certainly share my view—: our humans are nice fellows, but they really are stupid. My Heinz is definitely very dumb— otherwise he wouldn't be so happy that your Wilhelm has become an "honorary sponsor" of this meeting. Now one can get excited about a good bone, especially when there's still a good bit of meat on it, but about an "honorary sponsor" . . . ? Oh well. Be sure to tell your Wilhelm what you've heard from me and tell him that for this information he should give you a nice piece of knackwurst.
Cordially yours,
Mops

1. Wilhelm Solms-Rödelheim was a psychiatrist at the University of Vienna and a medical school colleague of Kohut. See Huber, *Psychoanalyse in Österreich*, pp. 125–27, 190–95.

March 3, 1973
Rudolph M. Loewenstein, M.D.
New York
Dear Rudy:
How nice of you to have agreed to be a member of the Honorary Committee for the meeting on June 2nd. I feel deeply honored and pleased that you will be one of the Sponsors. And I understand also that you might well come to Chicago for the occasion. That would, of course, please me beyond words. The meeting does seem to be shaping up nicely: Alexander Mitscherlich will speak, perhaps about anarchy; the eminent Princeton historian Carl Schorske will present a paper on Gustav Klimt and the Sezession, (discussed by Mary Gedo the art historian, and her analyst-husband, John); and Paul Parin from Zurich, Switzerland, will present an essay on "Psychoanalysis as a Social Science," undoubtedly an important contribution which should tell us something about the currents active in Europe at the present time. I think that you would enjoy the meeting and I am certain that your presence and participation as a discussant would enrich the occasion. After all, you are from way back an important contributor to "Psychoanalysis and History"—I still remember vividly my first encounter with your great book on anti-Semitism.[1]
Betty joins me in sending you our best.
Cordially yours,
Heinz Kohut, M.D.

1. Rudolph Loewenstein, *Psychanalyse de l'antisémitisme* (Paris, 1952).

March 23, 1973
Dr. Fritz Morgenthaler
Zurich
Dear Fritz:
I just read your review of my monograph in *Psyche* [27 (1973): 183–

86] and would like to tell you what a pleasure it was for me to see what you had to say. I felt thoroughly understood and appreciated, and I feel deeply satisfied that the labors and sleepless nights of all these years of work are receiving now such a rich reward of acceptance. And yet, we both know how much there is still left to be done. I extended my work somewhat in the paper on rage from which you quoted in your review, and I have gone still a little beyond that in some unpublished writings even though my steps are again very small and tentative. I have just finished an essay on Freud's self-analysis which branches out in a number of different directions, in particular in the form of thoughts concerning group psychology, the influence exerted by charismatic and messianic personalities, and the possibility of a psychoanalytic theory of the historical process.[1] In another examination, which, however, unfortunately, is still far from being ready for publication, I made some excursions into the psychology of the courage displayed by those who are able to (or feel forced to) resist the influence of mass movements and totalitarian regimes.[2] And I even tried to show that thinking disorders may be open to analysis.

I am telling you all this because I really don't know how to express my gratitude to you in any other way. What I am saying is simply that I'm still working and still trying hard. How wonderful it would be if you could come to Chicago in June.

Warm regards,

Yours,

Heinz Kohut, M.D.

1. *Search*, 2:793–843.
2. *Search*, 3:129–81.

April 19, 1973
Frederick J. Hacker, M.D.
Beverly Hills, California
Dear Dr. Hacker:

The delay of my response to your letter of March 26 had a number of reasons. First, I am, myself, absorbed in work which is not totally unrelated to the topics of your interest and it is hard for me to force my thoughts beyond the framework of my own goals. And, second, the questions which you ask me are very difficult ones.

Let me, however, assure you that I was not damning with faint praise when I said "that, on the conscious and preconscious levels, you are describing the facts of this social state [terror; terrorism] very well." I do not know what the unconscious factors are which account for our paralysis vis-à-vis terror—as a matter of fact: they might be very different in different people and under different circumstances. To be surrounded by nameless impersonal attackers might repeat the experience of the vague fears of a very archaic mental state in us or it might revive specific fears from later developmental stages. It seems to me—as I at least implied in my earlier letter—that here your research has to become based on empirical data: the fears of specific patients, the fears of specific groups vis-à-vis specific attackers, etc.

Only if we recognize the specific nature of the fear, can we recommend specific antidotes. The only *general* remedy that I know about is increasing awareness, i.e., clearly given information about the enemy and his motivations rather than the pretense that the enemy does not exist. Activity and organization of the potential victims rather than their passivity and isolation.

Again, my good wishes for success in your research.

Sincerely yours,

Heinz Kohut, M.D.

May 6, 1973 [original in German]

Frau Gertrude Fröhlich-Sandner

Deputy Mayor of the City of Vienna

Dear Frau Bürgermeister!

The birthday greetings of the city of Vienna on the occasion of my sixtieth birthday that you sent me in your letter gave me great pleasure. In spite of my long absence from my hometown [*Heimatstadt*], I still feel myself strongly rooted in Viennese soil [*Boden*]; and, as you correctly noted, my contributions to psychological science are definitely marked by the influences of the Viennese culture to which I belong.

I have recently received many honors—among others, a scientific gathering held on June 2 here in Chicago, an honorary doctorate from the University of Cincinnati—but I am happy to say to you that the recognition of my work on the part of my hometown expressed in your letter will have a special place in my heart.

With best wishes I remain

Your

Heinz Kohut, M.D.

P.S. I enclose a program for the Chicago meetings that might interest you because of the various European participants.

June 10, 1973
Dr. Jeanne A. Lampl-de-Groot
Amsterdam
Dear Jeanne:

Warmest thanks for the birthday greetings which you and Bets sent to me on the day of the Chicago meetings. Thank you also for your letter of May 10. Please forgive me the delay in replying to it, but I was absorbed with the preparation of a long address ("The Future of Psychoanalysis") which I presented on June 2.[1]

The ease with which you are able to relate to criticism of your work is very impressive. How truly great to be able to respond so rationally. I know I *should* feel the same way, but I am unable to do so. I am usually not certain about the validity of the criticism and it is very difficult for me to learn from it directly. It has its effect on me, whether constructive or destructive, and it leads me to re-think my formulations and re-examine my findings. But it is only very rarely that I am able to accept a direct, concrete emendation to the results which previous work has led me. I used to consider this aspect of myself as a serious flaw—some unresolved old grandiosity, or the like—but I don't think so anymore. It is not that I believe that the critic may not be right or that I can't conceive of being wrong myself, it is simply that the critic is generally not in tune with where I am working and struggling at the time. And I can interrupt my internally motivated cognitive struggles only with the greatest loss to my ultimate results. But all this needs much further thought and there is no question in my mind that your attitude, especially your philosophical tolerance of the uncertainty of all knowledge, is really not so very different from what I'm saying about myself, i.e., I may be experiencing the same thing in a somewhat different way.

Your intention to clarify the difference between the biological aspects of narcissism and the psychological aspect is laudable. It's at the same time an area which is very complex and difficult but which one can also handle in a comparatively simple way. I struggled with these basic problems long ago when I wrote my paper on introspection and empathy (in the *Journal of the American Psychoanalytic Association*, 1959) and I have continued to deal with this issue in a more peripheral way in a number of places in *The Analysis of the Self*. The definition which

I gave in the footnote on page 39 of *The Analysis of the Self*, in connection with the basic consideration presented in the 1959-paper, outlines my fundamental theoretical stance in these matters. The central issue then, as I see it, depends on the question whether the subtle but decisive shift in defining the libido theory and its subsidiary conceptualizations which I suggested in 1959 is considered to be relevant. If analysts can accept the point of view which I advocated in 1959— namely, that it is the safest and most consistent stance for the depth-psychological theorist to maintain that his concepts are abstractions and generalizations which relate to an introspected and/or empathically grasped reality—then the unbridgeable inconsistency between a biological and a psychological libido concept disappears.

But enough concerning all these heavy issues! Once more my thanks for your telegram and, beyond that, for having been a friend for all these years.

Affectionately yours,

Heinz Kohut, M.D.

1. *Search*, 2:663–84. This paper was presented at a banquet in celebration of Kohut's sixtieth birthday.

June 18, 1973
Dr. Martin James
London
Dear Dr. James:

For obvious reasons I am writing to you in great haste since I am nourishing the hope that something can yet be done to prevent the worst from happening. This afternoon I sent two telegrams to England. One to you which reads: "Deeply disturbed by allusion to plagiarism in last sentence of review. Letter follows."; the other to Dr. Sandler which says: "Read manuscript of Martin James' review of my book. Deeply disturbed by allusion to plagiarism, especially in last paragraph. Letter follows." This present letter goes to you with copies to Dr. Sandler and Dr. Gillespie.

Let me begin by quoting the last sentence of your long book review as contained in your manuscript. You say, ending your discussion of my book: "It seems that, since unconscious plagiarism is an endemic force in psychoanalytic writing and theorising, this is really a synthetic

book much influenced, in fact but not in attribution, by those preoccupied by the theory of development in the earliest mothering period."

I was stunned, of course. I had read your long review with somewhat mixed feelings. You not only call my book "less a scholarly work
and more a work of popularisation," but you also see it increasingly
as your discussion goes on, from the local viewpoint, i.e., as finding
its position between orthodox Freudianism and Melanie Klein and her
followers o[r] "offshoots" as you call them. You repeatedly impute
"nervousness" to me and describe my attempts at theoretical clarification as defensive manoeuvres, undertaken out of fear of offending
orthodox Freudians. Well, while I feel that you are doing my position
an injustice and don't realize that in the morass of conflicting and
poorly based theoretical speculation I turned back to the direct observation of clinical material and constructed formulations which would
accommodate my observations, an author must, unfortunately, expect
such treatment and has no recourse if he does not want to appear as
being unable to take criticism.

But the thunderclap at the end of your review is something else
again. I have puzzled and puzzled, especially in view of the fact that
you wrote to me several times during the last year and, unsolicited,
gave me the greatest pleasure by telling me how much of a contribution you think my book makes and how much it has meant to you.
Let me, for example, quote from your enthusiastic letter of September
6, 1972. You say that you have been "reading and rereading" my book
and want to tell me "how insightful and theoretically valuable" you
found it. After reading my book, as you say later, "I found that your
100 lines or so on Klein have done more to clear my mind about her
contributions than Waelder, [Edward] Glover, or Bibring could do for
me in many pages." And finally, of specific interest in view of the
public slap in the face to which you expose me with the last sentence
of your review, you say: "I hope praise to the face is not too much
of a disgrace, but <u>since plagiarism is endemic in psychoanalysis</u> [my
underlining], I thought that before I use your ideas and forget where
I got them I had better acknowledge that I found this an important
book. And there are really not so many of them, although there are
many books on psychoanalysis. . . . My work with adolescents, family
consultations, and schizoid patients is already affected and explained
by you. Incidentally . . . , your metapsychology of borderline, psychotic and narcissistic personality cases is most helpful." Reading
these lines after reading your review makes me gasp with amazement.

But perhaps you have changed your mind since September 1972?
Hard to believe because on 17. February you wrote to me "I find that

you have markedly affected my forms in technique and made a lot clear to me." And on 11. June 1973 you say that after reading most of my other papers you value my book more now and you add that you find "especially the paper on narcissistic rage and the other on the transformations of narcissism a complete breakthrough. Not only do you describe clinical phenomena, which people know about but have never systematically studied, but you make them respectable." You announced that you will send me a type-script of the review for the *International Journal of Psychoanalysis* and comment: "I know one can never do justice to what an author has attempted, but I sincerely believe that this is a bridge book which joins many departments of theory and explains many areas metapsychologically and in terms of classical theory." And finally, accompanying the manuscript which ends on the note of the innuendo concerning plagiarism, you wonder, in your letter of 14. June, 1973, whether I might come to London and you asked me and my wife to dine with you.

It all boggles the imagination. It is clear that you don't see what you have said, that you don't see how your review (in particular the last sentence) looks to others, what message it gives to the reader.

Please, don't reply that you used the word "unconscious" plagiarism; after all, you go right on with "in fact but not in attribution." The mere position of this crucial sentence as the last one of the review speaks volumes.

I don't know what more I can say. Please consult about this matter with Dr. Sandler and Dr. Gillespie and obtain their views. I do trust their judgement and sense of fairness. And notify me immediately concerning your plans in this matter.

Sincerely yours,

Heinz Kohut, M.D.

Copies: Drs. Gillespie and J. Sandler

June 20, 1973

Dr. William H. Gillespie

London

Dear Dr. Gillespie:

You are undoubtedly very busy now in preparation for the pre-pre-congress and the Paris meetings; and I assume that a situation will arise on July 25 which will make you even busier from that point on than you are now. I will nevertheless not excuse myself for imposing on your time and attention when I now turn to you once more in the matter of Dr. James's review. I know that your sense of fairness and responsibility [as a member of the editorial board] in matters which deeply concern a colleague who has devoted his life to psychoanalysis would not allow you even without my request to step back from the issue that is here at stake.

Two days ago I sent the two telegrams which I quoted in my letter of June 18 to Dr. James. In view of the fact that I have had no (reassuring) reply as I had hoped I might have received by now, I fear that the worst has indeed happened, i.e., that either the issue of the *I.J.P.A.* containing Dr. James's review has irretrievably been processed or that it has perhaps even already been published and distributed. When I reread your letter to me of 6 January in which you, to my deep satisfaction, responded so warmly to my book, my fear in this respect was increased because you mentioned already then that Dr. James told you that he was doing an extensive review for the *I.J.P.A.* In view of the fact that this was more than half a year ago the chances of the review being already published are of course increased.

Please allow me to discuss various issues separately because it is only in this way that I can separate the various layers of their relevance and significance.

There is, most broadly, Dr. James's overall evaluation of my work, an evaluation which is in such striking contrast to his personal communication to me as I pointed out in my letter of June 18. Leaving details aside, he praises my work as a popularizing contribution, not well written but with infectious enthusiasm and thus useful as some kind of propaganda—just as [Charles] Dickens on poverty would compare with let us say a series of scientific essays in sociology. Although I disagree with the view that this is not a scholarly scientific contribution, I probably have no right to complain if a critic, idiosyncratically, sees my work in this light, in fact appears at times to praise me for this supposedly non-scholarly approach. Dr. James does apparently not accept my research methods [(1) careful variegated clinical observation of the material which unfolds in the analytic situation; (2) theoretical formulations of the data thus obtained] as scientific and believes that I should instead have undertaken a scholarly study and synthesis of the psychoanalytic literature. But, as I said, unjust and erroneous though I believe his view of the scientific essence of my work to be, such idiosyncratic approaches by reviewers (although rarely quite as much determined by a preconceived point of view as is Dr. James's) are not infrequent and the author must not openly complain.

But now to the narrower area which is closer to the real issue: Dr. James's conclusion that I have plagiarized the work of those who have studied childhood directly, that—in my words; but I don't know how else I can understand what he says—that I have seen in adult analyses what had been told me by the child analysts without, however, acknowledging my real source. This narrow, central area where the real issue lies must be further divided into two separate sections. (1) Is Dr. James correct in his accusation? And (2) did he, in accusing me, express himself within the bounds expected and permitted in a scientific dialogue?

There is no doubt concerning the answer to the first question: Dr. James is wrong. I have in essence not drawn from the reports of child observers and child analysts, but have relied fully on the empathically worked over material obtained in the psychoanalytic situation with adults. The formulations thus obtained (first spelled out in my paper on "Introspection and Empathy" presented in Paris in 1957, published in 1959; see, for example, pp. 470–72; and then consistently broadened in a series of publications ending with my recent paper on narcissistic rage) do also clearly demonstrate that this method leads in certain respects to results of a different order of refinement that can be obtained via the direct examination of children. My major formulations (the independent line of development from [a] self nuclei via [b] certain specific aspects of the relationship to self-objects and their support to [c] a cohesive self with [d] cohesive ambitions and ideals and other transformations of narcissism) were not obtained through direct child observation. Even the importance of "good mothering," to which Dr. James refers, pales as a vague generality when seen from the vantage point of my work. To be able to allow the establishment of the precursors of a mirroring-, twinship-, and merger-by-extension-of-the-grandiose-self-transference between parent and child, or an idealizing relationship with an omnipotent object, are formulations which are vastly different from "good mothers," are vastly more specific.

Be all this as it may: if Dr. James had said, for example, in arguing with my discussion on pp. 218ff. of my book, that much further work needs to be done to bring together the results of psychoanalytic reconstruction and direct child observation, I would have responded with a hearty consent. Some such work has indeed already begun (see, for example, Marian Tolpin, one of my students, who in her paper "On the Beginnings of a Cohesive Self" (*Psychoanalytic Study of the Child* 26, 316, 1971) applied my concept of "transmuting internalization" to the study of the "transitional object"), but a vast area of relevant research remains of course still to be done.

Yes, integrating conceptual bridges need to be built—not only between the data of child observation and child analysis, on the one hand, and the data of adult-analytic reconstruction and recall, on the other hand, but also—on a totally different level—between analysts of different schools of thought. But the fact that these bridges have not been built yet does not make for "plagiarism," conscious or otherwise, and recklessly made statements will not build bridges but will have the effect of tearing down what conceptual integration and professional rapprochement might have been in the offing.

I've thus come to the last and crucial issue, the issue raised by the final sentence of Dr. James's review. It must have become clear to you that, apart from my horror at the accusation and the social consequences that its publication must have, I was also deeply puzzled about the inconsistency displayed by the reviewer—not only the enormous contrast between his private admiration of me and his public attack, but also within the body of the review itself, the contrast between numerous favorable details displayed quite inconsistently side by side with his subtle belittling and open disapproval and reprimand. Dr. James sees my work as plagiarized from (the modern) British child analysts, thus he sees in my work those areas (in my opinion of least importance) in which I am referring to the phenomenology of childhood experience as recalled by adults. He quotes a long passage from my book concerning the phenomenology of recalled childhood situations, just before his final statement about plagiarism—one of the few passages in my book, I suppose, that might perhaps remind some readers of descriptions in the literature on lonely, depressed, abandoned children with "poor mothering." I have no doubt that such descriptions exist—how could it be otherwise? But while this passage is contained in my book and truthfully reports what my patients told me, it does not refer to the essence of what my contribution is all about. If my book had indeed dealt with the phenomenology of childhood experience, Dr. James would be correct in asking me to devote years of careful study to all the available reports in the field and to compare and integrate them. But this was not my work: I concentrated on the adult psychopathology as embeddeed in the past, on the methods by which the past can be revived in the narcissistically disturbed, but neither on the content of the reconstructed childhood nor—and this even less—on the actual environmental deficiencies which brought about the trauma and the fixation.

I have gone far afield, but I think I had to spell out some of these details to demonstrate to you that something has gone astray in Dr. James's attitude. That something which could have been expressed as a creative suggestion for further work, became a concretely experienced preoccupation with a fight between warring factions in which I am seen, on the one hand, as fearful of the ego-psychological school of thought for over-stepping the bounds accepted by it, and, on the other hand, as dishonestly stealing from another group, the British child analytic group. I fear some concretistic attitude toward a conceptual scientific problem has here crept in which has brought about the unfortunate, the terrible situation in which I am finding myself; in which, I feel, we all are finding ourselves. I will not search for a psychological explanation because it would be irrelevant—all I can do is to worry about the result and hope that someone will find a way out of the seeming impasse. Do you know a way out?

Sincerely yours,

Heinz Kohut, M.D.

P.S. If you would like to share this letter with Dr. Sandler you may certainly do so.

June 23, 1973

Miss Anna Freud

London

Dear Miss Freud:

This morning, six days after I sent telegrams to Drs. James and Sandler, I received a phone call from Dr. Sandler telling me that Dr. James had, on his own, deleted the offensive last sentence about plagiarism from the manuscript which he had submitted to the *International Journal of Psychoanalysis*, but that he had sent to me a previous version which still contained that sentence. Sandler hoped that I would be pleased to know that and that I could now have a good weekend. For the rest he felt that, Dr. James being a very ambivalent person, his review of my book was therefore also very ambivalent. He thought, however—expressing himself here in a tone of philosophical objectivity—that it was not the prerogative of the Editor to interfere with the results of this ambivalence, i.e., with Dr. James' specific evaluation of my work. And there the affair has now come to rest.

Frankly, once the offensive sentence is gone, I am not greatly disturbed about the rest even though I find that neither Dr. James's criticism nor his praise are hitting the mark. Time and future work by others will have to decide whether my research will prove to have moved analysis forward or not. I am too much interested in my ongoing work to waste much time puzzling over this unanswerable question. I do hope, however, that the account which Dr. Sandler gave me concerning the previous deletion of the offensive sentence is correct. If so it not only exonerates him concerning any blame for not having stopped the manuscript when it was submitted to the *International Journal*, it also would go some way in soothing my anger toward Dr. James. It was strange, however, to hear Dr. Sandler wondering on the telephone why Dr. James had sent the old version of the manuscript to me.

Well, I will not further waste your time with this matter which I will soon forget, unless there are further surprises in the version of the book review which will in fact appear in the *International Journal*.[1] Please forgive me for having burdened you with my worries. But you understand, of course, what it meant to me to be able to turn to you at such a moment.

Fondly yours,
Heinz Kohut, M.D.

1. *IJP* 54 (1973): 363–68.

July 2, 1973 [from Anna Freud]
Dear Heinz Kohut,

Even though you told me to keep the information in your first letter to myself, I was so worried about it that I could not help asking Dr. Sandler whether the review had in fact been published. He reassured me and told me of the telephone conversation with you. I was very glad indeed. Thus, there is one worry less.

I expect the person Martin James really tries to "defend" is [Donald W.] Winnicott[1] to whom he was very devoted. But I can tell you that I have had a similar experience to yours with Winnicott himself. He wrote such a hostile and denigrating review of one of my books for an official journal here that it was refused. And afterwards he said that he was sorry, he did not know why he had done it, he really liked the book. So that is how it is.

As regards the copy of your address ["The Future of Psychoanalysis"] and the "Reflections [on the Self-Analysis of Freud]," I am sorry to say that I never received them. But if they were not made Airmail they may still come. Ordinary surface mail takes weeks.

Yours sincerely,
Anna Freud

1. Winnicott was an "independent" member of the British group of child analysts and the object-relations school.

July 3, 1973
Dr. W. H. Gillespie
London
Dear Dr. Gillespie:

Having participated in the first four acts of the tragicomedy, I believe that you should not miss the denouement in the fifth. Yesterday
I received (probably from Dr. Sandler) the "proof copy" of Dr. James's
review. Apart from the ending it appears to be identical with the
manuscript which Dr. James had sent me, except that my "nervousness" has now been transformed into "hesitance" and the sentence "Kohut, working as he does among Hartmann hard-liners, has
to defend his rear" has disappeared. It may amuse you, however, to
compare the two endings and I am enclosing them, xeroxed onto a
single page, the old one above, the new one below. Originally, as you
can see, Dr. James asserted that it is the aim of my work "not to
rely on anything but classical theory" and that my work is, therefore,
"especially convincing." Now, however, Dr. James claims that my
work will be familiar to British analysts because my approach "aims
not to rely on classical theory alone." I assume that this 180-degree
switch of the reviewer's opinion concerning my theoretical position
was necessitated by his wish to avoid ending his review on a positive
note. The missing period leaves everything fittingly open—but alas!
it will undoubtedly be inserted by the proofreader.

Sincerely yours,
Heinz Kohut, M.D.

P.S. I have not yet heard from Dr. James. Perhaps he does not
realize even now through what an emotional wringer he squeezed me.

Carmel, September 2, 1973
Dr. Morris A. Sklansky
Evanston, Illinois
Dear Morie:

I got your letter a couple of days ago in Chicago where, after our
long European vacation, we stayed for just one day before going on
to Carmel. We arrived here last night and are beginning to settle down
for a month which is to be devoted to some writing that I have to do.

I read your letter with compassionate interest and am glad that you are now feeling better and that you can reflect about your encounter with the ultimate reaches of human experience.

Concerning the obtuseness of the medical profession, I could sing you a song that deals with crudities which are almost as crass as those to which you were exposed by your surgeon. But even with individual good will and reasonable understanding from the side of more humanely constituted physicians, the individual patient is exposed to great emotional hardships within the web of our increasingly larger and thus increasingly more impersonal medical institutions. As you know, I alluded to this fact in my address on "The Future of Psychoanalysis"; I also once wrote a brief blueprint for a research project on this subject matter (referring to Kafka [1925], I called it "The Trial") which I sent to Dan Freedman, the Chairman of the Department of Psychiatry at the University of Chicago [see above, February 26, 1971], and to Bob Daniels, the Chairman of Psychiatry at the University of Cincinnati. In neither case did I get a response to my suggestion.

Your reaction to my June-2 speech pleased me a great deal—not only because you like my ideas but also because you responded with so much understanding to my intentions. I was glad in particular that you asked me whether I "had in mind the value of empathy for *all sciences,* or for the sciences directly related to human value and understanding," because this is the specific topic to which I will be turning in the next few weeks in preparation for the paper that I was asked to present at the University of Cincinnati—little Tommy Tucker sings for his supper—on the occasion of receiving an honorary degree from them. Nothing of this speech has been written yet, but I know its title ("The Psychoanalyst in the Community of Scholars") and have the message in mind that I want to give on that day. In essence I want to expand on those thoughts in my June-2 paper which deal with the increasing irrelevance of universities and will discuss this situation in the context of the tool-and-method pride of the specialist whose activities cannot attain their full significance unless they are rooted in a matrix of human ideals. The role of the university in providing this matrix, the role of the psychoanalyst in defining and explaining it within the social situation of a university, will be the topics that I hope to present convincingly on that day in Cincinnati.

Well, that's it for now. Take your time about returning to work. Let those muscles heal and the spasms subside. And, most of all, give yourself time after the emotional upheaval. All kinds of psychological work has to be done after the kind of experience to which you were exposed, and I think one needs to provide sufficient time for the homeostatic unconscious processes to run their course, before one can fully immerse oneself again into the psychic life of others.

Warm regards to Alice and the best to you. Betty, too, sends her best wishes.

Cordially,

Heinz Kohut, M.D.

Carmel, September 13, 1973

Dr. Serge Lebovici

Paris

Dear Dr. Lebovici:

Allow me first to give you my warmest congratulations at having become President of the International Psychoanalytic Association. I do not know you intimately, of course, but I have seen you on the Executive Council long enough to be glad that you have become now the leader of organized psychoanalysis. It gave me a somewhat melancholy feeling though that I was not nominated by the Nominating Committee to continue on the Executive Council, and I have wondered whether I should not have tried to counteract this move by letting myself be nominated from the floor. Should I do so next time, in London—or should I just bow out gracefully without making a fuss? I really don't know. Chances are that I would get elected. But, of course, one never knows and it's not pleasant to suffer the humiliation of a public rejection. Still, I'll think about it and wonder what your opinion might be in this matter, whether you would consider it worthwhile if I were to take this risk in two years.

The other problem on which I would like to ask for your view is the question of the fate of C.E.A. [See above, August 23, 1971.] Such a wonderful enterprise, such valuable work already done, such a constructive potential for the future. Yet, with the exception of [Olivier] Flournoy, there was again no European member present at the Paris meeting, which was very likely the last one of this study commission. (The only ones present were Flournoy, Solnit, Kligerman, and I.) Well: *tant pis* [so much the worse]! I really have done the best I could. Thus, unless you have some other suggestions, take this, please, as an unofficial announcement of our request to dissolve the committee; the official request will follow in a few months unless I hear from you to the contrary. About one thing, however, I will remain firm: while I am willing to continue as a member of the committee I will not remain its chairman—even though I am, of course, willing to help a new chairman to the best of my abilities.

Well, Dr. Lebovici, this is all for today. Even though I am not anymore a member of your official family, I hope that you will write to me concerning my present inquiry and that in general we will stay in touch with one another.

Once more my most cordial congratulations and all good wishes to you for a fine four years at the helm of the I.P.A.

Sincerely,
Heinz Kohut, M.D.

Carmel, September 14, 1973
Michael F. Basch, M.D.
Chicago
Dear Mike:

Thank you for your letter and the enclosed review from *Psychiatric Annals*. Yes, we had a very good vacation in Europe. Switzerland was perhaps the best, but Rome, Vienna, and Salzburg were not far behind. Vienna for us was a little like Berlin was for you, even though Tom had been there before with me. But now he is an adult, speaks German well, and could grasp some of the essence of the environment which has formed me. In Salzburg, apart from the usual aspects of returning to a town of which, too, I have many fond and important memories from way back, and apart from the musical pleasures which the festival provided, I had also the strange experience of spending a day with an old classmate from my Gymnasium days. The man, who has become a rather well-known historian, had heard about me through his friend and colleague Schorske who visited him immediately after attending the June-2 meetings [on "Psychoanalysis and History"] in Chicago. He got in touch with me in Vienna, and stayed an extra two days in Salzburg in order to see me. A strange, a fascinating, an eerie experience. A cultured, intelligent man who openly admitted that he had been swept along by the Nazi ideology during his days at the university (his teacher-ideal was the well-known Nazi sympathizer [Ritter von] Srb[i]k), that he had joined the Nazi party, and served in the Africa corps until he was captured by the American forces. But then, during his three and a half years as a prisoner in the United States, he underwent a deep-going personality change. It led, among other things, to his active enthusiasm for the democratic forces in history and to his marriage to an Italian woman who belongs to a family of active anti-fascists.[1] It all gives much food for thought—but it's hard to digest. Strange to say: it was, on the whole, a moving experience. What does it prove except that the passage of time does finally allow for a dialogue when formerly there could have been nothing but suspicion? I don't know the answer. But I am glad that I met the man and I would rather think that we will maintain contact now. He has already sent me a book that he has recently published (he has written a number of them) and says that he wants to study my work. He is clearly intelligent enough to understand it.

In the quiet of Carmel I have begun to do a little work again. I am writing a rambling draft of the address I will give in Cincinnati in November when I get the honorary degree. The topic is quite closely related to the address which I gave on June 2—only this time it will be directed at the universities and what they should learn from analysis in order to retain their relevance in our age—i.e., in order to shed the tool-and-method snobbishness which has tended to insulate modern science from the basic needs of mankind.

Your description of the impression which Freud's apartment made on you and your family touched me deeply and I was happy to know that this experience meant so much to you.

In about ten days I'm going to Princeton for a weekend with a group which, I understand, is rather inimical toward my work. Then I will return to Carmel for just a few more days, and will finally come back to Chicago to begin work again on October 1.

The best to Carol, greetings from Betty to both of you, and warm good wishes to you.

Cordially,

Heinz Kohut, M.D.

P.S. Did you get any clues concerning the question what Maetze thinks of my work? I had heard that he was very negative about it, but then, to my great surprise, he made the special trip to join the June-2 meeting in Chicago. I can't figure him out. Can you help?

---

1. See Adam Wandruszka to Kohut, August 28, 1971; Kohut to Wandruszka, July 3 and September 3, 1973; Wandruszka to Kohut, December 25, 1973; and Kohut to Wandruszka, April 22, 1974. Wandruszka (full name Wandruszka von Wanstetten) joined the Nazi party on May 28, 1938. On May 1, 1941, Wandruszka, along with his brother, was granted dispensation by Hitler himself to remain a party member in spite of not being of "pure Aryan descent." Berlin Document Center: NSDAP-Mitgliederkartei; Parteikorrespondenz. It is likely that this dispensation was necessitated by the fact of some Jewish ancestry.

October 23, 1973 [original in German]
Tilmann Moser
Frankfurt/Main
Dear Tilmann,

I've been waiting for a letter from you for a long time and even toyed with the idea of sending you an otherwise blank piece of paper with a large question mark on it together with my signature. But I kept thinking that it wasn't important to write and that our relationship would remain unchanged even in the absence of letters. When your letter [October 20] arrived today, with the small "f.m." [sic; *Familie* (family) Moser?] on the envelope, I immediately began to leaf through it even though I really shouldn't have taken the time then (between patients). I was sufficiently disappointed and distressed by the first reading that it was difficult for me to read it again through slowly. It was only this evening that I felt ready to undertake this task and now it is behind me.

First of all, I can say that your reaction was unexpected—not inexplicable, naturally, not without a "well, I should really have expected that" that I said to myself. But still in reality an unhappy surprise. That it was difficult for me to dedicate my time to you in St. Antönien [Switzerland], that I know.[1] But our walk, after all the other (superficial) friendly companionship, was such a joy for me that I felt especially happy afterwards and assumed the same about you.

Of course our relationship should not be built on one-sided admiration—not even on mutual admiration, although I've never hidden the fact that I admire you. And naturally we are "equal" ["*ebenbürtig*"], although you assume that I would be horrified by such a presumption on your part.

But, dear Tilmann, with equality, with non-idealization, belongs a tolerance for the weaknesses of the friend, for the limits set to his personality. I simply cannot open myself up to you in the way you expect. I also don't think that such disclosures—planned and in response to questions—belong in a friendship. It has to be spontaneous, at the right moment, in a crisis [*Notlage*]: for example, when one turns to a friend for help, but not at this or that planned hour, not even on a predetermined day or week. In spite of this I really did tell you a lot about myself; not only during our walk in St. A., but also earlier, especially in my letters.

I really should be angry that you assume that I enjoy the admiration ostensibly given me; that I can't get along without it. There you do me an injustice. I don't reject admiration, so long as it is sincerely intended, because I don't like to offend anyone. But admiration does not give me pleasure. You don't know how much I have had to suffer under the rejection of my colleagues. Most of the colleagues in my age group who earlier had been friendly with me have, since the appearance of my essays on narcissism, adopted an antagonistic stance toward me and what, for example, I have had to endure in the year before the birthday meeting [Kohut's sixtieth] in terms of antagonism is scarcely to be believed. One has to have lived through it in order to understand why some of the younger colleagues, as a counterreaction, adopted such an exaggerated positive attitude on that occasion [John Gedo, for one, had likened Kohut to Euripides].

What else can I say to you? That I like you, that you know. Whether I can fulfill your expectations, that I don't know. But I hope that your inclination toward me will remain and that our friendship will continue to ripen. More I cannot offer you. Like so much that is good in life, a serious relationship between people is largely wordless and without clear contents and conceptions. The maturation of the relationship consists in one slowly becoming clear about what the relationship is based on. But this growing clarity is not the basis of the relationship—it simply accompanies it.

I hope to hear from you again soon. I send you my warm greetings. I sincerely regret having disappointed you.

Cordially yours,
Heinz Kohut, M.D.

1. Betty Kohut recalls that the family felt somewhat intruded upon by Moser's arriving uninvited, especially since vacations, because of Heinz's heavy work schedule, were almost the only time the Kohuts could spend a great deal of time with each other.

October 27, 1973[1] [original in German]
Tilmann Moser
Frankfurt/Main
Dear Tilmann,

I've been thinking some more about your letter—especially concerning my disinclination to speak about certain chapters of my early life. You said that you were particularly interested in my past because you assumed it contained sources of my productivity that parallel those that compel you to be creative. I'm not sure, but the supposition has been going through my head the past few days that my sequestration of a part of my past perhaps preserves one of the sources of my productivity. I am also pondering the possibility that a split in the self not only can lead to neurotic formations but also to creativity.

These musings are not why I am writing you today, but rather the desire to tell you that I have read the book review in the *FAZ* and find it extraordinarily good. It is a masterpiece of understanding, simplification, communication that can scarcely been surpassed.

Cordially yours,

Heinz Kohut, M.D.

1. Since Kohut's thoughts about his past life inspired this letter to Moser (and the next; see below, December 4, 1973), it is perhaps not surprising that for the year Kohut originally typed "1937," a simple transposition which nonetheless is also the year of his father's death. Kohut corrected the error in pen after he had removed the letter from the typewriter.

October 28, 1973

May Weber, M.D.

Winnetka, Illinois

Dear May:

You ask whether I have an explanation for the fact that fifteen of the seventeen cases referred to in *The Analysis of the Self* are male. I was, of course, aware of this peculiar imbalance in the case material—others, too, have noticed it and had spoken to me about it—but I have not found a satisfactory explanation. I do not believe that narcissistic personality disorders occur with greater frequency among men, yet I do not believe either that the imbalance can be due to chance alone.

Let me give you, helter-skelter, some details which you don't know; perhaps they will assist you in your thoughts about the matter. (1) A small correction. The actual ratio of male to female is 14:3, not 15:2[1] (case _____ (p. _____) is a woman). (This change is a disguise.) (2) Of the seventeen cases, twelve were cases of mine. Of these twelve cases two were women. Of the five supervised cases (two of the analysts supervised were women) one was a woman. (3) The majority of the cases in my practice has generally been male (perhaps explained in part by the downtown location of my office), the predominance of male patients, however, has never been great; certainly there was never an imbalance which came close to the fifteen (male) out of seventeen (total) ratio of the cases in *The Analysis of the Self*. (4) My major insights concerning the mirror transference and the idealizing transference came to me during the analysis of women. (Concerning the mirror transference, it was Miss F.; concerning the idealizing transference, it was a case which, unfortunately, I could not disguise without the loss of essentials. Had it not been for this circumstance, I might well have used this case instead of Mr. A.)

Those are the concrete data which I can give you. The rest is speculation. Could it be that the case material from men is more easily
presented—perhaps because of more dramatic fantasies or because of
more striking conflicts in the social scene (such as problems concerning
work)? Could it be that the researcher when he steps into new and
unfamiliar territory avoids instinctively shouldering the additional
hardship of having to build an empathic bridge toward the other sex?
None of these answers seem fully satisfactory to me. But perhaps it is
the combination of several of them which accounts for the discrepancy
which you noted. To sum it all up in a nutshell: good question—poor
answer.

Greetings from house to house, with a special hello to Sarah. We,
too, would like to get together some day and will keep this possibility
in mind.

Warmly,
Heinz Kohut, M.D.

1. There is a possible parapraxis ("Freudian slip") in the original letter sent to Weber
in which the ratios of male to female are given as "14:17" and "15:17," an error Kohut
describes in a letter to Weber of November 14 as "a nonsense statement."

November 2, 1973
M. Robert Gardner, M.D.
Cambridge, Massachusetts
Dear Dr. Gardner:

You say that I know what I have done. Perhaps, for moments, I
feel that my efforts have led to results and I am grateful for this fleeting
feeling. But I have also been exposed to many attacks—that I have
ruined analysis, that what I have said is plagiarism, that I am insuffer-
ably vain, that I am fostering adulation. Much of the time I can take
these diatribes with that humor and wisdom—I have invented a
phrase in this context: "envy disguised as moral indignation"—to
which I have assigned a position in the schema of psychological development. But I can't always maintain equanimity. And that is the reason why I am deeply grateful to those who, like you, have the generosity to tell me without shame and hesitation that my contributions have
done something for them. Many thanks for expressing yourself—and
never mind the delay. The gift of your message is more welcome today
than it would have been at the celebration of my birthday when the
number of good wishes began to dull my capacity to react to them.

I trust that your work will remain gratifying to you despite local unpleasantness. To remain in touch with a few like-minded colleagues will surely sustain you, whatever the external hardships. Please continue to count me among those to whom you can turn for support.

Sincerely,

Heinz Kohut, M.D.

December 4, 1973 [original in German]

Tilmann Moser

Frankfurt/Main

Dear Tilmann,

Your writing appears to have made a lasting impression on me. At first I read through your letter quickly and was simply happy that you had gotten over your upset and that you did not hold my reticence against me. I read your interpretations with intellectual rather than emotional interest. I don't think I can find the old self again. The different phases of my childhood and youth—the lonely child; the soccer-playing Viennese kid; the idealistic young man in the youth movement; the confused, deeply disturbed young man—all these I remember well. And I know too that I can always best overcome the feeling of loneliness, of isolation through creative activity (poems, novellas, plays). The traces of my early creativity have all disappeared. Out of the masses of poems I can remember only two—why only these two tiny fragments? One is a song (from a lost libretto which I wrote for a friend [Franz Krämer] who was a composer and student of Alban Berg). It went: "As I was still there—With mother and father—And the rocking horse stood outside in the darkness—There led my life—Like a broad—Street into bright, open country.—But it's all mixed up—And my head is so small—One should not think—One should simply so be."[1] The other was called "The Crows." Here it is: "I saw a crow—In white snow—Maybe it's something.—Maybe.—But maybe as well—It was only black—And the snow so white."[2] One could assign all sorts of meanings to the content of these productions. Some almost force themselves upon one. But in writing down these verses it still strikes me with great sadness how lonely I was and how this loneliness found expression in my poetic stammerings. In spite of all the loneliness and confusion I had within me a great deal of early childhood vitality that never left me. And then came my American personality. The earnest work, the strengthening of the intellect; and then, as the schism of the artistic-childish and the scientific-adult weakened the collaboration of these (dividing) parts of my self, then came the creations that I no longer needed to throw away, that I could let be seen.

As I received the honorary doctorate in Cincinnati, to which I sent you the (symbolic) invitation, I became conscious of how strongly I had reacted to your letter. The President of the University had just presented me the doctoral diploma after he had praised me in his speech as the first truly American analyst. And then I stood up and, following the invitation of the President, began to speak. At this moment your letter must have worked its effect, because I took up the theme of being an *American* analyst. I didn't defend myself against this, although I confessed that I had been surprised by this appreciation. But then I went on to say that I was both an utter, true, and unredeemable European as well as a complete and true American— and that it was exactly this division within my self that had driven me to creativity, or more precisely, to research into the self.

You want a copy of my lecture. And naturally I want you to read it and to give me your impressions. But I don't know in what form I should send it to you, in the form in which I presented it the day after the bestowal of the honorary doctorate or in the longer form that I have prepared for publication. I'll send the short version for now.

Now a couple of quick answers to your questions. I am completely in agreement with the short "your Heinz Kohut."[3] I simply wanted to indicate that an ending to our letters was missing.

Tom's coming home on December 15 and will be here until shortly after New Year's. Susan will also be here—although she'll spend Christmas Day with her family out East. . . .

I would be very interested in seeing [Joachim] Fest's biography of Hitler [1973]. I would naturally prefer to read it in German and would be grateful if you could get me a copy.

Try to work out an occasion for a visit. How would it be if you spoke about the problems standing in the way of an analyst who wants to write an autobiographical book. (One could distribute a copy of my introduction if your lecture could be held within the small circle of the Institute.)

Cordially yours,
Heinz Kohut, M.D.

1. "Als ich noch war—Bei Vater und Mutter—Und das Schaukelpferd drüben im Dunkel stand—Da führte mein Leben—Wie ein breite—Strasse ins helle, offene Land.—Aber alles verwirrt sich—Und mein Kopf ist so klein—Man sollte nicht denken—Man sollt bloss so sein."

2. "Ich sah eine Krähe—Im weissen Schnee.—Vielleicht ist es etwas.—Vielleicht.— Vielleict aber auch—War sie nur schwarz—Und der Schnee so Weiss."

3. See Moser to Kohut, December 11, 1973. Kohut had proposed ending their letters with personal greetings, but Moser demurred, saying that their correspondence was too weighted with scientific material to end on a personal note.

December 27, 1973
Nathan P. Segel, M.D.
Chairman, Program Committee, American Psychoanalytic Association
Farmington, Michigan
Dear Dr. Segel:

It was very kind of you and the Program Committee to invite me to participate in a "Meet-The-Author" panel about *The Analysis of the Self*. I am pleased to see that the Program Committee is experimenting with new arrangements for scientific discourse and I believe that many authors will welcome the opportunity of being able to explain their thoughts to a large audience. As far as concerns me and my work, however, I must unfortunately decline. It has been a good many years now since I worked on the formulation of the clinical and theoretical problems of narcissism which I presented in *The Analysis of the Self* and the focus of my scientific interest has since then shifted into different directions. With the exception of my essay on narcissistic rage, no part of my newer work has yet been presented and most of it is in fact still unfinished. I know that under these circumstances I would do a serious disservice not only to my old ideas but especially to my new work if I entered a situation which would force me to become the defender of certain propositions—however hard we might try to avoid such a result. I am convinced of the fact that it is best for scientific ideas to be discussed in an impersonal way, preferably in small groups, and that a large public arena in which an author is asked to stand up for one of his publications is neither a favorable matrix for the growth of science nor is it likely to further the maintenance of that optimal fluidity and uncertainty of thought which must be preserved, especially in those scientific areas which constitute the growing points of scientific advance.

These considerations are of overriding importance to me; they compel me, with sincere regrets, to decline the warm invitation which you and the Program Committee extended to me.

Sincerely yours,
Heinz Kohut, M.D.

1974–1976

"It is strange to argue, when one agrees."

January 28, 1974
Professor Otto Pflanze
Department of History
University of Minnesota
Dear Professor Pflanze:

I owe a great debt of gratitude to my son who sent me a reprint of your essay "Toward a Psychoanalytic Interpretation of Bismarck."[1] Reading your essay gave me a good deal of intellectual pleasure. I see it as a significant contribution to the beginning interaction between two important sciences of Man, history and depth psychology—an interaction which I hope will someday lead to a new synthesis: not only the construction of a new scientific methodology for the investigation of Man and his actions but also to the emergence of new sets of questions and new scientific aims.

Your scientific interests may have moved into different directions by now and the problems of the psychological investigation of the personality of Bismarck may well have receded from the focus of your attention. But in view of the fact that you have demonstrated so clearly the importance which narcissistic elements played in shaping the personality of the life pattern of this powerful figure, I am taking the liberty of sending you a sampling of my own thoughts in this field. I hope that we will someday have the opportunity to meet and to discuss the area of our shared interests.

Sincerely yours,
Heinz Kohut, M.D.

P.S. If you have still copies of your Bismarck article available, I would be grateful for one or two of them which I want to give to certain colleagues whom I would like to acquaint with your work.

1. *American Historical Review* 77 (1974): 419–44.

February 9, 1974
Harry Trosman, Ph.D.
Department of Psychiatry
University of Chicago
Dear Harry:

Thank you so much for your warm note and for giving me the affirmation which comes from the expression of shared feelings. Your two points are well taken and, when you get a copy of my essay ["The Psychoanalyst in the Community of Scholars"] and can read it you will see that, here again, our attitudes are not far apart.

I am speaking about the acceptance which one part of analysis finds by the humanities—namely, its being accepted (see page 12) as "subtle phenomenology" and (see page 21) as "a specific, sophisticated art— an art of understanding people via the resonance of empathy." That this acceptance has desirable effects, I do not deny. In the context of my argument, however, I had to stress that this acceptance is incomplete, that it is restricted to only one of two "layers" of analysis.

Concerning the origin of the universities, you will notice that I speak (page 44) of the "university as we have known it" when I refer to "its humanistic beginnings in the Renaissance." (Cf. in this context also my remarks in "The Future of Psychoanalysis," in particular the paragraph which begins at the bottom of page 20 and ends on page 21.) I am, of course, familiar with the scholastic historical origins of the institutions of higher learning in the Middle Ages. But I am sure that it is the liberated individual of the Renaissance and the transformed university of the Renaissance which are the meaningful antecedents of the research oriented professor and the research oriented university of the 19th and 20th centuries on which I am focusing. (Should I add a footnote to the text on page 44, stating what I said in the preceding two sentences of this letter, in order to protect myself against a possible accusation of having exhibited a gross lapse of historical knowledge? Or is the phrase "as we have known it" sufficient?)

Thank you once more for the warm echo to my efforts and for your perceptive comments.

Sincerely yours,

Heinz Kohut, M.D.

March 6, 1974
Dr. Jacques Palaci
Nice
Dear Jacques:

Thank you for your letter and the enclosed announcement of your lecture in Nice in which you discussed my recent work on narcissism. I am grateful that you are interested in the paper which I presented in Cincinnati and that you want to submit it to French psychoanalytic journals and, if accepted, that you are willing to translate it. I would, of course, be very happy if your plans would materialize, but I wonder about the following. This is a paper for a broad university audience, not primarily for psychoanalysts. I would, therefore, think that it would be better to place it in a journal which is read by a wider circle of readers and not just by analysts. In addition, there is this consideration. Almost none of my papers (with the exception of my remarks in Stockholm when I chaired a panel on unconscious fantasy) has appeared in French psychoanalytic journals and, although my book has now been translated into French, is in print, and will appear in a few months (Presses Universitaires), none of my papers on narcissism has been translated into French so far. Now it might be said that since my book will be available, it is not necessary to translate either "Forms and Transformations of Narcissism" (1966) or "The Psychoanalytic Treatment of Narcissistic Personality Disorders" (1968). But my basic essay on "Introspection and Empathy" (1959) should be available to French analysts and, even more important, my paper on narcissistic rage (1972) should by all means be translated since it continues the work presented in my book and carries my ideas decisively farther. Thus, if a choice had to be made, I would rather see my paper on narcissistic rage (and my old paper on "Introspection and Empathy") published in a professional French journal,[1] and the Cincinnati address in a journal which has a broader circle of readers.

What do you think about all this? Please let me know if you need the reprints of the two papers which I mentioned and I will send them to you promptly. All these papers, by the way, and several others, have been translated into German and have appeared in *Psyche* as well as in several other volumes.

And now only once more my warm gratitude for your interest. It is nice to know that one has an old friend who is willing to be helpful.

Cordially yours,
Heinz Kohut, M.D.

1. "Reflexions sur le Narcissisme et la Rage Narcissique," *Revue Francaise de Psychanalyse* 42 (1978): 683–719.

March 15, 1974
Douglas D. Bond, M.D.
University Hospitals
Cleveland
Dear Doug:

I read "A Psychological Autopsy" with great interest, and I found it well written and hard to put down. If one accepts the specific theoretical framework used by the author [a student or young colleague of Bond's]—approximately a pattern of theories extracted from those presented by Freud in the Schreber case—one can only say that the author did very well with it and that he created a cohesive, internally consistent hypothesis. One could (and should), of course, raise the objection that the author's thesis is highly speculative since no deeper-going material could be obtained with the aid of the interview method. But, as an exercise, it is very appealing indeed, and, if it proves anything, it proves the author's intelligence.

What I, myself, find most regrettable, however, is the narrowness of the theories used. I do not believe that one can properly explain a severe psychotic disintegration, such as the one which underlies the paranoia of this insane mass murderer, by adducing oedipal dynamics. Freud showed already in 1911 that the "narcissistic regression" was of the essence; and (1924) that the delusional reality was an attempt to cover up the fact that the reality had been lost. What I would consider to be the essence (the fragmentation of the internalized idealized self-object; the replacement of these structures by "persecutors") is not even touched upon by the intricate oedipal (explanatory) formulations; and the only door available that could perhaps give access to the deep disturbance in this man's self-cohesion, the assessment of his mother's personality—is she a woman with deeply disturbed empathic capacity, e.g., an ambulatory schizophrenic?—remained totally closed.

Thank you for letting me see this interesting report. Despite my objections to the psychological level of the theoretical framework of this essay, I still admire the intelligence of the author and the zeal with which he collected the empirical data which were made available to him.

Cordially yours,

Heinz Kohut, M.D.

P.S. I will give this case report to the librarian of our Institute.

March 20, 1974

Dr. Jacques Palaci

Nice

Dear Jacques:

I hasten to reply to your informative and very helpful letter [March 14]. I am glad that you are learning so much about the French contributors who have worked in the field of narcissism. It is clear that they will react to my work by saying that they have known this all along—as has been said by some British critics. To the best of my understanding, this reaction is almost totally the expression of a narcissistic injury (I am hearing similar statements from various quarters in the United States also) and I will not undertake the thankless task of quarreling about priorities in this realm. The area of the self—its development and its vicissitudes—is a vast one, and there are undoubtedly statements made by Winnicott or [Bela] Grunberger, by Mahler or [Edith] Jacobson, which deal with the problems that I have tried to master in recent years. But I also know that my specific systematic approach, and the specificity of my insights, differentiate my work from those of the others, however great the value of their work might be.

Now to the specific question of the publication of my papers in French. I think that the paper on narcissistic rage should have priority and I suggest that you follow through with your idea and submit it to the *R[evue]. F[rancaise]. [de] P[sychanalyse].*, giving them your reasons why you think it should be published by them, telling them that I would very much like to have it published because it is a continuation of *Le Soi* which will appear shortly, and, finally, tell them that you will translate this paper as soon as it is accepted by the *R.F.P.*

"The Psychoanalyst in the Community of Scholars" should, I believe, have second priority. I wished that it could be published by a periodical which addresses itself not only to analysts, but to a broader, academic audience. I am certain that such publications must exist in France. Again, if you feel that you have discovered a dignified place for this paper, I would suggest that you submit it for publication in the same way that I outlined with regard to "Narcissistic Rage."

Warm regards,

Heinz Kohut, M.D.

March 28, 1974

Professor Edward Teller

Berkeley, California

Dear Professor Teller:

Friends of mine who are familiar with my work pointed out to me your recent contribution to the Forum for Contemporary History,[1] which is in striking support of a position which I have held for a long time—to the displeasure even of my own colleagues, not to mention my friends in the "hard" sciences.[2] At any rate, I was glad to see your eloquent statement; and I hope that my own views, as expressed in the enclosed address ["The Psychoanalyst in the Community of Scholars"], will help to dispel some of your own misgivings about the possible abuse of this indispensible [*sic*] instrument [see below, May 3].

Sincerely yours,

Heinz Kohut, M.D.

1. Edward Teller, "Neither Social nor Science," *Skeptic* 3, no. 2 (February 1974): 6–7. Teller, a nuclear physicist, was the developer of the hydrogen bomb.

2. See Center for Psychosocial Studies memorandum of March 25, 1974, in which Teller is quoted on the need for empathy in the social sciences.

April 18, 1974
Dr. K. R. Eissler
New York
Dear Kurt:

Thank you for your phone call and for your warm response to my having received an honorary degree. As far as your critique is concerned, I will admit that it gave me a feeling of despair. I fully agree with the views which you are expressing in your letter [April 13], but why you would have felt the need to emphasize them after reading my address ["The Psychoanalyst in the Community of Scholars"] is unintelligible to me. I must have failed completely in communicating the message that I intended to give. (Did Ruth, too, understand my speech as you did?) Out of the complex weave of my argument a critic can, of course, pull out a number of selected strands and demonstrate that I have given an exhortation which parallels an appeal to cure the ills of the world through Christian love. But I would not have believed that a conscientious and fair-minded reader like you could overlook the central points which I am making. They are: (1) a prescription to the universities to shift from the dominant preoccupation with those sciences which, through the acquisition of knowledge, serve man's mastery over his historical destiny; (2) the exhortation for a light but important shift in the hierarchy of values of the scientist: from tool-and-method pride (which should be transformed into the enjoyment of ego functions) to the goal of the survival of humanness (which should become the matrix in which specialized scientific aims should be pursued); (3) the plea that empathy as a scientific instrument should not be denigrated—that we should recognize that it can become a rigorously controlled tool of observation in the field of complex human experiences, that its value for science should not be discarded on the basis of the do-gooder's traditional distortion that empathy—which (as vicarious introspection) is a means of gathering data about the inner life of man—is nothing but an aim-inhibited form of love.

But enough! It is strange to argue, when one agrees. But try to think yourself, for example, into my sense of feeling thoroughly misunder-

stood when you are telling me that many people are trying to human-
ize hospitals, and are implying that I am advocating nothing more
than that by what I said. There are indeed some sentences which
express dismay at the machine-like stance of modern medicine (and
of other aspects of modern life)—you failed to notice, however, that
my aim was not to appeal to good will in order to create a friendlier
atmosphere in the big hospital but I was describing a research project
[see above, February 26, 1971] which could serve the investigation not
only of the individual's reactions in a big hospital but, by extension,
his reactions as he feels caught in the impersonal milieu of the mass
organizations which dominate and threaten human life and its values
more now than the "storm and plague" of yesteryear.

Tomorrow we are going to Cincinnati and I will participate in a
panel on my two papers on these topics. I am curious to find out
whether some of the representatives of the various departments will
have interpreted my intentions as you have done.[1]

Warmest regards to Ruth and the best to you from your,
Heinz Kohut, M.D.

1. See Kohut to Eissler, April 21, 1974; and Eissler to Kohut, April 24, 1974.

April 18, 1974 [original in German]
Mr. Jürgen vom Scheidt
Munich
Dear Mr. Scheidt,

Many thanks for the sending of the collection, *The Treatment of Drug
Addicts* [1972], edited by you which I received today. I read your introduction carefully and enjoyed it. Since you are an expert in the area
of addicts—and particularly with regard to your lovely contribution,
"Sigmund Freud and Cocaine" [*Psyche* 27 (1973): 385–430]—, I would
like to ask your view (and help) on the following matter. There exists
a rather comprehensive work by me (English: "Reflections on Freud's
Self-Analysis") that will appear in German in *Psyche* [29 (1975): 681–
720]. The manuscript originally contained the following sentence:
"Furthermore, one might hypothesize that his [namely, Freud's] intense oral-respiratory cravings (cf. his cocaine addiction as a young
man, and his increasing, unbreakable bondage to cigar-smoking later
in his life) were related to. . . ." A colleague who read my essay
wrote about this remark: "Is it correct to call Freud's use of cocaine an

addiction? As far as we know he had little difficulty in breaking himself of this habit." Since my remark is unimportant in the context of my work, I decided to leave it out. I would, however, like to ask your opinion (and also refer me to the sources that would support the view that Freud's use of cocaine actually carried traces of addiction).[1]

Once again many thanks for the book. I am with cordial greetings

Your

Heinz Kohut, M.D.

1. Scheidt replied on April 22 that the literature suggested that Freud was *not* addicted to cocaine. See also Kohut's preface to vom Scheidt's *Der falsche Weg zum Selbst* (Munich, 1976) in *Search*, 2:845–50.

May 3, 1974 [from Edward Teller]

Dear Dr. Kohut:

I read your address [see above, March 28] with interest and pleasure. In criticizing "social scientists" for their lack of empathy I certainly did not have the psychoanalysts in mind. I am fully aware of the fact that in this regard psychoanalysis is a great and wonderful exception. (Having been born long ago and at a distance of approximately 100 miles from Vienna, I had a relatively early exposure.)

There is one particular point that bothers me about psychoanalysts. While I have learned much from them that is important and interesting, I do not recall any occasion where a psychoanalyst has been permanently stumped. In your address you do mention a case that worried and puzzled you, and of such cases there are many. But I still have to meet the psychoanalyst who concludes a story of this kind by saying "and I have never understood it. It still worries me, maybe something that we believe in is not quite right." Yet statements of this kind are not only quite usual in the kind of science in which I am engaged, they are also among the most fruitful of statements because they lead· to real novelties.

In case you have experienced such a situation, or in case you have heard of one from a colleague of yours, I certainly would enjoy hearing about it.[1]

Again, thanks for sending me your manuscript.

With best regards,

Edward Teller

1. *Search*, 2:888–91.

May 19, 1974 [original in German]
Professor Dr. Clemens de Boor
Sigmund-Freud Institut
Frankfurt/Main
Dear Clemens,

Your letter from Holland gave me special pleasure. The work that you have undertaken there appears to promise much and I hope that the intellectual spoils will lead to a broadening of our understanding in the realm of narcissism and especially narcissistic rage—a possibility you indicate. Would you like to come to Chicago again and report on your experiences in the prison? If you are interested in principle in such an undertaking I could then try to take the necessary steps for its realization. Not only would the Institute be a possibility (and perhaps the "Society"), but also in particular the Center for Psychosocial Research, which I believe has some money available and is concerned, among other things, with the area of asocial behavior. So let me know if this is a possibility.

I myself am working rather busily. I have just finished a small essay. Right now it bears the title "Remarks on some principles of scientific research" and was written as a letter to a student at the Institute.[1] The occasion was a report for a regional conference in which a student had summarized the results of my research for the last few years. In this report he complained that I had been much too careful in my theoretical formulations, that I too often only "imply" rather than clearly "state" them. This reproof led me now to set forth what I have long had in mind: namely, to underline the fact that analysis is an empirical science and that the theorizing which (especially through Hartmann) has become the crown jewel of analytic conceptualizing must once again return to the place that Freud had originally reserved for it.

It was very nice of you to reassure me that my work is not being neglected in Frankfurt. I would very much like to visit you again, but don't know whether there is enough interest for such a visit. What is more, on my last visit to Frankfurt there was this unhappy tension between the analysts who work at the institute and those who are in private practice. I would not want another visit from me to contribute to a revival of these tensions. But perhaps—it is to be hoped!—they have in the meantime subsided or even improved. These family squabbles [Bruderzwiste] among analysts are universal. Their bases are as unintelligible to the outsider as they are compelling to the conflicting parties. And so often the attempt at an objective position is perceived as insult, since each side appears to make a clear distinction between right and wrong. I hope that my long essay ("Reflections on Freud's Self-analysis"), which will appear in *Psyche*, will also make the group tensions within analysis more understandable.

Tom and Susan are as before in Minneapolis. Tom appears to be working hard and is academically successful. Susan has found a small civil service position, which at least provides some small income. In about ten days we fly (for the first time) to Minneapolis for a visit. The occasion is a lecture at the University to which I have been invited.

Let us hear from you again, give my best greetings to your wife and daughter (Betty also sends greetings to you and your family) and in particular my heartiest greetings to you from your
Heinz Kohut, M.D.

P.S. Dr. E. Wolf, who coincidentally just called me on the phone and to whom I explained that I was just writing you, mentioned that he had written you some time ago about a visit to Chicago. Now you've heard it a second time—twice is better.

1. *Search*, 2:737–70.

July 20, 1974 [original in German]
Prof. Dr. med. Helmut Thomä
Ulm, West Germany
Dear Dr. Thomä:

I cannot give a rational reason for the optimism with which I undertake the work of responding to you, for I really should doubt whether the unbridgeable gap that appears to have opened up between us over Moser's confession and my introduction to it[1] can be bridged. Perhaps my relatively hopeful attitude toward this task is partly explained by the fact that I am in the middle of scientific work. During the last three weeks I have been working on a difficult essay that deals with the problem of the termination of analysis of narcissistic personality disorders—especially with a detail of these terminations, namely, that the analysand sometimes turns to a creative task, that he withdraws from the analyst (as self-object) the narcissistic tensions gradually transformed during the analysis and now brought to expression in a new way. I have already written many pages about the details of this process—for example, about the nuances of the not yet transformed and the already transformed narcissism which are discernible in these works of the analysand—and I don't want to try to give you a short summation of my thoughts here. But it may well be—as I could often observe in myself in other circumstances—that I can best preserve my own narcissistic balance when I am able to treat an upsetting problem with scientific objectivity.

Now, as far as Moser's representation of his narcissistic disorder and its treatment goes, I can say that I was deeply impressed by it. That no analyst before him had done what he has does not necessarily mean that what he has done is bad. I know there was no time in my life when it would have been possible to undertake something like it. I am far too protective of myself and with the impression I make on others to dare anything similar. I had however, the feeling that Moser's self-revelation, in spite of its defects, is an important human document—how an analysand experiences his analysis; that it represents a completely unique source that contributes to the understanding of the forms of experience of modern man, especially to the understanding of the internal life of a particular postwar generation. It would not surprise me if one day his book were read as an important contribution to the history of human experience and if many heavy tomes of scholarship (like my own) are scarcely able to work a more direct influence.

But now to my foreword. I wrote it for different reasons—among which was a particular desire to help analysis in general—where I thought I could. In tone and content therefore I tried to be a worthy representative of this great science, to give the reader the feeling of the circumspection, the measured nature, the emotional depth, in short, the maturity of psychoanalysis. It especially pleased me when about two months ago I received a letter from Hans Strotzka (whom I scarcely know) in which he wrote to me: ". . . I've just read Tilmann Moser's book and want to thank you for giving him a boost with your foreword, which sets a standard for wise and elegant judgment."

We could certainly be of different minds—as well over the value of Moser's book as over the value of my foreword. I would scarcely worry about that. (In this connection it depends on to what degree Moser's narcissism has remained unsublimated in his presentation. But even if he has succeeded for the most part in sublimating, as I think, I must admit that literary sublimation is something different from the scientific. I have already discussed this in my book on narcissism [pages 348/9 of the German translation; pages 310–12 in original]). But that you see in the book and in the foreword a danger for analysis, that you assume that the book (and my foreword) is directed against analysis, that I do not understand. That Moser's book can be used as ammunition by those who are antagonistic toward analysis is very possible. But can one ever avoid such dangers? On the whole it seems to me that Moser, in spite of his ambivalence, praises analysis to the heavens, that in him, in spite of his evident adolescent rebellion and in spite of his socialistic conflict of conscience, there is an insufficiently bridled tendency toward idealization that arouses expectations in the reader that we (unfortunately) cannot yet fulfill. Perhaps you will say that Moser's idealizations hide his hostility—a hostility about which he however speaks openly. I don't believe that; in spite of Moser's tendency toward chronic rage: the chronic rage of chronic disappointment. He is still so young! But in spite of his confusion there resides in him (and in others like him) our hope for the future.

You point out that many patients make use of Moser's little book in order to make life difficult for their analysts. I know of such episodes only too well. I too have very often had to fight to keep my analytic objectivity under such circumstances. But let us assume that some of your patients criticize you for hiding behind the abstinence rule, whereas Moser reveals himself to his future analysands. I have often endured such criticisms and been under such pressure. It always seemed to me that the result of my efforts was good when I succeeded in not becoming defensive, but rather to explain (again) with deep conviction to the patient the correctness of the principle, to which I still hold, what the advantages of anonymity of the analyst holds—for the analyst and for the patient. And in the cases in which the distance of the analyst recalls the deep trauma of unempathic parents, I explain this situation with great warmth and great understanding for the complaints of the analysand who tells me that in other families ("in Moser's") the children are treated better. That one can also get by without anonymity (as I mentioned briefly in the foreword) I have no doubt. Over the years I've analyzed many colleagues who know me well and with whom I remain in (scientific and professional) contact. The unrivaled achievement in this realm is of course Freud's analysis of his daughter Anna—a masterstroke [Husarenstück] which even appears to me to have gone too far. But since I myself have never tried anything similar, I should not allow myself a final judgment here. I am always surprised when I again and again have the experience of how everything about the earlier relationship gradually recedes in a well directed analysis—not only because grass grows over the past, but because an active analytic process simply governs the proceeding and remains dominant. You know well, Mr. Thomä, that I could write much more. But I will close now. I began optimistically and I will end optimistically. I hope very much that your openly expressed anger with me will again make way for benevolence. For my part I have the feeling of having come closer to you. I enclose with this letter two addresses ["The Future of Psychoanalysis" and "The Psychoanalyst in the Community of Scholars"] that I gave in the past year. Perhaps you will find agreement with the thoughts that I express in these works and that will help to reduce your rancour and disappointment with me. In any case I trust you will continue to be as open with me as you were in your last letter. I remain, in old fellowship,

Your

Heinz Kohut, M.D.

1. Tilmann Moser, *Lehrjahre auf dem Couch: Bruchstücke meiner Psychoanalyse* (Frankfurt/Main, 1974); *My Years of Apprenticeship on the Couch: Fragments of my Psychoanalysis,* trans. Anselm Hollo (New York, 1977); see also *Search,* 2:725–36; Thomä to Kohut, July 12, 1974; and the review by Yela Lowenfeld in *Psyche* 29 (1975): 186–88. Moser's book provoked great controversy in Germany.

Carmel, September 1975
President Gerald Ford
White House
Dear Mr. President,

With many millions of Americans I sighed a sigh of relief when you became President—not because I share all your political views but because I felt that you were a sincere human being who did not nourish any lopsided ideas which would put you above the law and that you would not act precipitously in lonely splendor or after secret discussions with selected intimates.

Your decision to give unconditional pardon to Mr. Nixon has shaken my confidence.

The decision, based on the wish to spare us the agony of finding out whether, and how far, the man was guilty whom we had elected to be our President, demonstrates a misunderstanding of the basis on which our country rests. It treats us as if we were children who must not be exposed to the pain of seeing clearly the guilt of the man who was our elected leader. If democracy is to be preserved, then we, the people, must be trusted to be able to tolerate the truth. The truth might give us pain, but it will not destroy us. What will destroy us is the feeling that due process of law and equality under the law are abolished in order to spare our feelings, in order to let us maintain the illusion that our leaders will always be good men.

Respectfully yours,
Heinz Kohut, M.D.

September 27, 1974 [original in German]
Mr. Jacques Berna
Zurich
Dear Berna,

I share your sorrow over René[Spitz]'s death. He was a good friend of mine who in spite of his age did not shy away from the long trip to Chicago to take part in my birthday celebration last year. And I know that I received the highest compliment from him that he could give. He wrote me a few years ago that he valued my works very much. "There is only one thing wrong with them," he continued, "namely that *I* didn't write them."

We're looking forward to our visit with you and it is lovely that you want to pick us up. I'll let you know the exact time of our arrival, but please let me know if it causes you any difficulty to come to the airport. We can easily take a taxi. By the way, did I write you that the Swiss Radio Network will broadcast a lecture by Dr. Ernest S. Wolf on October 3 (originally broadcast by Southwest German Radio) that reports on my work on narcissism? I would be interested to hear how it goes.

Now for today only cordial greetings from your

Heinz Kohut, M.D.

P.S. Has Lambelet sent you my (I hope repaired) compass yet?

November 13, 1974
Mr. Robert E. Hampton, Chairman
Civil Service Chairman
Washington, D.C.
Dear Mr. Hampton:

I was taken aback by the news that the Civil Service Commission has negotiated a contract with the Aetna Insurance Company that includes serious cutbacks in mental health benefits. Since I have hardly any patients whose fees are paid by insurance I am not personally involved in this issue. But as a psychiatrist and citizen I am deeply distressed by the fact that a governmental agency gives evidence of what strikes me as a discriminating outlook on emotional disturbances and a biased attitude toward those who are experts in giving assistance to the emotionally disturbed. I do hope that further reflection about these matters will lead to more fair-minded decisions in the future.

Respectfully yours,

Heinz Kohut, M.D.[1]

1. This same letter was sent to Congressman James Waldie as part of an institute

campaign of protest. See George Pollock memorandum ("Re: *Insurance*"), November 11, 1974.

December 31, 1974 [from John Demos][1]
Dear Dr. Kohut:
I want to send you a message of special thanks for your part in the symposium Sunday evening. I liked the way the discussion developed, and your comments were instructive in many ways. A number of people from the audience spoke to me afterwards, to convey their own sense of interest and excitement about the new (to them) ideas presented. At the very least, an important seedling has been planted, and I look for valuable growth in the future.

I know you were disappointed by the relatively modest turnout—at least in comparison with the crowd that attended your lecture in Munich several weeks ago. I counted seventy-five heads at one point, and actually that is not bad by the usual A[merican] H[istorical] A[ssociation] standards. It is necessary to remember, too, that psychohistory is still a new and marginal enterprise for most historians, so the interest in a session like this one would be necessarily rather limited. The next step, I feel, will involve the application of your work to concrete historical problems and settings—something which I, for one, am eager to take up in the months ahead.[2]

Again, on behalf of the Center and of the Group for the Use of Psychology in History, many thanks for Sunday night.

With all best wishes for the New Year,
John Demos

1. Acting director, Center for Psychosocial Studies.
2. See John Demos, *Entertaining Satan: Witchcraft and the Culture of Early New England* (New York, 1982).

January 5, 1975
Arnold Goldberg, M.D.
Chicago
Dear Arnold:
The cooperation with your fine mind and sensitive personality gives me great pleasure—in the casebook [1978] venture, and now your willingness to respond to the Toronto attackers.[1] The cooperation with you (and with the other friends in our group—whatever the upheavals) reassures me more than anything else about the worthwhileness of my efforts and repays me, more than any other external reward,

for the deprivations which the hedonistic aspect of my personality has to suffer while I am engaged in my work.

Two remarks concerning the specific task posed by the Torontonians. (1) The quotation about "militant atheism" comes from the paper on narcissistic rage and is on page 364, nine lines from the bottom of the page. (2) I believe that much of the attack will fall in place if considered from this vantage point. Mystical propensities, conscious and unconscious, are present in all of us. Unconsciously persisting mystical attitudes lead to defensive hyper-rationalism which deprives us of the freedom of examining, dispassionately, the fact that non-rational systems, such as religion, may serve (and have indeed been serving) culture-building, humanitarian ends, while strict rationality may be in the service (and indeed has sometimes been in the service) of culture-destructive, anti-humanitarian ends. If one is free of strong unconscious urges toward mystical obfuscation, one is able to take an attitude of tolerant objectivity vis-à-vis man's need for non-rational supports on the way to rational goals. (I have, as you know, investigated this psychological area in my work on the lone resisters in Germany during the Nazi period. The discovery of a "transference of creativity" belongs here.) My remark about "militant atheism" must be understood within this context. In examining the dynamics of certain historical processes—the pre-history of Nazi Germany, for example—I came to the conclusion that the all-too-rapid destruction of established institutionalized forms of highly elaborated narcissistic commitments (among others: the sudden loss of belief in the powerful god-figure) leads not to firm and sustaining rational attitudes but to a regression to dangerous archaic narcissism—in the specific case of Nazi Germany: to the intense subject-bound grandiosity of being the "master race" and to the unquestioning commitment to an omnipotent Führer.

The narcissistic rage, by the way, which you feel emanates from the Toronto essay, may become intelligible in the context of my remarks in "The Future of Psychoanalysis" concerning the narcissistic nature of values and value systems. Even the most cautiously expressed advocacy of a shift in values (or even only of a shift in the hierarchy of values) tends to create the feeling that the core of the self has been attacked and mobilizes narcissistic rage.[2]

I am looking forward to your thoughts concerning this whole topic. I know that you will avoid a counter-polemic and present the positive contribution which our point of view is able to make.

Warmly yours,

Heinz Kohut, M.D.

1. C. Hanly and J. Masson, "A Critical Examination of the New Narcissism," *IJP* 57 (1976): 49–66.

2. Arnold Goldberg, "A Discussion of the Paper by C. Hanly and J. Masson on 'A Critical Examination of the New Narcissism,'" *IJP* 57 (1976): 67–70. Charles Hanly and Jeffrey Masson criticize Kohut's idea of mature narcissism and, in Goldberg's words, "go on to confuse narcissistic transformation with all religion and to condemn the latter as a universal neurosis of mankind" (68). Goldberg reproduces Kohut's observations from this letter in response. Goldberg also more generally defends the notion of a separate line of development for narcissism and argues for the viability of Kohut's theories as an expansion upon the classical theory espoused by Hanly and Masson.

February 11, 1975
Drs. Anna and Paul Ornstein
Cincinnati
Dear Anna and Paul,

I finished my first reading of your paper on the "Interpretive Process."[1] My reading took place in a piecemeal fashion and I am planning to read your essay again in one fell swoop, perhaps during some vacation period. Still, despite my less than ideal approach, I am sure that my very positive feeling about your work is well founded and that a later reading won't in any way change my favorable impression. I liked the details—both, the theoretical reflections and the case vignettes; they are instructive and make your outlook very clear. But what I liked above all is the total message. Your paper succeeds beautifully in bringing home the intellectual and emotional atmosphere which is a natural and unavoidable consequence of the theoretical stance which we all share.

A few helter-skelter suggestions, most of them unimportant.

(1) I have come to prefer the term "separate" line of development to the term "independent" line of development when I speak of the development of narcissism from its rudimentary archaic beginnings to its mature forms. What I have in mind here is the fact that object love does not develop out of narcissism, does not replace narcissism. I did, of course, never consider the idea that the two independent— whoops!, I mean: separate—lines of development were isolated from one another, that they did not influence each other. There is nothing in the psyche that could be called "independent" in this sense. But at any rate, as a self-protective measure, I suggest that we use the word "separate" and not the word "independent." (For example, on page 19, last line, of your paper.)

(2) I would state clearly at the beginning of each case vignette (per-

haps in footnotes) whether the case was in analysis with Anna O. or with Paul O. That makes the reader's task easier.

(3) I don't know whether the following remark should or should not influence your paper. At any rate, even if you do not want to incorporate into your present essay the point that I will be making now, you might want to think about it in the future—especially Paul, in editing and prefacing my papers. I am more and more inclined to replace the term "narcissism" with the term "self." I prefer, for example, the term "self-object transferences" to the term "narcissistic transferences." And I would also (see my previous point) speak rather of a separate line of development of narcissism. I think that if you reflect on the advantages of this terminological shift, it will become clear to you why I am inclined to advocate it. You mentioned to me, Paul, for example, that K. R. Eissler said that the narcissistic transferences had really been discovered long ago by Aichhorn. Perhaps so, in a rudimentary and implied sense. And it is indeed true that Aichhorn used the term "narcissistic transferences." Still, what he had in mind was in essence different from what my work is all about: he spoke about the phenomenon of which one now speaks as "therapeutic alliance," but not about a true transference. He intentionally acted the part of a super-delinquent, in order to attract delinquent adolescents to him— after he had them thus "hooked" to himself, however, he analyzed their oedipal neurosis. (My inclination, by the way, to use the term "narcissism" up to now, is related to my attempt to prevent a sudden break with tradition. See my remarks concerning this topic in the paper on Freud's self-analysis [pages 9/10 of the triple-spaced manuscript; page 8 of the double-spaced manuscript].)

(4) On page 63, line 16, you are referring to the paper I gave in Cincinnati when I received the honorary degree. The paper is called "The Psychoanalyst in the Community of Scholars"; it will appear in The Annual [of Psychoanalysis] III [1975]. Actually an even more concise reference to the problem of "understanding" and "explaining" is contained in the essay which appeared in The Annual I [1972] (on page 14).

(5) I would suggest that you do not include "intuition" as an equal to "introspection" and "empathy" (page 63, line 12). There exist intuitive introspective processes and there exist intuitive empathic processes—but intuition alone does not exist as an actual function or process.[2]

Enough for now. Please forgive the pettiness of some of my remarks. They should not obscure my great pleasure in the splendid overall impression that your work produces and my pride in the fact that I have found collaborators such as the two of you.

Congratulations!

Affectionately yours,

Heinz Kohut, M.D.

1. "On the Interpretive Process in Psychoanalysis," *International Journal of Psychoanalytic Psychotherapy* 4 (1975): 219–71.
2. In the margin here Kohut has written "(cf. Psa of Self 1971 p. 302)."

February 28, 1975

Lucia Elizabeth Tower, M.D.

Chicago

Dear Lucia:

The more I think about your tersely expressed opinion that Mayor Daley's decision to run for yet another term was motivated by his wish to get even with Alderman [William] Singer,[1] the more perceptive I think you were. It is, of course, impossible to know with certainty what influenced Daley most—the fear of leaving public life for good might well have been a very great incentive, too, in and of itself—but the motivational power of vengefulness after a humiliating defeat in a man who has obviously been carried from victory to victory by an unbounded belief in his omnipotence, might well have been decisive. It is strange—and it gives me food for thought—that I did not immediately catch on to the cogency of your suggestion. I should, after all, be expected to recognize the workings of "narcissistic rage."

Cordially yours,

Heinz Kohut, M.D.

1. In the 1975 Democratic primary Mayor Richard Daley, for the first time since 1955, faced a challenge, this time from a reform faction led by Singer. In 1971 Singer was one of two Democrats who successfully challenged Daley candidates in elections for the city council.

March 1975

My dear Gustl,

A birthday letter, sent by personal messenger from O'Hare [Airport] to Minneapolis, alongside Mom's birthday cake. The occasion of your having been around for a quarter of a century, that round number of 25, forces the awareness on us that time passes, that we are living in a strangely changing condition—upward as it is for you, downward as it unmistakably is becoming for me (at least as my running times tell me).

Well, many good wishes, Tom. I am happy about the fact that you are enjoying your work, that you are fascinated by your favorite teacher, that your skill and knowledge are expanding. And, of course, I am happy to know that you have found Susan, that you are lucky to have found the girl with whom you will go through life, just as I was lucky when I found Mom.

The gifts are not only symbolic (ten dollars for every year of your life plus ten "to grow") but also useful and, I hope, not unwelcome. I hesitated about the photograph. But someday you will be teaching and then you can look at the picture and see me there, reading, as some kind of forerunner.

All my love and many happy returns,
Dad

March 3, 1975
George H. Klumpner, M.D.
Oak Park, Illinois
Dear George:

I will not expose myself to the rejection by your unempathic machine and will address myself directly to you, even though it has to be via the written word. First of all: thank you for devoting so much time and care to giving me your reactions to my new work [*The Restoration of the Self*] in its present incomplete state.

The warm, personal asides did not remain unnoticed by me, of course; I was especially appreciative of the fact that you interspersed them in your otherwise objective assessment of my style, my methods of presentation, and of the soundness of my argument.

You were sincere and direct; and I cannot do less than try to react with sincerity and directness to your objections. And I must, therefore, tell you that I have not been able, so far, to recognize that I have done anything I need to be ashamed of. What you see as polemical, as a belittling of opponents, as a setting up of straw men, and the like, was not intended by me in that way. I wanted to be lively in my exposition and to communicate my views in a clear and intelligible way. You believe, for example, that I am nourishing some grudge at

Otto Kernberg and, in particular, that I had him in mind when I used the word "fanatic" on one or two occasions. But Kernberg does in fact strike me as anything but a fanatic. I don't agree with his view (probably derived from his Kleinian training in South America) concerning the *clinical* importance of *primary* aggression. But I do not consider this disagreement as a personal argument between him and me, or between the Kleinian school and me, or between others who hold these concepts and me. In using the word "fanatic" I wanted, contrary to what it seemed to you, to say that while there are a few oddballs to be found in any science, most analysts are hopefully level-headed, and can disagree with each other without fanaticism.

There are very many objections in your annotations and I cannot take them up here one by one. But I do want to give you my impression that you are chiding me a number of times for not proving my position at a point when I am only trying to make clear what my position is. The analogy with organic and inorganic chemistry belongs here. It proves nothing, of course. I used it only to demonstrate what I have in mind. The proof for my point of view must come from an examination of clinical material (my next installment will again deal with clinical material; and the whole long first part of the present essay concerned clinical, empirical data) with the aid of a conceptual framework that I am trying to outline as clearly as I can.

There is another implication to be derived from your annotations and, especially, from our brief verbal exchange on Michigan Avenue. It is the implication that the group which has been attending the previous readings (before you and a few others joined these sessions) consists of yes-men who do not discuss my thoughts but take them as gospel truth. This is, however, not the case. What may give you this impression is connected with the fact that the "older" members are in a different phase of their relationship to my work. Have you ever participated in months of committee meetings, discussing hundreds of objections and doubts concerning various suggestions, finally framing a report to a supraordinated body, presenting this report—only to find that the supraordinated body begins again right where the committee was at the beginning of their work? Our "committee," too, has questioned my suggestions assiduously in the past. But by now the "older" members are, at least for a while, in a different phase from those who came in more recently. That does not mean that the new members should not react; and their reactions should be responded to without impatience, indeed with the readiness to learn, and with the expectation that they will confront me and the "older" members of the group with cogent arguments. I trust that this has indeed happened, and I will try my best to have it happen again in our forthcoming meetings.

But now I will close. Once more my warm and sincere thanks for your devoted efforts. I will not disregard what you have said; I will read your remarks again and, if they have hit a defect in me, I will try to recognize it and will try to correct my errors.

Warmly yours,
Heinz Kohut, M.D.

March 11, 1975
George H. Pollock, M.D.
Director, Institute for Psychoanalysis
Chicago[1]

Thank you for letting me see the correspondence about the [Paul] Parin statement. Behind it all is, as you, of course, know, Anna Freud. Parin is in essence her spokesman, just as Jeanne Lampl-de Groot and the Dutch Society upheld her principles when they granted membership to people who received training which paralleled that at Hampste[a]d. No doubt: Parin is, in addition, a rebel from way back. He is a Marxist who (with Morgenthaler) fought the Nazis after being parachuted by the British to the Tito forces in Yugoslavia. [William] Gillespie, on the other hand (and, I suppose, Burnie Moore), is opposed to "lay-analysis" and, in framing the relevant By-Laws as he did, is not only rejecting the lay-analysis program in Holland and the free training program in Switzerland but is also building a wall around the Hampste[a]d Clinic which prevents the graduates of Miss Freud's training program from achieving the status of analyst. It's all very complex and sad. But the outcome is hardly in doubt: the solid, silent majority will carry the day.

As concerns my own feelings, I am emotionally drawn to the side of Anna Freud, Jeanne Lampl, and Parin, Morgenthaler, Berna, and the rest of the Swiss. But I also think that Parin's methods are wrong (and that the Dutch, although legalistically ok were wrong)—that one has to work through changes in the IPA or—as a last resort, resign from it. But can you imagine Anna Freud's resignation from the IPA? Here is the unresolved impasse.

1. Pollock, director of the Chicago institute, was also president of the APA for 1974–75.

May 3, 1975
John Gedo
Chicago
Dear John,

Today is my birthday, an unimpressive sixty-two. But inevitably it brings to my mind the celebration two years ago and among all the me[m]ories of those days one is foremost: I see you, intense, moved, speaking of my work and me. I will never lose this image; indeed, the way I am constituted, it becomes stronger and more vivid as time goes by [see above, October 23, 1973].

What is reality? The fleeting moment of the present? The still remaining tensions that point toward a still remaining future? Or such precious, ineradicable moments of the past as my vision of you two years ago? More and more I come to believe in the relativity of that nexus of experiences which we call reality. The belief is not the manifestation of a fuzzy, quasi-religious resignation but, on the contrary, a hard-won scientific insight concerning the unfissionable unity of observer and observed. Applied to my image of you, this means that you are my cherished friend and that, however the cloudiness of the moment might seek to veil the clearness of this reality, I know that it will never be inaccessible to me as long as I can think.

Yours,
Heinz Kohut, M.D.

June 17, 1975
Peter J. Loewenberg, Ph.D.
Department of History
University of California
Los Angeles
Dear Peter:

Last night I spoke with my son Thomas and he read to me the very nice and informative letter that you had sent to him in response to his having written to you. I was very touched by your kindness and I want to thank you most cordially. It is difficult for a father to be objective—but I cannot help but feel that Tom is a fine person who will be a good, imaginative, and, I believe, creative psychohistorian [see below, May 14, 1979].

My own work has, unfortunately, taken me more to the center of clinical and theoretical questions in analysis *per se*—a book on *The Rehabilitation of the Self; Thoughts about the Termination of Analyses and the Concept of Cure* is nearing completion. But there are some unfinished manuscript pages which contain a few psychohistorical thoughts to which I hope to be able to turn in the years to come.[1]

Will we ever have a chance to meet and to chat? I hope so.

Warmly yours,

Heinz Kohut, M.D.

1. See "The Self in History: A Symposium Discussion," *Group for the Use of Psychology in History Newsletter* 3, no. 4 (March, 1975): 3–10.

Carmel, September 4, 1975

William Offenkrantz, M.D.

Department of Psychiatry

University of Chicago

Dear Bill:

Thank you for sending me the pages of [Subrahmanyan] Chandrasek[h]ar's Ryerson Lecture that contain the paragraphs which echo some of my remarks at the Chicago Psychoanalytic Society.[1] My hunch is that a forward step of the first magnitude into new territory (such as Einstein's in 1916) leads to an irreversible freezing of the pioneer's mental abilities, to a loss of further flexibility as if an ageing process had taken place during the brief period of intense thought that in others takes place only after a lifetime of thinking. To look at our own field: Freud produced on the highest level throughout his long adult life. But he entered the field after a step of incredible magnitude had already been made in the encounter of Anna O. and Breuer.

Best regards,

Cordially yours,

Heinz Kohut, M.D.

1. Chandrasekkar had said that physicists, as opposed to artists, appear to lose productivity early in life. See Offenkrantz to Kohut, August 16, 1975.

Carmel, September 15, 1975

John E. Gedo, M.D.

Chicago

Dear John,

Your letter was a welcome gift. You are never out of my mind for very long, and since my work always involves the deeper layers of my personality, the hours over the manuscript that I am in the process of finishing now are always accompanied with a number of free associations concerning people who are important to me—and you have often appeared among them.

The vacation has been very good, so far. Tom and Susan are still with us to the end of this week. It will be hard to see them go. And there is tennis, and restaurants, and walks on the beach, and drives along the coast, and reading. But mainly, of course, there is work. It is quiet work, putting finishing touches on things, finding solutions for inconsistencies which always means: finding one's way to what one has known all along. It is a strange manuscript. And although everybody tells me that it will cause a storm of attacks, I don't worry about that. I think that people will have an easier time seeing my position in the open, rather than having to guess it through a veil of allusions. But I cannot do without interim stages—for their benefit and, I guess, also following an inner need that allows the penetration of reality only via gradual steps.

It was good to hear that you, too, are absorbed by creative work; and, yes, your return to Morocco must be a great adventure for you. I can be empathic with you—and with your need to protect yourself by the presence of your son. I will never forget my first return to Vienna after the war [in 1957]—without the presence of Betty and Tom my playing with psychological fire might well have led into chaos.

Betty and Tom and Susan send their warm greetings to Mary and you. Give my best to Mary—I am glad that she was not upset about the bibliographical error.

And warmest greetings from your old

Heinz Kohut, M.D.

P.S. I received a letter from Jeanne Lampl-de Groot yesterday. She had just read the "Creativeness, Charisma, Group Psychology" paper in *Psyche* and was enthusiastic. She was a good personal friend of Freud, is very close to Anna Freud—so her response was very reassuring to me.

Carmel, September 16, 1975
Mr. Lothar Wilk
Marburg, West Germany
Dear Mr. Wilk:

Your letter followed me on my vacation in California where I am concentrating on some work that is far away from the Danish Prince whose problems you want me to illuminate for you. I have never studied Hamlet extensively—for a thorough psychoanalytic investigation I refer you, apart from Ernest Jones's work, to K. R. Eissler's book.

I am sure that you are familiar with this extensive investigation. My theory about Hamlet—as you refer to my remarks on pp. 235/6 of *The Analysis of the Self*—relates only to one aspect of Hamlet's psychological disequilibrium and attempts to explain mainly the form of his behavior, not its content. Although I would have to refresh my memory (with regard to the "closet scene," and with regard to Hamlet's actions at the end of the play) by re-reading the relevant passages, my hunch is that evidence for Hamlet's traumatic state could be found in traces in these scenes, too, i.e., evidence of his being under great pressure, of acting under the impact of an undigestible value-degradation to which he responds with sarcastic pseudo-insanity. The following are examples of traumata that can lead to the shattering of the idealized parent imago and of the grandiose self: anything in the parental behavior that interferes with the *gradualness* of the disappointment in the parents' perfection and with the *gradualness* of the child's recognition that the parents' empathy for him and pleasure in him is not unlimited. (Specific circumstances are: parental psychopathology; the parents' physical illness or death; a significant defeat suffered by the idealized parents; etc.)

This is as far as I can respond to your inquiry at this point. Should I have further thoughts after my return to Chicago, I will let you know about them.

Sincerely,

Heinz Kohut, M.D.

October 8, 1975 [from Lloyd Etheredge, MIT]

Dear Dr. Kohut,

I wanted to write you about my pleasure in reading *The Analysis of the Self*. I think it has direct application to my own field of political psychology. There are some obvious examples among political leaders: DeGaulle, Woodrow Wilson, [Henry] Kissinger in some ways, Mao, Nixon, your own example of Churchill. Some preliminary research by Richard Fenno at the University of Rochester suggests that a substantial number of members of Congress do not enjoy their work. Lucille Iremonger in *The Fiery Chariot* [1970] presents evidence which suggests most British Prime Ministers in recent centuries would fit your model. I think the combination of stubborn grandiosity and lack of intimate affective ties to other people might facilitate political "success" and advancement in some situations. I sometimes think that part of the unpleasant, ambitious, status-conscious, manipulative maneuvering in Washington is a political culture generated by men with narcissistic character defects. Chris Argyris's social psychologic study, *Behind the Front Page* [1974], suggests that even the news media and *The New York Times* are part of it.

I am trying my hand at a few case studies and will write you further when they are at a later stage. I wonder if you have thought of extending your talents in the direction of political psychology? There are not many of us and we would welcome new colleagues.

You mention in your book the task of complementing social psychological perspective with the psychoanalytic. I thought you might enjoy the enclosed monograph I've written for my undergraduates.

Sincerely,
Lloyd S. Etheredge

October 14, 1975
James P. Gustafson, M.D.
Department of Psychiatry
University of Wisconsin
Dear Dr. Gustafson:

Your paper on the mirror transference in the psychoanalytic therapy of a case of alcoholism gave me a great deal of enjoyment. I read it attentively and found it well presented, convincing, and instructive. The application of my work to psychotherapy in general and to the psychotherapy of addictions (including alcoholism) in particular seems to be a very worthwhile undertaking and I congratulate you on the skill and perceptiveness with which you pursued your task.

A few random remarks as they occurred to me while reading your paper. With regard to your description of my formulation in the last few lines of page 6, I would also refer you to an early paper of mine (*Journal of the American Psychoanalytic Association 7*, 459, 1959; in particular page 476) which in general I consider as the most important basis on which all my later work rests. One of the most interesting aspects of your case is the relationship of the child to the aphasic mother. I would stress the likelihood that the language impairment accounts for only one aspect of the disturbance in the relationship. I would assume that without a broader disturbance in empathy (perhaps as a consequence of emotional dulling due to an organic defect in the basal ganglia) the language disturbance would not have been equally traumatic. With regard to your remarks about the patient's rage when his need for empathic mirroring is frustrated, I would suggest that you look at my paper on narcissistic rage (*The Psychoanalytic Study of the Child*, 1972) in which I attempted to illuminate the relationship between rage and narcissistic injury. I liked especially your remarks (on page 18) concerning the fact that the self-soothing functions are not necessarily created by the self-object but that one may conceive of them as autonomous, yet in need to be confirmed in order to become effective. Finally, with regard to the shift of the transference toward the father, I will tell you that I have just (more or less) finished a book (*The Restoration of the Self: Thoughts on the Termination of Analyses and the Concept of Cure*) in which I discuss the bipolar organization of the self; the child's turning from a frustrating self-object to the other self-object; the fact that narcissistic psychopathology occurs only when both attempts to gain the response of the two self-objects fail; and the fact, finally, that in treatment the cure seems to hinge on the re-establishment of empathic contact with the less damaging of the two early self-objects, i.e., often with the father. This movement is in general from mirroring toward idealizing. In your case—a more rare sequence—it seems to go from maternal to paternal mirroring.

I close by once more telling you of my great pleasure with your work and by sending you my best wishes for a productive future in our field.

Sincerely yours,
Heinz Kohut, M.D.

January 5, 1976
Dr. David M. Moss
Center for Religion and Psychotherapy
Chicago
Dear Dr. Moss:

I would like to add another request for a change in the essay "Narcissism, Empathy & the Fragmentation of Self: An Interview with Heinz Kohut" [*Pilgrimage: The Journal of Pastoral Psychotherapy* 4 (Summer, 1976): 26–43].[1] On page 7, line 18, under the (sideward-placed) heading "Treatment," [Robert] Randall [see below, June 7, 1981] speaks of the fact that the "Therapist needs to (1) understand the independent line of development . . . etc." The sentence *should* read as follows: "Therapist needs to (1) understand the separate line of development of narcissism and the vicissitudes of the narcissistic transference; (2) ". . ." The important point is not the stylistic one ("narcissistic line of development"—"line of development of narcissism") but the substantially different meaning of the words "independent" and "separate." The line of development of narcissism is separate from that of the line of development of object-love but the two lines do, of course, influence each other—they are usually interdependent, despite their separateness. A firm self may often be the basis for the capacity to love; and the capacity to love may increase self-esteem and self-cohesion. But not necessarily so. There exist indeed instances— e.g., of certain very creative people—where self-cohesion and self-experience in creative activity are well developed and, on the other hand, object-love is stunted. And there are instances—certain schizophrenics—in whom the capacity for object-love is relatively highly developed and stable, while the self is always in danger of disintegration. While all these exceptions are rare, they illustrate the need to view the two lines of development separately. It must not be forgotten that I made the statement concerning the "separateness" of the two lines of development in order to underline the fact that object-love does not develop out of narcissism, that narcissism is not *per se* immature or bad as compared with object-love which is mature and good, but that there are immature forms of narcissism and mature ones, just as there are immature forms of object-love as well as mature ones. And finally, in contrast to classical psychoanalytic theory, the statement about separateness takes into account the unquestionable fact that object-love enhances (not diminishes) self-esteem, i.e., that the one does not replace the other. Anyway: here is a long explanation for my wish to have you replace the word "independent" by the word "separate."

Have a good 1976!

Sincerely,

Heinz Kohut, M.D.

P.S. You might wish to share the preceding reflection with Dr. Randall.

1. This article by Moss also appeared in a German translation in 1977; see below, March 24, 1981. See also above, February 11, 1975.

June 13, 1976
Dr. Jacques Palaci
Paris
Dear Jacques:

It was so good to hear from you; and many thanks for the handsome book of [Theodor] Reik that you translated. I have always had a warm spot for Reik's artistry in my heart; but I also felt always that he lacked that scientific rigor which I believe analysis needs if it is to remain protected against the intrusions of fuzziness and sentimentality.[1]

I am disappointed that the narcissistic rage paper is still not published in French [cf. above, March 6, 1974]—that is not a good sign
with regard to the possible acceptance of my ideas in France. Do you
know whether *Le Soi* is arousing any interest? By contrast to the apparent lack of interest in France, the German public (especially at the
universities) seems to take to my ideas.

My new book (*The Restoration of the Self*) is making progress. The
manuscript is being processed, chapter by chapter, and I hope that it
will be ready to go into print in the late fall.

During August we will be in Europe (Zurich, Florence, Rome, Amsterdam). Then we will be in California (San Francisco, Carmel) where
I hope to put the finishing touches on the new book.

I trust that you and Diane are well and that you are leading fulfilling
lives.

Warm regards from house to house,

Yours,

Heinz Kohut, M.D.

1. Theodor Reik, *Listening with the Third Ear: The Inner Experience of a Psychoanalyst*
(New York, 1948).

July 25, 1976

Mrs. Siegmund Levarie

Lucca, Italy

Dear Norma:

Fancy getting a letter from me. Here is why. A new book of mine
is in the making. It will be published by International Universities
Press in New York late this year, they say. Its title is *The Restoration of
the Self*. Could you give any advice concerning a good design, especially for the dust wrapper? Or do you know of any good people to
whom the International Universities Press could turn?

The title refers to the consolidation of a fragmented self. Eugene
O'Neill's play *The Great God Brown* [1926] contains these evocative lines
which I quote: "Man is born broken. He lives by mending. The grace
of God is glue." Does all this give you any idea for a design? Nothing
flashy or sentimental, of course—it's a book for scientists. But then it
needn't be drab either.[1]

I trust you are having a good time in your Italian retreat. Say hello
to Siegmund, and love to both of you from both of us.

Warmly,

Heinz Kohut, M.D.

1. Mrs. Levarie did compose the design for the dust jacket.

December 26, 1976
Kate Rosenthal, Administrative Secretary
Institute for Psychoanalysis
Chicago
Kate—

The radiator knobs and their housing were invented by a sadist—at any rate, I have experienced them as instruments of torture ever since we moved to 180 North Michigan years ago. But, skinned knuckles and burned fingers notwithstanding, I managed until recently to turn the knobs and thus to escape the worst of the numbing polar cold of 8 A.M. and of the stifling tropical heat of 9:30. Now, however—whether due to my increasing senility or to mechanical causes—even this marginally performed feat has become unperformable. I am still managing the knob on the north; but the one on the south hardly at all—and that's the one that regulates the bigger of the radiators. Help, help, help! Can't we have the Goddam radiator covers removed and replaced?

1977–1978

"Over and over in life I have started afresh."

February 7, 1977
Evan Brahm, M.D.
Jewish General Hospital
Montreal
Dear Dr. Brahm:

Please forgive me for being so slow in answering your letter. The delay was due to the fact that I was busy putting the finishing touches on a book (*The Restoration of the Self*) which, I hope, will contain some answers to the questions that you are raising. As you will see, I suggest that we differentiate between two psychologies of the self: one in which the self is seen as a content of the "mental apparatus" and one in which the self occupies the central position. The first should suffice when we are dealing with classical transference neuroses; the second is necessary when we are dealing with the disorders of the self. Do classical transference neuroses exist? I believe that they do (notwithstanding the fact that the self is, of course, involved in them, too)—but I also think that we are encountering them very rarely in our present day practice. I believe that a shift in the human condition has been taking place during the last fifty to one hundred years which accounts for the increasing prevalence of self-disorders. Formerly children were overinvolved with their parents and developed structural neuroses; now they are understimulated and develop self disorders.

In the new book I am also discussing the position of drives in psychoanalytic psychology, and I believe that my conceptualization of aggression should become clearer to you. I have made some progress in this area since I wrote the paper on narcissistic rage in 1972.[1]

I am glad that the work of my friends (Drs. Goldberg, Wolf, the Ornsteins, etc.) is helpful to you and that you enjoyed the Chicago meeting on adolescence. Send me your thoughts about my work. While I cannot promise that I will be able to turn to any of your communications immediately, I will eventually do so. As concerns the question of supervision—either with me or with one of my colleagues—that is something that we must confront when you feel ready for it. As long as you are still a student at your institute, you must, of course, first get permission from your institute.

Sometime during the early spring I will be in Cincinnati on a Saturday for lectures and seminar. It would be nice if you could attend these. If you are interested you should write to Dr. Paul H. Ornstein . . . and ask for permission to attend.

Let me tell you in closing that your letter gave me great pleasure and satisfaction. Nothing is more precious to me than the response of the younger generation among analysts.

Sincerely yours,

Heinz Kohut, M.D.

1. *Search*, 2:615–58.

February 13, 1977

Philip C. Gradolph

Evanston, Illinois

Dear Phil:

The galleys of *The Restoration of the Self* are at the printers, the page proofs have not yet arrived, and I have a few days in which I can turn to other tasks. Your paper was near the top of my list and, although it deserves more than the single reading that I could devote to it, I will give you my responses at this time.

You have done an excellent piece of work; and I enjoyed it and profited from it.

While I have no criticism, only praise, I will spell out a few reactions. To begin with, I see no significant disagreements between my stance and yours with regard to the importance of adolescence as a period of "maturationally governed restructuring of the self," as you say. This statement does not mean, of course, that I know as much about adolescence as you do or that I could have written a paper concerning this period in the development of the self that would come up to the scope and quality of the contribution that you have made. But far from feeling that you have disagreed with me—a contingency that I would have had no trouble accepting without resentment—, I think that you have applied the psychology of the self to an area where such an enterprise is especially fruitful.

I asked myself the question why you came to think that we differed in principle, and I came up with these two answers. The reference to adolescence in "Thoughts on Narcissism and Narcissistic Rage" might have produced an erroneous impression concerning where I stand on this issue because I wanted to emphasize at that time the view—a view which I still hold, of course—that, in contrast to [Erik] Erikson's conceptualization of a person's "identity" as a socio-psychological configuration that may be said to establish itself primarily in adolescence,[1] my conceptualization of a person's "self" as a depth-psychological configuration refers to a structure that is primarily established much earlier in life.

It might well be that this, I believe quite legitimate and correct differentiating emphasis would not have led you to misunderstand my stance, were it not for the by you correctly perceived fact that I have made no contributions to the psychology of adolescence—that I have neglected this important phase of development in my writings. There are obviously many reasons for this fact, and it would not be difficult to expand on a number of them, i.e., I could say that this is an area for specialists, that my research has priorities that made it inadvisable to immerse myself into this phase of life, etc. But I would rather admit to you the belief that there are important personal reasons for my inability to do the kind of research concerning this phase that I was able to do with regard to adult life and reconstructed childhood. I will not go into details here but restrict myself to telling you that there is something in myself that refuses to consolidate in the way in which most people's selves consolidate in adolescence. Over and over in life I have started afresh—witness the fact that my scientific productivity has had a number of new beginnings, even quite late in life. This is a specific life style—while it is not the norm, I am by no means alone here—which relates also and importantly to my cognitive processes, i.e., I tend to look at things to a certain extent as if I were seeing them for the first time, as if I had not learned established ways of looking at them, even when it is a question of modes of looking at them (theories) that I have myself constructed in the past.

Now to another point. I was very glad to see how well you have understood the important difference between ego-ideal and idealized parent imago, and how clearly you were able to point up [Peter] Blos's misunderstanding of my concepts in this area. It might be of interest to you to hear that I have given a good deal of further thought concerning this whole sector of psychoanalytic theory and that I have to broadly based conclusions that will be spelled out in my new book. It is profitable, I believe, to differentiate between two complementary theoretical systems in psychoanalysis: (a) self-psychology in the narrower sense of the term, i.e., a psychology in which the self is a content of the mental apparatus; and (b) a self-psychology in the broader sense of the term in which the self is in the center of the theoretical system. The concept of the superego belongs in the first-named framework; it is a part of a mental apparatus. The ego-ideal, however (and its precursor, the idealized parent imago), belong into [sic] the second framework; it is a pole (a constituent) of the self. I will not expand here on the relation between the two complementary theoretical frameworks—*The Restoration of the Self* undertakes this task, and I hope that my book should be available before long.

Let me close this letter by telling you once more how much enjoyment your paper gave me as evidence of the fact that my work has been able to serve as a stimulus for your own enterprising mind.

Yours,

Heinz Kohut, M.D.

1. Erik H. Erikson, *Childhood and Society* (New York, 1950).

February 13, 1975

Charles Kligerman, M.D.

Chairman, Curriculum Committee

The Institute for Psychoanalysis

Chicago

Dear Charlie:

This is to confirm that I will be teaching the fall quarter of the new course that we are organizing for the not yet matriculated students. I think that these meetings are important because they are the student's first contact with the Institute as a center of learning—a contact that should go some way in defining the atmosphere in which their education will proceed and in supplying the impressions around which their future professional identity can crystallize.

I think that the Curriculum Committee made a wise decision when it chose senior members of the faculty as the teachers for these courses. The encounter between those who are making their initial steps toward becoming analysts and those who are at the peak of their career or, as is my case, reasonably close to its end, has a special significance: it gives the new students a sense of the continuity of our science, a sense of their participation in an important human enterprise that began before they came on the scene and that, we hope, will go on after they have left it.

These considerations will not only determine my overall attitude toward the beginning students and the style—warmly informal discussions—in which I intend to conduct these classes, they also explain my present plans with regard to the subject matter. I want to stimulate the students to think about certain broad questions for which they will later have no time and interest because they will be engrossed in the task of learning the details of their craft. Why did analysis come into being toward the end of the nineteenth century? Why was analysis isolated among the sciences? And why has it still retained a certain separateness, even in the world of today? What is the essence of psychoanalysis, as a profession and as a science?

I will not make many reading assignments—although, as we get to discuss this or that specific issue, I will give appropriate references. There are only two readings that I am at this point planning to suggest. I choose them because, in their contrasting mood, they will provide us with a good framework for our discussions: (1) Lecture 35 ("The Question of a Weltanschauung") of Freud's *New Introductory Lectures;* and (2) my own essay "The Psychoanalyst in the Community of Scholars."

Sincerely,

Heinz Kohut, M.D.

March 10, 1977 [from Shirley Braverman]

Dear Dr. Kohut,

I am writing to you at the suggestion of Douglas Levin whom I was recently telling about my gratitude to you and him, in an experience I had with my students in family therapy at the McGill School of Social Work.

I have been seeing Doug in consultation for the past 1½ years because I wanted to learn more about your concepts regarding the psychology of the Self. He has loaned me copies of your lectures, at my request, because yours were the first ideas that helped me understand some of the very fragile people I had seen in social agencies (I am a social worker) and, to a lesser extent, in my private practice.

My understanding of these people must have been creeping into the courses I am teaching in family therapy at McGill, without my being aware of anything different coming through to the students. In this semester my students are presenting case material linked to the literature on various social problems. Since they are placed mainly in social agencies the people they see are often single parent or multi-problem families where wife or child abuse and alcoholism occur quite frequently. I had been trying to find a way to help these students be responsive to such needy people, rather than accept the often prevailing attitude that these were the "garbage" cases that were dumped on the students because nobody else wanted them.

To my surprise, when the students began to present their cases in class what came through was that they were no longer avoiding these clients. They had not understood them previously, were therefore afraid of them and had tended to avoid contact with them. I have seen a real change—they are responding to them as people in need, intensely interested in understanding what's behind the observable behavior and struggling to find appropriate responses. They are much more available, both physically and psychologically, to these very needy clients. I was truly touched.

I would like to thank you for helping to give me insight with your concepts about the psychology of the Self. They have helped me tackle clients I would have felt quite helpless about in the past and have helped me, in turn, to pass this on to 25 eager young social workers.

Sincerely,

Shirley Braverman

March 23, 1977

Mrs. Shirley Braverman

Montreal

Dear Mrs. Braverman:

It was very generous of you to let me know that my concepts have helped you in your work as a teacher, especially since you are applying them in a field—serious psycho-social problems such as wife and child abuse, and alcoholism—with which I, myself, have no first-hand acquaintance. Have you ever considered writing a report on your experiences? Judging by the clarity with which you express yourself in your letters, it seems to me that you are able to write simply and effectively. And the content of your observations—(1) how "garbage" cases become interesting human problems once one has a conceptual key to understanding them; and (2) how the asocial behavior of these clients can be explained in the terms of the psychology of the self, e.g., as the appearance of self-fragments in the form of rage and of addictive behavior in consequence of the non-responsiveness of the environment, present and past, to the self in its totality—constitutes surely a very worthwhile subject matter for a report to your colleagues.

Once more my thanks for your friendly letter.

Sincerely yours,

Heinz Kohut, M.D.

March 19, 1977

Peter A. Martin, M.D.

Southfield, Michigan

Dear Dr. Martin:

My reply to your inquiry was delayed because I was busy with the page proofs of a new book, *The Restoration of the Self,* which should be available in a few weeks.

The new book, as well as *The Analysis of the Self,* are in toto pertinent with regard to the area of your interest, because the recognition of narcissistic transferences and of the specific working-through processes that are correlated to them allow us to do analytic work with a number of patients whom we formerly would have prepared by psychotherapy for the analytic task of dealing with their object-instinctual transferences.

Apart from making this specific point, I am of the opinion that preparatory psychotherapy should only rarely be employed. I think that in most cases we are doing our patients an injustice if we do not take them into analysis because we are alarmed by the severity of their symptoms or by the fear of their precarious adjustment. It is not analysis per se, the analytic situation per se, that makes such patients worse, leads to their disintegration, but faulty empathic understanding of their personality—erroneous interpretations that repeat the serious trauma of an emotionally flawed early environment.

While I therefore believe that preparatory psychotherapy is not generally advisable, I believe that psychoanalysis is contraindicated with patients who present the chronic defenses that I call schizoid personality (1971, pp. 12–14) and paranoid personality (1977, p. 192).

I know that your inquiry would deserve a much more extensive response, but I cannot at this time expand any further on this complex set of issues and must restrict myself to the overly simple answers that I gave you in the foregoing.

Sincerely yours,

Heinz Kohut, M.D.

March 19, 1977

Department of Health, Education and Welfare[1]

Washington, D.C.

Gentlemen:

This is an inquiry concerning the magnitude of the risk incurred by people over sixty who smoke small numbers of low-tar, low-nicotine cigarettes.

I have a number of patients, sixty years old or older, who, after smoking approximately twenty-five cigarettes a day between the age of twenty and fifty, stopped smoking altogether for about ten to fifteen years. Now, in their later life, they wonder whether they could not without incurring great risks enjoy a small number (five to ten) low-tar, low-nicotine cigarettes a day. It is my impression that the emotional well-being of these individuals would be significantly increased if they could smoke a few of these cigarettes every day without having to feel that they are possibly inflicting serious damage on themselves. Measured by the tar content (one milligram per cigarette), five to ten cigarettes a day would contain less tar than that contained by about one-half of one ordinary cigarette per day. And yet there are recent reports that seem to indicate that even low-tar, low-nicotine cigarettes still carry a great risk—to be specific that there is only a fifteen percent reduction in morbidity. Is this information correct, even with regard to such cigarettes as *Now* or *Carleton*, if smoked in small numbers, such as five to ten per day?

Please give me what information about this matter you have so that I can advise my patients intelligently and responsibly.

Sincerely yours,
Heinz Kohut, M.D.

1. This letter also went, on March 22, to the National Clearing House on Smoking and Health at the Centers for Disease Control in Atlanta. Kohut himself had finally quit smoking because he thought it dumb, although he subsequently enjoyed an occasional *Carleton*. See above, July 5, 1960; and John Witte (Centers for Disease Control) to Kohut, April 13, 1977; Witte advises against smoking if at all possible.

March 22, 1977
Ms. Margrit Hengärtner
Zollikerberg, Switzerland
Dear Ms. Hengärtner:

Thank you for your letter of February 28. I am sorry to be so late in my response—the delay is due to the fact that I had to devote all my free time to the page proofs of a new book, *The Restoration of the Self*, which will be published by the International Universities Press of New York around April 15. I am mentioning this book especially because it contains a good many answers to the questions you are directing at me in your letter. Now to some of your questions.

(1) The narcissistic personality disturbances are not new; but I do believe that they are more frequent now than they were let us say toward the end of the nineteenth century when Freud examined his basic clinical material. (Chapter Seven of *The Restoration of the Self* will expand on this point.)

(2) Yes, to some extent the diagnostic category of narcissistic personality disturbances is the result of a new viewpoint. Let me use, as a clinical example, two types of work inhibition. There is, on the one hand, the person in whom the work inhibition is the result of unsolved inner conflicts. To succeed in his work means to him to defeat the ambivalently loved and hated rival-father. In order to avoid this guilt-

producing eventuality, he fails. There is, on the other hand, the person in whom the work inhibition is the result of a defect in the self. Phase-appropriate greatness had not been "mirrored" in childhood by the mother; the phase-appropriate need to merge with an available omnipotent object had not been responded to by the father. As a result—an *indirect* result; see my considerations concerning optimum frustration via the increasingly selective parental responses—the patient lacks the self-confidence that is needed in order to succeed.

(3) Concerning self-esteem regulation I believe that the basic self-esteem regulation is acquired through the baby's and small child's merging with the omnipotent self-object. The child's narcissistic imbalance is empathically understood by the adult self-object who picks up the child (or allows it to merge with it by other means) so that the child can participate in the self-object's return to calmness. If, however, the self-object either fails to bring about the child's merger at such times, or if, after the merger has taken place, the self-object's mood swings are abnormal, then the process is interfered with by which (through many repetitions of the merger and through optimal failures from the side of the self-object) the child acquires the basic mood regulating mechanisms. (This point is discussed in Chapter Two of *The Restoration of the Self*.)

I hope that the foregoing remarks will help you in your work. I wish you success in your endeavors.

Sincerely yours,

Heinz Kohut, M.D.

April 2, 1977

Mrs. Elke vom Scheidt

Costermano, Italy

Dear Frau vom Scheidt:

I am glad to hear from your letter of March 28 that everything is now in good order. You mention that, when I read the definitive version of "Narzissmus als Widerstand, etc.," I will see that you did not have to change very much. Are you going to send me a copy of this definitive version? Or did you have the printed book (or the galleys) in mind?

Now to the differentiation between "pleasure" and "joy" and the question of the best German equivalents for these terms. I follow your arguments completely and agree with them—nevertheless I think that we must stick to the opposition *"Lust"* ["pleasure"] and *"Freude"* ["joy"] because, for better or worse, I want them to be accepted as specifically defined technical terms. Please read the paragraph about this topic on pp. 271/272 in "Die Zukunft der Psychoanalyse" (Suhrkamp, 1975) and note that the antithesis between *"Lust"* and *"Freude"* corresponds to the antithesis between *"Angst"* ["anxiety"] and *"Verzweiflung"* ["despair"]. And on page 44 of my new book you will soon find this paragraph: "I will add here that I do not use the terms joy and pleasure at random. Joy is experienced as referring to a more encompassing emotion such as, for example, the emotion evoked by success, whereas pleasure, however intense it may be, refers to a delimited experience such as, for example, sensual satisfaction. From the point of view of depth psychology, we can say, moreover, that the experience of joy has a genetic root different from that of the experience of pleasure; that each of these modes of affect has its own developmental line and that joy is not sublimated pleasure. Joy relates to the experiences of the total self whereas pleasure (despite the frequently occurring participation of the total self, which then provides an admixture of joy) relates to experiences of parts and constituents of the self. There are, in other words, archaic forms of joy relating to archaic developmental stages of the whole self, just as there are archaic stages in the development of the experiences of parts and contituents of the self. And one may speak of sublimated joy, just as one speaks of sublimated pleasure." You can see from the foregoing that we are now not at liberty to replace the words *Lust* and *Freude* by other words whenever we are talking about these experiences in the context of the *Genuss* [enjoyment] evoked by parts and the *Genuss* felt concerning the whole self. In other contexts, however, I would, in anticipation of the later work, try to keep the question in mind whether experiences of parts or of the whole self are involved and, if we can distinguish, choose *Lust* or *Freude*, respectively.

I wish you and your children a good and refreshing holiday* with your parents in Italy.

Sincerely,

Heinz Kohut, M.D.

*[handwritten] *mit* [with] *Lust, Freude, und Genuss!*

April 7, 1977
Dr. Henry D. v. Witzleben
Palo Alto, California
Dear Henry:

I was finally able to turn to your essay. As was true with regard to its predecessors, I enjoyed following the unrolling of your thoughts.

In fact, this *latest* of your contributions in praise of Goethe—like [Heinrich] Politzer in his charming postscript,[1] I refuse to believe that you are serious about its being the *last*—gave me even more pleasure than the earlier ones. To be exact: I was more moved by it, because it enabled me to understand more broadly, and to sense more deeply, the emotional sustenance that the relationship with the figure of Goethe (and Freud) has had for you throughout your long life.

My own commitment to great figures, I must confess, had never been as strong as yours; the choice of our heroes, however, Goethe and Freud, was the same. And then there has come to be another important difference in our attitude. During the past ten or fifteen years a change has taken place in me. Not that the content of my image of Goethe or Freud changed, or that I did not anymore look up to them. But my need for them lessened—I did not feel that I had to lean on them, to listen to them via their writings when I felt in need of self-confirmation or support. On the contrary, I felt that they and their works and values kept my gaze fastened too strongly upon the past. I wanted to look directly at the present—not from the point of view of their values and habits of thought, but from the vantage point of the child of the twentieth century that I felt I was, who still admired the world of Goethe and Freud—a world in which in essence I had lived since my adolescence and early adulthood—but now from the outside as it were, by glancing backwards at it as on something beautiful but past. Yes, I still admire Goethe and Freud profoundly. But other heroes have now gained stature as equals next to these two— some that had always been important to me, such as Dostoyevsky and Thomas Mann, others—foremost among them Proust, Joyce, and the aged O'Neill—who achieved a new and intense meaning for me that they had not had for me in earlier years. And with their aid, witnessing their suffering and participating in it via their work, I asked myself a question that I had never allowed myself to ask before. Is the present world worse, I asked myself, or is it rather different—different in a decisive way that demands new values, new yardsticks, new viewpoints, by which to evaluate, measure, and understand it?

Enough! Instead of talking about myself I must tell you that it is good to know that there are some unchanged values in this world, that there are men like you who continue to remain loyal to certain values of the past that will retain at least some of their original power as long as man walks on this earth. And even though I do not anymore cling to these values as fervently as I once did, I am happy in the realization that there are individuals who demonstrate by their whole

being that these old values are still alive and that, if the new ground
does not sustain us, we can return to them.

Warm regards,

Yours,

Heinz Kohut, M.D.

1. Henry von Witzleben, 'Im Dienste Goethens: Bekenntnis und Dank" (Paper presented at the Goethe Institute, San Francisco, January 27, 1977); afterword by Heinz
Politzer.

May 2, 1977

Jerome Kavka, M.D.

Chicago

Dear Jerry:

I finally was able to read your essay on "Ezra Pound's 'Beggar
Dream.'" Like all the others of your communications about your encounter with Pound that I have so far become acquainted with, I found
this one, too, of great interest. One is fascinated by the details that
are presented, they are excitingly evocative—yet, in the fragmentary
form that one confronts them in, one cannot be sure that the formulations one builds would stand up in the face of further information.

Still, I will give you in the following certain impressions that I would
consider as at least containing a part of the psychological truth about
your fascinating patient. I believe that one of the main themes in the
material is the theme of insanity—but not insanity in its social and—in
1946—current sense, but insanity in its essential and individual sense,
as it formed Pound's genius and personality. I would venture the
guess that there was a decisive break in continuity in Pound's personality development—a point at which he withdrew from the attempt
to build up a sane masculine self, a fragile structure that could be
maintained only so long as he was incessantly creating with the aid
of words and language. I think that Pound's need—the beggar's
need—was the need for masculine substance from his father. That he
was in fact denied the fulfillment of this need (transmuting internalization of maleness from the idealized father) by the mother who kept
the boy "in curls" (i.e., infantile, feminine), forcing him to construct
a psychotic-creative masculine self after splitting himself off from the
need, perhaps sexualized in the form of a fellatio fantasy, of obtaining
male substance (money, the "nickel," gold). In order to create, in order

to maintain this creative-psychotic masculine self, in order to remain a creative genius, to write poetry, he had to defend himself against the intrusions of his old need for real masculinity. This needful self—a self that admits the absence of masculine substance, admits that it has yet to obtain it in order to be healthy—is split off and rejected. This needful self he experiences as the greedy Jew in him, the beggar who has no pride, who wants to suck in order to get substance into himself. The powerfulness of this need that is split off is attested to by the idea of the Jewish conspiracy that spreads all over the world.

Did I make myself clear? If not—and perhaps even if I did—may I ask you to look at the case history of Mr. X. in Chapter Four of *The Restoration of the Self*. Mr. X., although not endowed with Pound's genius, and therefore capable of cure in the ordinary sense of the word, illustrates the psychological structure that I tried to outline in the foregoing.

Warm regards and good wishes in pursuit of psychological insights.

Yours sincerely,

Heinz Kohut, M.D.

May 19, 1977
John Demos
Chicago
Dear John,

I just learned from Mike Basch that you might undertake some steps to bring my new book to the attention of some important potential reviewers outside the narrow professional field of psychotherapy. I do thank you warmly for these efforts and hope that they will arouse the interest of the reviewers. I believe that the *Restoration* is much more accessible to people outside the narrow professional field than the *Analysis of the Self* of 1971. And there are, as you know, many other publications that could and should be noticed by people outside psychoanalysis. If somebody of some substance would to talk over my work with some of my colleagues or with me, that could be arranged. And, of course, if you are willing to give the necessary information, that would be great.

At any rate, thank you again. I am sending you a copy of the *Restoration*. Please let me know sometime what *you* think of it.

Regards,
Cordially,
Heinz

June 22, 1977 [from John Gedo]

Dear Heinz,

We received your very thoughtful gift, with its much appreciated memento of a treasured moment of the past, just as I was completing my reading of the review copy of your book IUP had sent a few days before. I have promised you a forthright account of my reactions to your new ideas, and I want to keep that pledge.

Many of your new proposals go in the direction I have espoused for many years, as you know, and I can only welcome them. You will recall that I urged you to define the self in terms of the broader criteria you now spell out when you came to Princeton to address my CAPS [Center for Advanced Psychoanalytic Studies] group. It is, of course, very gratifying to have been judged to be correct by a person of your caliber.

With most of your other hypotheses I do not find myself to be in sympathy; in particular, my clinical experience has not confirmed the adequacy of the developmental sequences you postulated a decade ago. But this is not the place to attempt to go into those details. Let me say only that the new book helped me to grasp the wide differences between your point of view and my own—divergences that were covered over for a number of years by my enthusiasm for the enormous service you had rendered us all in sweeping away the cobwebs that had accumulated over psychoanalysis in the past generation.

And I shall always remain grateful to you for setting me free through your work, not to speak at this moment of all the other kindnesses you once showed me.

As ever,

John[1]

---

1. As noted in the Introduction, Gedo and Kohut came to a somewhat bitter parting of the ways and this letter, according to Gedo (personal communication, November 5, 1991), "was my *ironic* reproach to him." See John E. Gedo, "Reflections on Some Current Controversies in Psychoanalysis," *JAPA* 28 (1980): 363–83; cf. his admiration for Kohut's work on narcissism: "The Hero of Our Time: The Dissidence of Heinz Kohut," in Gedo, *Conceptual Issues in Psychoanalysis: Essays in History and Method* (Hillsdale, N.J., 1986), p. 100.

Gedo sees the flaws in self psychology as a reflection of Kohut's personal struggles, both with his past (Gedo, personal communication, November 5, 1991) and with the cancer Gedo believes compelled Kohut to hurry to finish his life's work: "Barred from the Promised Land: Heinz Kohut in the Wilderness," in *Conceptual Issues in Psychoanalysis*, p. 131. Gedo (personal communication, October 3, 1991) came to regard Kohut, for all his brilliance and courage, as a "pitifully needy person." Gedo argues that Kohut is a utopian convinced of the remedial effects of the environment in compensating for early caretaking deficiencies and who therefore abandons insight in favor of cure: "Self

Psychology: A Post-Kohutian View," in *Self Psychology: Comparisons and Contrasts*, ed. Douglas W. Detrick and Susan P. Detrick (Hillsdale, N.J., 1989), pp. 415–28.

July 9, 1977
Miss Georgie Anne Geyer
Washington, D.C.
Dear Miss Geyer:
I, too, would like to talk with you sometime this summer, firstly because it's always fun talking with you, and, secondly, because I would like to get your advice on the following. Many of my colleagues who are well acquainted with my contributions feel that my ideas should become known beyond the narrow field of my profession—but nobody seems to have the skills to bring this about. There is no question that a review of my new book by some leading newspapers would help.[1] (This happened in Germany concerning my other writings with the result that I have a broad circle of readers among the educated, especially in the university communities there.)
Have you any ideas and suggestions in this matter? If so, I would love to hear them.
Warmly,
Heinz Kohut, M.D.
P.S. If you would just read the last chapter of my new book— Chapter Seven, called "Epilogue"—you would get a quick idea that the significance of my work transcends the confines of psychotherapy.

1. Georgie Anne Geyer, "Glue for a Broken World," *Los Angeles Times*, October 19, 1978.

July 19, 1977
Jacques Palaci
Paris
Dear Jacques,
I am following your advice and am sending a copy of the *Restoration* to de M'Uzan. I feel rather pessimistic about arousing the interest of the French in my work. The situation is so different in the U.S.A. and in Germany. The I[nternational]. U[niversities]. P[ress]. tells me that in less than 2 months, about 11,500 copies of the *Restoration* were sold. And Suhrkamp, having already published *The Analysis of the Self* in a regular edition and as a pocket book, and having also published two separate volumes of my essays, is eager to acquire the German rights of the *Restoration* and wants to bring it out in the fall of 1978. What a

contrast to France! But thank so much for all that you are doing.[1] I hope that it will ultimately be fruitful.—Have a nice vacation and let me hear from you soon. (Write to my office address during the summer for greater speed of forwarding.) Warm regards from house to house.

Yours,

Heinz

P.S. I am sending copies of some letters I exchanged with Daniel Lagache in 1963 to Mrs. [Eva] Rosenblum.[2]

1. See *Advances in Self Psychology*, ed. Arnold Goldberg (New York, 1980), pp. 449–56.
2. Rosenblum was editing the works of Lagache.

August 2, 1977

Judy L. Kantrowitz, Ph.D.

Brookline, Massachusetts

Dear Dr. Kantrowitz:

Your letter gave me a great deal of pleasure—and more. I was in fact deeply moved by your expression of gratitude for what my contributions have come to mean to you. What pleased me most was that the specific qualities and aspects of my writings that you value most highly are those that I, too, consider as the essence of my work. I knew, in particular, that you had thoroughly understood my work when you told me about the session with your patient in which you learned that offering a gift "was an unusual act for him." And I was in full sympathy with your communication to him that you had grasped the gift offer as being a step of initiative into a direction into which he had not moved before because of the rebuffs from the side of his mother.

These are crucial clinical insights that turn the tide in an analysis. And an analyst's continued failure to understand the patient's action bars the road toward the decisive structural changes. Even patients' lies are sometimes not to be censured as immoral but are to be acknowledged as first moves toward self-assertive initiative. I believe I talked about such moments in Cincinnati.

Let me end by thanking you once more for the generosity of your approval. Being at this time again exposed not only to scientific but also to personally insulting attacks, it is good for me to know that I do not need to rely exclusively on my inner resources but that I have the support of others.

Warmly yours,

Heinz Kohut, M.D.

August 10, 1977
Ernest S. Wolf, M.D.
Stratford-upon-Avon, England

Dear Ernie,

You left—but your letter [of August 7] reacting to my message to Heller[1] arrived to make it easier for me to do without being able to pick up the phone and call you as I do so often in the evening. I enjoyed your response, especially your remarks about the artist's creativity. In fact, I have expressed this thought before (peripherally in "The Future of Psychoanalysis" and, more directly, in Chapter Seven of *The Restoration of the Self*). Your elaboration of my thought, at any rate, in terms of the "group-self" hypothesis, I experience as fully congenial. To speculate even further, I would think that here is a useful analogy to biology: the individual cell, with its own life and, *sit venia verbo* [so to speak]—with its own personality, is yet subordinated to the overall design. There is a host of challenging problems to follow up here. On the one hand, this conception of the group-self might help us understand different types of social organizations—e.g., democracy, the absolutarian state—; on the other hand, it seems to me that here is also a novel approach to psychosomatic medicine—e.g., concerning the breakdown of the supraordinated pattern leading to states of biological fragmentation and disease (diminution of host resistance vis-à-vis infections or vis-à-vis malignancies).

Your remarks about my picking unworthy addressees also gave me food for thought—though of thought of a different kind. I do have the tendency—largely overcome—to elevate certain figures in my surroundings above their actual worth. And when I read about your uneasiness in this respect, I wondered whether you had put your finger on a remaining ill controlled need to do so. A remnant of this tendency may have indeed clouded my judgment with regard to E.H.—with regard to [Norman] L[itowitz].[2], however, that is not at all the case. The decisive issue at any rate lies elsewhere. When I form new lines of thought, an imaginary, yet simultaneously real person whom I can address with some emotionality—plead with, teach, argue with—is helpful to me. The important thing to me in the choice of this target is not at all its importance, but rather its haziness, its lack of interpersonal substance. I could never write such messages to people toward whom I feel strong emotions, especially not to anyone for whom I feel affection.

Have a fine vacation! Love from Betty and me to both of you.

Yours,

Heinz Kohut, M.D.[3]

1. *Search*, 2:914–27. See also *Search*, 4:577–91, 606–8. This debate over Erich Heller's criticism of psychoanalytic denigration of art began with Heller's lecture at the Chicago Institute for Psychoanalysis in November 1976: see Erich Heller, "The Dismantling of a Marionette Theater; or, Psychology and the Misinterpretation of Literature," *Critical Inquiry* 4 (1978): 417–32; and Heinz Kohut, "Psychoanalysis and the Interpretation of Literature: A Correspondence with Erich Heller," *ibid.*, 433–50. See also below, December 14, 1977; and December 11 and 28, 1978.

2. *Search*, 3:223–29.

3. Two postscripts concerning minor foreign publication matters have been omitted here.

Carmel, September 21, 1977

Lars B. Lofgren, M.D.

Los Angeles

Dear Borje,

Your fine letter followed me on my vacation and reached me here in Carmel after considerable delay. When it came I was in the middle of trying to work out a plan for some writing that I am now engaged in—a clinical contribution concerning a patient ["Mr. Z."] whom I analyzed twice; once before and once after I had made my decisive steps towards the new psychology of the self;[1] it is fascinating to compare how the same material takes on a completely different significance when seen from the new point of view—and I put aside all correspondence until the design that I wanted to use had become clear to me. Please forgive the slowness of my response.

That you understand and value my work gives me a great deal of satisfaction. To hear the echo to my efforts that comes from you and a few others like you far outweighs for me the inevitable attacks, often in the form of blows below the belt—that I don't know that one listens to dream associations, not just to the manifest content; that I don't know that there exists pre-genital, pre-oedipal infantile sexuality; that I am replacing science by philosophy; etc.—to which I am now frequently exposed.

I was in particular taken by the brief case vignette which I immediately understood and which rang many bells of the memory of similar experiences. Have you finished the *Restoration* in the meantime? I wonder how you responded to this new work?

Now to your two questions. As far as coming to Los Angeles is concerned, the answer is "no." I decided some years ago not to give any lectures anymore, in particular not to travel away from Chicago for such purposes. My energy is limited and I want to devote it all to further investigations. I was very pleased by your inquiry whether you could see me for consultation and I would very much like to accommodate you. The difficulty is that a number of other colleagues—four of them from Canada—have already a weekend spot on my schedule. In addition, I will, after some years of staying away from teaching, give a course at the Institute on alternate Fridays this fall. As I can see it now, I must regretfully tell you that I do not have an appointment for you in the fall. But I will keep your wish in mind and if, unexpectedly, there is a suitable opening, I will let you know immediately.[2] Two details which, I hope, won't deter you if I can make arrangements later: (a) my fee for consultations of the type you envisage is $100 per session; and (b) if case material or theoretical thoughts are to be discussed, they should be presented during the session. Again—and I hope that you will be tolerant of my needs here—I must husband my time and energy if I want to get things done.

Please let me hear from you. Once more, I enjoyed greatly receiving your letter.

Cordially yours,
Heinz Kohut, M.D.

1. *Search*, 4:395–446.
2. See below, Kohut to Lotte Köhler, December 14, 1977.

Carmel, September 26, 1977
Professor Lloyd S. Etheredge
Department of Political Science
Massachusetts Institute of Technology
Dear Professor Etheredge:

Thank you very much for your interesting letter (and the not yet read draft for your book on Political Confusion) which followed me on my vacation. I vaguely remember, but cannot check here, that I have in a former letter referred you to a paper written with Dr. Seitz in which mention is made of the fact that we feel as if we were looking up to the superego. I can now refer you also to the footnote on pp.

112/13 in *The Restoration of the Self* in which a related topic is touched upon within the framework of a psychology of the self.

Your question whether at the end of a successful analysis an individual might still experience his ideals and moral standards as superior to him—in space? in power?—is difficult to answer. I would think that the criterion that I have for a proper process of transmuting internalization applies here also. A successful analysis, in other words, should be expected to lead to a degree of de-concretization, of de-personalization of ideals and moral injunctions—the concrete features of the parental figures should fade and the ideal, the code as such, should now prevail.

Three further remarks about the process of transmuting internalization and its results. (a) In line with my shift from structural theory (the agencies of the mind: id, ego, superego, and their relationship to each other) to a psychoanalytic psychology of the self, the analytic results that you wonder about could be expressed in terms of the degree to which an analysis has achieved the establishment of a firm self, to the degree to which ambitions, basic skills and talents, and idealized values have become self and are, therefore, not anymore experienced as located outside (and therefore also not, in the concrete sense of the word, as "above" the self). The best analytic results, to put it still differently, are those in which the content of ambitions, the choice of skills and talents, the content and the hierarchical place of idealized values, have no relationship to the source (the parent of childhood; the analyst in the analytic process) from which the original crystallization points of these constituents of the self were derived. You may remember that in *The Restoration of the Self* I am in this context using the biological analogy of the building up of protein. Foreign protein is needed in order to build up and to maintain one's own. Yet via a very specific biological process a splitting up of the foreign protein into its constituents takes place and these are the re-arranged to form the specific proteins that characterize the ingestor. (We eat plant and animal proteins and transmute these into human protein.) (b) The aforementioned process is not only for practical purposes always incomplete—no analytic result can be perfect; no childhood, even the very best, can bring about perfect developmental results—it must also, in principle, remain incomplete. Traces of the corporeal, however, rarefied, must be retained by us or we cannot function. We think in images and in words which have auditory and visual features. The same holds true, I believe, for our idealized values and for our relationship to them. (c) A final remark. I believe that in general prohibitions tend to be more experienced as outside the self (located "above")—it follows that the framework of structural psychology can accommodate them reasonably well—than positive values—it follows that the framework of the psychology of the self is needed to deal with them. But even the latter—you may remember my evocative analogy that we are "pushed" by our ambitions but "led" by our ideals—must surely also retain traces of the concreteness that they once had before they developed further.

Allow me to end with two personal observations. Whenever I read your letters, I am struck by two differences between us. The first one concerns the fact that you know so much more than I about society. I think, with some embarrassment, how, for example, the Epilogue chapter of *The Restoration*, with its amateurish references to the influence of social, psychotropic factors must read to an expert such as you. The second one—and I must admit that I feel here that I need no excuses—concerns the fact that I feel that my outlook is more dispassionate than yours. You seem to me to have more of an axe to grind, that you are, in principle, somewhat of a reformer. While I have of course values, too—one could not speak of the evaluation of a "cure" of an analysis in the absence of a framework of values—I instinctively not only attempt to keep these at a minimum but I also, whenever I can, try to be dispassionately relativistic about them.

Best regards,
Sincerely yours,
Heinz Kohut, M.D.

Carmel, September 26, 1977
Dr. Jürgen vom Scheidt
Munich
Dear Dr. vom Scheidt:

I hope that time and the silently moving inner processes of reintegration are continuing to do their good work after the harrowing experiences of the past year. Judging by the intellectual level of your last letter (June 3) you have indeed succeeded in freeing yourself sufficiently and to return to creative thinking.

The outline of the ideas that you will be pursuing in your next book was fascinating. I followed the correlation of the various images of God as you sketched them out with the greatest interest and obtained a strong impression that you are on the track of important insights in this area. With your remarks concerning the influence of the experience of the group on personality formation I felt again somewhat less at home. I still think that group-experience influences later acquired layers of the personality—that the cohesive core of the personality must first have formed via transmuting internalizations acquired in the matrix provided by a few individuals who served as empathic self-objects before a person is able—generally in early adolescence—to open himself to the enriching stimulation of the group. Why, I ask myself—and you—does an early surrounding that is strongly weighted toward group experience (a childhood spent in an orphanage for example—even a very good orphanage) lead to the shallowness and psychological impoverishment that we so often encounter in adults who were deprived of a childhood matrix of father, mother, and a few siblings. And is it not even true that families with an unusually great number of children often produce flat and shallow personalities in the offspring—especially in those lost in the middle—unless unusual circumstances bring about more of the wholesome empathic closeness from the side of the parents, or from one of the older siblings who substitutes for them, than is most frequently found under such conditions? Do you have answers to these questions that are based on actual observation?

Let me close this letter by telling you that I enjoy your communications. It seems that, as I am getting older, the contact with young minds—especially those with a creative spark—gives me a sense of continuing participation in a world that will strive and think and create after I, myself, have ceased to do so.

Cordially yours,

Heinz Kohut, M.D.

P.S. Thank you also for sending me the nice article on your experiences in India with the impressive photographs.

Carmel, September 26, 1977
Robert S. Wallerstein, M.D.
Langley Porter Neuropsychiatric Institute
University of California
San Francisco

Dear Bob:

Your friendly note followed me on my vacation. Congratulations at having been elected to be a Vice-President of the I.P.A.! It's a job that I filled for quite a number of years and found very rewarding. I could have stood for election to the Presidency in 1969—as a matter of fact there was a good deal of pressure on me to do so. I have no doubt now that the writing of *The Analysis of the Self* and *The Restoration of the Self* and of several long papers to which I gave a good deal of thought

was more fulfilling to me than an election to the Presidency of the
I.P.A. would have been—however important a contribution to analysis one can make by handling decisions wisely. Actually, I don't think
that the Presidency must be very time consuming if one has the genius
for effective leadership that you have. To me, these things come very
hard and, when I had in the past undertaken them, they filled my
time and absorbed my energies almost completely. Anyway, these are
crossroads in life that each person has to face on his own. Small decisions, Freud is supposed to have said, one makes with one's head,
large ones with the belly.

Let me hear sometime what you think of the *Restoration*.

Warm regards,

Cordially yours,

Heinz Kohut, M.D.

P.S. Today I received your note that you had read and forwarded
the paper that I had written with Dr. Ernest Wolf. Unfortunately, we
received a note from the Swiss publishers of the encyclopedia for
which we wrote the article in which they now strictly prohibit us from
publishing the essay elsewhere. We have therefore written to the *International Journal* and have recalled the paper.[1]

1. This worked out in the end: "The Disorders of the Self and Their Treatment: An
Outline," *IJP* 59 (1978): 413–25; *Search*, 3:359–85; see also below, September 9, 1978.

Carmel, September 27, 1977
Douglas Levin, M.D.
Montreal
Dear Doug,

The Copies of [Fritjof] Capra's letter to you (8/29) and of your reply
to him (9/19) arrived here today, shortly before our return to Chicago.
But I will not delay my response in order to tell you immediately that
I am very glad about this positive feed-back from a scholarly physicist.
I also thought that your elaboration of the mind-body theme was, as
usual, full of surprising and thought-provoking vistas. Capra has not
phoned me here as you had suggested he might do, and I could,
therefore, not tell him that his assumption that my work, too, is in
harmony with the Cartesian mind-body duality is in error. You might
point out to him (at a suitable occasion) my 1959 essay on "Introspection & Empathy" where I unambiguously demonstrated a) that the
essence of reality is unknowable, and b) that the difference between
mind and body is operational, i.e., that we speak of psychological

processes when our observation employs introspection and empathy, that we speak of physical (e.g., biological processes if our observation employs (sensory) extrospection[)].

Once more the expression of my great pleasure about Capra's response to you. I feel encouraged and so, I hope, do you.

Cordially,
Heinz Kohut

October 3, 1977
Dr. Fritz Morgenthaler
Zurich
Dear Fritz,

Your letter awaited me on my return from California—it was the best welcome home that I could have hoped for. You end your letter by stating modestly that it is probably the longest and most comprehensive letter that you have ever written to me; and then you add that, despite its length it was fragmentary and incomplete.

My reaction is that it was the most satisfying response to my work that I have ever received from anyone. And I thank you for it with a deep feeling of gratitude.

I will not try at this point to discuss your searching comments, but they will not be lost—I will think about everything you said. Only two personal remarks. What you said about sexuality—including the attitude toward "pathological" sexuality—evoked an immediate sympathetic echo in me. I fully agree with you; indeed, I felt that you understood me well, even though I did not always express my convictions as directly as I might have.[1] But, there too, you understood my reasons; I am saying so many new things in the *Restoration*, am shifting the focus of psychoanalysis so decisively, that I do not want to provoke comparatively unimportant small skirmishes that would deflect the reader from joining the major encounter. With regard to the societal issues you raise, I feel on less secure ground in my reaction. That the psychology of the self as I see it is of the utmost importance vis-à-vis a meaningful understanding of group relations, is almost self-evident—to give an example: narcissistic injuries and the insecurely established group-self play a decisive role as a cause of international tensions and of war. But with regard to the fabric itself of society I feel my path less clearly defined. I vaguely realize that you may be right when you imply that here lies perhaps the most important application of my work; and I cannot help but agree with you that the professional sociologists will not be of great help to us. But whether *I* can be of help here is questionable. What is needed here is the confluence, in a creative personality, of a keen understanding of the vicissitudes of the self in the experience of the deprived masses, whether they live thousands of miles away in India or almost next door—in my case, in Chicago, on the other side of Sixtieth street—but emotionally almost as far away as the starving beggars in Calcutta.

Enough now. Except, once more, my thanks to you for your response. One letter like yours makes up for the hundreds of attacks, open and disguised, to which I am, of course, now exposed.

Warmly yours,

Heinz Kohut, M.D.

1. Morgenthaler (September 25, 1977) argues that after a successful analysis a homosexual remains a homosexual.

October 5, 1977 [from David M. Terman]

Dear Heinz,

Having finished reading *The Restoration of the Self* I want you to know how nourished and grateful I felt when, regretfully, I came to its end. I want to assure you that that which you stated as your deepest wish—to "motivate the rising generation of psychoanalysts to pursue the path . . . that will lead us further into that aspect of reality that can be investigated through scientifically disciplined introspection and empathy"—has been fulfilled with me. Your work and thought are always an inspiration to my efforts.

There is much that I admire in your new work, not the least of which is your courage in presenting it. For, inevitably, you will have to endure all manner of reactions of outrage and derision—or worse, those of disdainful dismissal. I can just imagine the howls of indignation in some quarters, for example, for your audacity in suggesting that Freud was limited in his comprehension of narcissistic experience, or that concepts of transference and resistance may not be the shibboleths which define our essential professional characters.

But though we may chuckle knowingly to each other over the narrowness and rigidity of those who would so respond, I think you would much rather have these (others) understand and value the insights you have wrested from your experience; and it is always with sadness—not just for oneself—but for the human condition—that ideas offered in good faith with such potential for extending our understanding and mastery of ourselves are met with such aversive reactions. So, in addition to my admiration for your courage, I send you my sympathy for your sadness.

But overwhelmingly, of course, I send my heartiest congratulations. There are so many good ideas and seminal insights. Some that come immediately to my mind are your comments on technique, the sufficiency of the establishment of a sector of wholeness of the self as a criterion of analytic success, and, of course, the importance of the reconstruction of the pathogenic personality of the parents in their self object function.

Though I may differ with you in some of the details of your ideas (the chief one being your separation of Guilty [oedipal] and Tragic [self] Man—a separation which I feel does not do justice to your own basic ideas)[1] I want to reassure you that I feel such differences are trivial and that my deepest and truest response to your work is one of sympathy, respect, agreement and enthusiasm. I am convinced that your work will stand as an important, perhaps crucial step in man's cultural evolution.

Again, congratulations, and my warmest regards,
David

1. See Terman to Kohut, December 4, 1975: "I don't think guilt is related only to conflicts over pleasure. It, too, (guilt) is an outcome of the vicissitudes of self development—perhaps most related to the fear of punishment or abandonment by the idealized parental self object."

October 6, 1977
Univ. Prof. Dr. Adam Wandruszka
Vienna
Dear Adi,

Many thanks for your interest in my possible election to Corresponding Membership in the Austrian Academy of Sciences. This would be an honor which I would be very proud to receive and I do hope that your plan will come to fruition.[1] In response to your request I sent you today not only a copy of *The Restoration of the Self* but also a volume of my essays, called *Introspektion, Empathie, and Psychoanalyse,* which was just published by Suhrkamp. It contains, so far as I can judge after a cursory look, a reasonably good bibliography of my writings. Suhrkamp and the International Universities Press, I might add, have already agreed on a contract concerning the German translation of the *Restoration* which is planned for publication in 1978.

It gave me a great deal of pleasure to hear that your daughter likes my contributions and that she approves of our long-established ties.

Give again our warm regards to your wife and let me hear from both of you from time to time. How strange the ways of life are! Who would ever have predicted forty-five years ago when we graduated from our Gymnasium that you would ever support my election to membership in the Academy of Sciences?

Yours,

Heinz Kohut, M.D.

P.S. Do you recall Marcel Proust's wonderful description of the negotiations between the Prince of Faffenheim and M. de Norpois concerning Faffenheim's wish to be elected Corresponding Member of the Academy of Moral and Political Sciences? If not, do refresh your memory and read it over. (In *Le Côté de Guermantes* [1920], about half-way through the volume, in the section about Mme. de Villeparisis.) It's priceless!

1. Wandruszka had knowledge of, and connections within, the nominating and election process of the Austrian Academy. See Wandruszka to Kohut, September 29, 1977; and his obituary of Kohut in *Die Presse*, October 13, 1981.

December 14, 1977

Dr. med. Lotte Köhler

Munich

Dear Dr. Köhler:

I was very much taken with your letter and was charmed by your thoughtfulness in sending me the Kleist-coin. I have also looked at your paper, have read it, here and there, and while I have not yet been able to study it carefully, it is my impression that your knowledge is solid and that you have produced something valuable. Dr. Wolf took your paper along to New York and since he will be going back and forth between New York and Chicago twice more this week (he also spent the last weekend there), he should be able to finish it. After that we will discuss it and perhaps come up with some suggestions concerning publication.

It is really too bad that Chicago is so far away from Munich. Our self-psychology study group meets about once a month. Our next meeting will take place on Saturday, January 14. We will be discussing a twenty-page letter I wrote to a colleague in Los Angeles who thought that in *The Restoration of the Self* I advocate incomplete analyses.[1] This colleague will join us for this meeting, and there is another colleague flying in from Montreal, but Munich, unfortunately, is much farther away than either one of these places. Still, despite the distance, you might at some time or other want to hop over here and get some relief from your narcissistic rage[2] in the warmly welcoming atmosphere I can promise you here.

It might interest you to hear that a world-famous Germanist, Professor Erich Heller, leveled a scathing attack against applied psychoanalysis in a paper called "Psychoanalysis and the Misinterpretation of Literature." The example he uses is a reductionistic psychoanalytic interpretation of [Heinrich von] Kleist's "Marionettentheater." The essay will appear in *Critical Inquiry*—with a long reply by me [see above, August 10, 1977]. Sometime in the future I might submit my reply to Heller to a German-language publication. Perhaps to *Merkur* where, I understand, Heller's article will appear shortly.[3]

Warm regards and the best for Christmas and the new year, also from Betty,

Yours,

Heinz Kohut, M.D.

1. *Search*, 4:711–24. According to the notation on Lofgren's letter to Kohut of October 27, 1977, and on the manuscript copy of the letter reproduced in *Search* (dated 1981), this letter was apparently written on December 17, 1977. See also above, September 21, 1977. On the Kleist-coin, see below, Kohut to Schaefer, December 11, 1978.

2. Köhler was upset by political conflicts within the Munich psychoanalytic community.

3. Erich Heller, "Die Demolierung eines Marionettentheaters oder: Psychoanalyse und der Missbrauch der Literatur," *Merkur* 31 (1977): 1021–85.

January 17, 1978
Prof. Dr. phil. Rudolf Heinz
Wuppertal, West Germany
Dear Dr. Heinz,

Thank you for your interesting letter of December 18, 1977. I am glad to see that you are now less rejecting of the form in which I presented my empirical findings in 1971. I am confident that you will find my position even more congenial when you will see the formulations which are contained in my 1977 volume, *The Restoration of the Self*. Only two points today. (1) I am very eager not to encourage a break in the development of psychoanalysis and am therefore proceeding with theory change in a gradual way. And (2) by basing myself on the investigation of transferences and by retaining a psychology of the self in the narrower sense, i.e., a psychology of a self within a mental apparatus (see *The Restoration of the Self*), I am retaining the concept of a dynamic unconscious (including that of an unconscious nuclear self) and remain therefore in the mainstream of analysis, i.e., I do not encourage the development of a dissident school.

I will be very interested in your reactions to the theoretical position which I take in *The Restoration of the Self*.

Sincerely yours,

Heinz Kohut, M.D.

February 18, 1978
Mr. Kenneth L. Woodward, General Editor
Newsweek
New York

Dear Mr. Woodward:

It was very friendly of you to write me a personal note, and I enjoyed it: I can recognize a good mind and it always gives me pleasure to meet one. I can put myself in the shoes of those editors who, "nervous about the importance of things they don't understand," as you say, will always carefully protect themselves against a possibly embarrassing misjudgement. But I am glad to see that there are also those like you who will go out on a limb and courageously present new ideas which, on the basis of a deep-down hunch, they have recognized as important.

Some lay people have been able to grasp the essence of my work better than many of my professional colleagues. I recently listened to a roundtable conference on my new book, three half-hour sessions over the Chicago A.B.C. station. Three of my colleagues—very well informed about my work and quite committed to its significance—discussed *The Restoration of the Self*. I was not surprised to see that they understood the book. But what surprised and delighted me was the understanding that the moderator—not a psychologist; simply an intelligent and educated man—had acquired after a single and, I believe, incomplete reading. He was always on target, realized the significance of the shift in the conception of psychological man that was presented here, and led my colleagues, by skillful questions, to a superb discussion.

Enough! I do hope to meet you sometime—perhaps at our first international conference on the psychology of the self in Chicago, next October. There will be many participants from Europe and representatives from many fields of human thought—including a number of theologians who seem to have found my work especially attractive.

Once more my thanks for your friendly letter. I am glad that your article [January 30, 1978] proved so successful for *Newsweek* and for you.

Sincerely,

Heinz Kohut, M.D.

February 21, 1978

George H. Pollock, M.D., Director

Institute for Psychoanalysis

Chicago

Dear George,

You remember that I recently mentioned to you that the demands on me for consultations and conferences, especially by out of town people, were mounting and that I was reaching the end of my capacity to handle them. Something needs to be organized in order to accommodate out-of-town visitors (and perhaps also people from Chicago), without further pressure on me. Since I do not want to make any move that could be construed as a step away from organized psychoanalysis, I hope that at least some of these activities can be carried out under the aegis of the Institute if I can be sure that they will be the responsibility of qualified people.

The tasks of which I speak are at the present moment not great; the people who are writing to me now (and also to a few others who have become known as experts in the psychoanalytic psychology of the self) want either private consultations, clinical supervision, or similar small-scale offerings. Such needs can, and should, be handled on a private basis, outside the framework of the Institute, even though they too need to be coordinated. But sooner or later these demands will increase; I think especially so after the October-conference. It's best to be prepared.

In order to get us started on plans for a more cohesive program of postgraduate education in the psychology of the self, I will in the not too distant future meet with a small group of colleagues who are especially closely associated with my work and outline a schedule of courses and supervision. (We might have to consider special programs for non-analysts; and we will have to find an answer to the question of how to respond to analysts who are not graduates of "approved" institutes.) We will then discuss our plans with you (and perhaps others involved with postgraduate education at the Institute). If we can come to a more or less firmly outlined program, we could then begin to offer it actively by announcing it—in particular in connection with the October conference.

Please let me know your reactions to these thoughts.

Sincerely,

Heinz Kohut, M.D.

April 27, 1978

Richard C. Robertiello, M.D.

New York

Dear Dr. Robertiello:

I was deeply touched by your dedication. The support of colleagues like you means a great deal to me and, when I feel shaken occasionally for a moment by the often rather harsh attacks on my work and me, I have no trouble regaining my balance by reminding myself that there are people like you to whom I have given something and that my efforts have not been in vain.

I am quite immersed in work right now and unable to turn to your book.[1] I will take it along on my vacation (late in August) and will read it then—I am certain with a great deal of enjoyment. But, quite independent of any time pressure on me, I decided that, at this juncture, I should not write either the preface or the quotable "opinion" that you mentioned to me.

Since you are familiar with my writings it will not come as a surprise to you when I tell you that I am trying hard to find ways of integrating the new psychology of the self with the main body of psychoanalytic knowledge and practice. At the moment this goal may still seem to be unreachable. But it may be reachable in the long run if I can resist the temptation toward angry withdrawal and if I can support my friends and colleagues to do likewise. You may ask me, of course, whether my wish for this integration is wise. You may even wonder whether it does not betray a degree of faintheartedness, i.e., whether I am afraid of going it alone. I have asked myself these questions, I have discussed them with my friends. My conclusion is that this wish is neither foolish nor cowardly. For better or worse, psychoanalysis, whatever its shortcomings, comes ever so much closer to the realities of human experience, in my opinion, than any other psychological approaches to the mind of man. And I feel therefore that going it alone, outside of analysis, while perhaps leading to short-run success, would, in the long run, bring about defeat. I am, despite my new views which, according to some analysts, constitute a kind of heresy, a dedicated psychoanalyst, and I am convinced that my work lies in the mainstream of progress of this vital science.

But enough of these reflections. I have said a great deal about these issues before and don't need to elaborate on my conviction that the continuity of the analytic "group self" must be preserved. And you can surely see how all this relates to my decision not to comply with your wish—a decision that I made reluctantly in view of your friendliness toward me and support of my work, To put it in the briefest possible form: your book is addressed not to analysts but to the intelligent public. And my participation in this venture, as valuable as I consider this type of publication to be, might, at this point, be held against me as proof that *I* am moving away from the center. But let me stress again that I am convinced that it is valuable to communicate the new insights to a broader audience. And let me assure you that I will undoubtedly use your book and recommend it to people who are in need of this kind of information. I will also undoubtedly find other ways of showing my appreciation to you.

Let me close by expressing once more my warm gratitude for the generosity of your approval. I am very much looking forward to seeing you in Chicago in October.

Sincerely yours,

Heinz Kohut, M.D.

1. *Your Own True Love: The New Positive View of Narcissism: The Person You Love the Most Should Be . . . You* (New York, 1978).

May 1, 1978

Arnold Goldberg, M.D.

Chicago

Dear Arnold,

This is now a totally impossible situation, the worst atmosphere in which to propose a postgraduate program to the Council. Rumors not only in Chicago *but all over the USA* that we are "splitting off" and setting up an Institute of our own.[1] I see no way of counteracting rumors. It all started of course with your informal proposal to our group that George [Pollock] took as an official document & distributed to a committee, from where it was "leaked" with the present results.

What to do? I see only 2 possibilities:

(1) You write a new proposal to Council—stressing this is the only official document—an earlier was taken as official via misunder-

standing, to be explained at the meeting. In the proposal you say that we want the Council's advice *whether, and if so, how* to set up a p./g. program via the IfPsa [see below, November 22]. Give reasons why we want it: the demands on H.K., the needs for careful learning. Then mention informally a *spectrum* of possibilities: a) to continue as now, informally, outside IfPsa except for the workshop; b) to expand the workshop—several workshops + supervision private; c) a more or less planned curriculum. Stress that the last possibility has great advantages because of the Class-1 (?) [Continuing Medical Education] credits for the participants.

(2) Give me the opportunity to express myself on my deep conviction that the psa of the self is a step *within* psychoanalysis, not outside of it. This may be done best before we even get to the discussion—but it's probably impossible to do that and will have to wait until an opportune moment during the meeting on May 22.

What do you think of all that?

Heinz

1. In a letter of November 6 to his son and daughter-in-law, Kohut mentions discussion ("*great secret* please!!") of the future establishment of an "Interdisciplinary Center for the Study of the Self."

June 7, 1978
George Pollock, M.D.
Director, Institute for Psychoanalysis
Chicago
Dear George,

Knowing your schedule and the rapid pace of your life and realizing—burnt child that I am—that quick interchanges can lead to misunderstandings, I would nevertheless ask you whether you could give me a little time for a talk. Basically the issues are broad and important—what the Institute should undertake, now and in the future; how we can—you and I, and the others who support our outlook—break through the restrictions imposed by the panic-reactions of some on council and faculty that oppose all movement into new directions. My specific focus, however, is your having bowed out of the Chicago Conference on the Psychology of the Self. Despite the initial reassurance I derived from what you told me over the phone, I keep worrying. It just isn't like you to move away from a promise to participate because something else has come up—unless I badly misunderstood the enormous, overriding importance of the Washington meetings [at the National Institutes of Mental Health] for you. (If so: you could still send a message of regrets and good wishes to our Conference that could be read at our meeting.) Still, there are things that can't be written but need to be talked about. You know that I wanted this conference run at the fringes of psychoanalysis (the choice was between 1) Boston University and Harvard, 2) U of Cincinnati, and 3) Michael-Reese). I ultimately favored Reese because it allowed a degree of non-committed participation by members of the Institute without exposing the Institute. But, in the future, with the hopefully growing acceptance of selfpsychology[1] as a step in psychoanalysis, that should change; and, if there is to be a second conference, I had hoped that the Institute might become more centrally involved. All this would have been eased by your participation. Still, I don't throw in the sponge—I have lived long enough in psychoanalytic organizations to know that, if one keeps one's sanity, in the long run the storms subside and other issues overshadow the former ones. At any rate, these are the things I'd like to talk with you about. Do you think you could set a luncheon time aside? Or some other time?[2]

Cordially,

Heinz

1. In handwritten letters from this time on Kohut always used "selfpsychology," although typed letters rendered it as two words or, rarely, hyphenated it. Subsequent publications in the field use "selfobject" and "self psychology." See below, September 9, 1978.

2. See Pollock to Kohut, June 8, 1978. Pollock and Kohut did talk and Pollock did write a message of greeting and support to the Conference on the Psychology of the Self.

June 1978
Dr. Lotte Köhler
Munich
Dear Lotte,

Please forgive me for answering in English—but the luxury of having my letter typed is becoming irresistible. The warmth of your birthday greetings touched me deeply. They came just at the right moment and assisted me as I was struggling to deal with an emotional hurt of some magnitude: the Faculty of the Chicago Psychoanalytic Institute, my last remaining psychoanalytic home, celebrated my birthday by not re-electing me to its Council,[1] i.e., to its leading body of about twenty people—a body to which I had belonged for more than twenty-five years and to which as I assumed I would belong until I myself decided to retire. My removal from the Council came about as the result of a carefully organized campaign among the Faculty. The ostensible reason was an informal proposal of our group to offer a series of postgraduate courses on the psychology of the self in order to deal with the demands for instruction that are increasingly put upon me and to which I personally cannot respond adequately. An additional motivation for the move by the Faculty came from the fact that I had given a lecture, within the framework of a postgraduate course organized by the Institute, in which I outlined the psychology of the self and said (1) that the selfobject transferences were different from the object-instinctual transferences because they dealt not with revived conflictual instinctual strivings toward childhood objects but with re-vived needs for the completion of a developmental task, i.e., with the reactivated need to fill defects in the structure of the self with the aid of selfobjects; (2) that, psychologically speaking, drives were not primary but that, from the beginning, they were elements integrated into larger, more complex psychological configurations (exhibitionism and idealization, on the one hand; assertiveness, on the other); and (3) that it was not Freud and his theoretical system, however admirable the man and however dazzling his intellectual contributions, that de-fined psychoanalysis, but that it was the modest and almost accidental event that took place between Anna O. and [Joseph] Breuer that should be considered as the basic step that defined a whole new di-mension of man's investigations—i.e., the field of psychoanalysis.[2] Among those who attended this lecture was a young member of the Faculty who apparently smelled the unmistakable smell of heresy as I was uttering the aforementioned statements and, since she had obvi-ously not read *The Restoration of the Self*, the shock was great. She alerted a number of other members of the Faculty who were apparently equally shocked since, as I must assume, they, too, had not obtained any previous knowledge about my ideas via reading and were there-fore equally unprepared. At any rate, the videotaped lecture was now inspected by various small groups and since this experience appeared to confirm their worst fears, they concluded that I had ceased to be an analyst and needed to be removed [see below, May 5 and 6, 1980].

You can see, dear Lotte, that your expression of gratitude for my work came just at the right moment and that it contributed to my ability to see things in the wise perspective of my old Vienna where at such moments we used to say: "Wenn's nit zum Weinen wär,' wär's zum Lachen." ["If it weren't so sad, it would be funny."] By now I have regained my composure almost completely. True, the rift between the Institute and me can probably never be healed anymore. But I know, of course, that I have many good friends among the Faculty who were deeply upset about what happened. It even seems now that the Institute will offer a postgraduate program on self psychology, after all—a move that I would welcome very much and with which I would cooperate to the best of my ability. The program that I hope will be instituted would consist of three courses (clinical theory and development; general theory; case conference). These courses would be given on weekends (perhaps Saturdays), every four weeks; and the students (graduate analysts) would, in addition, have the opportunity for private supervision (consultations) with some of my closest co-workers and myself. Thus, in the course of one school year (perhaps ten Saturdays) a respectable amount of learning could be achieved. I would be very pleased, indeed, if this plan could be realized. The decision should come within the next two weeks.

But enough now about these Chicago shenanigans. Hearing about them will, I hope, help you to see the Munich tensions in better perspective. Such tensions arise everywhere and one has to be philosophical about them. I only hope that our increasing knowledge concerning the injured self and, especially, concerning reactive narcissistic rage will help us in the long run not only to master these organizational tensions but also—am I here unrealistic?—to learn lessons that will even help us to deal with the dangerous tensions between the larger groups in the arena of history that threaten the survival of man.

The news that your paper was accepted by *Psyche* gave me great pleasure.[3] And it was also good to hear that Hans Kilian can apply my ideas in his work with teachers. Will he, too, come to our Chicago conference? (I understand, by the way, that interest in the conference is high and, what gives me special pleasure, that people from various fields—psychologists, sociologists, political scientists, philosophers, social workers, pastoral counselors, etc.—are sending in their registration. Have you received your program and registration form yet? Just in case you have not, I am enclosing forms for you and Dr. Kilian.

But now I must close. We will be in Chicago until August 12. Then we are off to California. We will, as usual, be in Carmel. . . . I hope that you will be having a very nice summer. Give my warm regards

to Dr. Kilian. Betty sends her greetings. We are both looking forward to seeing you in October [see below, October 13, 1978].
Cordially yours,
Heinz Kohut, M.D.

1. See George Pollock to Kohut, June 9, 1978. Kohut would subsequently be re-elected to the Psychoanalytic Education Council; see below, May 5, 1980.
2. This was Breuer's treatment of a case of hysteria from 1880 to 1882 which inspired Freud's innovation of the psychoanalytic method of free association.
3. Lotte Köhler, "Über einige Aspekte der Behandlung narzissistischer Persönlich-keitsstörungen im Lichte der historischen Entwicklung psychoanalytischer Theoriebil-dung," *Psyche* 32 (1978): 1001–58. Köhler and Kohut later agreed that *Psyche* had become dedicated to classical psychoanalysis and thus not interested in self psychology, while Kohut complained that his German publisher Suhrkamp was no longer mentioning his works in its literature: see Köhler to Kohut, February 20, 1981; Kohut to Köhler, February 28, 1981; and below, March 24, 1981. But cf. Köhler's report on the Boston Self Psychology Conference of November 1980: "Die amerikanische Psychoanalyse zwischen Ichpsychologie und Selbstpsychologie," *Psyche* 36 (1982): 343–54. See also Köhler, "On Selfobject Countertransference," *Annual of Psychoanalysis* 12/13 (1984–85): 39–56.

June 28, 1978
Kurt R. Eissler, M.D.
New York
Dear Kurt,
I know that in a few days you will be seventy. There is no virtue in growing old, as I am finding out myself, even if as is luckily the case for you one has the health and energies that allow one to carry on. Seventy is not predominantly an age for the forging of new plans but one of looking back and assessing the meaning and the value of a life. I do not know how you yourself feel about your life, but I know how I and many others feel about it to whom you have given the gifts of your intellect and the example of your moral commitment and loyalty. I can only thank you for myself since, after passing through many stages, I am now in the lucky position of being the spokesman for no one but myself. Therefore: thank you and thank you again. I hope that the gratitude that you have evoked in me and in many others, whether they now express it or not, will give you the sense of satisfaction with yourself and with your life work that you and your work deserve.
Affectionately yours,
Heinz Kohut, M.D.[1]

1. Kohut organized the writing of congratulatory letters from psychoanalytic insti-

tutes in the United States to Eissler and of contributions to the Freud Archives on the occasion of Eissler's seventieth birthday.

Carmel, September 9, 1978
Dr. Ninon Leader
International Journal of Psycho-Analysis
London
Dear Dr. Leader,

I am returning the corrected proofs of "The Disorders of the Self and Their Treatment: An Outline" with the expression of my appreciation for the skill & care with which it was prepared by the *Int. Journal*. As you will see immediately, we are facing only one problem—the spelling of the word "selfobject." You hyphenated it, we do not. We are here dealing not, I must stress, with a question of formal preference. When I first introduced the term, I hyphenated it as you do now. But about a year ago, after consulting with my friends and co-workers who all agreed with me, I decided that from now on we would dispense with the hyphen. In introducing this change we were prompted by two considerations. The first, a minor but not unimportant one, is indeed stylistic. Spelling "selfobject" without a hyphen allowed us to refer to the relationship between the self and its selfobjects by speaking of a "self-selfobject relationship"[1]—clearly preferable to "self-self-object-relationship." Important though this point may be, our second reason for introducing the change was the decisive one. The concept of the selfobject is, as you undoubtedly realize, of central importance in the psychoanalytic psychology of the self. By spelling the word without a hyphen we feel that we give expression to a significant firming of this concept—that we express more unambiguously the fact that we are here dealing not with an ad-hoc construct but with a viable concept which we hope will find an enduring place in analytic thought.

You can see from the foregoing why I urge you now strongly to make the necessary corrections, however timeconsuming [sic] this step might be. Nobody likes to spend money, and I hope we will not be charged for this work. But if the *Int. Journal* can make these changes only under the condition that we defray the cost, then do go ahead & charge us for it.

Once more my appreciation for the fine work you have done.
Sincerely,
Heinz Kohut, M.D.
Copy: Dr. E. Wolf

1. This term was soon dropped in favor of "selfobject relations." See Jay R. Greenberg and Stephen A. Mitchell, *Object Relations in Psychoanalytic Theory* (Cambridge, Mass., 1983), p. 354.

October 13, 1978[1]

CONCLUDING DINNER REMARKS
Heinz Kohut, M.D.
Chicago Conference on the Psychology
of the Self

I recall a personal incident which seems fitting as I reflect upon these last few days and the company of this evening. When I was a student of grade school level, I had the opportunity to play the role of a doctor in a class play. I became fascinated by this part and began to think about how things fit together, particularly the brain. My father, a musician, was perplexed by my behavior. I asked him questions that, at first, seemed to be the interests of the physician I had portrayed. In reality, these questions reflected my own interests.

I kept asking these kinds of questions. I can still remember his reactions. He became visibly annoyed with me and said, "Why are you interested in such questions? Why can't you be like the other boys?" I remember being very hurt. I had the feeling that there was some kind of gap—some kind of a distance that existed between my father and me—that there was something in me that I was deeply interested in which annoyed him. This was not his mode of living or thinking. He was a person who tried to express himself in art and sounds but he was not an inquisitive thinker. And I was. I was beginning to think inquisitively and continually asked, "Why is this?" and "Why is that?" I bothered him and it bothered me that he was not proud of my interests. Still, I felt that it was good that I asked these questions even though I knew that there was something unsettling about his not understanding me.

Well, it was a long, long hard road from that time on. I idealized him greatly. Yet there was a distance between the two of us, and I felt that he did not try to understand what I was after. But then came the time when I was a late adolescent and I got into medical school and I wrote several scientific papers and he was very impressed by my work. One day he said me, "You know, Heinz, you have done things that I could never do. I'm *very* proud of you." I was extremely pleased by this, as you can imagine. And there's something about this present moment here that reminds me of that moment. For many, many years now, perhaps for longer than I even realize, I have always felt I wanted very much to have a childhood like the other children. And I tried very much to do all the right kinds of things. However, in the long run, I couldn't. I grew up not quite like the other children. I continued to ask all the kinds of questions which annoyed the other "fathers" that I had. So often I felt very uncomfortable and stuck to myself, but I kept thinking my own thoughts, and I have attempted to rationally articulate new thoughts. Today it seems to me—after all these years— my *father* finally approves of me.

1. Recorded, transcribed, and edited by Dr. David Moss, The Center for Religion and Psychotherapy of Chicago.

November 22, 1978
Nathan Schlesinger, M.D.
Chairman, Continuing Education Committee
The Institute for Psychoanalysis
Chicago
Dear Nate,
I just received the leaflet announcing the Postgraduate Program for Analysts. It looks fine. Now let us hope that we will be getting eager and receptive participants. Numbers are important, of course. But the spirit of the undertaking is more important. I thank you and all those who worked with you in getting this significant enterprise to its present advanced stage. I know the great obstacles that stood in our way; and I also realize that they have not all been surmounted. Still, with patience, persistence, tact, and the ability to think ourselves into other people's feelings, we will be successful. I think that the Institute will look back with pride on having organized the first postgraduate courses in the psychology of the self.
Cordially yours,
Heinz Kohut, M.D.
Copy to Dr. George H. Pollock
         Dr. Leo Sadow
         Dr. Ernest S. Wolf

November 23, 1978
Miss Patty Ross
Hadley, Massachusetts
Dear Miss Ross,

I read your letter (11/18) attentively and I think that I understand the problem. Whether anything can be arranged for you in the short time that is still left I don't know. I phoned the Ornsteins & discussed the matter with them and, as far as Cincinnati goes, it would seem to me that you should not disregard this possibility. There is no center of training that would give you only self psychology—still, in Cincinnati you would have the opportunity to further your knowledge of our field via contact with the Ornsteins and others.

Here in Chicago there is Michael Reese Hospital—the organization which ran our recent conference so successfully. But whether they could provide you with what you need, I don't know. I will—there is unfortunately no time to ask your permission—I will ask Dr. Goldberg to look at your letter, and it may well be that he has something to offer you there. There exist, unfortunately, some serious tensions between the Institute here and the Michael Reese group.[1] The cooperation of those people at the Institute who would be most important in giving you supervision and consultations is, therefore, at the moment hard to get because they feel reluctant to associate themselves with any program that is run by Michael Reese Hospital. But I will inquire and let you know.

Could anything be organized by the Chicago Institute itself? I doubt it. But I will try to find out.

The idea of a consortium, as you describe it, is, in & of itself, a good one—but, unfortunately the tensions here are so great that it would be taken as a move to split off from organized psychoanalysis and thus, again, most members in the group to which you are referring would be reluctant to join in such an undertaking. The difficulty, as you can see, lies not with you but with the peculiar problem of selfpsychology. You and a number of other people feel that we have a hold on something new, exciting, important. But we have no position of power in the social field. We run no schools, influence no centers of learning, and, as far as psychoanalysis goes, our ideas are not only criticized but treated with hostility and scorn. What else can we do, under these circumstances, but to continue to think, learn, write—persuade others gradually of the value of what we have to offer. Whether you know it or not, you have by your interest in our ideas joined a pioneering group and you are experiencing the hardships of the pioneer. Don't let yourself be discouraged—despite many blows, and despite my age, I do not let myself be discouraged either.

You will hear from me. In the meantime warmest regards.

Sincerely yours,

Heinz Kohut

1. *Search*, 4:611–19.

November 25, 1978

Mrs. Marie Emond

Montreal

Dear Mrs. Emond,

Your letter [November 16] gave me great pleasure and I am grateful to you for having written it. I was in particular glad that the conference impressed you and that its effect on you was not just a momentary one.

Letters like yours are important to me. They sustain me because, being exposed to many attacks from many sides, from the side of total strangers and from the side of colleagues who formerly held me in high esteem, I sometimes forget that I have now many new friends and supporters and that my contributions have been helpful to many, known and unknown to me, in various places of the world.

Your remarks about the field "Beyond the Bounds of the Basic Rule" as I once called it were of special interest to me, as you must know not only from my writings but also from the "Narrow the Gap" symposium at our conference. I would be especially curious about the Louis XIV by Saint-Simon because the contribution is not tainted by conscious psychological knowledge. People like [novelist] Philip Roth and Francis Bacon [the contemporaneous Irish painter], despite their great talent, attract my attention less because of their at least partial awareness of the problems they are portraying. (One of the reasons why I feel so interested in the work of such artists as Picasso and [Ezra] Pound is that they express the problems of the crumbling self via the formal aspects of their art, not primarily through the content of their oeuvre.)

Thank you once more for the generosity of your letter to me. And good wishes for your personal, professional, and scientific future.

Sincerely yours,

Heinz Kohut, M.D.

November 25, 1978
Miss Giovanna Breu
People Magazine
Chicago
Dear Miss Breu,

I don't know whether you like to prepare yourself for an interview that you will be conducting or whether, in order to be in the same position as your future readership, you want to face your subject without knowing much about him or her. At any rate, in order to give you the opportunity to prepare yourself for our meeting, I put together some material that you might want to look at. I selected papers that are of comparatively non-technical nature and, especially, interviews, given in the past, in which the interviewer, not being a member of my profession, was in the same boat that you will be in when we meet.

When I spoke to you on the phone some days ago, I was, as you must have noticed, quite puzzled about a remark that you made to me. You said that "we have received permission to go ahead with the interview." When I asked who in the world could give such permission, you mentioned Dr. George Pollock of the Institute. I think that you must have misunderstood something here. While Dr. Pollock has for some years held the position of Director of the Institute for Psychoanalysis, and while I have been on the Faculty of the Institute for many years—long enough, I might add, to have been Dr. Pollock's teacher many years ago—, the Institute is neither the only place where I teach nor is it even the place with which I have had the longest affiliation. I have been on the Faculty of the University of Chicago since 1941 (I now hold an appointment there as Professorial Lecturer); I have been for quite some time a Visiting Professor at the University of Cincinnati, an institution that gave me the honorary degree of Doctor of Science some years ago, and I am the first and only honorary staff member of Michael Reese Hospital, an institution with which I have no working relationship but whose psychiatric staff considers me as having become, through my writings, a teacher of them all.

I trust that you realize that I am telling you all this only to dispel a misunderstanding which, if left uncorrected, could badly slant your perception of me and my work. At any rate, I would like to know what produced the impression that prompted your remark. I am sure that it would never occur to Dr. Pollock who is a good friend of mine and whom I hold in high esteem as a colleague and as a human being to think he was in any position to allow me to be interviewed by anyone.[1]

Sincerely yours,

Heinz Kohut, M.D.

1. Pollock had contacted *People* to express his desire that the institute receive some publicity in the Kohut article. See note above, March 5, 1967. The article mentions the Chicago Institute for Psychoanalysis as Kohut's "current base." *People*, February 16, 1979, p. 61.

December 11, 1978

Miss Margret Schaefer

Chicago

Dear Margret,

After I talked with you the other day—in the elevator and in front of 180 North [Michigan Avenue]—I walked away with a special springiness in my step which I don't feel frequently anymore nowadays. But I was profoundly glad that all anger about our public interchange seemed to have gone from your mind and that this whole dumb affair was behind us.[1] (I knew that Heller would still be heard—but I really don't care about Heller.) On the way home an idea came to me: I could send you a small but significant little gift for Christmas with a brief note telling you how happy I was that we had lived through a certain trial and have come out unscathed. And now comes Kurt Eissler's letter and turns it all topsy-turvy again [see below, Kohut to Eissler, December 11]. For a while I didn't know what to do. He is obviously (to me, obviously) using the chance to attack me and my work—even though he says he wants to continue to remain my friend. Well, that's between him and me. As you know, he is really just one of the great number of my colleagues who attack me & my work in the most violent way. But now—how about us? Will his letter start up your anger again? I must wait and see. Still, I decided to send you the little gift [a Kleist commemorative coin] anyway that I wanted you to keep as memory of our public debate. At least you must know that I am not the "bearlike adult" (my interpretation [of one of the elements in Kleist's story]) who pays no attention to the gifted child. Should you feel angry at me—either still, or again—please don't hesitate to return the gift to me. I will be sorry—but I will understand.[2]

Warm regards to Peter

Yours,

H. Kohut

1. Margret Schaefer, "Psychoanalysis and the Marionette Theater: Interpretation Is Not Depreciation," *Critical Inquiry* 5 (1978): 177–88; Heinz Kohut, "A Reply to Margret Schaefer," ibid., 189–97; see also *Search*, 2:900–901; 4:595–606; and above, August 10, 1977. Schaefer's article, "Kleist's 'About the Puppet Theater' and the Narcissism of the Artist," *American Imago* 32 (1975): 365–88, had served as starting point for Heller's criticism.

2. See Schaefer to Kohut, December 22, 1978; and above, December 14, 1977.

December 11, 1978
Kurt Eissler, M.D.
New York
Dear Kurt,
     In your brief note [December 6] enclosed with the copy of your letter [December 4] to Margret Schaefer you say "I do hope you don't mind I wrote that letter." I wished I could tell you that I don't mind but the fact is that I do. I think I will have to let time pass in order to see how I can deal with this blow.[1]
Yours,
Heinz

1. Both Schaefer and Eissler felt that Kohut had conceded too much to Heller in the debate, and Eissler in particular was concerned that this stemmed at least in part from Kohut's growing departure from what Eissler conceived of as genuine psychoanalysis.

December 28, 1978
Professor Sheldon Sacks, Editor
Critical Inquiry
University of Chicago
Dear Mr. Sacks:
     You are returning to Chicago, I hear, and will thus undoubtedly become again more involved in the day-to-day business of *Critical Inquiry* from which the distance between Chicago and London may have shielded you. I would therefore like to tell you about a problem that might arise in the near future in the wake of the publication of Professor Heller's essay on applied analysis, of my two letters to Professor Heller, and of the letter of Margret Schaefer and my response to it which were published in the issue that followed the publication of the basic debate. Here is the problem. As I have recently learned there is a move afoot in New York to speak up against my work and me in *Critical Inquiry;* that there is the wish to censure me for the positions that I took, namely, that I had been too soft vis-à-vis Professor Heller

and critical, instead of supportive, vis-à-vis Margret Schaefer. That some of my colleagues in New York should feel that way does not surprise me since, as you may know, or, if not, will undoubtedly have guessed, my contributions to a psychoanalytic psychology of the self have been strongly rejected by the classical school (which is the firmly entrenched establishment in New York) as not being biological enough, as a regression from a biologically based science to an experience-oriented, non-scientific branch of the humanities. A weighty set of issues is involved here—and who can clearly separate a right from a wrong?

Now I remember, of course, that you told me (at the nice lunch to which you treated me in the Quadrangle Club last spring) that except for Professor Heller's closing letter—I understand not yet received by *Critical Inquiry* and perhaps never to be written—you would not accept any further letters in this affair. Still, I know the persuasiveness and insistence of some of my New-York [sic] colleagues and realize that you might change your mind under their pressure and open your pages to them, indeed—who am I to judge here?—should perhaps give in to their request. I am thus not writing to you to remind you, in anticipation of such a request to you, of your promise to me that I would not be exposed to further criticism and the time-consuming necessity of taking up the pen again in defense of my ideas and me. I am writing this anticipatory—and, let us hope, unnecessary—letter in order to ask you to give me the opportunity to respond to an attack if it should indeed find its way into *Critical Inquiry.* Please do not consider this request as frivolous or made with a light heart. You will remember how reluctant I was to respond to Margret Schaefer's reaction to my letters to Heller, that I turned to it only—and with many sighs of resentment—after you told me that I *must* do so because I had been attacked personally, had been publicly accused of being two-faced because she quoted private communications from me to her that showed that I praised her essay while publicly, in the letters published by *Critical Inquiry,* I sided with Heller who had condemned it. Believe me, my reluctance has not changed and I would much rather go on doing my work unhampered by strife and debate. Still, if you publish a New-York [sic] attack on my work and me, I strongly believe, in view of the broad significance of the disagreement, that I should be given a chance to say my piece, too.

At any rate: welcome back! I hope that this opportunity to witness the quarrels in which psychoanalysts are prone to engage will not altogether wipe out whatever respect you may have for them—the intensity of their infighting is a function of their commitment to their profession.

Cordially,

Heinz Kohut, M.D.

P.S. Should you decide to reverse your stand and to open your pages to further debate I would, of course, also withdraw my objections to the publication of Dr. Robert Freedman's letter to you (May 20, 1978) and of my reply to Dr. Freedman (August 24, 1978;[1] copy enclosed) of which I sent a copy to you—as a matter of fact I would welcome the publication of this exchange under these circumstances.

1. *Search*, 4:606–8.

1979–1981

"While . . . the old and famous should be visibly represented, my heart belongs to the younger group"

January 2, 1979
Dr. N. Treurniet
Blaricum, The Netherlands
Dear friend Treurniet,
I am glad that you [December 22, 1978] felt positively about the emotional climate of our October meeting and am pleased about your follow-up with the aid of Basch, Goldberg, Kligerman, and [Evelyne] Schwaber.
One of the reasons why I feel that "integration" is not indicated at this point is that "selfpsychology" is in such an early phase of its development—continuously changing, with new findings, and new—and temporary—theories. My "Selected Papers" [i.e., *Search for the Self*], edited by P. Ornstein, will appear any day now (I already have the 2-volumes)—I believe that reading my essays in sequence will not only help you to get a deepening understanding of our work but will also give you the sense that this new development in analysis seems to have lost nothing of its initial momentum. Two long papers (a theoretical summary with E. Wolf and a clinical report)[1] will appear in the next 2 issues of the *Int. Journal of Psychoanalysis* [see below, August 28, 1979] and will I hope add to your understanding why I consider integration efforts at this time to be still premature.
I say all this even though I believe I can understand very well indeed why integration is so important to you.
Regards to Dr. Van Groeningen and to all my Dutch friends. And the best to you, also from my wife for now, all of 1979 and the future.
Warmly yours,
Heinz Kohut

1. "The Disorders of the Self and Their Treatment," *IJP* 59 (1978): 413–25; "The Two Analyses of Mr. Z.," *IJP* 60 (1979): 3–27.

February 9, 1979
Miriam and Alex Elson
Chicago
Dear Miriam and Alex,
Many thanks for the welcome gift and especially for the note [February 3] that accompanied it. Throughout my recovery period and convalescence [from coronary bypass surgery] I have over and over reminded myself that it is the life of the mind that is the true human life—your gift and your shared thoughts sustain me in my resolve to consider the physical discomforts as no more than a nuisance and silly

obstacle, standing in the way of returning to intellectual activity and constructive work. When I read the dustwrapper blurb Furbank immediately appealed to me since he wrote also a biography of one of my favorite writers—little known in the USA—namely, Italo Svevo.[1] I am looking forward to turning to the [E. M.] Forster biography [1977–78] as soon as I am done with the present voluminous tome on [Eugene] O'Neill[2] whose life and personality have fascinated me for some time now. Many thanks again and the hope that we will see each other when I am fully recovered.

Yours,
Heinz

1. Philip Nicholas Furbank, *Italo Svevo: The Man and the Writer* (London, 1966); see also John Gatt-Rutter, *Italo Svevo: A Double Life* (Oxford, 1988). Svevo (1861–1928) was of German-Austrian-Italian-Jewish ancestry and a pioneer of the modern novel. His *The Confessions of Zeno* (1923) was one of Kohut's favorite books.
2. Arthur and Barbara Gelb, *O'Neill* (New York [1964], 1979).

February 24, 1979
Siegmund Levarie
Brooklyn

Dear Siegmund,

Thanks for your lovely letter. I am not surprised to hear that you share our prejudice against "resorts." I guess it's in essence a snobbish attitude vis-à-vis the petit-bourgeois standards that pervade these institutions of pleasure, however expensive and "exclusive" they might be. Yes, we are senior citizens—that doesn't disturb me; and I can't even say that it sneaked up on me. In some ways I felt old before I became old in years—which does not mean, as you know, that I lost my vitality. But it's the vitality of many years of living and experiencing now. An old colleague approached me once in New York after I'd given a paper about the late stages of life[1] and asked me: How do you know all these things, you're still so young? (I was 52 at the time.) Also, the older I get, the more I feel some strange nostalgia—for Germany. I wouldn't dare tell this to many people. But the only times when, in recent years, I have felt thoroughly "at home" was when I was in Germany and/or with German friends. Not any real yearning for Austria, or for Vienna—despite their being so nice to me in recent times. I wonder why? Is my old *Bürgerschullehrer* [junior high school teacher] grandfather's *grossdeutsche Haltung*[2] seeping into me? Ah well, "gar nicht ignorieren"[3] is surely the best thing one can do. But down deep it gives me enormous pleasure that Tom studies modern German history, that he speaks German accent[-]free and that he is spending his second full year in Germany now.—

Quickly about your query: *American Imago* and [Harry] Slochower have, I believe, a good reputation. (I knew nothing about the man's political troubles.)[4] Do send me a copy of your review.[5] If I don't get to it: *tant pis!* But I think I will.

Much love,
Heinz

1. *Search*, 1:427–60.
2. "Greater German attitude," or the ideal of a united Germany including Austria.
3. "Don't even bother to ignore it," a Viennese dismissal of something "not even worth ignoring."
4. While at Brooklyn College Slochower was a member of a Communist "cell" and refused to give names to an investigating committee; see "Texts of the Majority Opinion and Dissents in Slochower Case," *New York Times*, April 10, 1956.
5. "Biography of a Composer," *American Imago* 36 (1979): 313–27.

March 2, 1979
Mr. Richard S. Pine
Arthur Pine Associates
New York
Dear Mr. Pine

I am glad that you enjoyed the *People* article. I am, however, unfortunately unable to prepare a book on "*how to raise neurosis-free children.*"

Sincerely yours,
Heinz Kohut, M.D.

May 14, 1979
Dr. Charles B. Strozier, Editor
The Psychohistory Review
Sangamon State University
Springfield, Illinois
Dear Chuck,

I'm sorry for the delay in replying to your note of March 16 but, as you may have heard, I have been quite ill and am only now gradually regaining my strength.

With regard to the specific questions that you asked me I would suggest that the issue of narcissistic rage in connection with the injured or weakened national self be considered as one of the major topics of the conference. As you may know, I have myself for some years been interested in certain specific problems that bear on the investigation of historical events such as (1) instances of unusual courage (resistors), (2) the fragmentation and other forms of weakness of the group self (see the final paragraphs in my narcissistic rage paper), and (3) supportive and non-supportive selfobjects for the group and the resultant cohesion and strength of fragmentation and weakness of the group. If my health permits it I might very well be willing to present my ideas concerning one or the other of these topics at your conference [at Michael Reese Hospital, June 1980].

Concerning names I can only think of one that would probably not occur to you, i.e., my son, Tom, who is engaged in an in-depth study of the personality of Emperor Wilhelm II and its influence on the outbreak of World War I.[1]

Cordially yours,

Heinz Kohut, M.D.

1. Thomas A. Kohut, *Wilhelm II and the Germans: A Study in Leadership* (New York, 1991). See above, January 5 and June 17, 1975; and below, May 15, 1980.

May 21, 1979
David Dean Brockman, M.D.
Chicago
Dear Dean,

I cannot tell you how touched I was by the warmth of your letter and by your deeply felt good wishes for my recovery. I was also very glad to learn how well you are doing and that you are even on the way to becoming an athlete. This is certainly a very laudable development if it is tempered by [former University of Chicago President] Maynard Hutchins well known advice that whenever one feels the urge to exercise one should lie down with a book and wait until the urge passes.

The best to you and Marty from Betty and me and hopefully a personal reunion at 180 North Michigan just as your dream depicted.

Warmly yours,

Heinz Kohut, M.D.

May 29, 1979
Dr. John Haag
Department of History
University of Georgia
Dear Dr. Haag:

I'm sorry to say that I can be of little help to you with the type of information that you are interested in.[1] On the whole I can say that those among the students who were not sympathetic to the Nazi cause shared with the rest of the world the illusion that the status quo would not change and that the Nazi bubble would burst.

Have you by any chance read the recently published book by Muriel Gardiner and Joseph Buttinger, *Damit Wir Nicht Vergessen* [*Lest We Forget*]?[2] I recommend it to you very highly. I would also suggest that you interview Dr. Gardiner who was a medical student in Vienna before and after the *Anschluss* [annexation of Austria].

Sincerely yours,
Heinz Kohut, M.D.

1. Haag to Kohut, May 21, 1979. See Haag, "Blood on the Ringstrasse: Vienna's Students 1918–33," *Wiener Library Bulletin* 29 (1976): 29–34; and Haag, "A Woman's Struggle against Nazism: Irene Harand and Gerechtigkeit," ibid. 34 (1981): 64–72.

2. See Muriel Gardiner, *Code Name "Mary": Memoirs of an American Woman in the Austrian Underground* (New Haven, 1983). Gardiner studied psychoanalysis in Vienna.

July 17, 1979
Arnold Goldberg, M.D.
Chicago
Dear Arnold,

What a lovely gift you're offering me! I accept it, in anticipation, with deeply felt gratitude to you and to Ernie [Wolf.].[1] Concerning the details of your plan, I will give you now my immediate reaction with the earnest request that the present communication should, if at all possible, be the last one between us concerning this enterprise. And so let me take the bull by the horn and tell you that I'm not in tune with the principles that guided your choice of potential contributors. If I deserve the gift that you will prepare for that chronological milestone of my life, I deserve it as an innovator. This list that you suggest, however, is one of people who, whatever their merits, are in essence committed to preserving the status quo.[2] I hope that some of them will accept when asked to make a contribution; but their motivation to [sic] doing so will be the mobilization of old loyalties to me, a sense of obligation rather than enthusiasm for the task. Don't misunderstand me: I think some of the old group who's [sic] names are household in our profession should be included in the collection. I would first approach those with lively, interesting minds rather than those who are most widely known—although you have only to think of Anna Freud [proposed to introduce the volume] to see that the second qualification does not exclude the first one. (Two names within this group of older colleagues I might also mention, though not with great emphasis: Paul Parin and Rudolf Ekstein.) The point I'm making is clear: while, for the sake of balance and of easing publication, the old and famous should be visibly represented, my heart belongs to the younger group (I will not mention the obvious choices here, e.g., those in Chicago, but give, as an example, Bob Stolorow and Joe Lichtenberg). Another idea: I believe there should be a minimum of regional representation and you might ask for help by finding a regional consultant (one for Europe and Israel, one for Canada, one for Latin America) who could make suggestions. Does all this show how I feel? I hope so. But let me end by telling you that I will be pleased with the gift and grateful for it, however you ultimately decide to put it together.

Affectionately yours,
Heinz Kohut, M.D.

1. *The Future of Psychoanalysis: Essays in Honor of Heinz Kohut*, ed. Arnold Goldberg (New York, 1983). This was to be in honor of Kohut's seventieth birthday in 1983.

2. Kohut was balking at such proposed contributors as Jacob Arlow, Charles Brenner, Kurt Eissler, Leo Rangell, Erik Erikson, Otto Kernberg, and Masud Khan, among others. The actual contributors to the volume included none of those Kohut would have regarded as a defender of the psychoanalytic status quo, rather they were by and large "Kohutians" such as Basch, Goldberg, Wolf, Ornstein, Tolpin, and others.

Carmel, August 20, 1979
Hyman L. Muslin, M.D.
Evanston, Illinois
Dear Hy,

Among the reading material I took along to California was the draft of your paper "Self Transformations in Medical and Surgical Illness."[1] I read it, in fits and starts, during the last few days and liked it a great deal, even though I think—I'm sure in agreement with you—that a good deal should still be done with it before it can be considered as ready for publication. The material is fascinating, especially the case vignettes that you are presenting. But to my taste your presentations do not focus sufficiently on the crucial issue: the detailed examination of the specific selfobject transferences with which these patients are struggling.

Please don't take it amiss when I tell you that, as far as I'm concerned, you write and think too much like a psychiatrist and not enough like a psychoanalyst—even though, I haste[n] to add, you clearly have the stuff of which the analyst is made.

But what an opportunity these patients present to the investigator! How much, it seems to me, one could learn, by inference about the actual way, the specific concrete steps, by which transmuting internalization takes place—how something that is not-self is gradually transformed into something that is self. I think that you are too much caught up in Freud's model of mourning, that you still think too much in accordance with a thought pattern that involves a reluctant relinquishment of the selfobject, instead of trying to determine what (perhaps in the need-motivated attitudes of the selfobject) interfered with the healthy movement toward the proudly displayed ideal-guided autonomous self that is creatively employing its talents and skills. I could show you in detail where in your paper you are especially hampered in your full understanding, on the one hand, and in your ability to pursue the issues more deeply and in greater detail than you are allowing yourself to do now.

Rather than pointing out to you the specific places in your essay that I marked and annotated as I went through it, I want to mention to you certain remarks contained in my writings that are especially relevant with regard to the issues that I am talking about. I'm thinking of (1) my remark about the significance of the addictive drug as a stand-in for the unavailable selfobject (in "Forms and Transformations of Narcissism" and in the preface to vom Scheidt's book); (2) the outline of the various steps involved in transmuting internalization (in *The Analysis of the Self*); and (3) the two-step (understanding-explaining) sequence in interpretation and its genetic precursor exemplified in the mother's empathically picking up the child and allowing it to merge with her, before in fact giving it food (in *The Restoration of the Self*).

One of the most beautiful contributions of your paper is the case vignette of the obese woman, in particular the description of her relationship to the refrigerator. But here again I think that you would overcome a significant obstacle in the pursuit of your investigations concerning the significance of the selfobject's body to a child if you saw this woman not as clinging to something that she doesn't want to relinquish (a drive-theory-derived moral attitude in the analyst) but, in tune with selfpsychology, a need to maintain the life-sustaining merger with a selfobject because the primary need was not fulfilled in consequence of the selfobject's own needs. In other words (but all this is open to detailed investigation) her selfobject mother did not mirror her display of an autonomous self but, by becoming alarmed, depressed, and possessive, forced the child to retain the merger she was yearning to leave behind.

Enough of science now! We are settled down nicely in a comfortable house. I am working slowly but steadily every day and, what is most important, am enjoying it. Physically there is still much left to be desired (the general muscular weakness is more noticeable here than in the city; and the labyrinthine imbalance is still quite bothersome at times, especially after drives along the curvey coastal road. But, in view of the fact that everything is so much better now than it was, I don't complain but am rather happy with my state.

I trust things are going reasonably well with you and yours. Let me hear from you sometime if you feel like doing so—I would enjoy a letter very much.

Cordially yours,
Heinz Kohut, M.D.

1. See Hyman L. Muslin, "Transformations of the Self in Cancer," *International Journal of Psychiatry in Medicine* 14 (1988): 109–21.

Carmel, August 28, 1979
Giampaolo Lai, M.D.
Milan
Dear Dr. Lai,

I am glad that your interest in psychoanalytic selfpsychology has continued. And I will, of course, respond to your questions even though I am afraid that I might not be able to answer them to your full satisfaction. Is my aim pedagogical and/or political, you ask, when in the two papers that appeared in the two latest issues of the *International Journal of Psycho-Analysis* [see above, January 2, 1979] I emphasized—quite unnecessarily, as you rightly say, in view of my unambiguous position all along—that the analyst refrains from blaming or exhorting his patient? The answer is that it is both. Its educational aim points into two quite different directions. There are those who, for reasons of their own, misinterpret selfpsychology and believe that it gives them licence [sic] to attempt to cure their patients by giving them love (for an example see the last of the letters in Volume Two of *The Search for the Self* (IUP, 1979)). And there are those among classical analysts who attack my work via the claim that I do indeed recommend the use of non-analytic attitudes and non-analytic curative means. (For an example see an essay by Martin Stein[1] who, leaning on *one* word but failing to consider the total, completely unambiguous context in which this word is used, accuses me of allowing my patients to idealize me, i.e., accuses me of "accepting" my patients' admiration rather than analyzing it. Stein, as I said, fastens on the word "accept" that I use—I believe it is in the chapter on countertransferences to the idealizing transference in *The Analysis of the Self*—namely, that one does not censor the patient's admiration or belittle it but that one has to allow the transference to unfold in order to interpret it effectively in genetic and dynamic terms—is unmistakable.)

You might rightly question whether my emphasis in order to refute such attacks should be called educational or whether it does not serve a political aim? It does the latter, of course. But then it is also and simultaneously an educational tool because I surmise that the very people who accuse me of "accepting" the narcissistic transferences (now called "selfobject transferences") are likely to respond in censorious and belittling ways to their analysands' re-activated narcissistic needs. Thus when I emphasize that my clinical stance is a truly analytic one, I am indeed trying to do a bit of educational work—though I know that its relevance will not be acknowledged by those at whom it is directed.

As you anticipated I am on vacation. I was quite ill during the past six months and I'm now taking a very long vacation (into October, in fact) in order to complete my recovery. I have, unfortunately, no books available here that I could look into to give you some references about the topic that you inquired about. But do read *The Restoration of the Self* (in German [Suhrkamp] *Die Heilung des Selbst*) which, so far as I know, is also already being translated into Italian. It contains a chapter called "The Psychoanalytic Situation" in which you will find the topics that you raised illuminated from a variety of sides.

Thank you again for your interest in my work. I am glad to hear that it has been helpful to you.

Sincerely yours,

Heinz Kohut, M.D.

1. *JAPA* 27 (1979): 665–80. See also Robert D. Stolorow to Harold P. Blum, *JAPA* Editor, December 20, 1979, protesting this review of *The Restoration of the Self*. Stein had been a close friend of Kohut's who in 1965 read Kohut's outgoing address as APA president after Kohut came down with laryngitis.

Carmel, September 25, 1979
T. T. S. Hayley. M.D.
Editor, *International Journal of Psycho-Analysis*
London
Dear Dr. Hayley,

Your letter (14. September) was forwarded to me to California and reached me yesterday. Dr. [Mortimer] Ostow's letter[1] needs a reply but, as I hope you will understand, I cannot give it. As you may have heard (perhaps Dr. Sandler told you), I have been quite ill during the past nine months. (A heart operation in January, followed by a series of complications—septicemia, a second operation, antibiotic treatment, etc.) While the worst is over, I hope, I am still in a rather precarious state and feel unable to do justice to the important letter that needs to be written. Luckily I am able to offer a substitute—in fact, even without any health problem, this is preferable since it is almost impossible for a person with some social sensitivity to defend himself, at my age, against the claim that he doesn't know the basics of his profession. I phoned Dr. Arnold Goldberg in Chicago (he is the editor of *The Casebook* referred to in "Mr. Z.," thus particularly in harmony with the task of replying to Dr. Ostow) and, to my great pleasure and relief, he agreed to write in reply to Dr. Ostow's letter to the Editor.[2] (I had read Dr. Ostow's letter to him over the phone & I am mailing him a copy today.) He will try to be as close to your deadline as possible but has really hardly enough time to come through—perhaps you can close an eye in view of the circumstances and allow him some extra days. At any rate, the important thing is that his letter gets published as soon as possible—whether in the immediate issue (which, of course, is best) or in the next one is not crucial, I would think.

I am sorry that I had to burden you with my personal problems but I could not see any way around it.

Sincerely,
Heinz Kohut, M.D.
Copy: Dr. Arnold Goldberg

1. *IJP* 60 (1979): 531–32. Ostow argues that "The Two Analyses of Mr. Z" shows that "the first episode of analysis was conducted imperfectly" in terms of classical analysis.

2. *IJP* 61 (1980): 91–92. Goldberg, in summary, responds: "Psychoanalysis is not a finished science." See also below, May 5, 1980.

March 4, 1980
Senator J. William Fulbright
Washington, D.C.
Dear Senator Fulbright:

Like millions of other Americans I have been an admirer of yours for a long time. Then I recently read the text of the address you gave at the University of Chicago where I am a member of the faculty, my appreciation of your wisdom became even greater than before, and I decided to drop you a line to tell you so.[1] But this is not simply a fan letter. I am a psychiatrist who for many years has sought to increase our understanding of man's behavior in history with the hope that I might in a small degree contribute to man's attempt to master his historical destiny. Some people—psychiatrists, historians—share my belief that the approach that I have been stressing is useful. I am enclosing a few samples of the application of my thoughts to the field of history and historical action. I hope you will glance at them. Certainly, if you should want further material I will be happy to furnish it. [See below, April 7, 1980.]

Sincerely yours,
Heinz Kohut, M.D.

1. "Fulbright Speaks on New Russian Policy," *Chicago Maroon*, February 22, 1980, pp. 4–5. Fulbright was a critic of traditional American Cold War foreign policy.

March 14, 1980
Charles Kligerman
Chicago
Charlie,

I am reading on, a few pages at a time, and am now on page 21. It's beautiful and makes its points to a "T."

At this point I have one question (which may well fall by the way-side as I read on), namely, whether you shouldn't discuss, even if only briefly, the intermediary homosexuality as the selfobject transference to you forms & he feels better. Among the most important clinical insights of selfpsychology is the re-evaluation of the significance of the perversions. Patients have (pcs [preconscious]) phantasies of sucking the analyst's penis, of having [the analyst's] penis ejaculate into their anus, etc., as intermediary symbols for their basic need to have male substance, i.e, transmuting internalizations (alternately) to fill the defect in the self. Self-defect, because of absence of sustained paternal interest in childhood, preventing optimum frustrations & structure building. The "homosexual" transference is the sexualized version of the need for [the analyst's] interest. It all lends itself beautifully to demonstrate the primacy of the self and the secondary nature of *these* drives. (Not all drives which, *ab initio*, may be the experiences of a healthy, strong self.)

The move from [the analyst] for whom he was "shit" to Charlie whose hamburgers he wants to take in—ultimately and on the deepest level not by oral ingestion (fellatio) but by psychological means. The sex is a symbol for the need of the self to be cured, to go on with (complete) its development.

The bad father (baked beans dream—paranoid, evil, poisonous food) vs. the good father "Charlie"—the delicious hamburgers, the male self he will achieve.

Ok?

Heinz

We are off to Cincinnati to visit Tom and Susan.

April 7, 1980 [from Senator J. William Fulbright]

Dear Dr. Kohut:

I apologize for the delay in replying to your cordial letter [see above, March 4, 1980] and the inclusion of some of your articles which I have read with a great deal of interest. It seems to me that you and your colleagues in the field of psychology could make a real contribution to the cause of our present difficulties with the Soviet Union. Judging from the recent developments, we have developed a paranoia with regard to the Russians which is fueling the arms race, and, I think, will lead us into a very difficult and dangerous confrontation if something isn't done to re-establish the principle of detente, if I may use that abused term.

It seems to me that our Government has overreacted to the Afghanistan affair and that our frustrations with Iran have exacerbated our fears and apprehensions of the Soviet Union. Obviously, I am not qualified to engage in an analysis of our motives, and I am suggesting that you would make a real contribution if you could apply your talents to analyze our current relations with the Soviet Union. I believe we are exhibiting an example of "group thinking" which was so well analyzed by Janis with regard to the Bay of Pigs.[1] The background of the impending elections tends to exaggerate this tendency because it is politically profitable.

I know that I would be, and I think everyone would be, interested in an analysis of why we have gone to such lengths with regard to the Afghanistan situation.[2]

Sincerely,

J. W. Fulbright

1. This was the ill-fated Cuban emigré invasion of Cuba in 1961 supported by the CIA. See Irving L. Janis, "Groupthink among Policy Makers," in *Sanctions for Evil*, ed. Nevitt Sanford and Craig Comstock (San Francisco, 1971), pp. 71–89.

2. *Search*, 4:662–64. See also Fulbright to Kohut, May 22, 1980. This refers to the crisis over the Soviet invasion of Afghanistan which culminated in the American-led boycott of the Moscow Olympics.

April 8, 1980

Ms. Susan Quinn

Brookline, Massachusetts

Dear Ms. Quinn:

Many thanks for "Voyages" [*Boston Magazine*, May 1977] which my wife and I read with great interest and profit. What a strange world it is in which we live! Odysseus over and over again—with the illusion of homecomings, but then, the puzzlement, the searching, all over again. We are a restless breed! And whether in the mental or physical realms, there are always a few of us who can't stay put and move into new countries—despite the discomforts, despite the readjustments needed, despite the anxiety-producing relinquishment of the familiar. Although my own "voyage" of the last fifteen years was mental, not physical, I can understand what the people feel whom you are describing. I, too, could have stayed put. I could have continued to live in the old country of familiar thought-patterns, just as the people you described could have lived on in their old country. Yes, the old scientific system has its serious discomforts, just as did Russia for the emigrés—but the move, for me, for them, created new problems. Yet, there is the adventurer in us that drives us on—some of us at least—despite the enmity that we encounter, and the anxiety that is evoked in us. Those who stayed in the old surroundings envy us and demean us because they would have liked to do what those did who moved into new regions. But they will not admit that they feel that way, even to themselves.

Enough! I was pleased to see the evidence of your skill and percep-

tiveness. I know that you will put your great gifts to good use as you describe the mental adventure of the psychology of the self.[1]
   Sincerely,
   Heinz Kohut, M.D.

1. Susan Quinn, "Oedipus vs. Narcissus," *New York Times Magazine*, November 9, 1980, pp. 120–26 +. See also below, December 16, 1980; and Quinn, *A Mind of Her Own: The Life of Karen Horney* (New York, 1987).

April 22, 1980
Paul Tolpin, M.D.
Chicago
Dear Paul,
   Thank you for your (4/21) letter to [Donald] Kalsched.[1] You did as well as one can in responding to his comments. As is often the case such inquiries as K.'s about our use of "Unconscious" and "Depth" are really taunts—they refer to values not to concepts. I sense the (hidden) accusation that we have abandoned the Ucs and are dealing with surface phenomena. The reply to such digs must be—quite in line with the way in which you handled K.'s challenges—that the self-selfobject experience has many layers, including archaic-ucs ones, and that the frustrated need for selfobjects as activated in the transference is often buried (ucs) behind a wall of defenses and may remain inaccessible for a long time.
   Thank you for your dealing with K.
   Yours,
   Heinz
   P.S. I especially liked your analogy to "the body plan of humans derived from ancestral forms." (Last sentence on page 1 of your letter.)

1. See also Kalsched to Kohut, October 9, 1979; and Tolpin to Kalsched, January 28, 1980. Kalsched's thesis, "Narcissism and the Search for Interiority," was written for the C. G. Jung Institute for Analytical Psychology in New York.

May 5, 1980
Arnold Goldberg, M.D.
Chicago
Dear Arnold,
   Our talk left me vaguely upset. I was out of sorts most of yesterday, slept fitfully, and have still not reached inner peace. You say that no-one understands how *you* felt (and feel). I would say that I have

no trouble understanding it because we are both in the same boat, feel equally rebuffed and hurt. The fact I was now renominated to the Council and might get elected back into it makes no difference in this respect. If anything it makes my situation worse because, by accepting the nomination, I had to swallow my pride and knuckle under—while a prideful refusal would have left me with a lesser wound.

Up to the time of our not being re-elected to the Council [see above, June 1978], I felt loyal to the Institute, identified with it—however great the disagreements, the gaps in viewpoint that separated me from the majority. And I assumed naively that these feelings were shared by the others—that however much they disagreed with me (and with you), the disagreement would not influence their vote, would not interfere with the unquestioned wish to retain us as members of the Council. The disappointing fact that their disagreements with us prompted them to vote against us has created a [sic], as far as I can judge, unalterable shift in my attitude. The Institute does not have the importance to me now that it once had. I resent that I might have to spend the Monday hours at the Council, and I will continue to resent it if I get elected.[1] Yet I think that by choosing to accept the nomination I chose the lesser of two evils. Will my attitude ever change? It seems unimaginable now—but then I have been around long enough to know that one cannot make such predictions with any degree of reliability.

All this leaves the main question unanswered. How will our relationship be affected by my agreeing to the nomination? As far as I can see, not at all. But I worry. You told me once before—at the time when you generously jumped into the breach for me and answered the Ostow letter [see above, September 25, 1979]—that I couldn't put myself into your shoes, couldn't see how it felt to you to sign your name under a letter to which I had made substantial contributions. Yes, I could understand what you felt then and I can understand how you feel now. But to me the overriding issue, transcending your feelings and mine, is the promulgation of the ideas with which we are working, of the new mode of thinking in depth psychology that we are trying to present. I know that one can say much against such an attitude, and perhaps you will feel prompted to doing that if you wish to respond to this letter. But these are deeply-grounded choices in our personalities that transcend argumentation and logic. Perhaps the *emptiness* of *my* birthday parties as a child vs. their *absence* when you were a child has something to do with the difference in our outlook and our responses.

I don't know whether you understand French but I will close with

a little poem—delightfully Gallic not only in language but in spirit—
that I find helpful when I get buffeted around by my colleagues.

"Dans la vie òu tu veux courir
Songe bien ce que tu hasardes.
Il faut avec courage également offrir
Et ton front au lauriers et ton nez aux nasardes."[2]

Fondly,
Heinz

1. Kohut was elected for a three-year term; see George Pollock to Kohut, May 29,
1980; and above, June 1978.
2. "In the life where you want to rush / Think well of the risks you run. / You have
to offer with equal courage / Your brow to the wreath and your nose to be tweaked."
This is possibly a verse from a group of French cabaret singers and poets known as *Le
Caveau* (1726–1939). See Goldberg to Kohut, May 6 and 7.

May 6, 1980
Arnold Goldberg, M.D.
Chicago
Dear Arnold,

I respect your feelings and arguments as you again expressed them
in response to my letter. There is only one thing that I hope you will
think over—an issue that I feel, indeed know, concerning which there
is a real distortion. It is not "nice" for me to return to the council. And
when I said that I could never return to it, this statement was in
essence correct—even though I did not at that time think it through
& differentiate between a possible physical return & an emotional one.
At least as far as I can see it now I will never be able to be there as I
once was there.

With regard to the Institute's refusal to allow Paul and Anna
[Ornstein] to teach I am also not on your side. There are times when
I, too, would put my loyalty to friends above the loyalty to ideas, but,
much as I am chagrined about the Institute's refusal to ask Anna, I do
not think that this issue is a sufficiently clear-cut one. The "Institute"
and those who run it have their "pride," too, and need to assert their
autonomy. But there may be an opportunity for me to argue the
Ornsteins' case if I get elected to the Council.

Was there a gloating in "Ernie [Wolf], Paul & the others" about
your not being reelected? I don't know—perhaps a trace. But these
are things that will come out in the wash—they should be insignificant
even though I admit they cause hurt and anger.

For the rest, the to me most important part—your feelings toward me now—, we will apparently still have to wait and see.

But I have a good deal of hope and confidence.[1]

Yours,

Heinz

1. See Goldberg's obituary of Kohut in *IJP* 63 (1982): 257–58.

May 15, 1980

Mr. Carlo Pietzner

Camphill Village, U.S.A., Inc.[1]

Copake, New York

Dear Carlo:

Your warm response pleased me a great deal—reading your words and enjoying your old intelligence and sensitive perceptiveness seemed to close a circle and mend the discontinuity of our individual existence. You want to hear about me and I will do your bidding and give you some details, even though we both know that such facts tell little of the essentials. I am a psychoanalyst and psychiatrist with academic appointments at the University of Chicago, the University of Cincinnati, and the Chicago Institute for Psychoanalysis. I have been happily married for 32 years and we have one son, married, who is a historian. (This June Tom and I will for the first time be both on the program of the same scientific meeting [see above, May 14, 1979].) I have written a good deal, but my work is "controversial." It is rejected by many but also accepted by quite a few. My focus, in a nutshell, is not the traditional Freudian one, the drives, but the self and its development and destiny.

Please say hello to your friend [George] Kalmar. Although I do not believe that we ever knew each other well, I do remember him and am glad to hear about him. Loewenherz is a musicologist whom you can frequently hear in the intermission broadcasts from the Metropolitan. His name is Siegmund Levarie. He and I are not infrequently in touch—he sends me the books he writes and I send him mine. Franz Kramer is in Canada. After having been in Montreal with the C[anadian].B[roadcasting].C[ompany]., he moved to Toronto where he was in charge of the Center for Performing Arts. He is now in Ottawa and works for the Canadian government, in charge of supportive grants in the musical field.[2] I tried to get in touch with him but, though outwardly urbane and friendly, he was clearly not eager to pursue the opportunity I offered to him.

Will there ever be a chance to see each other again? We will be in Boston around November 1 to participate in scientific meetings and, even though I will be extremely busy then, there might be a chance for a meal together if you could come down. I have no idea, however, what the distances are.[3]

Enough for today—only warmest good wishes from your old Heinz Kohut

1. See below, Kohut to Pietzner, June 22, 1980, n.1.
2. See Franz Kraemer to Kohut, October 11, 1943. Kohut's friend changed the spelling of his name after leaving Austria, dropping the umlaut over the "a" and substituting the English "ae"; Franz Kraemer, personal communication, April 15, 1992.
3. See below, June 20, 1980; and Kohut to Pietzner, June 22, 1980.

May 29, 1980
Kenneth M. Newman, M.D.
Chairman, Program Planning Committee
Fiftieth Anniversary Celebration Meetings
Institute for Psychoanalysis
Chicago

Dear Kenneth:

It cannot have escaped your notice and that of others in your committee that I hesitated for some time before coming to a decision whether to accept your invitation to participate in the Fiftieth Anniversary Celebration, undertaken jointly by the Chicago Psychoanalytic Institute and the Chicago Psychoanalytic Society. When I first heard that it had been suggested that I give the Academic Lecture on this occasion, I was gladdened by what I took to be clear evidence for the fact that, given an occasion of historical significance, analysts could rise above the factionalism of the day, could for a time allow themselves to set scientific disagreements aside, and make a choice mobilized by the wish to underline the specificity of specialness of the occasion. And I spontaneously responded in the same way in which I had responded ten years ago when I had received the invitation to be the principal speaker at the fiftieth anniversary of the oldest of all psychoanalytic institutes, the Karl-Abraham Institute (Berlin) [see above, December 26, 1970]: with a spontaneous outpouring of thought, mobilized by the wish to say something that would do justice to the occasion. Since twenty-five years ago I had spoken at the Twenty-Fifth Anniversary of the Chicago Institute[1] I assumed that the idea to give Academic-Lecture status to my presentation was prompted, at least in part, by historical considerations—by the realization, in other words, that my availability provided for the organizers of the Anniversary Meeting the opportunity to underline that point that despite the passage of time, the essential continuity of scientific effort and commitment is maintained. I am, therefore, disappointed that, under the pressure of some of our colleagues, the special recognition that was to be given to my lecture was withdrawn and that an important symbolic move is now not made.

What more is there to say? I cannot see myself refusing the invitation of two institutions to which I have belonged for thirty years, and I will, therefore, prepare an appropriate scientific paper. I would only make the following requests to which, since they do not counteract the decision not to assign Academic-Lecture status to my paper, I trust the Planning Committee will accede: (1) I would like to speak on Saturday morning, perhaps at 10:00 or 10:30; (2) there should be no discussion after my address; (3) no other program should be scheduled on Saturday morning following my presentation; and (4) I would like a person who feels friendly toward me to chair the session and introduce me briefly.

I am sending you my warm personal regards.

Cordially yours,

Heinz Kohut, M.D.

cc: John E. Gedo, M.D.
    Paul H. Tolpin, M.D.

1. *Search*, 1:205–32.

June 9, 1980
Kenneth M. Newman, M.D., Chairman
Program Committee
Dear Kenneth:

I want to confirm our verbal agreement by letter in order to be sure that I have understood all details accurately. My Fiftieth-Anniversary celebration lecture[1] will be scheduled for Saturday, November 7, 1981, at 10:45 A.M.; it will not be followed by any other pre-lunch break activity; the chairman who will introduce me will be friendly toward my work and me. Do I have it right?[2]

Sincerely,

Heinz Kohut, M.D.

cc: John E. Gedo, M.D.
    Paul H. Tolpin, M.D.

1. *Search*, 4:537–67. The completed paper was read by Tom Kohut. The institute was interested in the essay for an in-the-end unrealized volume of papers presented at the celebration: see Kohut to Gedo and Pollock, May 19, 1981; and George H. Pollock, "The Presence of the Past," *Annual of Psychoanalysis* 11 (1983): 3–28.
2. See Newman to Kohut, June 12, 1980.

June 20, 1980
The Rev. Peter Roth
The Camphill Village Community
Botton Village
North Yorkshire, England
Dear Peter,

I have now received responses from Thomas [Weihs], Carlo [Pietzner], and you [May 23, 1980]; plus an unexpected letter from George Kalmar who remembered me from the Gymnasium. (G.K. is in Copake with Carlo.)[1]

I wished I could remind you of our past. I, myself, remember it vividly. Our long discussions in various coffeehouses[2]—about Walter Marseilles with whom we were both in analysis; about [Rainer Maria] Rilke, arguing the meaning of the angel in the *Duineser Elegien* [1923]; about a million and one things. One evening we sat together in your apartment, talking for hours, drinking Cognac as we talked. When we wanted to get up we couldn't, either of us. But you could reach over to the coffee-maker & brewed us a strong cup of coffee or two, and that got us going again. I remember Alix [Roth], of course. Meals with your parents. Once your father said that you need[ed] a plate with a *Gatterl* [railing] around after you had spilled a bit of food—and you felt hurt and belittled by him. Oh, there are so many memories but there is surely no use talking about them since that part of your life seems to be gone from you.

It might interest you that I met Marseilles twice after the Vienna days. Once in Chicago—he was a commercial graphologist* for a mail-order course, evaluating credit-applications via handwriting, and once, just perhaps 5 to 6 years ago in Munich. He had heard that I was giving some lectures with the University, found out where I was staying, and then sought me out. I also got a strange transatlantic call from him a bit later—he felt he was being persecuted by the U.S. State Department and wanted me to do something about that. I learned that he died a bit later.

Franzl Krämer, my old friend, is in Canada & clearly doesn't want to be approached. I met him, in Montreal, in 1948—he was with the CBC then & asked me to be interviewed for a shortwave broadcast to Germany/Austria, etc., in German. He is now in Ottawa, close to retirement after working in the field of music for the Canadian government for many years. At present he is involved in grant-assignments for musicians.

Sorry, but as far as I can see there is no possibility for our meeting in late July in Copake or Beaver Run [Pennsylvania]. It would be nice to see you though and I won't exclude the hope for a future occasion. We have been to Europe many times over the years but hardly in England. Still, should we ever fly over I will certainly let you know about that.

Warm regards and good wishes,

Yours,

Heinz

*[original in German] Yet another memory: a lecture by [graphologist Ludwig] Klages that we attended in the Urania.[3] (Remarkable that I suddenly lapse into German.)

1. See above, May 15, 1980; and below, Kohut to Pietzner, June 22, 1980.
2. Steven Beller, *Vienna and the Jews, 1867–1938: A Cultural History* (Cambridge, 1989), pp. 40–41.
3. A center for popular continuing education.

June 22, 1980 [from Peter Gay, Department of History, Yale University]

Dear Dr. Kohut:

It was kind of you to send me a second installment of papers (and thank your wife in particular for making the suggestion!).

There is obviously much to talk about, but I want to take just a moment to concentrate on your comment on the Weimar Republic, and my comment on your comment. If I gave the impression that I thught you simple-minded, or even simplistic, then I did not express myself well.[1] What I had in mind essentially was this: the reasons for Hitler's accession to power were many—even more than most historians have been willing (or able) to see. By this I mean more than "reasons from the outside world" alone.

I really mean, rather, the great variety of psychological causes that played into one another with the calamitous results we all know. Many who had suffered deprivation in war, occupation, inflation, unemployment did *not* become Nazis. Many, who had so suffered, did. Many who did pretty well (one would have surmised, psychologically as well) in the '20s played ball with Hitler. Many of his supporters (for example, in big industry) were not even anti-Semites.

In short, what Fred Weinstein had in mind when he spoke of heterogeneity in social movements is what I had in mind in responding to the point you were making [see below, April 27, 1981].

One more comment. I agree with you about focus. Some historians (most) remain mired in the particular, and some who aspire to larger views sometimes do so at some cost to themselves. It is hard to drift from one to the other, though I, as you can imagine, would like to think that I am among those historians who make the effort. And I would agree also that in taking a larger view of historical events, the historian might do well to acquaint himself with the insights that psychoanalysis can provide for him. So we're not that far apart.

Again my thanks for the reading materials!

Very sincerely yours,

Peter Gay

1. *Search*, 4:665-66 and 667-68. On June 20 Kohut had written to Lottie Köhler that Gay had attacked his views at the Psychohistory Conference in Chicago. Gay holds to a more or less traditional Freudian point of view: see his *Freud for Historians* (New York, 1985).

June 22, 1980
Carlo Pietzner
Copake, New York

Dear Carlo,

I have now heard from all three of you, and, there can be no doubt, your response was the most congenial of the three by far. I don't know clearly why your letter [June 5] struck immediately such a harmonious chord in me. Your handwriting? Your stationery? Your warmth and freedom in expression? All of it, I think; but not because of the details but because I recognized in it a piece of my past that is still alive in me despite all the profound changes the years have wrought, a reverberation of some essential heritage that I took along when I left Vienna that is also still alive in you. (Do you remember, by the way, that you also designed an "ex libris" for me—the "H" of my signature it was. I still see it now and then in some old books, even though I don't use any "ex libris" labels anymore in any books.)—But I must answer your questions. How I heard of you all. Well, my son, a psychohistorian, interested in European history, in particular Wilhelm II and the outbreak of the First World War—spent a (second time) year in Germany with his wife. Became acquainted with a family there (Siebe[ck] in Bonn) via a friend of mine in Munich. When the youngest son of the Siebe[ck]s came to the USA we reciprocated the hospitality (he spent Christmas with us, for example) and, quite recently, he stopped over with us in Chicago with a visiting German girlfriend. At dinner I asked her where she had learned her remarkably fluent English and she said she had been a camp councillor in a Rudolf-Steiner[1] camp in Scotland. When I then mentioned your three names, she immediately said yes, she knew all these names. I asked for and received the Central Office address in Scotland. I wrote and got a friendly reply from Thomas plus the addresses of Peter and you. You expressed some interest in my work and I will be glad to send you some of my books if you want me to (they have also been translated into various languages, so I could send them in German if you prefer). But after some *Kostproben* [sampling] my writings might be a bit away from the fields you are familiar with—I really cannot judge that. At any rate I will first send you a few reprints of essays with a more general theme, then, if you want more, I can send you books and collections of essays for broader study. Finally the idea of a get-together. I really would love that & I don't believe that the risks are great—I know from the way you write and think that we will have no trouble with each other. But the mechanics of it are a different story. I cannot combine my Boston stay with a sidetrip to Copake. The meeting will be essentially about my work and I will be busy for 3 days, from morning to night—I will undoubtedly be very tired at the end of it and must get back home directly. But I can't believe that there will not be other possibilities sooner or later; now that we know of each others' whereabouts we must simply keep the possibility in mind and then make plans. (All of August and September my wife and I will be in Carmel, California. . . .)

And now only my warm regards. My wife joins by sending her greetings (*"unbekannterweise"*)[2] and, I hope, *ein Auf Wiedersehen* before all too long.

Yours,

Heinz

P.S. We just finished a "Psychohistory Meeting" in Chicago—for the first time my son and I were on the same scientific program. I was a proud father, of course. Please thank George Kalmar for me—he wrote me a long letter [June 24, 1980] with various bits of information. I hope to get to respond to him, too, before long.

My reprints will be sent from my office in a day or so.

1. Rudolf Steiner (1861–1925) was the founder of "anthroposophy," a philosophical system of "spiritual science," and of an elementary school movement in Germany and England. The Camphill–Rudolf Steiner–Schools with which Weihs, Roth, and Pietzner were associated were dedicated to "children in need of special care" as well as to mentally handicapped adults (see Weihs to Kohut, April 8, 1980; and Pietzner to Kohut, April 21, 1980).

2. "Without being acquainted."

June 27, 1980
Robert Jay Lifton, M.D.
School of Medicine
Yale University
Dear Dr. Lifton:

It was very kind of you to send me such a full letter [June 6] in response to the reprints I had sent to you. Actually when I talked about the "social therapy" of the Mitscherlichs in the workshop, as you said I did, I must have been quoting myself because, as you will see if you look at the Peace Prize Laudatio I gave in Alexander's honor in 1969—I believe I sent you the English translation which appeared later in the *J. A. Psa. A.*—I elaborated on that theme at that festive occasion. *The Inability to Mourn* I own, both in German and in English. I must admit I read it only in German when I prepared the Peace Prize laudation and your preface* thus escaped me. I will read it at an early opportunity. While I thus do not need this volume, I am certainly looking forward to getting your *Broken Connection*[1] which, if it arrives in time, I will take along on my vacation in August. (Reading is unfortunately still not easy for me at this point. After heart-surgery, septicemia, and six weeks of penicillin i/v, I developed a labyrinthitis or something of the sort. At any rate my right labyrinth is non-functional now and prolonged reading makes me seasick and dizzy. But it's getting better slowly.)

I will not be East until Oct./Nov. when we will have a "Self-psychology" conference organized by the Boston Institute. It would certainly be nice to be able to say hello to you then—although the Program Committee has assigned so many tasks to me that I am sure that I will be too tired for the exchange of views that you envisage and that, at a different time, I, too, would value very much.

It's so nice to have made your acquaintance! We will surely see each other again before long.

Cordial regards,
Heinz Kohut, M.D.

P.S. See pp. 25/26 of ". . . Chance of peacefully working out conflicts" (1970) and pp. 27–29 of "Alexander Mitscherlich" (1969).
P.P.S. I have not had any illumination yet about Freud's "da kann ich nur hassen" ("there [the Nazis] I can only hate") but I'll pursue it and let you know if I am successful [see below, July 9].
*Anyway, it was written much later as I now realize since the translation appeared in *1975*.

1. *The Broken Connection: On Death and the Continuity of Life* (New York, 1979).

July 9, 1980 [original in German]
Miss Anna Freud
London
Dear Anna Freud,
    Today I'm doing something that I have never done before, something that for me goes completely against the grain and that I hope you will not hold against me. For the last few weeks I've been racking my brain, leafing through books, asking friends and experts—all in the search after a wonderful phrase that your father once spoke or wrote. Someone had asked him what he thought about anti-Semitism (or about the Nazis, or something similar) and he answered—he, the greatest interpreter of human behavior—that when it came to anti-Semitism (or the Nazis and their atrocities, or something similar), there he could not explain, there he could only hate.
    I know of course that your father had many, and profound, explanations for anti-Semitism—but there was a moment in which he, more profoundly than any explanation, said to someone that he could only hate. (I know that I have not made this up—I don't have what it takes for the wisdom of such an utterance.) Well, are you familiar with these words? Do you know if it appears in print? Have you yourself perhaps related this anecdote?[1]
    How are you? Despite the passing of years during which we have not seen each other, I feel myself still bound to you. As you perhaps know, my newer works have made me a very controversial person—often, it appears to me, because people twist what I am saying. But I really don't want to burden you with all that now. I trust in your inner greatness which, in spite of growing questions with respect to my

works, will not lead you to see me with the eyes of my contemporaries who treat me in a most unworthy fashion.

On August 1 we go again to Carmel. A few weeks ago Tom and I were for the first time on the same scientific program (Psychohistory Conference in Chicago). That was a great experience for me.

All the best, also from Betty, from your faithful

Heinz

1. See Anna Freud to Kohut, July 21, 1980, in which she expresses the doubt that her father would ever have said such a thing. She does go on to say, however, that her father was often asked to write about anti-Semitism, but that he always refused, saying he was too personally involved to be objective. Cf. *Search*, 3:259–60; and Kohut, *Self Psychology and the Humanities*, p. 94. Anna Freud died in 1982.

July 11, 1980
Peter Barglow, M.D.
Chicago
Dear Peter,

Arnold [Goldberg] and Mike [Basch] told me that you will write to the Editor of *Commentary* in order to take exception to their having dignified [Frederick] Crews' outburst of narcissistic rage by including it in their most recent issue.[1] I am glad that there will be a reply and I am pleased that you will write it. If handled appropriately, setting oneself above the anger of the moment, this is a valuable opportunity to present to a broad, cultured readership a brief glimpse at the new psychoanalysis. Crews' use of isolated old statements of mine about female sexuality, while disregarding pp. 776/7 and pp. 783–792 in Volume 2 of the *Search for the Self*, should give you an excellent opportunity to show both his defamatory method *and* a sample of selfpsychology. The man even holds it against me that my essays were published—I allowed them to be published, he says, or something of the sort. Now what is wrong about essays being published? And why—if one understands my theories about the self in general & the group-self in particular—is it political expediency when I remain convinced that the new, even the radically new, must be built on the old? That the continuity of the group-self should be preserved?

I wish you success—for your sake, for my sake, for our sake, and above all, for the sake of ideas that have moved our therapeutic efficacy forward, both in individual therapy and in the socio-historical arena, even if only an inch.

I am looking forward to your response to Crews & *Commentary* with keen anticipation.
Warmly yours,
Heinz

1. Frederick Crews, "Analysis Terminable," *Commentary* 70 (July 1980): 24–34. Crews, a former practitioner of applied psychoanalysis, had decided that psychoanalysis was an intellectual and scientific fraud. Here he observes that "if Freud's couch were passed along like the throne of St. Peter, it might well find itself today in Dr. Kohut's office in Chicago" (30). Crews thus ignores the growing divide between classical analysis and self psychology in concluding that Kohut's emphasis on the clinical data gathered "from remarks by supine adults" (32) is "a matter of scientific rhetoric rather than true rigor" (30). Barglow argues that Kohut's work represents an advance on the pioneering efforts of Freud; see *Commentary* 70 (October 1980): 6–7, 10; Kohut to Levarie, August 30, 1980; and Linda B. Martin, "The Psychiatrist in Today's Movies: He's Everywhere and in Deep Trouble," *New York Times*, January 25, 1981.

Carmel, August 7, 1980
Mr. Michael Ferguson
Chicago
Dear Mr. Ferguson,
Your letter [July 31] followed me to California. To your question: I read [Harry Stack] S[ullivan]'s *Conceptions of Modern Psychiatry* [1947] around 1948–50—remember it as interesting, but undisciplined.[1] More the expansion of a gifted but pathological mind than a scientific contribution. Perhaps it looks more orderly from the hindsight of selfpsychology. Did he "influence" me? I don't know. I suggest you look at the 1951-discussion of "The Function of the Analyst" etc. in Volume I of *The Search for the Self* (pp. 159–66). Perhaps you can discern something Sullivanian there. I doubt it. The basic dichotomy of human experience—Guilty Man and Tragic Man—I treated already [at] age 18 (1931) in an essay in which I compared the Cyclops episode in Homer's *Odyssey* and in Euripides' Satyr play *Cyclops*.[2]
Perhaps we can chat about these questions sometime in the future.
Good luck as you pursue your work. Keep at it. I believe you have something to say.[3]
Friendly regards,
H. Kohut

1. Sullivan was the leading American proponent of the trend in psychoanalysis toward interpersonal dynamics in place of the emphasis on drives.
2. "Greek Language Final Examination: Euripides' 'The Cyclops,' 1932," Heinz Kohut (1913–81) Papers, Box 1, Folder 13, Institute for Psychoanalysis, Chicago.

    3. See Michael Ferguson, "Progress and Theory Change: The Two Analyses of Mr. Z.," *Annual of Psychoanalysis* 9 (1981): 133–60; and *Search*, 4:395–446, 658–60.

October 2, 1980
Evelyne Schwaber, M.D.
Brookline, Massachusetts
Dear Evy,

    Among the large stack of mail that greeted me on our return from California I found two items that stem from you, one directly, the other via George Pollock. At this time I can unfortunately do no more than to tell you that I received a) your paper "Empathy: A Mode of Analytic Listening" with your warm accompanying note of September 24; and b) your paper "Narcissism, Selfpsychology, and the Listening Perspective."[1] with copies of the correspondence between George Pollock (September 3, September 23) and you (September 19).

    As things are now I cannot, must not turn to this material. I hope you will understand and forgive. I am rather doubtful that I will be able to read these papers before our trip to Boston—there is just too much pressure on me at this time. As you have heard I am working on a new topic, perhaps to be called "How Does Psychoanalysis Cure? (Contributions to the Psychology of the *Self*)." In this work I am taking up a number of topics—incomplete analysis; castration anxiety; agoraphobia; etc., etc., plus, at the end a theory of therapeutic action. The empathy issue is a peripheral one and I remain open-minded about different ways in which one can formulate the role, both as a determinant of the nature of the theory with which we work and as a factor in the therapeutic process. That there is some debate and that people within our ranks have different opinions about some issues is a very fine thing. We have reached the point where we can make progress almost exclusively via debate among ourselves—even though I insist that we must carefully examine criticism from those who reject us more or less *in toto* because now and then we might find something of value even from that side.

    Betty and I are very much looking forward to seeing you and Julie in Boston. We have—not unexpectedly to you, I am sure—decided to keep to ourselves during the meetings in order to husband my energies. (We will probably eat in our hotel room, for example, most of the time.) Still, we will play it by ear and see how things will go. At the moment I feel much stronger and in general healthier than I have for a long, long time.

Warm regards and see-you-soon
Cordially,
Heinz

1. See Evelyne A. Schwaber, "Narcissism, Selfpsychology, and the Listening Perspective," *Annual of Psychoanalysis* 9 (1981): 115–31; Schwaber, "Psychoanalytic Listening
and Psychic Reality," *International Review of Psycho-Analysis* 10 (1983): 379–92; and
Schwaber, "Empathy: A Mode of Analytic Listening," in *Empathy II*, ed. Joseph Lichtenberg et al. (Hillsdale, N.J., 1984), pp. 143–72.

October 6, 1980
Charles Kligerman, M.D.
Chicago
Dear Charlie,
The letter [September 23] you wrote to me a couple of weeks ago
finally reached me on the weekend. Even though you had in the meantime told me personally some of the things that you also mentioned in
your letter—the [Victor] Calef-[Edward] Weinshel twins vs. [Samuel]
Guttman affair, for example—,[1] the real message of your lines to me,
the reinforcement they gave to my better self (the self that disregards
petty criticism and pursues the directions that force themselves on it
via intrinsic necessities). was as fresh as when the letter finally came
to me two days ago as it would have been had the mails been more
efficient in getting it to me.
You must know that you are very special to me—quite different in
your significance than anybody else I know. I realize that you have
your doubts about certain aspects of my work at times and that your
full acceptance concerns only a limited portion of it. But I also know
that you remain openminded about the rest—that you are not rejecting
it contemptuously but that you are considering it. I am not surprised
[*sic*] abôut your caution and slowness—I don't forget, I am cautious
and slow myself and my intellectual and emotional commitment to
the analytic traditions is intense. But I have worked my way toward
new positions and I believe that, in the long run, you, too, will be
closer to them than you are now. But that is not, at this point[,] of the
greatest importance. What counts for me is that, independent of your
judgement about this or that line of new thought that I have pursued,
you are friendly toward me and respect and support my serious efforts.[2] Many thanks then for your encouraging presence in general
and for the last letter in particular.
Yours,
Heinz

1. Scholastic conflict that arose at a conference in Aspen.

2. See Charles Kligerman, "Address delivered at the Spring Dinner of the Candidates' Association of the Chicago Institute for Psychoanalysis—June 16, 1978."

December 6, 1980
Douglas Detrick, M.D.
San Francisco
Dear Doug,

You may have learned about the fact that I have been very ill, specifically that I came down with a serious, life-threatening pneumonia shortly after returning to Chicago from Boston. But I am on the mend now and even though the doctors are imposing a 2-months convalescent period on me, I will not be inactive, I hope, but, while not going to my office until February, see some patients at home and do some work at my desk—thesaurus et al.

You have correctly recognized a slight shift in my thinking about the types of selfobject transferences. They correspond to the 3 parts of the bipolar self (mirroring—alikeness—idealization) and they make good sense experientially. Each of them has its own development line, from archaic forms to mature forms, and each can be easily discerned during development and in the therapeutic transference (in which old defects are remobilized & offer themselves to be healed). With regards to the sustaining effect of the presence of human sameness I have in mind the early security that the baby must sense in the mere presence of humans (voices, smells). I also think of the little guy just working next to daddy in the basement or "shaving" while daddy shaves (corresponding to the developing "intermediate" area of skills and talents), the fact that an inimical environment, even one trying to harm you, is better than an "exterminating" one (KZ experience, the atmosphere in Kafka's *The Trial*),[1] and also the experience of the astronaut I described in my letters to Professor Heller.

I hear that you recorded my Sunday PM remarks in Boston & I am glad about that since, as you heard, the official system failed.

I felt that the Boston meeting was successful in all essential ways. Did you feel the same?

Warm regards,

Cordially,

Heinz

P.S. Your observation that shared enthusiasm is similarly sustaining is very cogent—I would not stress it though at this point because people will translate it immediately into the classical Freudian formula of "group-psychology" & play up the *social* value while disregarding the increment of self-esteem. Still, later, we should point out that all effects do in fact co-exist. (Maybe you could do this some day.)

1. KZ-concentration camp (*Konzentrationslager*).

December 13, 1980
Phyllis Greenacre, M.D.
New York
Dear Phyllis,

Although I am still weak after a bout with pneumonia, I want to write to you in response to the material (copies of your letters to Dr. Marian Tolpin) that you had sent to me. I am not certain of the role that I am playing in the issue you raised with Dr. Tolpin since, despite the fact that you said in your letter of October 28th to Dr. Tolpin that you had read her chapter in "Heinz Kohut's *Recent Advances in Self Psychology*," the "*Recent Advances*" is not my book. Michael Reese Hospital and Medical Center had held a conference on self psychology in Chicago in October, 1978—a similar conference was organized one year later by the [*sic*] UCLA, and a third one just recently by the Boston Psychoanalytic Institute—and "*Recent Advances*," edited by Dr. Arnold Goldberg, a senior member of the Michael Reese Faculty, is almost exclusively a collection of the major papers and discussions from the Chicago conference on self psychology. I spoke only twice during this conference: I introduced the panel on applied analysis and I made a summarizing statement at the very end concerning all the panels and symposia of the conference. These summarizing remarks were included in the "*Advances*"—also two letters about scientific topics that I wrote shortly before the conference—and I am, therefore, one of the many contributors to this book. To speak of "*Recent Advances*," however, as "Heinz Kohut's *Recent Advances*" is clearly in error.

I must admit that I have read only a few of the essays contained in "*Recent Advances*." I had, however, listened attentively and carefully to the presentations as they were made during the conference. Some of them had been favorable to my work, others questioned the accuracy, usefulness, or relevance of various aspects of my work, others, finally, rejected much of my work (or important aspects of it) with great vehemence. As I listened I made notes and, when I gave my summarizing statement on the last day of the conference, I tried to respond as fairly and objectively as I could to these contributions—whether they approved of my work or were critical of it. This was the actual context for which the essays of *"Recent Advances"* were originally written. The publisher, however, decided to disregard the fact that the content of a conference was presented. Instead the volume became simply a series of essays and my final summarizing statement was presented in the book as my reactions to the essays contained in the book. These changes, I understand, were undertaken in order to make the volume more attractive to the reader. There was no intrinsically significant reason for them—it was simply a matter of offering the material to the readership in an appealing form.

But now back, specifically, to my attitude to these contributions. Let me admit first that, while I listened attentively to the speakers, I cannot say that the opportunity offered by a single hearing allowed me to form opinions about details. While thus, in particular, I remembered Dr. Marian Tolpin's discussion and responded to it in my summary, I did not recall then that she had attacked or demeaned Dr. [Margaret] Mahler's work. As I heard it, she took sides with regard to the question that had been raised earlier in the panel of which her discussion formed a part, namely, whether the observations of Mahler, on the one hand, and my reconstructions from certain transferences in the analysis of certain adult patients, on the other hand, could be integrated or whether they could not. If you read the relevant statements in my summary, you will see that I took Tolpin's attitude as supporting the viewpoint that I held then and that I still hold now— which, by the way, does not rule out the possibility that I might change my mind about this issue in the future—namely, that such an integration is precluded by the fact that the basic conceptions of a psychology that puts the self—its wholeness or fragmentation—into its center and that considers psychological life as a succession of changing but forever persisting experiences of self-selfobject units, from birth to death, do not lend themselves to be integrated with those of a psychology that focuses in essence on conflicts concerning object relations, in particular as regards the separation from the object and the achievement of autonomy.

This is as much as I can say for myself—if you are sufficiently interested in these issues, please do read my summarizing reflections in *"Advances"* where I tried to express myself as clearly, simply, and unambiguously as possible.

Now with regard to the issue raised by Dr. Mahler and you, I cannot believe that there is no way that should be satisfactory to you without pursuing the matter with the, it seems to me, excessive firmness of your insistence that a wrong be publicly righted. Since you say that Dr. Tolpin misunderstood what you had said about Mahler's theories or, to say the least, that she had misinterpreted the significance of your statements, Dr. Tolpin would surely have no qualms about admitting that she was mistaken—it is you, after all, who must know best what you were aiming at in what you said.

Still, these issues are not clear cut. Once a scientific statement is made, it has become public property, as it were, and is open to be interpreted by others in ways that the author does not agree with and to which he may feel impelled to object. The choice of whether or not he will object and, if he does, the selection of the form in which he will voice his objection, is a matter of personal preference, a matter of taste. Just take my own case, for example. It cannot have escaped you that my work has been the target of severe criticism. What you do not know is that I feel that almost all of the censure to which my work has been exposed is based on serious misunderstandings. Quite frankly I feel that the most devastating attacks on me and my work that you can read in our scientific journals are not dealing with what I really said or meant but with interpretations of my work that I consider to be grossly distorted. I have become resigned to these facts and have decided not to engage in polemics but to use my remaining years to express as clearly as I can what I believe to have discerned, trusting that in the long run attentive and unbiased readers will be able to recognize that some of my most severe critics had misunderstood what I had said.

I believe that these reflections will speak for themselves and I will, therefore, not try any further to plead with you not to be unforgiving in your attitudes toward a younger colleague who as you feel has misunderstood your intentions but to allow the emergence of a debate on impersonal, scientific levels.[1]

At the end I would also like to express the hope that your former friendly feelings toward me have not diminished. I assure you that my warm feelings toward you, my gratitude for what you have given to all of us, and my admiration for your work are as great as ever.

Sincerely,

Heinz Kohut, M.D.

Copy to Peter Hartocollis, M.D., Ph.D.

Marian Tolpin, M.D.

Arnold Goldberg, M.D.

1. According to Greenacre, Tolpin had wrongly asserted that Greenacre discredited much of Mahler's work on infant psychology. Greenacre insisted on a public correction, which appeared as "Statement of Correction," *APA Newsletter* 15, no. 2 (June 1981), p. 2. See Greenacre to Tolpin, October 28, 1980; and Mahler to Arnold Goldberg, October 30, 1980. See also Tolpin to Peter Hartocollis, editor of the APA *Newsletter*, December

14, 1980; Tolpin to Arnold Cooper, member of the APA Executive Council, December 14, 1980, and Greenacre to Tolpin, December 18, 1980.

December 16, 1980
Mr. Walter Demsyne
Crawford, New Jersey
Dear Mr. Demsyne,

Thank you for your thoughtful note.[1] We certainly appear to think along similar lines. If you want to learn more about my work you might look at the *New York Times*, Sunday, 11/9/80, where, in the Magazine section, my work is discussed at length in a rather clear, and, on the whole, correct way [see above, April 8, 1980].

With regard to your feeling that "ulterior reality" becomes "contiguated into existence" I can only say that, as a scientist, I must stay with the observable fact and avoid teleological assumption of higher purposes being fulfilled, of pre-existing patterns to which reality is subordinated, etc. Still, this might simply show that science and scientists are limited in their outlook and that a broader conception of the essence of reality, of a reality beyond reality, is needed.

Sincerely yours,
H. Kohut

1. December 10; Demsyne had read an article in *Time* about Kohut: see below, June 24, 1981.

January 12, 1981
Robert S. Wallerstein, M.D.
University of California
San Francisco
Dear Bob,

It was thoughtful of you to send me your letter [January 6] to Ms. [Jean] Dietz.[1] I can well understand your puzzlement—although I didn't do more than skim the article in question I noticed some completely unintelligible gibberish that was attributed to me. But I am so used by now to be exposed to utter distortions of what I say—and not only by journalists but, par excellence, by colleagues (I have said jokingly that some of my most severe critics read only between my lines but assiduously avoid reading the lines themselves)—that I have become quite numb about these (what shall I call them?) "misunderstandings" and don't even begin to ask questions or demand corrections. You know, of course, that I have always felt that your critique has addressed itself to ideas and issues and that I am grateful to you for that.

Warmly, as always,

Yours,

Heinz

1. Wallerstein was complaining to the editor of *Psychiatric News* that he had been misquoted in an article about Kohut in the December 19, 1980, issue, pointing out that he maintains a critical stance toward self psychology while also accepting the value of some of its insights.

January 26, 1981 [original in German]

Tilmann Moser

Münstertal, West Germany

Dear crazy, gifted friend Tilmann,

I too am glad that you wrote and, believe me—do you believe me?—: there is nothing in your letter that seems to me to be thoroughly unfriendly. And, although in my works I do not expatiate on the return of preverbal experiences, I know well how much that is primitive emerges in some transferences—in sounds, in bodily closeness or distance, in bodily smells, in the sound of the voice. I'm working once more on a book—*How Does Analysis Cure?* will be the title—and hope that it will at least instruct semi-courageous analysts, like those of yours in Freiburg, that courage grows and that "classic" feelings of guilt on behalf of a necessary abstinence standing in the way of free and generous emotional response can be cleared away. I speak in my book of a two-stage basic unit of psychoanalytic healing process—understanding and explaining—and the juridical figures of speech about which you write belong to the first stage. (And I also know that in some cases the first stage is the only one that is necessary and bearable. But not in all cases and even in the former not to the last—but lasting for years.)

Idiot that I am I've again been ill. After the Boston meeting (a great success: 960 registrants—1200 wanted to participate) I was exhausted [and that led to] pneumonia. But now I'm working again—see maybe 3 patients a day (at home) and write away at my manuscript. Sometimes at night I worry myself with the same stupid classic-analytic conscience from which I try to help free others.

Otherwise not much is new. I'm being attacked from all sides and sometimes it's hard to bear. On the whole, though, I manage it well. A trip to Europe is hardly likely—at the moment I am not even going downtown. At best, when the weather is nice, Betty and I take a walk.

In the summer (August/September) we'll again be in Carmel. Then, at the beginning of October a meeting—this time in San Francisco (actually Berkeley), organized under the auspices of the University of California.

And now love to all, also from Betty, Tom and Susan. (The children now have a dog—*we* naturally wish for a grandchild.)

As always,

Yours,

Heinz

February 14, 1981

Dr. Pietro Castelnuevo-Tedesco

Vanderbilt University

Nashville, Tennessee

Dear Dr. Castelnuevo-Tedesco,

I read your letter & the enclosures carefully and wished that I could respond to your proposal to meet with me for clincial consultations & theoretical discussions with a clear & unambiguous "yes, of course." But, unfortunately, there are certain circumstances that prevent me from doing so. Two years ago I had heart surgery with a series of incredible complications that made it impossible for me to work at my usual speed and with my usual vigor and vitality. Finally, last summer, I began to feel almost like my old self again. I undertook my participation in the Boston meetings in Oct./Nov., 1980 with great enjoyment but, on my return to Chicago, came down with a 2-lobe pneumococcal pneumonia which, while antibiotics pulled me through, left me again quite weakened. I have not yet returned to my office, see my patients on a severely restricted schedule at home and what energies I have are concentrated on a perhaps 4/5-finished book *How Does Analysis Cure?*. All this in explanation for my inability to respond to your proposal with the "yes" I wished I could say.

What can we do? There are various possibilities. We could wait, and perhaps I will be firmly in the saddle sometime in the late fall of this year, i.e., after the meetings of the Chicago Society & Institute at which I will, as I promised quite a while ago, present a major paper on which I hope to work during the summer (the 50th Anniversary mtg. of the Chicago Soc. & Inst. will take place in November).

Another possibility is for you to have the consultations you envisage with someone else in Chicago: Arnold Goldberg, Michael Basch about theory; Marian and Paul Tolpin concerning clinical work; Ernest Wolf in either theory (in partic. re applied selfpsychology) or practice. Also:

we have a workshop which meets once a month on Saturday AM (10–12) which you could attend if the members accept your application.

So there we are. I am sorry I can't be more positive at this point, but I hope you will believe me when I say that I am very regretful about having to give you this answer. Please let me know what you feel about the possibilities that I wrote about.

Sincerely,

Heinz Kohut

February 16, 1981
Robert D. Stolorow, Ph.D.
New York

Dear Bob:

I should have written to you sooner in response to your having sent [January 26] to me a copy of the splendid discussion that you presented at the San Diego Symposium in January. I read it quickly and cursorily, but carefully enough to know that it was excellent; and I intended at first to read it more carefully in the near future in order to respond extensively and in detail to the three major points that you made. Unfortunately, however, I did not take into account a specific emotional obstacle that stood in my way. Can you guess what it is? Well, that is simple. It is the fact that I am working on the second part of my book, while the "unpublished paper," as you call it, to which your discussion responds, is, as you undoubtedly know, nothing else but a draft of the first part. This is where the obstacle lies. It is, to spell out my problem most distinctly, a prohibitive enterprise for me to immerse myself at this point into topics which I have now temporarily put behind me with which I was preoccupied earlier (during the early fall and, right after my illness, in the beginning of December) when I was working on the first part of my book, using the draft that you discussed in San Diego as my starting point. I am, therefore, postponing my point-by-point consideration of your discussion to the time when I return once more to the first part of my manuscript—i.e., as I hope, just before it goes to the publisher—and I will then insert references to your discussion into my manuscript if it seems appropriate to do so. In the following I will give you my preliminary reactions.

(1) Concerning the discrepancies in the structure of *your* case of agoraphobia and the outline of the psychopathology of agoraphobia that *I* presented, I can say only that I was extremely pleased to learn about your experiences. Chances are that there are several subgroups

of agoraphobia and that they are distinguishable not only with regard to symptomatology (e.g., whether or not the fear is absent when the patient is accompanied by an older woman) but also, which is of the greatest interest to us, whether the sequence of the transferences as they are unrolling during the treatment varies in accordance with the specific structure of the underlying disturbance.

(2) Concerning the different conception of complementarity that you suggest, it is my impression that further clarification of both of our conceptualizations [is] still needed. We must take into account not only that we may in each of the two types of psychopathological constellations—self disorders, structural neuroses—be dealing with different dynamic and genetic data, we must also take into account that we may use two different approaches—the socio-psychological (the emphasis of the observer is on the scrutiny of interactions); the depth-psychological (the emphasis of the observer is on the scrutiny of inner experiences)—as we examine each of these two constellations. The problem with the idea of "a psychology of conflict-ridden but firmly consolidated psychic structures" is not with how to contrast it with "a psychology of missing, precarious, and disintegration-prone psychic structures." That is easy enough, I think, and I have up to recently used this particular schema, knowing full well that I would sooner or later discard it again. The real hurdle, as I see it, the truly knotty problem, in other words, arises when we begin to try, as we must, to spell out the difference between pathological and pathogenic conflict, on the one hand, and non-pathological and non-pathogenic conflict—whether the latter is resolved or unresolved; whether the latter is experienced with moderate tension or with great anxiety—, on the other hand. The mental-apparatus model has allowed us to visualize this difference by differentiating between (a) normal conflicts which are conscious or preconscious and (b) potentially pathological and pathogenic conflicts which are wholly or in part unconscious and which, in consequence of the ego's lack of suzerainty, may result in the formation of (structurally conceived) transferences and neurotic symptoms. My present solution, already outlined in the oedipus-conflict chapter of *The Restoration of the Self* and now spelled out with greater assurance and elaborated further, is to dispense to a certain extent with complementarity of theory. I now say that all forms of psychopathology, including the oedipal-conflict neuroses, are ultimately disorders of the self. Still, not only in deference to tradition but also in recognition of the fact that we must in some cases focus first on the important intermediate area of pathological and pathogenic conflicts, I am still willing to retain the structural model as serviceable

during the period of the clinical work when this intermediate area claims our attention and think that we should dispense with it only if extensive clinical experience should prove to us that a prolonged and separate focusing on the drive-conflicts of the oedipal and preoedipal periods, instead of being appropriate attitude that is in harmony with the old technical principle that we must analyze from the surface to the depth, is in fact in error, perpetuated by us only because we have not been able to free ourselves from the misleading governance of an erroneous tradition. If, in other words, we should come to recognize that we should never focus on the conflicts but always, *ab initio*, on both the conflicts and on the selfobject failures that were responsible for the emergence of pathogenic drives and pathogenic conflicts, then, I believe, we should indeed discard the old model once and for all.

All these considerations rest, as you know from my "unpublished paper," i.e., from the draft of the first part of my book, on my conceptualization of the conflict neuroses as disorders of the self. This conceptualization, I will add, rests, in turn, on my assertion that conflict leads to psychopathology only when it arises in consequence of a disorder of the self. Still, the subdivision of the analyzable psychic disturbances with which we have been working can be maintained if we now add the self disturbances that lead to the pathogenic conflicts about drives (and, par excellence, the conflicts of the oedipus complex that lead to the symptoms of conversion hysteria, anxiety-hysteria [phobia], and compulsion neurosis, i.e., to the symptoms of the classical transference neuroses) are of a delimited specific kind, disturbing the self only during a specific, delimited period of its development and interfering with its cohesion, strength, and harmony only with regard to specific (e.g., and par excellence, oedipal) experiences and functions. One of the virtues of this present conceptualization—but as I said above, I am willing to discard and replace it if clinical experience (and your case of agoraphobia is a piece of evidence pointing in this direction) bids us to do so—is that the classification of analyzable disorders that is derived from it can accommodate all kinds of variations and all kinds of transitional forms of psychopathology.

(3) With regard to the differentiation between (a) borderline pathology and (b) severe narcissistic personality and behavior disorders, we are, contrary to what you believe to be the case, in complete agreement and, as a matter of fact, I have said on numerous occasions (I am not sure whether this view of mine has ever appeared in print or whether I have only upheld it verbally in our Chicago workshops and in other meetings) that this is simply an issue of nomenclature. I have also said many times (and I am expanding on this view in my present work—

the pages containing the discussion of this topic were apparently not part of the section of the manuscript that you read) that I am a relativist with regard to both the concept of borderline pathology and the concept of psychosis. Insofar, in other words, as the therapist is able to build an empathic bridge to the patient, the patient has in a way ceased to be a borderline case (a crypto-psychotic) or a psychotic and has become a case of (severe) narcissistic personality disorders.[1]

But now I must stop—my manuscript is calling me. As I said earlier: I will think about each of your points carefully when I return to the first part [of] *How Does Analysis Cure?*; and I will refer to your discussion and to the work that [Bernard] Brandchaft [see note 1 above] and you are doing together on which you remarked if such references seem appropriate.

Let me close by telling you again how much I enjoyed your discussion. Far from seeing in it the expression of "certain minor differences from some of your views," as you wrote, I see in it the thoughts of a cherished colleague and collaborator who is moving with me into the new territory that the insights of self-[sic]psychology have opened for us.

All the best to you and to your family. I am deeply grateful to know that you are one of our team.

Warmly yours,
Heinz Kohut, M.D.

1. See Stolorow to Kohut, March 4, 1981, requesting permission (granted March 9) to quote (p. 344n) this sentence in Bernard Brandchaft and Robert D. Stolorow, "The Borderline Concept: Pathological Character or Iatrogenic Myth?" in *Empathy II*, pp. 333–57. According to Kohut, Stolorow was one of the few psychologists in the psychoanalytically conservative New York City area familiar with self psychology; Kohut to Roger Petti, August 19, 1979.

March 4, 1981
Mr. Michael Ferguson
Chicago
Dear Mr. Ferguson,

I liked your letter [February 21] about rock music and it explained the impact of "rock" very well. I do think that there are some loose threads in your argument—why does our satisfaction with the political system prevent us from idealizing political hero[e]s; why is the "rock" movement a great success in countries (England, Germany, etc., etc., even Russia) where the political system diverges from ours?—but, still, I believe your explanations are right (or at least on the right track).

It's emergency idealization though and, in that sense, similar to religious cults (the "Moonies"). It doesn't provide the reliable, long-term sustenance to our selves that more highly nuanced idols—I call them our cultural selfobjects—provide for us.[1]

At any rate it's nice to witness your thinking and reading; and I for one am glad that you are able to idealize some lofty and defined targets and feel uplifted by them and that the stimulating beat provides only part of you with needed sustenance.

Regards,

H. Kohut

1. Although Kohut appreciated the cultural significance of such youth idols as Bob Dylan (*Search*, 2:708–9), he worried about the kind of "mass craziness" which accompanied the death of ex-Beatle John Lennon in 1980; see "Idealization and Cultural Selfobjects," in *Self Psychology and the Humanities*, p. 225.

March 7, 1981 [original in German]
Tilmann Moser
Münstertal, West Germany

Dear Tilmann,

Warm thanks for your charming and candid letter [February 9], which gave me much pleasure—especially since it indicated the possibility of your making a trip to America. From August 1 until the end of September we will be in Carmel, then from October 1 to 5 go to Berkeley in order to participate in the Selfpsychology Conference that is being held at the University of California.

Otherwise not much to report that is new here. I'm still at home, that is, I don't go downtown, but see some patients in our apartment. I'm working on my new book and am making slow progress—it's a difficult topic.

I don't know how I should react to the notion of a breath of too great a degreê of self-assurance and touchiness [*Verletzlichkeit*]. As for the place of my works (and those of my friends), I have certainly made myself clear (see pp. 546–52 of *Advances in Selfpsychology* [*sic*]). I cannot see that such candor is to be equated with arrogance. Friendly colleagues argue that the bipolar self represents a new paradigm. That seems to me not to be the case. All of selfpsychology (Jacobson, Winnicott, my works) since Hartmann's modest beginning appear to me to belong to analysis, to be an advance in analysis—id psychology, ego psychology, selfpsychology. Strangers remove our works from analysis and I resist that. Enemies say that what we are doing has nothing more to do with analysis and that it represents a regression to a "corrective emotional experience." I am convinced this is unjust.

Arguments, however, don't offend me. What offends me is the fact that former friends no longer greet me, that colleagues who take selfpsychology seriously cannot become training analysts, that the works of my friends are accepted (onto programs, in journals) only on the condition that they don't quote me, etc., etc.

I know your advice is well meant and I would not be surprised if you could show me that here and there I write with too much self-assurance. But that seems to me like torturing someone and then complaining when the victim occasionally makes unpleasant sounds. But I will keep your advice in mind and try to suppress any personal reactions. Whether I can succeed at this, I don't know. On the whole only my work interests me, the problems that I can yet solve, the insights into human experience that I can yet have.

Enough—one can discuss such things untiringly. You mention your touchiness and I can only say that certain important insights can be achieved only by vulnerable personalities.

But I am very happy that you wrote, that you study the psychological world in your own way, and that I, in spite of your [partial?] alienation from me, once meant a great deal to you and still do.

Love to all, also from Betty, and let us hear from you

Yours,

Heinz

March 24, 1981
Roger Petti, M.D.
Kings County Hospital Center
Brooklyn, New York
Dear Dr. Petti.

Sorry about the delay of this response to your letter of 1/26. I was glad to learn that you are feeling more put together than before and that you are enjoying your work. I have been busy in my own fashion—working on a book (*How Does Analysis Cure?*) the end of which always seems to be in the near future—but I always seem to be just as far away from completing it as before. Still, there is this manuscript the bulk of which is done, & so I assume that I'll get done with one more section that I want to add + a beginning & an end chapter that are not yet written.

You ask me whom I am idealizing now. I don't know. I respect Freud and his pioneering contributions greatly but I don't think that

I am idealizing him. He doesn't seem to have been exuberant enough for my taste—no pleasure in music really, a bit stuffy about modern art, & quite closed up vis-à-vis the average mixtures of failure and success in living—; and so "idealizing" is not my attitude, rather respect and admiration. I guess I am very much a child of the 20th century and Freud was clearly a man of the 19th. I still idealize the Thomas Mann of *The Magic Mountain* [1924], Franz Kafka, the O'Neill of *Long Day's Journey [into Night]* [produced 1956], and Picasso. I guess I idealize works, not people—or people only insofar as they produce something that puts me in closer touch with man's deepest experiences.

You ask about my writings in German. They were all published by Suhrkamp in Frankfurt:

1) *Narzissmus*, 1974 (*Analysis of the Self*)
2) *Die Zukunft der Psychoanalyse*, 1975 (essays)
3) *Introspection, Empathie und Psychoanalyse*, 1977 (essays)
4) *Die Heilung des Selbst*, 1979 (*The Restoration of the Self*)

Also: "Narzissmus, Empathie und die Fragmentierung des Selbst: ein Gespräch mit Heinz Kohut," in *Wege zum Menschen* 19, 2/3, Feb/M. 1977 (Vandenhoeck & Ruprecht in Göttingen).

I am sending you a few German reprints, enclosed.

Warm good wishes as always,

Yours,

Heinz Kohut

P.S. The reprints were too heavy—they'll be sent under separate cover.

April 2, 1981
Siegmund Levarie
Brooklyn, New York
Dear Siegmund,

Thank you for honoring me with "Music as a Structural Model."[1] The details are largely beyond my scope; but I read every word and got the gist of the whole. Trying to translate your message into my language, my experience (which I probably should not do), I ask myself: What is the difference between so-so music and a great work of music? Both partake of the harmonious and perfect relationships that you are laying out, and yet there are worlds between "My Old Kentucky Home" and, forgive the comparison, the piano Sonata opus 111 [Beethoven]. And the same is probably true for the human communal life. Institutions in the abstract are fine—*The Federalist Papers* [1787–88]

were one of my great experiences when I read them in the 1940[ies]—
but the difference between going to war in Vietnam vs. fighting against
Hitler is almost as great as the musical one I addressed above (while
the institutions that organized us were still the same as regards Vietnam as they had been with Hitler). Questions, questions.

It was good to hear from you & see how beautifully your mind is
producing thoughts & connections. And such care for language!

I am still not 100%—but working hard: a book (90% done): an essay
(50% done); a lecture (20% done). My mind works still ok but my
stamina are [*sic*] limited.

How is the grandson?

Fondly,

Heinz

Betty sends much love to both of you & so do I.

1. *Journal of Social and Biological Structures* 3 (1980): 237–45; see also Siegmund Levarie,
"Opera and Human Emotions," *Annual of Psychoanalysis* 12–13 (1984–85): 415–20.

April 27, 1981

Professor Fred Weinstein

Department of History

State University of New York

Stony Brook

Dear Professor Weinstein,

Today I received your *Dynamics of Nazism* from the Academic Press.[1]
I don't know whether you had told them to send your book to me;
but if you did: thank you very much.

You know, of course, that I am extremely interested in this topic
since it appears to me to be a fine illustration of my hypothesis that
people turn to archaic modes of self-esteem support when access to
the mature forms becomes inaccessible. You heard me talk about this
in Chicago [June 1980] & may still remember it. So you can see that
I am eagerly looking forward to studying your volume with care—I
know that I will be rewarded by many new insights. (I admired your
contribution in Chicago.)

Best wishes &, once more, my thanks.

Sincerely,

Heinz Kohut

1. *The Dynamics of Nazism: Leadership, Ideology, and the Holocaust* (New York, 1980);
see also above, Gay to Kohut, June 22, 1980.

May 8, 1981
Richard F. Gallagher, M.D.
Downers Grove, Illinois
Dear Dr. Gallagher,
   Thank you for returning the negative and two prints. I am inscribing one for you & will send it to you. Your idea of "translating" selfpsychology into everyday language is an interesting one. I certainly believe that the insights of selfpsychology, filtering through into public awareness, should be helpful in taming man's propensity to react with unbridled & demonic narcissistic rage in the arena of politics, both inside nations & in their relationships to each other.
   Good wishes, and thanks for expressing your positive feelings about my work so openly to me.
   Yours,
   H. Kohut

June 7, 1981
George H. Pollock, M.D.
Director, The Institute of Psychoanalysis
Chicago
Dear George,
   I was glad to learn of the continued financial support granted to me during the forthcoming year. And I thank the faculty, staff, and Board of the Institute for the continuation of the grant and for the good wishes, and I am, of course, especially grateful to you.[1]
   This financial help is not only of significance to me as a gesture of good-will from the side of an institution to whom I have devoted a great deal of my work, time, and energy during the past three decades, it is also of practical importance, I should say, since my powers are now limited and, in order to move on with my scientific contributions I am forced to curtail my clinical practice (barely over 20 sessions per week, including consultative work) and to take extended (working) vacations.[2] I believe, however, that this régime is paying off. A new book (*How Does Analysis Cure?*; you may have seen it advertised already by the eager-beaver IUP) is 90% finished. A long theoretical essay taking up some key questions that selfpsychological ideas have had to confront is in essence done (it is in the hands of the editor; and will be published by the I.U.P. in a volume [*Reflections on Self Psychology*, 1983] devoted to a debate about selfpsychological issues, pro & con).[3] I am working on an essay dealing with what one might call "a new look on the concept of defense and resistance in psychoanalysis"

(that's perhaps 50% done). And I hope, during the summer, to collect my thoughts with regard to the talk for the 50th anniversary of the Institute/Society: introspection & empathy, 25 years after my analogous presentation at the celebrations when [Therese] Benedek & I were the contributors to the scientific proceedings. I am also collaborating with a historian who is engaged in putting together my published & unpublished writings in this area;[4] and I did some work with a Chicago area minister who wanted my ideas concerning modern analysis & religion & who plans to write them up in a broader presentation[5] than I, myself, could produce in view of the time that would be needed for such an enterprise.

All these foregoing remarks were simply meant to tell you that the support I receive is real support for real work—that indeed I could not do what I am doing, however limited it might be, without support.

Once more: my gratitude.

With warm regards,

Heinz

1. See George Pollock to Kohut, June 5, 1981. The money for this grant most likely came from an outside benefactor long cultivated by Pollock: see Pollock to Anne Lederer, September 23, 1971; and Kohut to Lederer, October 3, 1971, and April 12, 1973.

2. During 1981 Kohut, at age sixty-eight, became a training analyst emeritus (faculty emeritus status was ordained for age seventy); see Pollock to Kohut, July 14, 1981. Earlier the same year the Chicago Psychoanalytic Society had elected Kohut to Life Membership; see Robert J. Leider to Kohut, March 9, 1981.

3. *Search*, 4:489–523.

4. *Self Psychology and the Humanities: Reflections on a New Psychoanalytic Approach*, ed. Charles Strozier (New York, 1985).

5. Robert L. Randall, "The Legacy of Kohut for Religion and Psychology," *Journal of Religion and Health* 23 (1984): 106–14. See Kohut to Randall, February 26, 1981; and "First Meeting with Heinz Kohut, M.D.," March 22, 1981; "Second Meeting with Heinz Kohut, M.D.," April 12, 1981; and above, January 5, 1976.

June 24, 1981

Mr. Anthony T. Di Iorio

New York

Dear Mr. Di Iorio,

Time forwarded to me your letter of June 19 with the enclosed lovely poem celebrating the deep feelings you have for your daughter.

I cannot tell you how strongly I agree with all the sentiments that you expressed in your letter.[1] The trouble is that you have everything I said topsy-turvy. That's decidedly not your fault. Nor is it mine. The trouble is with the mass-media who distort in order to be challenging, sensational, to get people upset and interested.

There are thousands of (often very difficult) pages I have written—and all this work is condensed into one totally distorted page in *Time* [December 1, 1980, p. 76]. What can I do? Grin and bear it & learn my lesson about giving interviews, even if the interviewer is clearly intelligent and shows good will. The distortion occurs probably in the re-writing before the article goes to print.

What *do* I say? I say that the love that you feel for your daughter is an expansion of yourself, that it rests on identifying with her, on giving our self-love to the next generation. I militate against this kind of love being a "sublimation" of the "sexual instinct" & I propose instead that it is a transformation of the original self-love of the small child. But I am afraid I am trying the impossible; that I do myself what I blamed *Time* as having done: to condense the work of a lifetime into a few lines.

Only one more bit of information: the word (term) "narcissism" is almost totally absent in my recent writings & is replaced by the word (term) "self." I am not speaking anymore of childish, self-centered narcissism, maturing into the capacity to be empathic, creative, wise, parentally-affectionate, but of the maturation of the self. Your criticism of the term "narcissism" is, therefore, to my mind quite cogent and, rooted as it is in the traditional theory that love derives from sexuality, it has now become discarded in my work. It would take too long to tell you why I originally used the old term—but, if you try to extend your empathy toward me and imagine that I was speaking to fellow scientists steeped in a particular scientific tradition, maybe you will be able to figure it out.

Good wishes,
Sincerely,
Heinz Kohut

1. Di Iorio argues that narcissism is anti-social and imprudently celebrated by contemporary psychologists and doctors.

July 20, 1981
Marion F. Solomon, Ph.D.
Los Angeles
Dear Dr. Solomon.

Thank you for your letter of 7/10 inquiring about my views on "borderline patients" and implying that I may have changed my mind about their "analyzability." So far as I am aware I have not changed my mind but, perhaps, my original meaning is now beginning to be understood more clearly. *I was not giving a clinical judgement, I was suggesting a definition.* My intention was to bring classificatory clarity to a hazy area & thus I suggested that analyzable disorders of the self, even severe ones with temporary delusions or hallucinations (I adduced examples) & even if exposed to serious fragmentation with psychotic-like manifestations, should be called (severe) narcissistic personality disorders—while those cases that do not develop a selfobject transference, however seemingly cohesive to the surface view, should be referred to as "borderline." I have often stressed that the distinction is relative—depending, for example, on the empathic potentialities of the therapist. Specifically, a therapist with special responsiveness to a particular analysand will be able to discern the development of a self-object transference and tolerate the (often enormous) demands it makes on him—the patient is then a "serious narcissistic personality disorder"—, while another therapist who does not possess the same empathic capacity will not see, or will not be able to tolerate, the archaic selfobject transference that does emerge. With the latter analyst the patient is now "borderline" or "psychotic." I do not believe that diagnoses are ever to be made in isolation from the (potential) selfobject milieu of the patient.

Sincerely yours,
Heinz Kohut

July 26–27, 1981
Marjorie Taggart White, Ph.D.
New York
Dear Dr. White,

I liked your letter [July 20] very much—it was nice to see myself quoted so intelligently—and the idea of a conference on the question whether human civilization can save itself from selfdestruction [*sic*] is fascinating.[1]

Not easy to organize, though. Such things can quickly degenerate into generalities, pep talks, & the like, and it needs to be planned carefully to be rigorously scientific.

As far as I am concerned: I will not be able to participate either as an organizer or as a contributor. But I would certainly endorse it if I can be sure that the scientific standards of selfpsychology are firmly applied in its planning. The participation of historians is needed, as well as of political scientists, in particular selfpsychologically well informed people. But what is most important: we need a liaison person from those who are immersed in (applied) selfpsychology who is actively and responsibly participating in the planning and organizing stages of such a project. It is only if I can be assured of the participation of such a person—the *active* and *decisive* influence of such a person—in planning and organizing such a conference that I would be willing to endorse it and support it.

I will try to find such a person willing to undertake the task in cooperation with you and will let you know if and when I've found him.

In the meantime my very best regards. It gives me great satisfaction to see that my ideas are finding such a warm and intelligent echo as those that you expressed to me.

Sincerely,

Heinz Kohut

1. *Search*, 4:683–84; and see also White to Kohut, August 21, 1981.

Carmel, August 17, 1981

Dear Tom,

I received your note with xerox of the Lovejoy page.[1] Thanks! . . .

I trust progress has been made toward fixing an acceptable air-routing to Monterey. Both of us are looking forward with strong emotions to your arrival. But, please, take me as I *am* now, not as what you would like me to still be!

My mind is ok, my courage unbroken, my work proceeds.

Love to both of you,

Dad

1. Arthur O. Lovejoy, *The Great Chain of Being: The History of an Idea* (Cambridge, Mass., 1936).

Select Bibliography

Detrick, Douglas W., and Detrick, Susan P., eds. *Self Psychology: Comparisons and Contrasts*. Hillsdale, N.J., 1989.

Goldberg, Arnold, ed. *Advances in Self Psychology*. New York, 1980.

———. *The Future of Psychoanalysis: Essays in Honor of Heinz Kohut*. New York, 1983.

———. *Progress in Self Psychology*. 2 vols. New York, 1985–86.

———. *The Psychology of the Self: A Casebook*. New York, 1978.

Kohut, Heinz. *The Analysis of the Self: A Systematic Approach to the Psychoanalytic Treatment of Narcissistic Personality Disorders*. The Psychoanalytic Study of the Child, Monograph no. 4. New York, 1971.

———. *How Does Analysis Cure?* Edited by Arnold Goldberg. Chicago, 1984.

———. *The Kohut Seminars on Self Psychology and Psychotherapy with Adolescents and Young Adults*. Edited by Miriam Elson. New York, 1987.

———. *The Restoration of the Self*. New York, 1977.

———. *The Search for the Self: Selected Writings of Heinz Kohut*. Edited by Paul H. Ornstein. 4 vols. New York, vols. 1 and 2: 1978, vols. 3 and 4: 1991.

———. *Self Psychology and the Humanities: Reflections on a New Psychoanalytic Approach*. Edited by Charles Strozier. New York, 1985.

Lee, Ronald R., and Martin, J. Colby. *Psychotherapy after Kohut: A Textbook of Self Psychology*. Hillsdale, N.J., 1991.

Lichtenberg, Joseph D., and Kaplan, Samuel, eds. *Reflections on Self Psychology*. New York, 1983.

Magd, Barry, ed. *Freud's Case Studies: Self-Psychological Perspectives*. Hillsdale, N.J., 1993.

Stepansky, Paul, and Goldberg, Arnold, eds. *Kohut's Legacy: Contributions to Self Psychology*. Hillsdale, N.J., 1984.

Wolf, Ernest S. *Treating the Self: Elements of Clinical Self Psychology*. New York, 1988.

Index